Nietzsche's Naturalist Deconstruction of Truth

Nietzsche's Naturalist Deconstruction of Truth

A World Fragmented in Late Nineteenth-Century Epistemology

Peter Bornedal

LEXINGTON BOOKS
Lanham • Boulder • New York • London

Published by Lexington Books
An imprint of The Rowman & Littlefield Publishing Group, Inc.
4501 Forbes Boulevard, Suite 200, Lanham, Maryland 20706
www.rowman.com

6 Tinworth Street, London SE11 5AL, United Kingdom

Copyright © 2020 by The Rowman & Littlefield Publishing Group, Inc.

All rights reserved. No part of this book may be reproduced in any form or by any electronic or mechanical means, including information storage and retrieval systems, without written permission from the publisher, except by a reviewer who may quote passages in a review.

British Library Cataloguing in Publication Information Available

Library of Congress Cataloging-in-Publication Data Available

ISBN: 978-1-4985-7930-8 (cloth)
ISBN: 978-1-4985-7932-2 (pbk)
ISBN: 978-1-4985-7931-5 (electronic)

Contents

Introduction	ix
1. Naturalism versus Metaphysics	ix
1. Naturalist Deconstruction of Truth	ix
2. Nietzsche versus Derrida	xii
1. Incompatibilities between the Naturalist and Deconstructive Project	xii
2. Nietzsche's Philosophy as Play	xv
3. De Man's Rhetorical Nietzsche	xvii
4. Deconstruction as Anti-Epistemology	xviii
3. Outline of the Work	xviii
1. Questions of Interpretation; Inessential Contradictions	xviii
2. Questions of Interpretation; Essential Contradictions	xxi
3. Nietzsche's Thinking as Consistent Development of the Naturalist Paradigm	xxii
4. Introducing the Nietzsche-Machian Theory of Knowledge	xxiv
5. A Bilingual German/English Version of Wahrheit und Lüge	xxv
Part I: Nietzsche's Early Theory of Truth and Knowledge	**1**
A: Part I of *Truth and Lies*	1
1. Preliminary Remarks	1
1. Paradigm and Text	1
2. Nietzsche's Intellectual Context from 1862 to 1873	2
2. Human Insignificance and Self-Deceptive Pride	4
3. Genealogy of the Pragmatic Notion of Truth	8
1. Genealogy of Truth in a Pragmatic Sense	8
2. Nietzsche's 'Correspondence Theory of Truth' and Its Limitations	11
4. Nerve-Stimuli, Images, and Sounds	16
1. The Development of a 'Truth Drive'	16
2. What Is a Word?	17

    3. Replacing the Unknown with 'Metaphors' — 23
   5. Word *and/or/versus* Concept? — 25
    1. The Distinction between Images and Words/Concepts — 25
    2. The Tenuous Distinction between Words and Concepts — 27
    3. A Later Pragmatic Resolution of the Distinction between Word and Concept — 31
   6. Truth as "Dead Metaphors" — 33
    1. Transferences Instead of Correspondences — 33
    2. God as 'Dead Metaphor': Feuerbach and Nietzsche on Anthropocentrism — 37
   7. The Rationalizing Concept — 40
    1. Reason as Constructive Human Intelligence — 40
    2. Unreason as Imaginary Divine Intelligence — 42
   8. Biological Perspectivism — 45
    1. The World according to Homo Sapiens — 45
   9. Nietzsche's Empiricist Neo-Kantianism — 48
    1. The Reversal of Thing and Predicate — 48
    2. The Proto-Forms of Knowledge: Time and Space — 51
    3. Active versus Passive Receptivity in the Neo-Kantian Tradition — 54

B: Part II of *Truth and Lies* — 58
   1. Regressions to Romantic Arts-Metaphysics — 58
    1. The Distinction between Authentic and Inauthentic Conceptualizations — 58
    2. Mobilizing the Metaphor-Drive of Intuitive Man against Intellectual Man — 61
    3. Nietzsche and 'The Romantic School' — 65
    4. The Young Nietzsche's Romantic-Aesthetic Program — 68
    5. Nietzsche's Later Self-Criticisms — 71

C: Human Knowledge from *Truth and Lies* to *Human, All Too Human* — 72
   1. 'Vanity' as the Specifically Human 'Thing-in-Itself' — 72
   2. Will to Truth as Will to Immortality — 74

Part II: Nietzsche's Positivist-Pragmatic Paradigm — **77**

A: Nietzsche's Later Theories of Truth and Knowledge — 77
   1. Nietzsche's Critiques of the In-Itself as *Cause* in the Middle Work — 77
    1. Associations to Hume — 77

2. Causes Interpreted as Deeds	79
3. The Cause-Effect Relation as Imitation of Subject-Predicate Logic	80
4. The 'Fear-Factor': How Knowledge Is Created Out of Fear of the New	85
5. The Naturalist Deconstruction of 'Causality' and the 'Synthetic A Priori'	86
6. Nietzsche's Irony: The Analysis of Kant's "Vermögen" as a 'Paralogism'	88
2. 'Chronological Reversal' of Cause and Effect	89
1. Chronological Reversal as Humanization of Nature	89
2. De Man's Reading of Nietzsche's Chronological Reversal as Rhetoric	93
3. A Surface without Abyss	97
1. Nietzsche's Development of His Epistemological Positions	97
2. Attempts to Un-Think the 'True World' in Twilight of the Idols	100
3. Senses Do Not Falsify	103
4. Nietzsche's Struggle with Structural Linguistic Language-Constraints	106
4. Three Pillars of Nietzschean Positivism: Phenomenalism Perspectivism Relativism	108
5. 'Long Live Science' as the 'Best Possible' Falsification	111
1. Objective Relativism	111
2. The Nobility of the Scientist	111
B: Nietzsche and Critical Positivism	113
1. From Materialism to Agnosticism	113
1. Laplace's 'Universal Mind' vs Du Bois-Reymond's 'Ignorabimus'	113
2. Different Interpretations of the In-Itself in Helmholtz, Spir, and Ueberweg	120
2. From Agnosticism to Positivist Nihilism	124
1. Epistemological Positivism and Affirmative Nihilism	124
2. Sunrise for the Gay Scientists	129
3. A Nietzsche-Machean Theory of Knowledge	132
1. From Substances to Appearances	132
2. Elements, Relations, and Construction of Objectivity	137
3. Filtration, Simplification, and the General Economy of Signs	141
4. Knowledge as Sign-Economy	146

5. A Critical Discussion of an Anti-Phenomenalistic Conception of Mach's Epistemology	147
6. The Exaggerated Fear of Solipsism	152
7. Claude Monet's Impressionism as a Model on Positivism	154
4. The Fictional Concept in Vaihinger and Nietzsche	155
1. "Fictionalism" as Radical Neo-Kantianism	155
2. The Biological Theory of Knowledge in Vaihinger, Avenarius, and Nietzsche	160
5. Nietzsche's Positivism According to Habermas	167
C: Final Assessment	171
1. What Is 'True' and What Is 'False' in Nietzsche's Discussion of Knowledge?	171
Appendix: "On Truth and Lies in a Non-Moral Sense"	175
Notes	193
Abbreviations	245
Bibliography	247
Index	263
About the Author	273

Introduction

1. NATURALISM VERSUS METAPHYSICS

1. Naturalist Deconstruction of Truth

There can be no doubt that Nietzsche in his *Ueber Wahrheit und Lüge im außermoralischen Sinne* (1873; "On Truth and Lies in a Non-Moral Sense" [TL])[1] performs a 'deconstruction' of sorts of 'Truth.' During the brief essay, he introduces us to different possible candidates for 'truth,' only to demonstrate that none of them touches any profound transcendental principle that could give them the permanence and universality that is required in the classical definition of truth as 'Truth' (let us here and in the following indicate this concept by using the capital 'T'). In other words, this concept comes across as 'false,' or in Nietzsche's formulation in TL, as 'illusion.'

However, this fundamental postulate of the essay does not entail, (i), that we live in a 'false' *world*. Rather, when it is the classical concept of truth itself that is 'illusory' or 'false,' embracing this insight consigns us quite to the contrary to a fundamentally 'real' world, albeit to a 'real' world that as 'chaotic ground' we cannot fathom in itself.[2] It is also not the case, (ii), that we after determining 'Truth' as illusion have unleashed in ourselves a certain playful-creative potentiality that has been held back by traditional 'Western Thinking,' as deconstructive criticism had a tendency to reiterate in the second half of the twentieth century.[3] To declare 'Truth' 'false,' is rather to declare a highly imaginative-creative-fictional notion false; it implies that we put new constraints on our poetic abilities to form fantastic and fanciful metaphysical universes. Finally, (iii), when Nietzsche 'denounces' or 'deconstructs' the concept of Truth, the implication is not that knowledge herewith is absolutely destabilized, because that assumes that we take 'Truth' to be that stabilizing power that Nietzsche precisely denounces that it is. Applying that hasty judgment, we falsely conclude that if Truth is gone, we are left with fictional-rhetorical inventions instead of knowledge; we then assume that all knowledge collapses because we start questioning the *false* metaphysical concept of 'Truth.' However, to question the *false*, is still to seek the *true*;

to question the classical dogmatic concept of 'Truth,' is still to seek a true pragmatic concept, endowed, of course, with entirely different attributes than the classical concept.

Therefore, when Nietzsche performs a naturalist deconstruction of truth,[4] he is deconstructing only *a* concept of truth, not *any* concept of truth; not the plain fact that we can utter sentences that are true or false in various practical contexts according to certain accepted conventional requirements (cf. Part I, A.3: "Genealogy of the Pragmatic Notion of Truth"). Our social-legal-pragmatic concepts of the true, of a distinction between truth and lies, although understood by Nietzsche as indispensable in social interaction, cannot be 'True' or 'False' in the absolute metaphysical sense, but in this, Nietzsche does not question that we in local circumstances and unique contexts continue to express judgments concerning falsehood or truthfulness qua the fundamental *structure of speech-acts. Assertions* will continue to express truth-claims that typically can be verified or falsified without further ado in the unique context of the speech-act. However, as soon as we are removed from these local contexts, we need to know in what *sense*, in what *context*, or according to what *criterion*, something is being asserted as 'true' or 'false.' Removed from the practical context, it is apparent that to state that something is 'true' or 'false' needs additional qualification and specification. It is symptomatic that we, after Nietzsche and his peers, feel that we in our writing need to write *true* in scare-quotes. We no longer want to indicate that we submit to a categorical absolutistic understanding of *Truth*, but still accept a practical.

Specifically, when the theological-metaphysical concept of *Truth* is seen as a *fiction* it implies that it does not make up a permanent ground that we can hit or miss in our statements or even perceptions. We still perceive and we still form statements, but our perceptions cannot be described as truthful conditional upon their correspondences to a thing-in-itself connoting 'Truth,' nor can our concepts be described as truthful conditional upon their correspondences to a permanent ground, beyond that conventionality of language that is the resource of all conceptuality. Denouncing the theological-metaphysical Truth-mythology as a fiction starts a chain-reaction, where references to Truth start collapsing like dominoes, but it does not to Nietzsche (nor to the peers he follows or follow him) imply that our perceptions or conceptualizations vanish into absolute irrelevance, or that our practical determinations of the true or the false are suspended. The implication is rather that knowledge is no longer validated by something called 'Truth,' but by an empirical universe presented as appearance to an observing and rationalizing subject. As we shall see, Nietzsche's background in the contemporary neo-Kantian paradigm is already clear in early writings, and it will in later writings incline him towards schools emerging from the same background, such as Central European versions of Positivism and Pragmatism.

We may notice that from a strictly pragmatic perspective, nothing is changing in this fundamental interrogation of the supposed *foundation* of knowledge. Nietzsche and peers are expressing their strong reservations about the *grand narrative* of Truth with its Christian connotations to the unconditional and the pre-established, but that does not prevent us from drawing up distinctions between the truthful and the deceptive, the honest and the dishonest, the sincere and the insincere. Perhaps the insight into Truth as non-truth indeed helps us to detect *deceit*, *dishonesty* and *insincerity* regarding appeals to Truth in manipulative and doctrinaire discourses of religious, political, ideological, or ethical nature. It teaches us a rather pertinent and healthy skepticism of ideologues with their inevitable appeals to the Truth of their various self-serving causes. Instead of appealing to empirical facts or to argumentative logic, ideologues habitually appeal to *Truth*, the easiest and laziest means of persuasion, which at the same time demands the most unconditional subjugation in the audience. Woe to those who do not subject themselves to *Truth*.

When we assert that Nietzsche's 'naturalistic deconstruction' of truth is a revaluation of the true-false distinction, we must hastily add that Nietzsche's famous 'revaluation of values' does not imply that we simply turn a hierarchy around. It does not mean that what was before 'false' is now 'true' and what was before 'true' is now 'false.' Such an automatic reversal achieves exactly nothing except restating the original structure of the binary. 'Revaluation' implies rather that the classical metaphysical-ontological foundation has been pulled away from under this binary and that we are now 'beyond' it, as well as we are 'beyond' that other famous 'good and evil' binary that preoccupied Nietzsche.

In 'naturalistic deconstruction,' Truth in the metaphysical sense is denounced as a purely constructed 'nothing' (and a 'no *thing*' as well), which to Nietzsche and peers is meaningless after the nineteenth century's scientific revolutions especially regarding our biological evolutionary history and psycho-physiological limitations. Still, as Nietzsche always emphasizes, this purely constructed nothing has been beneficial in the civilizational process. It has given the human being ideals to pursue, aspirations to fulfill, tasks to accomplish, goals to achieve. Looking up instead of down, looking to the stars instead of into the fireplace gave us ideals and drove us beyond ourselves. We became a species of dreamers, insatiable in our appetite to confront the impossible. The metaphysical-fictional nothing called 'Truth' had utility in the advancement of us as social-cultural species, and Nietzsche is often writing in awe of what this particular species accomplished thanks to what he nevertheless regards as a fundamental misunderstanding of the concept of truth.[5]

When we get rid of this fundamental misunderstanding, our world is de-fictionalized (but simultaneously also open to a new and original re-fictionalization), because, however readily Nietzsche accepts and even embraces the human weakness for imagery, myth, and poetry, his ultimate project is to defend an uncompromising 'nihilism' as the ultimate chaotic ground on which all our idealistic projects are erected. The charmed, enchanted, and magical world is gone. Instead, we encounter, like any other animal delimited by its physiology, a world with whatever receptive capacities we happen to have evolved under the sun (e.g., visual perception able to discern light, given that we quasi-randomly have evolved into perceiving a world illuminated, not a world of electro-magnetic forces). Still, our quasi-randomly developed visual perception has evolved in synchrony with that externality we call 'world,' which consequently we are able to perceive from *our* perspective. After this recognition, Nietzsche and peers no longer dare to claim that we perceive *The World* (i.e., as a thing-in-itself), what to them would be about as wrongheaded as denying that we perceive *a world* (i.e., a relativized perspectival world).

2. NIETZSCHE VERSUS DERRIDA

1. Incompatibilities between the Naturalist and Deconstructive Project

"There is nothing outside text," J. Derrida once famously declared.[6] A theoretical writer much closer to Nietzsche in time and spirit, Fr. A. Lange, has an equivalent dictum, which significantly reads, "There is nothing outside nature."[7] The two dicta capture *in nuce* the differences between the deconstructionism of Derrida and the naturalism of Lange and Nietzsche. They give significantly different answers to the ontological question, *what is*? One says 'text,' another 'nature.' Between 'text' and 'nature,' there is seemingly no connection. If or when Derrida in several essays has insisted on regarding 'nature' as 'text,' 'nature' is merely absorbed into the textualist paradigm. That is a colonization that should fool nobody; the original distinction prevails as antagonism (if 'nature' *is* 'text' it is obviously no longer nature).

Hence, when deconstructionists read Nietzsche, the naturalist dimension of his thinking vanishes. His intellectual context is never addressed and one will look in vain for references to the developments of neo-Kantian, psycho-physiological, and evolutionary schools of the nineteenth century; we rarely find references to Kant and Schopenhauer, and never to Darwin, Lange, or

Mach. Deconstructionists will continue to emphasize their overlapping interests with Nietzsche qua his deconstruction of 'truth,' but without considering his context. He is consequently read in isolation as the intellectual hero *per se* questioning the metaphysical tradition *as such*. If he is related to any other philosopher, it is usually forwardly to Heidegger.

In Derrida's early *De la Grammatologie* (*Of Grammatology*; 1967),[8] Nietzsche is seen as having 'discovered' *writing* before anybody else.

> Nietzsche has *written what* he has written. He has written that writing—and first of all his own—is not originally subordinate to the logos and to truth. And that this subordination has *come into being* during an epoch whose meaning we must deconstruct.[9]

Although Derrida is right that Nietzsche 'deconstructs truth,' we cannot feel certain that Derrida is in actual agreement with Nietzsche, because he does not attempt to determine *in which sense* Nietzsche might be deconstructing truth, e.g., by understanding how truth was discussed in the nineteenth century's naturalist tradition. By being abstract and formal, Derrida's concept of truth is not identical to Nietzsche's. Much against the general intention of deconstruction, Derrida refers to a notion of truth that is universalistic and absolute; it is, for example, characterized by its repression of something called 'writing.' This repression has allegedly been exercised since Plato and is continuing in the most recent philosophers (Lacan, Austin, Foucault, Searle, etc.). It is this abstract form of truth that Nietzsche allegedly is deconstructing by writing that writing is writing: "Nietzsche has *written what* he has written." The deeper meaning behind this apparently vapid statement must be that writing is a performance in which we produce differences. If Nietzsche is writing *that* or *what* he is writing, i.e., writing that he is producing differences, his theoretical merit is to have discovered that his content is mirroring his performance. As such, he apparently never refers to anything more significant than his own activity as writer.[10]

Ditto, even if Derrida with some right declares that Nietzsche is deconstructing 'presence,' it is 'presence' unspecified except in contrast to something called 'trace.'

> This deconstruction of presence accomplishes itself through the deconstruction of consciousness, and therefore through the irreducible notion of the trace *(Spur)*, as it appears in Nietzschean discourse.[11]

Derrida is not referring to the 'thing-in-itself' as presence, which unquestionably is an object of Nietzsche's deconstruction. He seems to presuppose a notion of 'presence' as the perceived and experienced 'now.' In his early work, Derrida emphasizes that this 'now' is an impossible notion, nonexistent as such but always woven into a 'trace' of the past. Several other thinkers in the Western tradition have realized a problem with the concept of 'now' (from Aristotle to Husserl and beyond), but not, so Derrida, to the full extent of the most radical consequences of this realization, namely that the absence of the 'now' (whether in the sense of an empirically sensed 'now' or a 'now' of rational intentions) implies that we live in a net of differences of which 'writing' is our best model (and often not only our model, but in extrapolation, our de facto available reality). Although Derrida casually knows that we live in a sense-world, his theoretical focus becomes the world of 'writing'; 'writing' or 'text' become deconstruction's new 'for-us,' while theoretically, the sense-world is demoted to a new 'in-itself.'

Derrida therefore concludes that Nietzsche—as well as Freud in another of his readings[12]—questions the notion of the 'now' for sense-perception, insofar as they both regard sense-perception as an interpretive activity (what they do, in an adequately qualified sense). The reading is not plainly wrong, but it is reductive, because regarding both Nietzsche and Freud, this understanding of perception comes about because they are inspired by the new psycho-physiological insights emerging in the nineteenth century, thanks to a number of physiologists (influential are, for example, J. Müller, Th. Fechner, Du Bois-Reymond, and H. von Helmholtz; cf. discussions in Part II, B: "Nietzsche and Critical Positivism"). Emerging from the psycho-physiological paradigm, Nietzsche and Freud are not interested in deconstructing the 'now' *as such* or in contrast to the '*trace.*' They are interested in understanding what consequences these new insights in psycho-physiology have for human knowledge of the outside world. In Derrida's purely abstract and formal 'deconstructions' of the 'now,' he ends up confirming the 'trace,' 'proto-writing,' or 'différance.' Original scientific discussions of physiology, perception, and mind are displaced and redirected to discussions of abstract-formal principles in their transcendental-universal manifestation.

Moreover, if all disciplines are reduced to 'text,' the sciences are neither as objective nor as progressive as they like to proclaim, and deconstructive critique of metaphysics must necessarily include also Empiricism, Naturalism, neo-Kantianism, Positivism, and Scientism. That these Schools in their own self-understanding were critical of the metaphysical and foundational project is ignored in the ultra-critical deconstructionist environment because they are never *sufficiently radical* to exclude sense-perceptions from their critique. They leave a space open for scientific 'observation' and subsequent 'conceptualization' of an empirical world.

2. Nietzsche's Philosophy as Play

Derrida not only refers to Nietzsche as predating his own critique of truth-metaphysics, he also seems to think that Nietzsche's style predates that deconstructive playfulness that is seen as a consequence of a critique of truth. However, Derrida's critique of truth-metaphysics comes from another place than Nietzsche's, since Nietzsche writes within the nineteenth century's neo-Kantian, naturalist, and pragmatic paradigm, while Derrida, in his initial critical engagements comes from Husserl's Phenomenology and French Structuralism (engagements precipitously expanded to Western Thinking as such).

The 'isms' we have discussed above as Naturalism, Phenomenalism, Perspectivism, and Relativism have in the definitions they got in Nietzsche's paradigm no place in Deconstruction. If Nietzsche attempts to *re-think* theory of knowledge qua this new set of concepts, Derrida attempts to *un-think* theory of knowledge as an impossible project according to a universalistic dogma of différance.

To Derrida, truth-critique is an implication of Saussure's insight that the language-system is a play of 'differences without positive signs,' but universalized and applied to all theoretical discourse. This means in Derrida's interpretation that philosophers as well as scientists are writing under this self-undermining and self-deconstructing condition in a futile attempt to produce 'positive signs.' Nietzsche's truth-critique, in contrast, invites us to draw the virtually opposite conclusion, since the nihilistic condition impels and encourages us to *construct* 'positive signs' as our best knowledge of the *for-us world*. In this, Nietzsche becomes a 'constructivist' and a 'pragmatist,' while Derrida remains stuck in his explicit *de*-constructivism, which cannot be translated back into constructivism, nor into pragmatism (as I will argue in disagreement with R. Rorty; cf. section 5).

Derrida's Nietzsche is not a Nietzsche constructed but a Nietzsche deconstructed, as well demonstrated in Derrida's book on Nietzsche, *Éperons: Les Styles de Nietzsche* (1978; *Spurs: Nietzsche's Styles*).[13] In this small work, Derrida has obviously not been able to see a serious motivation behind Nietzsche's critiques of metaphysics, theology, and ideology. Derrida applies in his small essay a radical hermeneutics according to which we ultimately cannot understand Nietzsche in his theoretical engagements, as he suggests that Nietzsche's work is as enigmatic as a sentence he jots down in one of his notebooks: "I have forgotten my umbrella."

Derrida starts by doing what he often does when he focuses on such isolated sentence-fragments, namely applying a free associative speculation about what the author could have intended in jotting down such a fragment. He is implementing the Freudian 'technique of free association,' but with ironic futility, since Derrida's associations do not and are not meant to lead us anywhere. Regarding Nietzsche, he states explicitly, "we will never know *for sure* what Nietzsche wanted to say,"[14] implying that our purposes for reading Nietzsche is to know what Nietzsche *wanted* to say. Generally, in Derrida, whenever we read texts, we endeavor to restore the original intentions of the author, but in vain, since the intentional context of the original inscription is a forever lost past that cannot be restored.

Paradoxically, it is Derrida who here and elsewhere takes for granted that the most important issue in philosophical commentary has been to understand what the author *wants-to-say*. In the case of Nietzsche, Derrida thinks that the umbrella-example has obsessed the "impulsive reader or hermeneut ontologist" trying to construe "this unpublished piece is an aphorism of some significance. Assured that it must mean something, they look for it to come from the most intimate reaches of this author's thought."[15] The urgency of this polemics against the 'impulsive reader' is puzzling, since the umbrella-fragment to the knowledge of undersigned never has been discussed by Nietzsche-commentators other than Derrida.[16] Derrida seems rather to be doing here what he does elsewhere as well, namely inventing a caricature, a straw man, onto whom he imposes a blatantly silly position, as such facilitating his own refutation of the manifest absurdity.

It is paradoxically Derrida who is preoccupied with 'intimate thoughts' emerging from the underground of unconscious intentions, which are thereupon quickly denied as accessible in the black mirror of his predictable deconstructions.[17] It is these 'intimate thoughts' that we as recipients always will be ignorant about, as Derrida claims, concluding that if we do not know what motivates Nietzsche to write, "I have forgotten my umbrella," if this fragment is "structurally liberated from any meaning,"[18] we must draw the conclusion that Nietzsche's philosophy *as such* escapes meaningful interpretation. "To whatever lengths one might carry a conscientious interpretation, the hypothesis that the totality of Nietzsche's text, in some monstrous way, might well be of the type 'I have forgotten my umbrella,' cannot be denied." To draw such a radical conclusion is of course only logically applicable, if one (that is, Derrida) presupposes that 'intention' is the precondition for understanding meaning.[19]

Derrida's witticism implies that as little as we are able to access the intention and/or context motivating Nietzsche to write his fragment, as little are we able to understand what in general motivated Nietzsche's writings. Any interpretation we happen to apply to Nietzsche ultimately relies on nothing but our own inventive subjectivity. As such, the umbrella-fragment becomes a model for Nietzsche's entire textual corpus. Derrida and fellow deconstructionists obviously admire Nietzsche for his playfulness; he is praised for writing on writing as a play without referent, and Derrida is in *Éperons* doing him one better when he is writing on Nietzsche's writing as a forgotten umbrella without references.

3. De Man's Rhetorical Nietzsche

De Man and Derrida's deconstructive projects share many identical features, as readily acknowledged by them both, but de Man is more explicit in translating traditional metaphysical and epistemological vocabulary into rhetorical figures and tropes. De Man appreciates that Nietzsche in the beginning of *TL* labels two transformations as metaphorical, the formation of stimuli into perceptive images, and the formation of perceptive images into sounds or words. And when Nietzsche draws the conclusion that truth is a "movable host of metaphors, metonymies and anthropomorphisms," that truths are "metaphors that have been worn out,"[20] de Man sees this as an explicit reference to literature as model for epistemology. "We can legitimately assert therefore that the key to Nietzsche's critique of metaphysics [...] lies in the rhetorical model of the trope or, if one prefers to call it that way, in literature as the language most explicitly grounded in rhetoric."[21]

Nietzsche's epistemological project becomes as such literary criticism, because epistemological distinctions are transferred into the field of rhetoric. The distinction between 'appearances' and 'things-in-themselves' is for example seen as an application of *antithesis* as rhetorical figure, implying that psycho-physiological and -linguistic discussions of stimuli, perception, cognition, and conceptualization concerning perceptive, cognitive, and conceptual knowledge of an inaccessible world are essentially reduced to a rhetorical binary. At this point, the deconstructionist cannot take seriously the epistemological discussions of the 'thing in itself' and the 'appearance,' since these two realms are no longer understood as having scientific relevance; they are best described by the 'antithesis' as tropical figure. Like Derrida, de Man, too, sees Nietzsche's 'critique of metaphysics' as a universal formal-abstract project, and like Derrida, he replaces Nietzsche's historically specific critique with a universal abstraction (cf. related discussions in Part II A.3: "Paul de Man's Reading of Nietzsche's Chronological Reversal as Rhetoric").

Nietzsche is certainly not blind to the indispensable role of language in conceptualizing our world, but as we will see, he suggests a three-stage model including a thing-in-itself, a world of images/appearances, and the conceptualization of images/appearances, which de Man reduces to a single level for figurative language in which we speak about the world.[22] If the deconstructionist is pressed to admit our banal encounter with a world of appearances, the admission comes reluctantly, perhaps in an exasperated 'of course' to the bemused philosopher insisting on the issue. In any case, the issue is without consequences for the deconstructive project according to which language 'as writing' has become a self-sufficient realm.

4. Deconstruction as Anti-Epistemology

On these arguments, it seems clear that the deconstructive project has little or nothing to do with the anti-metaphysical project of Nietzsche and peers despite certain word-to-word resemblances. Deconstructive readings do not, will not, and cannot discuss the importance of insights in biology and psycho-physiology emerging during the nineteenth century and are generally opposed to the scientific background that inspires Nietzsche into his criticisms of traditional metaphysical and theological positions. Whether it is seen or not, the abstract critique of the "presence of the self-present" as the *general form* of the now for sense-impressions must necessarily include Nietzsche and peers as preeminent *targets* of deconstruction, i.e., granted their inherited Empiricism, Kantianism, Naturalism, and Positivism; granted their insistence on a 'for-us' as *the sense-world of appearances*—evidently not 'writing/text,' which does not exist as a subject-matter occupying these discussions.

Hence, despite word-to-word resemblances, despite Nietzsche's 'friend status' on the Deconstructive Facebook, the paradigm from which he draws his critical insights does not serve postmodern ends. This is perhaps why a certain foreshortening of Nietzschean epistemology was necessary in much late twentieth-century commentary. If he was going to be a true friend of deconstruction, it was necessary to dislodge him from his intellectual context; it was necessary to construct a Nietzsche unrelated to the prevailing nineteenth-century positive, pragmatic, and naturalist Schools. When Nietzsche was questioning 'Truth' or 'Reason,' he was supposedly better in sync with Heidegger than with Darwin, Lange, or Mach. Moreover, given his aphoristic style, he could be perceived as a poetic and language-experimenting writer, mobilized against all meaning-imperialism, like Derrida and late Heidegger.

3. OUTLINE OF THE WORK

1. Questions of Interpretation; Inessential Contradictions

The first part of the present work is a critical hermeneutical exposition of Nietzsche's TL, the simple principle being to start with the first passage and proceed to the last, with a few necessary modifications of the principle because Nietzsche at times repeats the same ideas in different passages in his essay and it seems best expository practice to bring these ideas together.

In a recent debate, M. Clark and D. Dudrick has suggested the necessity of an 'esoteric' reading of Nietzsche in order to make sense of putatively conflicting theses in his work.[23] The reading here performed is in principle *anti-esoteric*, implying that it does not attempt to decode meaning behind expressed meaning or reconstruct hidden logic in Nietzsche's texts. It takes Nietzsche's formulations, arguments, and concepts seriously as they are explicitly expressed. This straightforward hermeneutical exposition of the text, I see as an elementary or a *primary elaboration* of the textual material necessary in order to piece Nietzsche thinking together as a conceptual whole in a more advanced *second elaboration* of the material. According to this methodological approach, one would want to confront only the observable text and adopt deliberate indifference to Nietzsche's putative ideological positions or intentions and, at least provisionally, hand over all authority to Nietzsche. i.e., we take his thinking as a learning experience: He talks and we take notes. To the extent we are capable of deliberate indifference and neutrality, this primary elaboration will precede the 'secondary elaboration,' which implies a 'reconstruction of the text,' i.e., of the notes we have been taken with deliberate neutrality. In this, we necessarily need to be far more explicitly involved, as we need all our rational acumen to re-organize the material so it makes the best possible sense. In the interaction between these two aspects of 'objective' reconstructive interpretation, it is often possible to rescue several of Nietzsche's alleged self-contradictory formulations as consistent statements from the point of view of Nietzsche and his time. Only insofar as they are in conflict with the inherent logic of *the paradigm* that he tries to expose do I question their consistency (as on one occasion below, cf. Part I, A.10: "Regression to the Romantic Concept of Concept"). That is, when Nietzsche in lack of oversight seems to betray himself and introduces issues that conflict with his primary concerns, I suspect that he is under counter-productive influence of another competing intellectual paradigm.

On this strategy, the reconstructive reading requires knowledge of the context of *the paradigm*, because it is the intellectual context that determines the *epistemic premise*—not the positions of various contemporary schools of philosophy. Hence, in the present exposition of Nietzsche's essay, we frequently introduce references to peers discussing theoretical concerns identical to Nietzsche's, peers that he refers to and sometimes even paraphrases. Thanks to these considerations, several classical 'puzzles' regarding Nietzsche's early epistemology disappear, whether they have been proposed by his supporters or his detractors. For example, as already indicated, (i), there is no contradiction in Nietzsche's insistence on 'truthfulness' in some passages of the essay, and in others, declaring 'Truth' for an illusion. On a sufficiently indifferent reading, the distinction is adequately explained by himself and comes about because the concept of 'truth,' on Nietzsche's general view, has a history and a genealogy. As such, it is not an abstract formal concept with a fixed logic, but a dynamic concept with an etymology, a history, and a development. It means something in one historical context and develops into meaning something else in another. When Nietzsche in one part of his essay identifies positively with the social requirement of 'truthfulness,' but elsewhere in his essay rejects the existence of a universal 'Truth,' he applies two entirely different concepts of 'truth.' It is a case of apples and oranges, and their differences do not imply paradox or contradiction. (ii) When he in the essay as well as in later work applies the universal concept of 'Truth' to the idea of 'reality' as a *thing-in-itself*, it has been regarded as contentious, because his 'anti-Truth' or 'falsification thesis' seems to imply that there is *no thing-in-itself* in the sense of *no reality*. However, in the thinking of Nietzsche and several of his peers from the Kantian tradition, so-called 'objective reality' is seen as asserted by a biologically evolved subject necessarily seeing the world from its own perceptive-cognitive perspective. So-called 'objective reality' is consequently de-objectified according to this new biological-physiological- psychological perspective. Nietzsche and peers on the contrary tend to regard the thesis of universal 'objectivity' as regressive anti-scientific metaphysics ignoring the (by the new sciences) established fact that we format so-called 'reality' already in perception, and continue this formatting on higher levels in language and finally in conceptualization. On this epistemological position, the human being is always *imbedded in reality* from its own perspective; indeed, it is imbedded in *too much reality*, since this super-abundance needs *simplification* on several levels. (iii) If we cannot adequately see, and even less, adequately talk about 'objective reality,' it is not far-fetched to call the concepts that we use to refer to 'reality' for *metaphors* or *illusions*, and in later writings, *falsifications*. Our formation of concepts has as such a creative aspect, which the speculative metaphysical traditions forget and/or repress when they confuse conceptual metaphors with 'Truth.' When this happens, former creative metaphors coagulate into 'dead metaphors,' implying that they are raised to the status of fetishes, and the conceptualizing human alienates itself from its creative ability to form knowledge about its appearing world for the sake of survival and self-advancement. Instead of knowledge being human-driven, it becomes God-driven. The putative divine origin of knowledge is always under criticism in Nietzsche, who emphasizes the anthropocentric character of knowledge. In this, we notice that Nietzsche in his critique of knowledge is associated with Feuerbach's critique of religion (cf. Part I, A.6.2: "Feuerbach and Nietzsche on Anthropocentrism").[24] (iv) Finally, despite Nietzsche's emphasis on 'interpretation' as characterizing various levels of our passive and active reception of our environing world, his thinking is not declining into idealism or subjectivism, because his appearing reality is not primarily constituted by the individual subject, but by the human species. Reality is not '*my* idea,' but '*our* perception.' The most important aspect of his much-discussed 'perspectivism' relates to the biological fact that different organisms have different perceptions of the world. It is a view, which Nietzsche shares with several peers such as Fr. Lange, R. Avenarius, E. Mach, and H. Vaihinger, to who it was as self-evident as it was to Nietzsche. From the biological fact that species perceive and experience the world differently, one must conclude that no species perceives an 'objective reality,' that *our* so-called 'objective reality' at best refers to a reality perceived by the human species with its unique human sense-apparatus. Insofar as we accept the authority of the naturalist paradigm, reality is necessarily constituted by the human species, therefore never 'objectively' as thing-in-itself, therefore 'perspectival' as a matter of fact (cf. Part I, A.8: "Biological Perspectivism").[25]

2. Questions of Interpretation; Essential Contradictions

Within the intellectual paradigm, these and other 'puzzles' have rational and straightforward solutions that seem to render them self-evident.[26] I do, however, notice a tension in Nietzsche's TL, which seems impossible to bridge. Nietzsche's essay contains two Parts, the larger Part I and a much briefer Part II. As we proceed from Part I to Part II, we encounter a Nietzsche almost transforming himself from a naturalist to a romanticist, as he turns up the volume of his rhetoric and persuades himself to defend the romantic-aesthetic paradigm inherited from the Romantic School, Schopenhauer, and Wagner. The few pages of the last part reads like a leftover from his newly published *Die Geburt der Tragödie* (1871), and is composed like a manifest directed against conceptual language and reasoning, which is not the conclusion we most reasonably would draw from the first part, where Nietzsche for example establishes that concepts in a naturalist epistemology must take the place of 'Truths' in the classical metaphysical sense. He has as such established that human knowledge harbors a creative aspect, epitomized in his talk about 'metaphors.' In Part II, he now devaluates this creative aspect when it is applied to the positive sciences, the indeed *most interesting* application of the thesis, as we are instead introduced to the old romantic dichotomies between concept and trope, science and poetry, reason and feeling, death and life, where the first position in these oppositions always is discarded.

This aesthetic romanticism of Nietzsche has been attractive in several deconstructive receptions (e.g., S. Kofman and P. de Man[27]), but in the reading of undersigned, it is the most problematic aspect of Nietzsche's essay. I see it as *regressive* as well as *paradigmatically inconsistent* with the more important naturalist paradigm that he does such a good job introducing in the first part.

However, as a consolation, the tension in the early essay between his adherence to the new 'naturalist' paradigm and his continued commitment to the older 'romantic-aesthetic' paradigm seems resolved in later writings.[28] In a manner of speaking, Nietzsche starts his career as an epistemologist with his right foot planted in the developing naturalist paradigm and his left planted in the older romantic-aesthetic paradigm, and he ends by realizing that also his left foot belongs where his right foot is already solidly planted. His early schizophrenia has consequences for his different evaluations of, for example, the important concept of 'concept' in early and late writings, and with this, his evaluations of the significance of science and 'the man of science.' It takes time for Nietzsche to leave the romantic paradigm behind, but when it happens, he arrives to a relatively consistent anti-metaphysical naturalist position, already competently sketched out in the first part of his early essay (cf. Part I, A.10: "Regression to the Romantic Arts-Metaphysics").

3. Nietzsche's Thinking as Consistent Development of the Naturalist Paradigm

When we read Nietzsche's notebooks from the years immediately following the publication of BT, constituting the groundwork for TL, it is as if Nietzsche has already stepped into the entirely different project of advanced neo-Kantian discussions of biology, perception, and cognition. Many of his early notebooks anticipates epistemological positions of his later years. His *Notebook 19*,[29] spanning a period from summer 1872 to beginning 1873 is particularly precocious as it introduces a series of observations that we will find, almost unmitigated, in much later works such as *Götzendämmerung* (1888; *Twilight of the Idols* [TI]) and in the late Nachlaß material preparing his unfinished magnum opus, *Der Wille zur Macht*. Is he 'source-mining' his own early notes when writing his later work, or has he internalized fundamental epistemological positions in 1872/1873 to such an extent that they essentially never change after that point?—In any case, the discussions of 'Nietzsche's periods' seems in need of revaluation or perhaps reclassification. My suggestion is that Nietzsche makes a false start in his earliest work, because he, as Nehamas has convincingly suggested, as young and impressionable is under the spell of the charismatic Wagner,[30] best manifested in his BT and traceable also in TL2, but in subsequent notes from as early as 1872 and in TL1, has adopted a 'naturalist' position that he essentially never changes.

Given this modification of his early position, which especially relates to his theory of art, one may notice certain reformulations of his epistemological positions from his early work to his late, but no radical shift in position as has been argued by several contemporary Analytic commentators (since initially suggested by M. Clark in 1990[31]). In order to understand this development in his thinking, we turn in the second part our attention to Nietzsche's later work such as *Die fröhliche Wissenschaft* (1882/87; *The Gay Science* [GS]), *Jenseits von Gut und Böse* (1886; *Beyond Good and Evil* [BGE]), *Zur Genealogie der Moral* (1887; *On the Genealogy of Morals* [GM]), *Götzendämmerung* (1888; *Twilight of the Idols* [TI]), and the notes for his planned but unfinished work, *Der Wille zur Macht: Versuch einer Umwertung aller Werte*, in order to understand his later discussions of Truth and the thing-in-itself.

Nietzsche's development may be seen as a response to the developments of the intellectual paradigm during the latter part of the nineteenth century. Outlining the brief history of the most relevant interpretations of the *thing-in-itself*, we see them developing from the Materialist, the neo-Kantian, to the Positivist understanding. We notice in this development that the thing-in-itself, *first*, is taken *literal* as one looks for substances that can adequately constitute such a 'thing'; *second*, the thing-in-itself is increasingly understood as mere *metaphor* or fiction, asserted with a possible heuristic purpose, but without referring to a corresponding reality; in order to, finally, being dismissed as *superfluous*. Add 1. In the so-called 'literal' interpretation, the 'thing' is seen as a unitary, substantial entity supposedly existing independently of the perceiving being; it is seen as an actual cause of and corresponding to appearances as their material or substantial counterpart, representing 'truth' antedating them. The view is defended by mechanical materialists as the 'literal thing' becomes placeholder for newly discovered 'atoms' and their associated 'forces.' Some philosophers of mechanical materialism (e.g., Ludwig Büchner and Maximilian Drossbach[32]) attempt to reconstruct the possible correspondences between atoms, our physiological receptions of them, and our psychological perceptions caused by them. On this increasingly discredited view, atoms and forces explain perception and cognition according to a linear mechanical model, where atoms and their associated forces affect the sense-apparatus and causes mental images. Increasingly, the view rejected as impossible and self-contradictory Kantianism, and replaced with, *add 2*, a 'metaphorical' interpretation of the 'thing,' in which it is merely seen as an expression of the unknown as such. It is a *limit-concept*, cf. Du Bois-Reymond, von Helmholtz, and Fr. Lange.[33] The new sciences have convincingly demonstrated that our perceptive-cognitive apparatus is a product of random evolution and furthermore is imperfect in its reception of the world. On this interpretation, Kant's original critique is regarded as revolutionary and rehabilitated as foreshadowing scientific advances in evolutionary biology and psycho-physiology. From a strictly scientific point of view, Kant has been proven right, we demonstrably cannot access 'things-in-themselves.' *Add 3*. Toward the end of the century, phenomenalist-positivist inclined thinkers such as Lange, Avenarius, Mach, and Vaihinger reject the 'thing' from a pragmatic position.[34] The concept is regarded as useless, and fulfills no purpose for the scientific researcher, who is on surer ground if he ignores it and focuses on observations and conceptualizations of relations between phenomena.

We notice an overlap of this brief history of the 'thing' and Nietzsche's development. Nietzsche too offers different interpretations of the Kantian 'thing.' The first 'materialist' interpretation of the 'thing,' he consistently rejects and nowhere do we find him defending the 'thing' in the form of substances, causes, or atoms. However, he adheres to the second interpretation especially in his early essay discussing the 'thing' as an "enigmatic X" to which we have no access. And he adheres to the third interpretation in especially his final work, where he in several passages attempts to *un-think* the Kantian thing—with greater or lesser success since this *un-thinking* is fraught with conceptual and logical problems. Thanks to the resilience of the age-old dichotomy between 'thing' and 'appearance,' it is frustratingly difficult to claim the existence of an appearing world without admitting to a corresponding thing. This frustration is often, in Nietzsche as well as in several of his peers, resolved by appealing to sense-reality as the only available reality. The resolution is in brief that sense-impressions are our nether limit of knowledge, and that they, upon being received by our biologically evolved sense-apparatus, are undergoing modification and reinterpretation, first in perception properly speaking and since in cognition. In this respect, Nietzsche begins in later work to see a task for the sciences and the scientists; they re-format not *objective* but *sensational* reality in formal languages meant to bring this chaotic realm under abstract control.

4. Introducing the Nietzsche-Machian Theory of Knowledge

In the last part of the essay, I compare Nietzsche's theory of knowledge to that of his likeminded peers, first and foremost, Ernst Mach and Hans Vaihinger. That the theoretical Nietzsche has affinities with the Central European positivists and pragmatists of the late nineteenth was generally accepted by proponents of these schools at the turn of the century. Since then the idea was forgotten and/or repressed and became unfashionable in the late twentieth century (*mutatis mutandis*, by Continental and Anglo-Saxon schools alike), until it in the beginning of the twenty-first century started up again and today is finding a still growing number of adherents.

Vaihinger was enthusiastic about the similarities between his own and Nietzsche's thinking; followers of Mach, such as Hans Kleinpeter and Phillip Frank, were so too.[35] It is unsurprising that we are able to see this overlap since they are all heavily invested in the same discussion emerging from neo-Kantianism, and adhering to the new naturalist and cognitivist turn of theory. They are all addressing conceptual systems that belong now to Kant, now to Darwin, now to Fechner, now to Comte, etc. In his letters to Mach, Kleinpeter is for example happy to report that Nietzsche is a naturalist, a Darwinist, a positivist, and a pragmatist. Vaihinger sometimes calls himself a 'naturalist,' sometimes a 'positivist,' sometimes a 'pragmatist,' and sometimes a 'fictionalist.' The many labels indicate a 'naturalist-scientific-positivist' paradigm still in development and with porous borders, but where members share certain fundamental creeds. Polemically, they all see themselves as anti-metaphysical, anti-transcendental, and anti-theologian. They all tend to put a strong emphasis on the 'given,' the 'available,' and the 'apparent,' and emphasize perception and observation since metaphysics, transcendentalism, and theology are demoted belief-systems dismissed as superstition. They share the criticism of the absolutistic notion of Truth and its associated true-apparent distinction. They begin to see science as the most promising of disciplines because it is preoccupied with the empirical and apparent universe, therefore starting from the senses, but with the never-ending task to form various conceptual languages about the appearing sense-material. They often see themselves as participating in a new 'enlightenment' thinking that in its emphasis on human intellectual autonomy points in the direction of atheism and nihilism.[36]

In a fluid situation where the new paradigm is under development, branching out in different directions, we cannot see participants like Nietzsche as belonging in a single box without any overflow into multiple other boxes. It is not particularly reasonable, for example, to insist that he is a 'Naturalist' but not a 'Positivist, a 'Pragmatist' but not a 'Fictionalist,' a 'Phenomenalist' but not a 'Cognitivist,' because the paradigm has not yet stabilized as such a clearly defined classificatory system with neat little boxes for each different school. It is at best the sum of the ongoing theoretical labor of its many individual members and it must quasi-randomly rely on its members for further demarcation and determination of its core creeds.

5. A Bilingual German/English Version of Wahrheit und Lüge

In an appendix to the present work I introduce a new translation of Nietzsche's *Über Wahrheit und Lüge*, arranging in two columns Nietzsche's German original to my own English translation. During my discussion of the essay below, I consistently translated Nietzsche's original essay into an English version that seemed most fluent and made best sense to myself. I opted to juxtapose this translation as a whole to Nietzsche's German essay in the appendix to this volume, instead of adding his many poignant German expressions in brackets to my quotes in the main text. Hopefully, this bilingual presentation of the essay may facilitate the study of the essay by meticulous readers who are inclined to crosscheck translations.[37]

Part I
Nietzsche's Early Theory of Truth and Knowledge

A: PART I OF *TRUTH AND LIES*

1. Preliminary Remarks

1. Paradigm and Text

When one embarks on presenting Nietzsche's 'naturalistic deconstruction' of truth, it must be imperative to understand the paradigm in which he was embedded thanks to his studies of peers of the nineteenth century. To say that he is 'imbedded in a paradigm' is the same as to say that he shares epistemological positions that many of his contemporaries at the turn of the century advocate as well.

The interest of the reading is not here to try to assess who says what first, who is inspired by whom, etc., according to a linear cause-effect model, because these attempts to determine 'ownership of ideas' may be simplifications of more complex situations. It may be correct that x is 'inspired' by y. However, it is sometimes the case that participants imbedded in the same paradigm—the same grid of conceptual positions and criticisms—*cannot help* but reiterating identical issues and draw from them identical conclusions. Since the paradigm is larger than any individual, the single participant imbedded in the paradigm, given a modicum of logical ability, often arrive to results that other participants can think as well—dependently or independently, with or without reading or being 'inspired' by peers. It should therefore not surprise us that we find agreements between theorists such as Lange, Nietzsche, Avenarius, Mach, Vaihinger, Peirce, James et al., many of who worked out their universe independently of each other. They came from *the same*, they thought about *the same*, they developed *the same*, such as newly discovered areas like biology, physiology, and psychology, and they criticized *the same*, such as the classical metaphysical and theological traditions. It would rather be extremely surprising if neo- or post-Kantian philosophers somehow develop isolated positions, defending unique philosophical agendas completely distinct from beliefs entertained in their age. As in biology so in intellectual history, never do we experience the evolution of a uniquely new species without ancestors, and never do we experience a jump from one form to an entirely new form.[1]

Nietzsche's TL can as such be seen as his preliminary summary of the multiple representations of the new naturalist paradigm that he throughout his career found convincing. In that sense, Nietzsche's brief essay creates order in a chaos of ideas, often combining areas not combined before in the predominantly scientific paradigm, such as perception, cognition, and linguistics, or metaphysics and morals. In all its brevity and notwithstanding certain significant flaws, the essay is the ambitious groundwork for a work Nietzsche continues in matters of psychology, cognition, epistemology, and metaphysics until his late notes. It is like a sketch he will continue to elaborate, develop, and modify.

2. Nietzsche's Intellectual Context from 1862 to 1873

It would require super-human learning to know the entire library of the nineteenth century and super-human intelligence to comprehend all possible conceptual connections, but to understand the paradigm in which Nietzsche is imbedded we may take a shortcut around what literature he read. It is manageable to read a selection of the work that we thanks to scholars know that he was reading in a decade from the beginning of the 1860s into the 1870s.

I have found a list of readings provided by Thomas Brobjer in an appendix to his *Nietzsche's Intellectual Context* (2008), in addition to Sarah Scheibenberger's account of Nietzsche's sources in *Kommentar zu Nietzsche's, Ueber Wahrheit und Lüge im außermoralischen Sinne* (2016), especially helpful in my attempt to identify the epistemological readings that would have been formative for Nietzsche's discussions in TL.[2] Exactly *how* Nietzsche was inspired from these readings, whether positively or negatively, that we cannot understand from simply looking at a list, but we can minimally assume that his readings have situated him within the particular intellectual paradigm indicated by the list. TL is a discussion of this paradigm, addressing, summarizing, criticizing, and sometimes offering solutions to the theoretical problems it suggests.

If we focus on Nietzsche's epistemological readings from the early 1860s to 1873, the year he finished *Wahrheit und Lüge*, we notice that he from early on is familiar with Ludwig Feuerbach's *Das Wesen des Christenthums* (1846), apparently read in 1861 and again in 1862. Arthur Schopenhauer turns up on his list of readings in 1865 where Nietzsche engrosses himself in several of his major works such as *Über die vierfache Wurzed des Satzes vom zureichendend Grunde* (1813), *Die Welt als Wille und Vorstellung* (1819/1844), the essays, *Über den wille der Natur* (1836) and *Die beiden*

Grundprobleme der Ethik (1841), and *Parerga and Paralipomena* (1851). Schopenhauer will reappear several times, and is the uniquely most important source of Nietzsche in his formative years. Fr. Albert Lange shows up as another important source in 1866 with his *Geschichte des Materialismus* (1866), and so does Kuno Fischer with his *Immanuel Kant* (the third and fourth volume of his monumental *Geschichte der neuern Philosophie*, 1854–1877) and Otto Liebmann with his *Kant und die Epigonen* (1865). Friedrich Ueberweg with his three volume *Grundriss der Geschichte der Philosophie von Thales bis auf die Gegenwart* (1863–1866) is acquired by Nietzsche in 1867 and will continue to reappear on his list of reading. Nietzsche reads Hans Rosenkranz's *Geschichte der Kantschen Philosophie* (1840) in 1868 where he also returns to Kuno Fischer and to Schopenhauer. In 1869, he becomes acquainted with Eduard von Hartman's *Philosophie des Unbewußten* (1869), to which he will return in the years to come (as he becomes increasingly critical of Hartman). In 1872, we find on his list Zöllner's *Über die Natur der Kometen* (1870), Afrikan Spir's *Forschung nach der Gewissheit in der Erkenntnis der Wirklichkeit* (1869), Schoperhauer's *Die Welt as Wille* appears again, and finally, Kant's *Kritik der reinen Vernunft* (1781–1787) is now included on his list. Brobjer and Scheibenberger mention Gustav Gerber's *Die Sprache als Kunst* (1871) as a library loan of Nietzsche's, and his reference to Gerber is obvious since entire sentences and passages of Gerber's work have been copied into Nietzsche's essay.[3]

I have here allowed myself to select only *nineteenth-century theoretical* literature among Nietzsche's variegated readings, and have left out multiple works from the classical Greco-Roman tradition or dealing with other topics that he was reading as well. On a survey, it is unsurprising that Schopenhauer followed by Lange and Gerber are primary sources. It is perhaps more surprising that we find several references to neo-Kantian commentators, such as Fischer, Ueberweg, Rosenkranzt, Liebmann, and Spir, rather than to Kant himself; we notice that Feuerbach, Hartman, and Zöllner, too, constituted important sources.

However, on the reconstructed list, we notice a glaring *absence of references* to proponents of evolutionary biology and psycho-physiology, although in TL, Nietzsche is profoundly inspired by these new naturalist, psycho-physiological, and evolutionary paradigms (cf. discussion Part II, B). Charles Darwin is not mentioned, neither are physiologists Johannes Müller, Theodor Fechner, or Du Bois-Reymond; although an essay by Hermann von Helmholtz apparently appears as a library loan. This inspiration we may assume that Nietzsche has received second-hand from Schopenhauer, who was introducing physiological considerations in his *Über die vierfache Wurzel des Satzes des zureichenden Grunde* (1847), from Lange, who had extensive discussions of the psycho-physiologists and dedicated a chapter to Darwin in his *Die Geschichte des Materialismus* (1873), from Ueberweg, who was discussing the nineteenth century's naturalists and scientists in the last volume of his *Grundriss der Geschichte der Philosophie* (1902), and from Hartmann, whose last volume of *Philosophie des Unbewußten* (1870) was a discussion of descent-theory.

2. Human Insignificance and Self-Deceptive Pride

Nietzsche starts *Truth and Lies* [TL] with the outline of a cosmology.[4]

> In some remote corner of a universe in which numerous flickering solar systems are scattered there was once upon a time a star upon which clever creatures invented knowing. That was the most arrogant and dishonest minute of "world history," but it was after all only a minute. After nature had drawn a few breaths, the star froze and the clever creatures had to die. One might invent such a story, and would still not have adequately illustrated how miserable, how shadowy and transient, how aimless and arbitrary the human intellect looks within nature. There were eternities during which it did not exist; and when eventually it is over, nothing will have happened. For this intellect has no additional mission which takes it beyond human life. Rather, the intellect is human, and only its possessor and creator takes it seriously, as if the axis of the world was turning within it.[5]

We notice that Nietzsche is guilty in a minor mistake, since we live on a planet and not on a "star" (*Gestirn*) as he has it; and he continues to confound the two celestial bodies when he describes the fate of our sun, destined to burn out and 'freeze,' as if this is the fate of Earth. Earth does not burn out, although it eventually will freeze in step with the Sun's burning out.

Regardless the minor glitch, the important message in the passage is that we live on borrowed time. On a cosmological scale, the eventual implosion of the sun will leave us dead on a dead planet in a trice of time: "After nature had drawn a few breaths, the star froze and the clever creatures had to die." Nietzsche wants to express the idea that on a cosmological time-scale, our existence is almost ludicrously irrelevant. As human species, we live "only a minute" in a universe, which Nietzsche in agreement with the cosmology of his day sees as infinite in time and space. Still, our pride, pretense, and narcissism prevent us from acknowledging this irrelevance, as we choose to ignore the greater context that reduces our idle activities to futility.

In the Theologian-Christian paradigm, the human with its divinely inspired reason was the center of the universe, but according to the new scientific-naturalist paradigm now adopted by Nietzsche and peers, 'nature' has assumed center stage. As explicitly expressed in the passage, nature now determines and contextualizes human reason: "how miserable, how shadowy and transient, how aimless and arbitrary the human intellect looks within nature" (ibid.). *A fortiori*, the human being is not only situated "within" nature, it is itself nature. With the reluctant recognition of this new situation, we are losing our former sense of self-importance, self-control, and self-determination, which we ascribed to ourselves in the grand Theologian and Rationalist narratives. We find instead ourselves as the random outcome of natural selective and evolutionary processes. This 'naturalistic' interpretation of human existence becomes the most obvious epistemological frame of the essay, and it will be reiterated in later work. It is an understanding the young Nietzsche undoubtedly adopts from his two most influential 'educators,' Schopenhauer and Fr. Lange.[6]

It is clear that Nietzsche in TL is indebted to Schopenhauer in the passage above, as he here rephrases (if not paraphrases) a passage from the second volume of *Die Welt as Wille und Vorstellung*, where Schopenhauer too compares humans in their idle activities to endless space.

> In endless space countless glowing spheres, around each of which a dozen smaller illuminated ones revolve; hot at the inside and covered with a hard cold crust, on which a musty film has produced a living and knowing being—this is the empirical truth, the real, the world. Yet for a being who thinks, it is a troublesome position to stand on one of those numberless spheres freely floating in boundless space, without knowing wherefrom and whereto, and to be only *one* of innumerable similar beings that press, and push, and suffer, restlessly and rapidly arising and passing away in beginningless and endless time.[7]

In this passage, Schopenhauer, too, describes the human being as ignorant of any deeper meaning or higher purposes. Situated in endless time and space, its relentless "pressing and pushing" are manifestations of an idle 'will to live,' a struggle for survival and reproduction that it shares with other creatures. We are again beyond the reassuring theological and rationalist narratives when Schopenhauer reduces the human being to "only *one* of innumerable similar beings that press, and push, and suffer . . . in beginningless and endless time" (ibid.).

To bring home the point that major writers from the period subscribe to the same scientific-naturalist paradigm, echoing the same depreciation of human self-importance against "infinite space," let us finally listen to H. von Helmholtz, one of the great scientific minds of the century, when he writes:

> We: bits of dust on the surface of our planet, itself hardly worth calling a grain of sand in the universe's infinite space; we: the most recent race among

the living on earth, according to geological chronology barely out of the cradle, still in the learning stage, barely half-educated, declared of age only out of mutual respect, and yet already, through the more powerful force of the causal law, grown beyond all our fellow creatures and vanquishing them in the struggle for existence.[8]

Again, the human being is described as a speck of dust in an indifferent universe, biologically and instinctually conditioned to carry out its struggle for existence out of simple self-preservation and survival concerns. Again, Helmholtz's description implies a loss of importance, purpose, and rational foundation for the human being.

These, and multiple other writers, have all adopted the new naturalist narrative. Their pessimistic assessments of the human condition come about thanks to three important scientific discoveries of the time: The discovery of the enormity of our universe, the discovery of our animal ancestry, and the discovery of our unreliable perceptive apparatus. The still influential Christian idea that the human being is the center-piece of creation is now being devalued and deconstructed thanks to these three major discoveries. 1) Research by C. Messier in the eighteenth century and Herschel in the nineteenth establishing the existence of numerous distant galaxies beyond our own.[9] It is against this perceived enormity of the universe that the human being dwindles to an insignificant speck of dust and its perception of itself as privileged center of the universe seem to be mere vanity. Nietzsche is likely to have found a discussion of the new universe in Zöllner whose *Über der Natur die Kometen* (1870) he reportedly had been reading (cf. Part I, A.2). 2) After Darwin (and contemporary natural philosophers, like Lamarck in France and Ernst Haeckel in Germany),[10] one begins to understand the mechanisms of evolution and realizes that the image humans have created of themselves in the image of God is hopelessly self-centered and self-congratulatory. The Darwinist proposals, that man descends from ancestors more animal than human, implying that our animal origin is an inherited and inherent part of us (moreover, a part lately evolved and therefore never fully superseded by and replaced with reason), is reflected in Nietzsche when he describes our intellect is merely an "accessory" to man. The intellect is a superficial veil over instincts more original and powerful than hitherto understood.[11] 3) The emerging understanding of human physiology becomes the third scientific discovery that contributes to raise doubt about the human capacity for knowing. Physiologists and psychologists such as J. P. Müller, G. Th. Fechner, E. du Bois-Reymond, and H. von Helmholtz[12] had begun to understand the limitations of human perception. They had observed that the perceptive image we produce of a world 'outside' us is an inadequate and inaccurate representation of something of which it is supposed to be an image. This theory of human perception becomes another aspect of the emerging naturalist paradigm. Even if Nietzsche may not have read the research of these scientific writers, it had been widely reported by philosophers such as Schopenhauer, Ueberweg, and Lange, who he positively did read. For example, it was generally known that the image received by the retina was different from the image which we consciously perceived (for example by picturing the exterior upside-down). From receiving impressions to perceiving them consciously, our brain had to play an active interpretive role. Helmholtz suggested that consciously appearing images could hardly be regarded as more than "arbitrary signs" of something outside, which we apparently did not see and could not properly know, and Lange discussed the thesis extensively in his *Geschichte*).[13]

After these three scientific discoveries, the vanity and pretention in *assuming* that we *know* truth almost prompts a sense of indignation in a writer like Nietzsche. A human being reduced to a dot in space and a blip in time can and should not pretend to know anything at all about the absolute and the universal. Reduced to an indiscernible vanishing point in the ocean of space and time, the narcissistic sense of self-importance seems misplaced in the devalued human, comparable to the self-importance of a "mosquito" in Nietzsche's comparison:

> Could we understand the mosquito, we might learn that it too glides through the air with such a self-importance, feeling itself as the flying center of this universe. There is nothing in nature so repugnant and low that it would not immediately swell up like a balloon at the slightest puff of the power of knowing. And just as every doorkeeper wants to have an admirer, so even the proudest of men, the philosopher, supposes that everywhere around him he sees the eyes of the universe telescopically directed at his action and thought.[14]

If a mosquito could think, Nietzsche suggests, it would be as 'mosquito-centric' as we are anthropocentric.[15] Our self-evaluations are 'human, all too human,'[16] and our so-called 'truth' is merely something we *call* or *hold to be* true.

We notice *en passant* that whereas Nietzsche here starts his essay by expressing insights well-known in the intellectual context of his day, he will eventually, as he further develops his thinking, realize the consequences of these insights and radicalize them as no one before him. Nietzsche seems to be the first to fully realize that a de-centered human ready to embrace the random and relative in the new scientific paradigm requires a new human self-understanding. The old human understanding of itself as divinely created and therefore a center of knowledge in a permanent and stable world needs to be replaced with a new human type ready to actively destroy this old theological anthropology. As Nietzsche sees it, this new human type is extended between its realization that nature in the traditional sense of 'objective order' is unknowable *and* the conviction that relative knowledge of nature self-assertively formed by the new human paradoxically is on firmer ground than ever before, i.e., in the articulation of an anthropology corresponding to the new epistemology, Nietzsche oscillates between a firm 'no' to the dependent and subservient self 'receiving' or 'discovering' objective knowledge, and a firm 'yes' to the independent and autonomous self 'constructing' or 'creating' knowledge. Eventually, this new self-assertive human type is dramatized as his *Übermensch*.

Later, at the entry into the twentieth century, this scientific, rational, and enlightened doubt regarding *foundational certainty* will continue in several writers from the epistemological, psychological, and linguistic traditions, such as, for example, E. Mach, S. Freud, and F. de Saussure. With their different projects and vocabularies, they too will question how rationally we 'know'—for example, how consistent our scientific theories are, how well we control our desires, or whether our language is an adequate representation of things. They are all rational thinkers of the random, the non-rational, or the irrational; they may indeed be seen as the latest offshoots of the enlightenment tradition emphasizing the emancipative ideal in cultivating the post-religious and post-metaphysical ultra-autonomous human. In the new emerging paradigm, we are as humans denied our empty claims to divine and objective knowledge, and impelled to embrace our biological roots and our random evolutionary inheritance as a *freedom*.[17]

3. Genealogy of the Pragmatic Notion of Truth

1. Genealogy of Truth in a Pragmatic Sense

During the century, one started to question the validity of the theological and metaphysical notions of knowledge in step with the growing scientific realization that we are, firstly, infinitesimally small compared to an infinite universe, secondly, random outcomes of evolution, and thirdly, poorly equipped to perceive our surrounding world. The new discoveries deliver a triple blow to human pride and are formative for Nietzsche's critical discussions of 'truth' and the 'true world.' We notice already here that Nietzsche's skepticism regarding 'Truth' is less an irrational romantic-idealist impulse, than a reflection of the scientific progress of his age. Truth is becoming an endangered species in the new paradigm. In an interesting reversal of the common understanding of the issue, the *defense of Truth* is now decried as traditionalist religious and metaphysical speculation, while the *rejection of Truth* is applauded as the new progressive naturalist-scientific view.

Despite this state of affairs, Nietzsche of course understands that humans during centuries have developed notions of what counts as true and in their societies interact according to ideas of what is true or false. In two paragraphs, he offers a genealogical analysis of how this apparent commitment to 'truth' has been evolving and introduces a narrative to which he will return in later writings, such as *Jenseits von Gut und Böse* (1886) and (especially) *Zur Genealogie der Moral* (1887). He assumes that before we were able to invent abstract notions like truth, law, and morality, we were living in dark ages where survival by any means was the order to the day. Again, the explanation starts with the Darwinist-naturalist assumption that human beings in their origin are animals, more nature than reason.

> The intellect develops its greatest powers in its capacity for pretense, as this is the means by which the weaker, less robust individuals preserve themselves, since they are denied the horns or sharp teeth of the predators in the struggle of existence. [...] Insofar as the individual wants to preserve itself over and against other individuals, it needs in the natural order of things the intellect mostly for pretense.[18]

Ironically, in an essay investigating 'truth,' Nietzsche proposes that the first impulse of prehistoric man was *never* to tell the truth. The genealogical origin of truth is quite paradoxically *the lie*. The prehistoric human was indisposed to 'truth' but predisposed to 'lying'; i.e., had a "capacity for pretense" (ibid).[19]

In these early days, we were animals and had no *use* for truth. On the contrary, in the struggle of survival we used pretense and dissimulation as compensation for our physical weakness, our lack of "horns and sharp teeth." We needed to be able to outsmart other species and one another between ourselves, in order to preserve ourselves and survive. Dissimulation was necessary. Therefore, Nietzsche submits that nothing in our biological existence gives us any inkling of abstract notions of 'truth,' nor establishes a distinction between 'truthfulness' and 'lying.'

Nietzsche's naturalized human has constitutionally an impulse to lie and deceive, as he sees this impulse as an advantageous feature in the struggle for survival; but our familiarity with lies and lying go even deeper, because we are so "deeply immersed in illusions and dream-images," so entrenched in a surface-world of appearances that we have never evolved any senses for detecting another world of things-themselves and transcendences. Our perceptive apparatus cannot penetrate into 'essences,' but is necessarily consigned to the surfaces of appearances, i.e., to a purely empirical world. We understand neither the 'inner workings' of the world around us nor the 'inner workings' of our body inside of us.

Briefly, deception is deeply ingrained in at least three aspects: a) in our social interactions as a means of survival and self-preservation; b) in our perception of our inside as well as our outside world; and c) in our cognitive attempt to understand, give meaning to, or interpret the world.

> They [humans] are deeply immersed in illusions and dream images; their eyes merely glide over the surface of things and see "forms"; nowhere do their senses lead them to truth, but make them instead content with receiving stimuli and to play a fumbling game on the back of things.[20]

Nature withholds knowledge from the human being and confines it instead to its deceptive consciousness. Thereupon she [nature] "throws away the key," and the only option of humans is to peer out of the cracks of their small chamber of consciousness, completely deluded about their capacity to understand the outside as well as the inside world. When 'Nature' is described as withdrawing herself and withholding her secrets ("throwing away her key"), Nietzsche does not here mean to suggest the existence of a secret world of things-in-themselves that we will recover when eventually we find 'the key.' He is implying, rather, that the key is *forever* lost, not merely *temporarily* lost. Access to the secret world in the form of 'things' and 'essences' is absolutely denied. Du Bois-Reymond's *Ignorabimus* (i.e., 'we shall never know') is by Nietzsche taken for granted as the given condition (cf. Part II, B.1).[21]

In the end of the paragraph, Nietzsche asks a straightforward question that propels him into his genealogical investigation of the 'origin of truth' in the subsequent paragraph: "If this is the condition, how on earth did the drive for truth derive?" (ibid.).

In Nietzsche's narrative, the concept of 'truth' has in itself a genealogy and undergoes evolution. In his suggested outline for a 'history of truth,' truth first appears among humans as 'truthfulness,' but not in the Kantian sense of a 'good will' in the form of a moral categorical imperative spontaneously springing out of the prehistoric individual.[22]

To be 'truthful' rather than deceitful is imposed on us as a *necessity* insofar as humans begin to gather in societies and need to accommodate themselves as group. Now they must enter a "peace treaty" for pragmatic purposes, and they assume a social code according to which it is better to tell the truth than the lie—mostly in order to facilitate trading and commerce. This expedient and pragmatic social code will eventually develop into a moral obligation.

The explanation is reminiscent of Hobbes, who is explicitly recalled in Nietzsche's reference to the *"bellum omnium contra omnes."* In Nietzsche as well as in Hobbes, we begin from the chaos, anarchism, and lawlessness of "the war of every man against every man." They both offer a narrative according to which humans in the beginning live without law, without sense of right and wrong, justice and injustice, and where only the rule of power applies.[23] Like Hobbes, Nietzsche uses this lawless origin as a springboard for introducing the necessity for people to enter a contract. In order to escape their anarchistic "solitary, poor, nasty, brutish, and short" existence, people are eventually compelled to give up their weapons and to rely on each other. Hobbes's 'covenant' and Nietzsche's 'peace treaty' are beginnings of social order, enabling peoples to unify and coexist without fear for their lives. In Hobbes, the covenant is guaranteed by a third party, the ruler, who compels the former antagonists to hold their peace and perform according to the letter of the contract.[24] Nietzsche will later return to the question of institution of law in *The Genealogy of Morals, II*, where he will introduce the notion of a "sovereign" as the guarantor of Law, in this paraphrasing Hobbes in language albeit not in content, since they have different determinations of their 'sovereigns.'[25]

2. Nietzsche's 'Correspondence Theory of Truth' and Its Limitations

In TL, we find no references to a sovereign. Nietzsche takes the discussion in another direction.

> When men from necessity and boredom also want to live socially and as group, they need a peace treaty and attempt to banish at least the worst *bellum omnium contra omnes* from their world. This peace treaty brings with it something which seems to be the first step in acquiring the enigmatic truth-drive. From now on that which shall count as "truth" is being established; that is, one invents a uniform and binding designation for things, and this legislation of language gives also the first laws of truth. From here emerges for the first time the contrast between truth and lie.[26]

Nietzsche is still engaged in answering his leading question, "how on earth did the drive for truth derive?" And he gives us a first hint when suggesting that truth emerges only when a *community agrees* on something to be *counted as true*. The first step in the evolution of our "enigmatic truth-drive" is that something is *established* as "truth"; notice here that Nietzsche puts 'truth' in scare-quotes indicating a cautious distancing himself from the traditional metaphysical concept of truth, i.e., truth understood as absolute, universal, transcendental, and a-historical. One instead "invents" truth as a "uniform and binding designation for things."

The 'invention' or 'establishment' of truth requires minimally the community's consensus on linguistic values; when we talk about legal values the requirement is a legislative body able to decree law. The *community* decides how we may and may not use language, prescribing the proper *correspondence* between given designations and things;[27] it is this *conventionally* decided correspondence between designation and thing that is established as truth. In this important but elementary sense, Nietzsche has a "correspondence-theory of truth."

However, as we immediately realize, it is a 'correspondence-theory' that makes no grand epistemological claims because it *is* conventional. Its elementary purpose is to distinguish the honest from the lying individual. Only after the fixation of a correspondence between sign and thing is it possible to recognize the difference between individuals obeying or violating the social code. Before the existence of this fixation, the lie cannot be recognized; but after the fixation, the liar can be seen as using conventional designations contrary to the value they have according to the community.

The liar uses valid designations, the words, for making the unreal appear as if it is real, says Nietzsche.

> He says for example, "I am rich," while "poor" would have been the correct designation for his condition. He abuses the established conventions by means of arbitrary substitutions or even reversals of names. If he does this in a manner that is selfish and causes harm, society will no longer trust him and will thereby exclude him. Humans do not so much shun being deceived as being harmed by the deceit. Even at this stage, they actually do not hate the deception as much as the bad and harmful consequences from certain kinds of deceit. In a similar limited sense, man wants only truth: he desires the pleasant and life-preserving consequences of truth, while he is indifferent toward pure knowledge without consequences; he is even hostile toward perhaps harmful and destructive truths.[28]

In a pragmatic sense, 'truth' is *conventional fixation of correspondence*. In Nietzsche's example, explaining what constitutes 'lying,' the liar tells people that he is wealthy, while he is in fact poor, and makes thus "the unreal appear to be real." Still, as Nietzsche specifies, it is not the lie as such that bothers society, but only the lie that has harmful consequences. If the liar tells people he is wealthy because he wants to attract investors, secure himself a career, present himself as a worthy suitor, etc., while he is in fact poor, he may be deceiving the community, but worse than the deceit is it that other members of society may suffer consequences from his lies that are harmful.[29]

The passage above is anticipated in *Notebook 19* in a slightly different variation. Here Nietzsche makes the following observations:

> One anticipates the bad consequences of reciprocal lies. This is the origin of the duty of truth. The epic storyteller is allowed to lie, because in that area no harmful effects are to be expected—Thus, where the lie is regarded as pleasant it is allowed.[30]

> If the state of war is to cease anywhere it must begin with fixing the truth, i.e. with a valid and binding designation of things. The liar uses words in order to make the unreal appear as real, i.e. he misuses the firm foundation.[31]

As Nietzsche points out in the passages, society punishes only the harmful lie; it reacts out of concerns for self-preservation; harmless deceptions like the poetic 'lies' we encounter in the theater or in novels, cause no alarm. As a pertinent example, we recall that in the history of criticism, the apologists for poetry in late medieval criticism would defend poets against the religious zealots with the catchphrase, 'Poetry lies, but it lies with delight'; i.e., poetic lies are harmless and poets should not to be blamed, since they are merely entertaining and delighting their audiences.[32]

May we from this reading of a few pages in TL conclude that Nietzsche 'believes in truth' and indeed has a 'correspondence theory of truth'—to paraphrase a concern of especially the Analytic schools of Nietzsche-commentary? Insofar as we talk about *truth as truthfulness*, we must answer in the positive.[33] Nietzsche has not suspended the commonsensical fact that humans are able to be truthful or deceitful, sincere or insincere, tell the truth or tell a lie. In this sense, Nietzsche 'believes in truth,' and may even be seen as, to paraphrase M. Clark, "truth-friendly."[34]

Truth as truthfulness is promoted by society, because it is necessary to have truthful rather than deceptive individuals. The liar abuses established social conventions, by for example defaulting on promises; and in enterprising, mercantile, and trading societies, such deceptions are inadmissible. Truth as truthfulness is tantamount to *accountability*. To be *accountable* means to act in accordance with the established convention; it even implies that one obeys what counts as *existing* in one's society. This implication is emphasized, not in TL itself, but again in the *Nachlaß* material from 1872–1873:

> In a political society, a firm agreement is necessary, which is founded on the habitual use of metaphors. Everything unusual upsets and annoys [*regt sie auf*], yes, destroys. Therefore, it is politically convenient and moral to use every word like the masses use it. To be true means from now on not to deflect from the habitual meaning of things [*Sinn der Dinge*]. The true is that *which is* [*Das wahre ist das Seiende*], in contrast to the non-existing [*Nichtwirklichen*]. The first convention is about what ought to count as 'being' [*seiend*].[35]

It is an issue Nietzsche will address again and in better detail in *The Genealogy of Morals*, where he will emphasize the importance of cultivating a human capable of making and of keeping promises. *Truth as truthfulness* and *accountability* has so far a practical economical purpose, the preservation of society with its social, economic, and political institutions. Man desires the "life-preserving consequences of truth."

However, we notice that Nietzsche regards this notion of *truth as truthfulness* as of "limited value." Since it does not aspire to access and understand reality 'in-itself,' it hardly gives us information beyond that which we can easily look up in the existing dictionary of the society, as Nietzsche explains later in his essay:

> If I create the definition of the mammal and then, after observing a camel, declare: "look, a mammal," then a truth is brought to light, but it is of limited value. I mean, it is anthropomorphic through and through and does not contain a single speck that apart from man would be really and universally "true in itself."[36]

In pointing at a camel and declaring it a mammal, I have essentially only confirmed that I know my dictionary and its most elementary definitions, and I have in this very obvious linguistic-pragmatic sense *told the truth*.

In the last sentence of the section, Nietzsche asks again a leading rhetorical question meant to introduce us to the next stage of his investigations; in paraphrase, 'what about linguistic conventions themselves; do designations and things correspond; is language an adequate expression of reality?' In this questioning, he seems to dispute the 'correspondence theory of truth,' which we just argued qua our reading that he was defending. Is he confused or caught in self-contradiction? —The answer must be in the negative. He is rather addressing 'correspondence' or 'adequation' from two different perspectives, conventionally and transcendentally. Sometimes he focuses on the *actual* correspondence established by linguistic convention, and sometimes on the *alleged* correspondence between language and reality as such. In the linguistic-pragmatic sense as discussed above, correspondence between discourse and thing as established by the community is not in question, but on an epistemic level we may doubt how deep our conventional languages reach into (or 'correspond to') the nature of things. His own example differentiates precisely between these two levels: we are as language-users compelled to call a 'camel' a 'mammal,' but this linguistic convention does not give us any knowledge of the nature of the camel. The postulate of a 'mammal-nature,' 'mammal-essence' of the camel is indeed highly dubious from Nietzsche's point of view.

Later in his essay, Nietzsche returns to this discussion of the pragmatic origin of truth. Here he uses the term 'lie' in an inflated sense insofar as words are regarded as 'metaphors' without direct correspondences to what they represent. In this inflated sense, we 'lie' simply by speaking, whether we are sincere or insincere, since words are coagulated metaphors randomly established by society, but fundamentally lacking correspondence to their various linguistic references.

> To be truthful implies that one uses the common metaphors, or expressed morally, one follows the obligation to lie according to the established conventions and in a herd-fashion lies in a manner applying to everybody. Obviously, man forgets that this is the case, and he therefore lies in the indicated sense unconsciously and according to century old habits; precisely thanks to this unconsciousness and forgetfulness, he arrives to a sense of truth. From the sense that one is obliged to designate a thing as 'red,' another as 'cold,' a third as 'silent,' a moral impulse emerges regarding truth. In contrast to the liar, who nobody trusts and everybody excludes, the person demonstrates to himself the venerable, trustful, and useful aspects of truth.[37]

Despite this, our so-called 'lying' in the inflated and general sense, Nietzsche adheres to his explanation of the pragmatic origin of truth. When we in "herd-fashion" "lie according to established conventions," we are actually telling the truth in the *pragmatic* sense. His critical analysis of the *transcendental* concept of truth is still a precise explanation of the *pragmatic* concept of truth, because the latter emerges from the forgetfulness and repression of our conventionally accepted 'lies,' i.e., there *is* no (transcendental) Truth, but there *is* the repression of this fact, resulting in the pragmatic belief in truth.

In our beliefs in Truth, we have merely adjusted ourselves to conventions and "century old habits" completely "forgetting" that this adjustment has a history and genealogy. I point at something 'red' and calls it without further ado 'red,' and if I have observed convention and the thing pointed out is called 'red' within my linguistic community, I have told the 'truth' and have demonstrated trustworthiness. However, on this analysis, we may still legitimately question whether nature in-itself harbors anything 'red' (or anything 'cold,' 'warm,' 'great,' or 'small'). We then question whether 'redness' or 'coldness' or 'greatness' are inherent qualities of things and suggest instead that these qualities exist only from a human perspective.

4. Nerve-Stimuli, Images, and Sounds

1. The Development of a 'Truth Drive'

The notion of truth as 'truthfulness' is for most readers uncontroversial. Most readers would grant that we as social and communicating agents must abide by the linguistic conventions that make what we say meaningful to other members of the community, as well as society compels us to obey the moral-legal imperatives that bid us to speak with honesty. Under these social obligations and at least *ideally*, we say what we mean and mean what we say. This elementary prescription is inherent in the idea of *truthfulness* and *accountability*, which eventually develops into the much more dubious "truth-drive."

Nietzsche alternately speaks of a *Trieb zur Wahrheit* and an *Erkenntniß-trieb* in his essay (cf. WL 877). To talk about a *drive* [*Trieb*] for truth or knowledge is hyperbole, because a 'drive' strictly speaking is biological, hereditary, and innate. Situated in the naturalist paradigm, we readily accept for example sexual and aggressive drives, because the human species could not have survived if there had been no sexual incentives to propagate the species or no aggressive instincts to preserve it in the competition with other species. 'Truth' on the other hand had no biological necessity, as Nietzsche recognized above when discussing 'lying' as the primordial human condition. According to that discussion, human beings had an innate 'drive to lie' rather than an innate 'drive to truth.' When nonetheless Nietzsche talks about a 'truth-*drive*,' it must be because he sees that the *belief in truth* has been so strongly internalized during the civilizational process that it from his civilizational vantage-point seems *as if* a 'drive.'

This cultivation of 'truth' has a history and a genealogy that Nietzsche attempts to explain, and as discussed above his explanation begins in the linguistic-pragmatic notion of 'truth as truthfulness.' The problem of the 'truth-drive' emerges when this self-evident notion of truth is applied or rather *misapplied* to *nature* as the possibility of *nature's truthfulness*. Then we encounter the beginning of a misunderstanding that will reverberate throughout centuries of Western thinking. At one point we are no longer satisfied with "mere tautologies," "empty husks" like 'a camel is a mammal,'[38] we instead apply the human truth-requirement to nature. If first truth is merely analytical (or 'tautological' in the typical vocabulary of Nietzsche and peers), then, applied to nature, it becomes synthetic.

> It is only by means of forgetfulness that man arrives to the illusion that he possesses "truth" to the extent just indicated. When he is no longer satisfied with truth in the form of tautologies, that is, is no longer content with empty husks, then he will always exchange truths for illusions.[39]

According to this misapplication, we falsely conjecture that nature is following the same rules as *us,* as if *nature* could be and ought to be *speaking truth.* We transfer 'truthfulness' from man to nature in the false belief that as well as *man* is able to be truthful, it is possible also for *nature* to be 'truthful.' Thanks to this false transference, we impress upon nature what was from the beginning merely a *social-moral-legal* requirement. In *Notebook 19*, Nietzsche is explicit about this transference: "But the drive to be true, transferred to nature, produces the belief that also nature has to true to us. The drive for knowledge [*Erkenntnißtrieb*] relies on this transference."[40]

2. What Is a Word?

When Nietzsche starts next passage with the abrupt question, 'What is a word?' thereupon beginning a discussion about the arbitrariness of language, he seems to be interrupting his line of thoughts. However, posing this question, Nietzsche is actually continuing his reasoning. It is by means of words that we judge something to be true, both in the modest pragmatic and in the grandiose metaphysical sense. Therefore, it is relevant and even necessary to understand what kind of relationship *the word* has to 'truth.'

> What is a word? The copy of a nerve-stimulus in sounds. But to infer from the nerve-stimulus to a cause outside us is already the result of a false and unjustified application of the principle of sufficient reason. If in the genesis of language truth alone had been the deciding criterion for the certainty of designations, how could we then say, "the stone is hard," as if "hard" were already known to us, and not merely a purely subjective stimulus? We divide things into gender when we describe the tree as masculine and the plant as feminine; but what arbitrary assignments![41] How far does this not exceed the canon of certainty! We talk about a "snake," but this designation touches only upon the coiling and twisting and could apply equally to the worm.[42] What arbitrary demarcations, what one-sided preferences for soon this soon another property of a thing! Juxtaposing different languages shows that regarding words, it is never truth, never the adequate expression that matters, because otherwise we would not need so many languages.[43]

Let us reserve the discussion of nerve-stimuli to the following section, and focus on two of Nietzsche's examples intended to refute the idea of a logical relationship between word and reality: (i) the word *hard*, as in "the stone is hard," relates to the merely subjective impression that the stone feels hard to our touch, but it makes no sense to talk about the hardness of a stone-in-itself. Here, it is not Nietzsche problem that the word 'hard' is arbitrary as sound-image, i.e., that we in different languages find different word-representations for the physical sensation of hardness. His point is that in whatever language, the stone is always *arbitrarily described* as 'hard,' since hardness is a specific human perception uniquely placing the stone in relation to the human touch. When we describe the stone as 'hard,' we add to the stone's substance an attribute that only makes sense within *its relationship to humans*. The stone-in-itself is neither hard nor soft, but to the human touch, it feels 'hard.'[44] The example illustrates the anthropomorphism of our language, which we find in his other examples as well; for example (ii) when we divide things in gender and describe some as masculine, others as feminine, others again as neutral. This gendering of language is an equally arbitrary division of the multiplicity of things that are in themselves neither masculine, nor feminine, nor neutral.

Nietzsche anticipates here something that later Saussure makes into a principle in his formulation of a scientific linguistics,[45] namely that language as arbitrary and conventional is a system of differences that *as system* corresponds to nothing in the outside world. Nietzsche talks about difference, convention, and arbitrariness too, when he questions the "arbitrary demarcations" of language (e.g., the genders in German language, indicated by the male, female, or neutral articles, '*der*,' '*die*,' '*das*,' are nonexistent in the references to which they refer). Nietzsche and Saussure are not denying that we live and breathe in a world, but they are asserting that our *knowledge of the world* is mediated by language, which adds an inevitable anthropomorphic component, since we cannot subtract *human perspective and interest* from *knowledge* and capture objectivity in its pure and uncontaminated self-presence.[46]

In the passage above, Nietzsche resorts to indirect proof, the *reductio ad impossibile*, by arguing that if language *was not arbitrary*, but was a transparent medium for truth, we would not have and did not need different languages. As well as species evolve randomly in evolutionary biology, languages evolve randomly in historical linguistics. However, in a hypothetical world *ad impossibile* of a single language providing a unique correspondence between word and thing, this diachronic aspect of language would be suspended. One language would universally fit peoples of all nations, suggesting an original creator of language, an original 'linguistic designer.' The proposal is suggested in order to be rejected as absurd. Since we live after the Tower of Babel, in a world of multiple languages, we are consigned to a sign-world where correspondences between words and things are arbitrary and conventional.

Nietzsche is here and elsewhere in his essay rephrasing discussions introduced by some of his peers, so for example by Fr. A. Lange, E. von Hartman, and G. Gerber as noted by other scholars.[47]

Nietzsche is in the subsequent passage still guided by his leading question, 'what is a word,' as he continues his examination by now suggesting that words emerge in the last stage of a perceptive-cognitive process, where *first*, nerve-stimuli are transformed into images, and *second*, images are transformed into words. The outside world, the 'thing-in-itself' (which is equivalent to 'pure truth') is irrelevant in this process of *becoming conscious*, and is therefore never included in Nietzsche's model, which simplified has the following form: *nerve-stimulus → image → sound/word*.

The origin and beginning of the process is always the 'nerve-stimulus' (as is was explicitly stated above, "to infer *from the nerve-stimulus to a cause outside us* is already the result of a false and unjustified application of the principle of sufficient reason" [ibid.][48]); the view is reiterated in the passage below, where the thing-in-itself is explicitly "not worthwhile striving for at all."

> The "thing-in-itself" (which would exactly be a pure truth without consequences) is also for the creator of language quite incomprehensible and is not worthwhile striving for at all. He designates only the relations of the things to humans, helped to expressing them by the use of the most audacious metaphors. A nerve-stimulus is first transferred into an image! First metaphor. The image is again transformed into a sound! Second metaphor. Each time there is a complete leap from one sphere right into the middle of a completely new and different one.[49]

When Nietzsche's transference-model, *nerve-stimulus → image → sound/word*,[50] leaves out the 'enigmatic X' (the 'thing-in-itself') and posits the nerve-stimulus as the nether limit for knowledge,[51] we are thrice removed from Truth understood as the *"enigmatic X of the Thing-in-Itself."* Nerve-stimuli remove us one step, the transference of these into images removes us another, and the transformation of images into words removes us a third (when we add the transformation of 'words' into 'concepts' in the expanded model (cf. below), we are removed an extra step). When these processes remove us these several steps from the 'enigmatic X,' it only becomes so much more inaccessible. The 'nerve-stimuli' become the raw material from which we form a world from 'images' and 'words,' according to intellectual processes necessary for the apprehension of an empirical world. The so-called 'objective world' is therefore a created construction thanks to these preceding processes originating in our mind; it is at best so-called 'objective' constituted intellectually or by our 'understanding.'

The framework of this idea was already elaborated in Schopenhauer's early essay *On the Fourfold Root of the Principle of Sufficient Reason*.[52]

Here Schopenhauer introduced the distinction between 'sensations' and 'perceptions,' where *sensation* indicated the mere reception of impressions, i.e., Nietzsche's 'nerve-stimuli,' and *perception* indicated a process where our 'understanding,' qua the brain, collaborates in creating the perception of an object, i.e., Nietzsche's 'images.' According to Schopenhauer's neo-Kantian thinking, the world does not exist in-itself, but is a cognitive construction we owe thanks to his three 'categories' time, space, and causality (a reduction of Kant's set of twelve). Especially the *causality-category* adds to the flow of sensational data, the necessary conception of cause *as if* data have an objective cause (this is the meaning of the so-called "unjustified application of the principle of sufficient reason" that Nietzsche referred to above). It is necessarily an *as if* construction, because it is to Schopenhauer as well as to Nietzsche absurd to believe in an actual objective cause imprinting itself on our mind. Schopenhauer is as always explicitly rejecting this possible misinterpretation.

> One must indeed be forsaken by all the gods, to imagine that the outer, perceptible world, filling Space in its three dimensions and moving on in the inexorable flow of Time governed at every step by the laws of Causality, which is without exception, and in all this merely obeying laws we can indicate before all experience of them that such a world as this, we say, can have a real, objective existence outside us, without any agency of our own, and that it can then have found its way into our heads through bare sensation and thus have a second existence within us like the one outside. For what a miserably poor thing is mere sensation, after all![53]

It is to Schopenhauer the *understanding* that creates the objective world thanks to the category of 'causality.'

> The understanding [*Verstand*] has first to create the objective world, for this cannot just walk into our heads from outside, already done and fully finished, through the senses and the openings of their organs. Thus the senses furnish nothing but the raw material [*rohen stoff*], and this the understanding reforms [...] into the objective understanding and apprehension of a corporeal world governed by laws. Accordingly, our daily *empirical intuitive perception is intellectual* [*unsere alltägliche empirische Anschauung ist intellektuel*].[54]

Explicitly, our brain accounts for the transformation from mere sensations (nerve-stimuli) to proper perceptions (images).

> It is only when the Understanding begins to act, a function, not of single, delicate nerve-extremities, but of that mysterious, complicated structure weighing from five to ten pounds, called the brain only when it begins to apply its sole

form, the causal law, that a powerful transformation takes place, by which subjective sensation becomes objective perception. For, in virtue of its own peculiar form, therefore a priori, i.e., before all experience.[55]

With Schopenhauer as his source, Nietzsche could therefore never endorse an atomistic or materialist theory explaining atoms and their forces impacting first the retina, then the understanding, and thus *transporting 'reality' into the 'mind.'*[56] Nietzsche carefully avoids suggesting such a linear and causal relationship between any of the three orders in a vocabulary insisting on describing the processes as 'transferences,' 'translations,' or 'metaphors.'

The former model had been suggested by Maximilian Drossbach,[57] who had defended this model on the assumption that 'forces' from the outside impress themselves on the physiological system, which again impresses them on the mind, which somehow translate the different gradations of intensities into adequate ideational objects. Suggesting this linear model, Drossbach attempted to restore a cause-effect relation between object and representation in order to rescue the idea of correspondence to (i.e., a logical relationship to) an outside world (cf. discussion Part II, B.1).

There is no anchoring point for the entire tripartite structure in the form of the self-identical and singular object as thing-in-itself, when the processes are described as transferences or translations of one order to another *type-different* order.[58] A neurologically defined reality is *replaced* with the phenomenological reality of a sensational image. Images are thereupon replaced with another completely distinct order, the linguistic reality of words, which finally, when we include epistemic conceptual knowledge according to the expanded model, is replaced with the meta-linguistic reality of concepts. Stimuli are not *effects* of things, images are not *effects* of stimuli, and words are not *effects* of images. Nietzsche is deliberately careful in his choice of words when he says that stimuli are 'transferred' or 'carried over' into perceptions. He shows proper philosophical modesty when talking about these processes as 'transferences' and the results of these transferences as 'metaphors.' Later in the essay, Nietzsche describes, even more vaguely, transferences as 'stammering translations' of something from one language into a completely different language.

> Between two absolutely different spheres, as between subject and object, there is no causality, no correctness, no expression, but at best only an aesthetical relation; I mean a suggestive transference, a stammering translation into a completely foreign language—for which one at any rate needs a freely poeticizing and freely inventive mediating sphere and mediating force.[59]

A cause-effect relationship between the orders would have suggested a *deterministic sequence of events*, a single linear *force* operating freely through the entire psychic system 'carrying' something from one system into another system, where it miraculously changes its state (i.e., Drossbach's suggestion). When Nietzsche describes his translation-, interpretation-, or replacement-processes as *arbitrary* and *unknown*, the outcome of these processes are appropriately described as 'metaphors.' In contrast, suggesting a freely operating *force* "causing" changes in the psycho-physiological system is by Nietzsche and his peers typically seen as lazy thinking pretending to give us the false assurance that processes are simple, linear, and grounded in *objectivity as such*. This lazy thinking does not realize that a 'force' is as much an unknown as is Nietzsche's 'metaphor.'

In this admitted *ignorance*, Nietzsche is continuing the skepticism of some of his important peers, such as Du Bois-Reymond qua his 'limits to our knowledge of nature,' his 'world-riddle,' and his 'ignorabimus' (we do not know and will never know absolute essences), often seen repeated in debates from the 1860s and 1870s (e.g., in Lange and Helmholtz; cf. Part II, A.1).

On a first glance, Nietzsche's model might appear like a variation of Locke's linear model from *Essay Concerning Human Understanding* (1690),[60] where he suggests that sensations from the outside drifts into the mind where they fix themselves as ideas. Although Locke introduced a distinction between ideas of sensation and ideas of reflection, he wanted to reduce the latter to the former, in order to emphasize the importance of sensory impressions received from without. The origin of human knowledge was therefore sense-experience in which the world was passively received from a set of elementary sensory building blocks that would form the simple foundation for the more complex conceptual constructions we would build in thought. To Locke, the mind was receptive rather than creative. He saw the ideas formed in the mind as similar to the represented objects, which were in turn seen as the sources of the formed ideas. As such, he suggested an empirical correspondence theory of truth.

We notice several significant differences between Nietzsche's transference-model and Locke's early empiricist thinking. First, as already emphasized, it has no 'outside' thing-in-itself, but begins in the nerve-stimulus. Second, there is no *cause-effect relationship* between one stage in the sequence and the following, the linear itinerary from one stage into another is broken, and causal-linear thinking is replaced with the idea of arbitrary transferences. Thirdly, the conclusion of Nietzsche's tripartite sequence is not the 'idea' as sensory representation, but the word (or in his expanded model, the concept).

Nietzsche's "first metaphor" is an image copying a nerve-stimulus, and his "second metaphor" is a sound copying an image. Images copying stimuli are metaphors in a non-linguistic sense, while sounds copying images are linguistic. We can thus answer Nietzsche's leading question, 'what is a word?' —A 'word' is a linguistic metaphor for a perceptual metaphor, a discursive copy of a pictorial copy.

3. Replacing the Unknown with 'Metaphors'

We see that when Nietzsche, following the thinking of his day, introduces a psychic apparatus consisting of three orders, first a physiological (for the nerve-stimuli), next a perceptive (for the formed images), and finally, a linguistic (for the word or sound), he is not (nor does he pretend to be) in the position to tell us how *exactly* we get from the physiological to the perceptive to the linguistic order. How exactly, according to what processes, stimuli become images and images become sounds, he cannot know and does not pretend to know.[61] To require him to provide a more precise description is empty criticism, because his *Age* cannot accurately describe this processes. He has, however, no doubt ascertaining that these two transferences are 'arbitrary.'[62] It is thanks to the *arbitrariness of sensible and linguistic signs* that he describes them as 'metaphors,' that is, *random replacements* of something, which does not inhere as their 'nature' or 'essence,' and may have existence only through the metaphorical description.

In the last part of the paragraph, Nietzsche offers a celebrated example in order to illustrate this essential disconnect between world and language. He refers to an experiment carried out by the physicist Ernst Chladni, in which Chladni made a violin-bow glide across the edge of a metal plate whose surface is covered with a thin layer of sand. The vibration of the string causes the sand to form a pattern on the metal-plate, and gives as such the researcher a visual representation of the tone produced by the violin string.[63]

> One can imagine a person who is completely deaf and never has had the sensation of tones and music. He would in astonishment look at Chladni's sound-figures in sand, might discover their cause in the vibrations of the string, and thereupon swear that he knows what humans call 'tone.' The same applies to us all with respect to language. We believe that we know something about the things themselves when we talk about trees, colors, snow, and flowers, although we relate to nothing but metaphors of things, with no correspondence at all to the original essences. Like the tone as sand-figure, so is it with the enigmatic X of the things in themselves appearing first as nerve-stimulus, then as image, and finally as sound. In any event, language does not originate logically, and the entire material in and with which the man of truth, the researcher or the philosopher, works and constructs, derives—if not entirely from an imaginary never-never land—at least not from the essences of things.[64]

This experiment is what Nietzsche refers to as 'Chladnian sound-figures in sand.' In his analogy, we are in the position of the deaf person who can only perceive the sand-figures, but has no perception of sound. Especially for a music enthusiast like Nietzsche it is a potent analogy, because the deaf person is robbed of an experience of the noblest order, music, and left with a substitute of the poorest kind, sand. Ditto ourselves as human beings, in our attempt to 'know' or 'understand,' we have no perception of the world in-truth and in-itself, but are left with linguistic representations as poor substitutions. It is clear that Nietzsche in his example refers to how language produces *scientific or theoretical knowledge*, not the commonsense knowledge we communicate between ourselves in everyday language, since he is referring to "the man of truth, the researcher or philosopher." It is this man, who like the deaf person can at best only infer something called 'tone' (i.e., truth) from looking at 'sand-figures' (i.e., appearances). The formal expression of Nietzsche's analogy is A is to B as C is to D: i.e., *our knowledge (A) is to the 'mysterious X of the thing-in-itself' (B) like Chladnian sand-figures (C) is to music (D)*. The example was well-known from nineteenth-century scientific literature, and Nietzsche's great source of inspiration, Fr. A. Lange, was using it as well.[65]

Nietzsche introduces an interesting caveat in the last sentence of the paragraph above. It is granted that in our search for knowledge we look at 'sand-figures' and do not possess genuine knowledge, but thereupon he objects to himself, 'sand-figures' are after all not entirely fictional and they do not emerge as if from some "imaginary never-never land."[66]

> If a painter in the absence of hands had to express an image in front of his eyes in song, he would with this confusion of spheres always reveal more, than the empirical world reveals about by the essences of things. Even the relation between a nerve-stimulus and the resulting image is in itself not necessary. However, when the same image has been generated a million times, and hereby have been inherited through numerous human generations, and finally by the entire humanity appears every time according to the same events, then it finally achieves for humans the same meaning, as if it is the only necessary image and as if every relation between the original nerve-stimuli and the appearing image is a strong causal relationship. It is like a dream, which eternally repeated is finally regarded as reality and judged as such. However, a metaphor's becoming hard and rigid does not reveal the necessity and the decisive verification of this metaphor.[67]

He seems to say—to stay within the logic of the analogy—that the deaf person may not perceive sounds, but he must perceive, besides the sand-figures, a violin-string gliding across the metal-plate. Nietzsche as such introduces a minimum of objectivity into his analogy, something that at least helps the sand-figures to form. He does not tell us in TL what the candidate for this objective 'something' might be, but in later work, such as TI and notes later collected as his *The Will to Power* [WP], he endeavors an explanation, as we will discuss below.

5. Word *and/or/versus* Concept?

1. The Distinction between Images and Words/Concepts

Conceptualization implies a generalization of individual cases under the heading of a single abstract label in Schopenhauer and Nietzsche. This removes the concept from the sphere of the concrete to the sphere of the abstract; the *concept* is no longer a perceptive but a linguistic representation, although it is still unclear in what sense it is different from the *word*.

Schopenhauer insists, and Nietzsche concurs, that the original root of concepts, however abstract, must be perceptions. So Schopenhauer: "Although the concepts are fundamentally different from intuitive-perceptive representations [*Anschaulichen Vorstellungen*], they still stand in a necessary relation to these, without which they would be nothing."[68] And further: "The whole world of reflection rests on, and is rooted in, the world of perception. All ultimate, i.e., original, *evidence* is one of *intuitive perception* [*ist eine anschauliche*]."[69] Nietzsche reiterates the view in *Notebook 19* (1872/1873) when he writes: "The concepts can only emerge from intuitive perception [*Anschauung*].[70] [...] The concept corresponds first and foremost to the image; images are proto-thinking [*Urdenken*], i.e., the surfaces of things are condensed in the mirror of the eyes. [...] Images in the human eye! This determines all human essence!"[71]

In our most primitive constitution, we *think* in images, and this proto-thinking [*Urdenken*] we share with animals (it is reactivated in dreams, which also unfold as imaginary proto-thinking, as Freud would later underscore).[72] Proto- or image-thinking therefore constitutes a first primary condensation (an abbreviation and thus interpretation) of the surface of things.

The distinction between image and word ('thing-representation' and 'word-representation') seems unproblematic. However, an elaborate distinction between 'word' and 'concept' is more challenging, and Schopenhauer often confounds the two stages. He often condenses word and concept as a single position in opposition to images, organizing this distinction hierarchically where words/concepts are second-order representations of first-order image-representations of the appearing world (cf., *Die Welt als Wille und Vorstellung*, vol. I).[73] In Schopenhauer, the word/concept becomes a representation of the image-representation, as it replaces our phenomenal reality with an abstract linguistic reality. Accordingly, words/concepts are rendered as "representations of representations [*Vorstellungen von Vorstellungen*], [...] as "abstract representations of reason," [...] as "abstract, non-perceptive, general, not in time and space individual representations,"[74] while images are "particular representations of perception."[75] Words/concepts are to that extent artificial given their distance to the perceptive world, although they still have first-order perceptive representations as their indispensable root. This remove from immediate sense-reality adds according to Schopenhauer a distinct unnaturalness to (especially) the concept, and the reflective and intellectual processes it represents: "Reflection is necessarily the copy or the repetition of the originally presented world of perception though a copy of quite a special kind *in a completely heterogeneous material.*"[76] [...] "The concept does not preserve what is perceived or what is felt; rather it preserves what is essential thereof in *an entirely altered form.*"[77]

The unnatural concept (now separated from the 'word') is able only to *describe* a surface-reality of phenomena. If these *descriptions* pretend to be *explanations* added to phenomena as their alleged causes, they are deceptive. According to Schopenhauer, we see, observe, organize, count, order, etc., the world, but we cannot penetrate into the 'causes' or 'essences' of what we perceive. As he famously put it, we "walk around a castle, in vain looking for an entrance, and in the meantime sketching the façades"[78]—i.e., we are at best able to observe the outer walls of this castle, but we will never be able to find an entrance into its interior (i.e., the 'thing-in-itself'). In this proto-positivist conception, all explanation only repeats what is already self-evident from observing the surface.

Nietzsche repeats Schopenhauer in the view that conceptualization is ultimately a piece of human folly and pretension, indicating a certain human tenacity for creating meaning-structures and classificatory systems that interpret a perceived world, but merely in our own light. Our 'truth-drive' is to be found in this 'will-to-knowledge' formed in concepts (Nietzsche, confounding 'word' and 'concept' as often as Schopenhauer, eventually seems to decide in TL that 'concepts' rather that 'words' are to blame for that unnaturalness).

We intend to reflect essences ('truth'), but the concepts that we use are uniquely human and therefore foreign to nature in-itself; cf. the following note from *Notebook 19*.

> Our understanding [*Verstand*] is a surface-ability [*Flächenkraft*], it is superficial [*Oberflächlich*]. It understands [*Erkennt*] through concepts [*Begriffe*]; that is, our thinking is classification, a name-giving [*Benamsen*]; therefore, it is something that derives from the human condition and never touches on the thing itself

[*Ding selbst*]. Man has absolute knowledge only when he calculates and only in the forms of space, i.e. the ultimate limits of everything knowable are quantities; [man] does not understand quality, but only quantity.[79]

2. The Tenuous Distinction between Words and Concepts

If or when the terms 'word' and 'concept' are not confounded in Nietzsche or in Schopenhauer, they describe two different stages in human abstraction of its environing phenomenal world. In that case, the 'word' is an abstraction of the 'image,' and the 'concept' an additional abstraction of words.

Despite the frequent confusion of the terms, Schopenhauer does indeed realize in various passages that they cannot be the same thing, since the concept removes us an extra step from phenomenal reality. In Schopenhauer's vocabulary, the concept becomes a "representation of a representation of a representation," where the word was only a "representation of a representation." Now, the *concept* is entirely "different not only from the word to which it is tied, but also from the perceptions from which it originates."[80] While the word is authentically tied to the perceptive image, the concept has lost this authenticity; it has become an "abstract representation of reason,"[81] and as such, "it does not preserve what is perceived or what is felt; rather it preserves what is essential thereof in *an entirely altered form*, yet as an adequate representative of those results."[82] Now, it is dangerously floating around in the abstract.[83]

We will discuss Nietzsche's adoption of this tenuous distinction between 'word' and 'concept' in especially his second part of TL, where he will describe both word and concept as 'metaphors,' but inspired by Schopenhauer argue that the 'word' is a more authentic metaphor than is the concept. He will here like Schopenhauer argue that the word retains its connections to sense-impressions, while this connection is lost in the concept. He will turn the hierarchical distinction into a theory of the possibility of a poetic metaphorization of the world, based on the original spoken word, in contradistinction to a scientific metaphorization, based on a now dogmatic and alienating concept. In effect, he will use this theory of Schopenhauer to defend a 'true' romantic world conception contra a 'false' naturalist (cf. further discussion in Part I, B.1).

In Part I of TL, Nietzsche nonetheless endeavors to explain the *concept in distinction to the word*. "Let us specifically consider the formation of concepts,"[84] Nietzsche starts suggesting, adding here to his initial model of the perceptive-cognitive apparatus, *nerve-stimulus* → *image* → *sound/word*, the transformation of word into concept. His extended and final model will consequently have the following abbreviated form, *nerve-stimulus* → *image* → *sound/word* → *concept*.[85]

Nietzsche's account of the last transformation is as ambiguous as is Schopenhauer's. Sometimes the distinguishing characteristics intended to distinguish word and concept happens to be applicable to both; occasionally, he uses 'word' and 'concept' interchangeably, by using the term 'concept' when he must be referring to proper word-forms, and vice versa.

In his attempt to argue for a value-hierarchy between the terms, positive and negative evaluations are applied to respectively word and concept; like in Schopenhauer, the concept is artificial and intellectual. Also like Schopenhauer, he regards the phenomenal surface world as an authentic world-manifestation, and words as removing us one step from that authenticity, while concepts remove us an additional step, but these attempts to consolidate a hierarchical authentic/inauthentic dichotomy of word and concept are often collapsing, or, as it were, self-deconstructing. This is for example what happens in the passage below, where he explains the *word* as a help to memorize the "unique," "individualized," and "original" experience, and thinks that it is transformed into a *concept* when it supersedes the unique, individual, and original. He suggests here that when the word "*no longer* serves as a reminder of the unique and completely individualized original experience," it "becomes a concept"—as if he presupposes that 'words' refer to the 'unique and individualized experience.'

> Every word immediately becomes a concept when it no longer serves as a reminder of the unique and completely individualized original experience to which it owes its origin, but also fits the numerous more or less similar—which strictly speaking means *never* similar—non-identical cases. Every concept emerges by equalizing the unequal.[86]

'Every concept emerges by equalizing the unequal,' he says, but every word 'equalizes the unequal' as well.

This is unfortunate theory, because if 'words' per chance were referring to particular individualized instances, individual *images* or *thing-representations*,[87] they are uniquely referential. It is also not a theory that is otherwise defended. From the beginning of TL, he has repeatedly stated that images as well as words 'equalize the unequal,' and this can only mean that they never capture unique and particular images as if directly referring to them. In this theory, only *thing-representations* may be 'unique' and 'unequal,' never *word-representations*. Equalization and simplification must start already in the earliest formation of language, because otherwise we had languages able to capture unique and individual instances, i.e., languages potentially infinite, languages with never-ending dictionaries referring to all possible instances of perceptive thing-representations.

So, in my analysis, Nietzsche is right when he asserts that words equalize and simplify, but confuses matters when he thereupon asserts that, "the concept emerges by equalizing the unequal," as if it is the *unique job of concepts* to *equalize, in contrast to words*. On his first (correct) theory, equalization cannot be a process that starts only in concept-formations, but must start already in the elementary 'naming' process (and even in image-formation or perception, as he is aware of in later work).

In an attempt to further elucidate the distinction between 'image,' 'word,' and 'concept,' Nietzsche gives us these two famous and often-cited examples, 'leaf' and 'honesty.'

> As certain as it is that one leaf is never completely identical to another leaf, as certain is it that the concept leaf is formed thanks to arbitrarily discarding these individual differences. In forgetting these differences, the idea is now formed that there is something in nature which besides the leaves gives us *the* "leaf," something like an arché-form according to which all leaves have been woven, outlined, measured, colored, curved, and painted, but by incompetent hands so that no copy ever turned out as a correct and faithful true imitation of the original form.[88]

As image or thing-representation, one leaf is always different from another leaf, and two leaves are never the same, what must be a correct observation insofar as we are taking leaves to be thing-representations or *appearing* reality. Given our practical need to orient ourselves in the world, we disregard all these individual differences between leaves and 'equalize' them all by means of the *word* 'leaf,' enabling us to organize all instances under a single label, enabling us to see all instances as belonging to the same class. The implicit process must be that we see a leaf, then another leaf, and another leaf, etc., and we eventually agree to call them by a single *word* as if all the individual instances are the same. In the passage, Nietzsche calls the outcome of this naming-process a *concept*, although 'leaf' is a *word* by his and Schopenhauer's own definition, i.e., 'a representation of a representation.'

In Nietzsche's narrative, we encounter here the beginning of the metaphysical scandal (what possibly accounts for the formation of the *concept*), because from leaves as images and 'leaf' as word, we seem inclined to mistakenly believe in the existence of something like '*the* leaf,' i.e., we erroneously deduce the existence of an abstract 'leaf' and we falsely infer from the name that leaves have a single property in common, perfect as a Platonic form—as if this property corresponds to all leaves, as if *the Leaf* exists as an origin of all the imperfect actually appearing leaves. This introduces into our immediate and intuitive world-experience a Platonic double-world consisting of 'leaves' as instances on the one hand and *the Leaf* as transcendental form on the other. In that sense, the concept represents a downfall from a world of *perceptive presence*, i.e., a world of *appearances*, into a transcendental otherness of false abstractions.

Nietzsche's next example is repeating the same line of thought, but is especially interesting because it returns us to the question of truth, namely to the discussion of *honesty*.

> We call a person "honest." Why did he act so honestly today, we ask? Our answer usually is, because of his honesty. Honesty! That is to say that the leaf is the cause to the leaves. We know nothing whatsoever of an essential quality called "honesty," but only of numerous individualized, and therefore unequal actions, which we because we ignore the unequal equalizes and now designate as an honest act.[89]

Again, Nietzsche assumes that when we observe instances of 'honest' behavior, we encounter "numerous individualized" thus "unequal actions," which we equalize and simplify when we designate these behaviors 'honest.' The *word* 'honest' is responsible for this necessary equalization of 'unequal actions.' However, as soon as word is introduced, we are again precariously exposed to the introduction of the deceptive *concept* of honesty *as such* or as an inherent quality. When we ask *why* the man behaved 'honestly,' and offer the question-begging answer, 'because of his honesty,' we have added a metaphysical form to the person's behavior. Nietzsche uses his two examples, leaf and honesty, to illustrate how the *conceptualization* of instances of 'leaves' and 'honest behavior' is generating a false formality of *arché-forms* and even *transcendental forms*, producing a non-existing "*qualitas occulta*" for individual perceptions and actions.

> We articulate out of this [the honest act] a *qualitas occulta* with the name, "honesty." By overlooking the individual and the real we get the concept which also gives us the form, while within nature there are no forms and concepts, therefore also no species, only a for us inaccessible and indefinable X. As such, also our opposition between the individual and the species is anthropomorphic and derives not from the essence of things, although we would not dare to claim that it does not correspond to them; that would namely be a dogmatic assertion, and as such, just as indemonstrable as its opposite.[90]

Nietzsche is saying that the idea of a '*qualitas occulta*' comes about already qua the word-form, by simplifying the perceptive real; but he must mean that only when words are taken to be surface-manifestations of occult qualities do we arrive to the metaphysical concept-form, not if words are used as practical expedients to equalize the unequal. Otherwise, he cannot assert a distinction between the authentic 'word' and the inauthentic 'concept.'

Also, Nietzsche must still take for granted that people can be honest and tell the truth (cf. Part I, A.3: "Genealogy of the Pragmatic Concept of Truth"). What he is here attempting to criticize must be the idea of *Honesty* in itself, assuming an abstract life of its own, as such explaining our registration of a well-known behavior we ourselves have classified (qua words). Ditto the leaves; instead of being individual thing-representations, and thereupon becoming general word-representations, according to innocuous linguistic processes, one asserts a *transcendental concept* of *the Leaf* as the supposed 'proto-form' [*Urform*] for leaves ("according to which all leaves have been woven" [ibid.]).

If the thinking is to make sense, we must distinguish between three, not two, different stages: thing-representations, word-representations, and concept-formation, where only the latter is precarious. We notice that already in TL, Nietzsche is describing a process that he will later label 'chronological reversal'; i.e., metaphysical thinking understood as a reversal of the order of two activities, the 'authentic' activity of perceiving and naming, and the 'unauthentic' activity of inventing 'reasons' or 'causes.' Nietzsche's point is that the explanatory cause is nothing but a generalization of the initially observed phenomenon (cf. Part II, A.3: "Chronological Reversal of Cause and Effect"). Qua generalization, a *concept* has been formed from observing a behavior we conventionally name 'honest,' namely, the concept of an 'honest' quintessence that uniformly informs a multitude of individual human behaviors. The 'authentic' stage is to identify a behavior as truthful and thereupon to name it as such, while the 'inauthentic' activity consists in the claim of the existence of a *qualitas occulta* called 'Honesty.' The same analysis applies to truth (to be honest and to tell the truth is after all the same thing), one ends up asserting 'Truth' as preceding as form a truthful statement. Nietzsche warns us that there are in nature no such 'forms' or 'concepts': "Within nature *there are no forms and concepts*, therefore also no species, only a for us inaccessible and indefinable X (ibid).[91]

3. A Later Pragmatic Resolution of the Distinction between Word and Concept

Let us note that (early) Nietzsche's *concept of the deceptive concept* is far from the only possible concept of concept that one may find among Nietzsche's contemporaries or near-contemporaries. Theorists like Avenarius,

Mach, Vaihinger, Pierce, James, and Nietzsche himself in later writings, tend to regard concepts as pragmatic tools for classification, schematization, and formalization of language, i.e., as a *technique* applied by the methodic mind in order to *further simplify* an already simplified linguistized world. In this pragmatic sense, concepts are merely another level in an ongoing 'equalization,' 'simplification,' and 'abstraction' of chaotic complexity. Conceptualized language adds an extra layer of abstraction to ordinary language; the 'concept' simply represents a further condensation of an already familiar linguistic surface. In this secondary condensation, the particular is generalized, and the unequal is equalized. If plain language qua words simplify, conceptual language adds another level of simplification to this first-order simplification, the reason why we often describe conceptual language as meta-language. We may illustrate the idea by way of one of Nietzsche's own examples: a 'camel' may be seen as a *word-representation* organizing multiple distinct, unique, and individual animals sharing certain features into one set. The 'mammal' is a concept including several sets of animals of which the set of 'camels' is a member.

We see this much more pragmatic concept of concept defended in a note from the later *Nachlaß* material, where Nietzsche revisits his early discussions of differences between sensations, words, and concepts. Now he suggests the following sketchy, but more satisfying, solution to the problem:

> First images—to explain how images arise in the mind. Then words, applied to images. Finally concepts, possible only when there are words—a subsuming of many images under something not intuitive but audible (a word). The small bit of emotion that arises with the "word," hence with the intuition of similar images for which there is a single word—this weak emotion is the common element, the basis of the concept. The basic fact is that weak sensations are regarded as equal, sensed as the same.[92]

We notice that the distinction between word and concept is clear. Words are applied to images, and become thereupon the basis of concepts. Concepts therefore organize something audible, the sound-images or the words, rather than the perceptive images themselves. We do no longer find traces of the artificial distinction between the *authentic word* and the *inauthentic concept* from the early essay. Words as well as concepts simplify the world according to a principle of 'weak sensations.' If there are weak emotional responses to different elements, they are regarded as equal and we organize them consequently under a single heading. These 'weak sensations' may exist between perceived images, in which case we organize them under a single word, or they may exist between words, in which case we organize them under a single concept.

6. Truth as "Dead Metaphors"

1. Transferences Instead of Correspondences

In his attempt to explain human acquisition of knowledge, Nietzsche has so far been introducing five different realms: (i) the 'thing-in-itself' as the objective world 'outside' us, and therefore beyond our comprehension; (ii) the nerve-stimulus as our first physiological reception of this incomprehensible 'outside'; (iii) the perceptive image resulting from our processing of these stimuli; (iv) the word, as our conventional linguistic labeling of perceptive images; and (v) our concept-formation, as our epistemic classification and organization of the world. Furthermore, he has attempted to account for the dynamics between the realms, *except* in the case of the transformation between (i) and (ii), of which he has nothing to say apart from reiterating the incomprehensibility of the "thing-in-itself," the "enigmatic X," etc. This would arguably have been a most interesting transformation to see explained, but an explanation-attempt is usually rejected in neo-Kantian thinking because it for obvious reasons is seen as self-contradictory (what is the purpose of addressing the absolutely incomprehensible?).

In describing the other transformations, Nietzsche has been emphasizing their *arbitrariness*. The transference of (ii) to (iii), from stimuli to images, is like a jump where something belonging to one order is transferred to something of an entirely different order. The transformation of (iii) to (iv), from images to words, is arbitrary for the same reason, the perceptive world of images is incompatible with the linguistic world of words. Finally, the difficult-to-explain transference of (iv) to (v), from words used as simple references to thing-representations into an artificial conceptual language is arbitrary because concepts give us general forms where words (putatively and confusedly in Nietzsche's early presentation) refer to individual thing-representations. This arbitrariness between realms Nietzsche sums up in one of the most famous passages in his work, a passage that half a century ago became like a battle cry for the postmodernist and deconstructionist reception of Nietzsche, and became influential in the general understanding of 'theory' according to the same school.[93]

Let us reread this important passage within the context so far discussed.

> What is then truth? A mobile army of metaphors, metonymies, and anthropomorphisms; in short, a sum of human relations, which, poetically and rhetorically intensified, have been transferred, embellished, and after long usage of a people seem fixed, canonical, and compulsory. Truths are illusions, which one has forgotten that that is what they are, metaphors, which have become outworn and sensuously powerless, coins, which have lost their stamp and now only are regarded as metal, no longer as coins.[94]

Immediately preceding the passage is Nietzsche's discussion of 'leaf' and 'honesty' as concepts, where he argued that concepts are on several removes from the impossible 'thing-in-itself,' which they supposedly pretended to represent. It is coming from this context he now asks, 'What is then truth?' implying, 'what is the truth of these conceptual constructions we call truth (i.e., *the* leaf and honesty *as such*)?' Since Nietzsche consistently has argued against the self-present 'thing,' what is now truth, i.e., what is truth in the form of concepts, if they have *no correspondence to 'things'*?

The answer we get in the famous passage, "a mobile army of metaphors. " So, 'Truth' is not just *a* metaphor in the singular, but an entire legion of metaphors, and highly flexible to booth, ready to be inserted at any trouble spot. They are words or concepts (it is unclear which, since Nietzsche continues to confound them) that in any case have undergone a particular processing, a so-called 'poetical and rhetorical intensification,' to the extent that they now seem "canonical and compulsory."

We recall that Nietzsche earlier in the essay described also images and sounds as "metaphors": "A nerve-stimulus is first transferred into an image! First metaphor. The image is again transformed into a sound! Second metaphor" (ibid.). Therefore, *images* as well as *words* as well as *concepts* as well as *truth* are 'metaphors.' This inflates the standard notion of 'metaphor,' because from a professional rhetorician's point of view, only 'words' and 'concepts,' belonging in the linguistic domain, could adequately be described as 'metaphors'; neither 'images' nor 'truths' fit the standard definition comfortably. Perceptive images can clearly not qualify as metaphorical expressions from a rhetorical point of view; a perceptive image cannot replace another perceptive image of which it becomes a symbolic representation, because we are compelled to see what we see and cannot at will re-create what we see into something else for rhetorical purposes. In visual perception, I see a house, but never a 'metaphor' of the house—although we in language may interpret the house as a symbol of a number of things and although we have the philosophical license to *call* perceptive images 'metaphors' for the visual processing of stimuli happening in my brain, as Nietzsche does.

When Nietzsche describes images and truths as 'metaphors,' he must be adhering to a tacit but presupposed theory where (i) *replacement* of something with something else is granted as a fundamental characteristic of 'metaphor,' and furthermore, where (ii) the term that is *replacing* (e.g., the image) has no *objective correspondence* to that which it *replaces* (e.g., the nerve-stimulus), and where finally (iii), the new replacing term *supersedes and suspends* the old term that disappears in the process.[95] When a neurological defined reality is *replaced* with a sensational sign (an image), the replacement is *arbitrary*, since the neurological defined reality is incompatible with the perceptive image; i.e., we do not perceive 'quanta,' 'forces,' or 'electrical impulses' in the perceptive image; we also do not perceive the processes by which sensational 'impulses' are transformed into perceptive 'images' *for-us*. Our perceptive image has completely superseded and suspended the forces that putatively affected it. From the complex psycho-physiological process, there is nothing left but what we *see* and that what we *see* does not reveal any leftover from the neurological processes underlying the image-formation.

Thus conceived, Nietzsche can argue that his transformation-processes have features in common with the fundamental metaphorical structure, and the resultants of these processes may thus (leniently) be described as *metaphors*, because also according to classical rhetorical theory, the 'metaphor' is described as 'replacement' of one term with another term disappearing or dropping out in the process.

For a more detailed explanation of the process Nietzsche is describing, let us briefly return to Aristotle's classical theories of poetry and rhetoric in order to see how Aristotle's theory of metaphor accords with Nietzsche's explanation of psycho-physiological transformation-processes. To Aristotle, a metaphor is produced when one posits an analogy between *two sets of two terms*, and then abbreviate this total of four terms into a two-term expression. If we have the analogy, *A is to B* what *C is to D*, a metaphor emerges when we cancel a term on each side of the equation and create an expression that takes one term from one realm and another from another. To paraphrase Aristotle, we can create the following analogy: evening (A) is to day (B) as old age (C) is to life (D). From this analogy, we create a metaphorical expression when we cancel the two terms, (B) and (C), and get, 'the evening of life.' There *is* no 'evening' of life, but the phrase gives us a *metaphorical expression* for the *literal expression*, 'old.' Instead of saying, 'he is old,' we say, he is in "the evening of his life," as we repress the fact that life has no 'evening.'[96] According to the metaphorical expression, we subconsciously conceive of life as an analog clock, life starts in the morning, reaches its highest point at noon, its maturity during the day, and old age in the evening—the least desirable stage of life, therefore the metaphorical amelioration.

The metaphorical expression is a pleasant expression of the blunt fact, 'he is near death' or 'he is old.' The metaphor replaces something factual with something poetic, but distracts us from (possibly represses or belies) the cruel fact of deterioration and death (an 'evening' is after all followed by a new day). To summarize, we see again that metaphors, (i) *replace* (ii) *arbitrarily*, in order to (iii) *supersede and suspend*, a term that now disappears in the equation. Cf. 'evening of life' replaces and supersedes 'old' that disappears in the equation.

After having stipulated that 'truths are metaphors,' Nietzsche thinks it safe to argue that "truths are illusions." We can now understand that truths are illusions since they are metaphors; they are illusions because they (i) *replace* (ii) *arbitrarily*, in order to (iii) *supersede and suspend*, some-thing. The particular 'something' we are talking about in this context happens to be the impossible 'thing,' the 'thing-in-itself,' the so-called "*unzugänglichen und undefinirbaren X.*"

Since Nietzsche's metaphor replaces his X as a non-existing purely postulated essence, we can indeed argue that Nietzsche's metaphor does not 'replace' anything at all.[97] At best, it 'replaces' *a void*, the *void of the non-existing 'X'*; but this, we immediately realize, is improper and illogical language. We cannot strictly speaking replace a nothing, but we can *create* a *metaphorical expression* or a *sign* in the stead of nothing. Truths are illusions that assume sign-function, because they insist on referring to an extraordinary something, which is nothing.

Nietzsche famous passage continues by specifying in which sense 'truths' are illusions, namely in the sense of having been forgotten as metaphorical illusions. They are metaphors, "one has forgotten that that is what they are; metaphors, which have become outworn and sensuously powerless; coins, which have lost their stamp and now only are regarded as metal, no longer as coins" (ibid.). This is an important additional stipulation in Nietzsche's understanding of the 'truth-metaphor.' Paradoxically, truths are metaphors, but metaphors no longer functioning as metaphors. They have been habitualized up to a point where everybody takes them for granted as literal language.

If the poet, rhetorician, theorist, or scientist knows that they create metaphors, and their audiences are recognizing and perhaps appreciating powerful metaphorical language, fixated truth-metaphors have instead stabilized as literal expressions. A language originally metaphorical has become a flat language of 'used-up' or 'worn-out' metaphors naming the inexpressible and ineffable, the flat language is now elevating this naming as a picture of objective reality. Literalized metaphors are therefore like "coins having lost their stamp," now worth only their metal; they have become sensuously powerless [*sinnlich kraftlos*]; they have lost the figurative power they once had. These flat so-called 'metaphors' have in themselves undergone a transformation and as a result they are no longer metaphors according to the classical rhetorical definition; they no longer lend figurative power to language as metaphors supposedly do. They have instead become *literal, rigid,* and *reified* as if they as words refer to distinct things.

Nietzsche's thinking seems to be that *originally* they served the human community as metaphors, perhaps as the most expedient and economic expression for certain states-of-affairs, but then they coagulated and it was forgotten that they only provided convenient and practical model-expressions. Now they are "dead"; they are *signs* no longer understood as signs, but as directly corresponding to *things* existing in the order of the *real*.[98] They designate a reified, coagulated, and petrified language of sorts as if they have started to live a life of their own like Marx's commodities on the capitalist market detached from their means and relations of production. The problem is here that language, which is *only symbolic* (which can only be *about something*), has been turned into reality, and that the word at best *representing* the thing is confused with the thing.

According to reified language, a camel *is* a mammal, not only *designated* and *classified* as a mammal, the latter implying the acknowledgement of a certain biological paradigm with its intellectual history of emerging rules of classification. If we go back to the origin of the biological paradigms, the first intellectual contexts in which it was asserted that certain animals according to certain rules had to be classified as 'mammals,' we may breathe life back into 'dead metaphors.' We may regard Nietzsche's *genealogy*, as discussed in later writings[99] and M. Foucault's *archaeology*,[100] as such noble attempts to revive 'dead metaphors' by revisiting their early epistemological and etymological origins.

2. God as 'Dead Metaphor': Feuerbach and Nietzsche on Anthropocentrism

The relation between Feuerbach and Nietzsche has not often been under discussion, but to give an example of a civilizational master-metaphor, we may regard Feuerbach's 'God' as a preeminent example of a repressed 'metaphor' raised into the order of the real as *God himself*. The religiously conceived God is the 'dead metaphor' par excellence. A religiously conceived God can obviously only be 'as such,' a 'thing-in-itself,' because *God* cannot religiously be seen as a mere sign, as a linguistic convention, as a "poetically and rhetorically intensified" expression. For the believer, the sign 'God' necessarily transforms into *God himself* as it (i) *replaces* (ii) *arbitrarily* in order to (iii) *supersede and suspend* the non-existing X, and in this process instantiates the real and living God.

This was precisely Feuerbach's analysis in *Das Wesen des Christenthums* (1846; *On the Essence of Christianity*), which Nietzsche had studied a few years before writing his essay,[101] and although Feuerbach is never mentioned in the essay (and rarely in Nietzsche's work generally), they share certain ideas about essential human anthropocentrism followed by unconscious self-alienation.

In Feuerbach as well as in Nietzsche, humans produce knowledge of an outside world by projecting into it their own 'nature.' Although the outside stands over and against man, it is in Feuerbach seen as man's own nature *projected* into the outside as its objectification. Following Hegel, man's nature cannot be recognized in itself, but needs to come out of itself and find itself in the outside object: "The object to which a subject essentially, necessarily relates, is nothing else than this subject's own but objective, nature."[102] This means that when man starts to reflect on the object, he essentially reflects on himself 'as species': "Consciousness of the objective is the self-onsciousness of man."[103]

This idea applies preeminently to God, where we are thinking the purely imaginary, no longer constrained by our actual perceptions of an appearing world. The only restriction on thinking the god-image is man's own nature, because the god-image reflects the ideals that humans project into their god, i.e., everything which society holds to be precious, but in its god is seen in augmented and perfect form. Thus, the god-image reflects human nature as its ideal expression; cf. Feuerbach.

> Man cannot get beyond his true nature. He may indeed by means of the imagination conceive individuals of another so-called higher kind, but he can never get loose from his species, his nature: the conditions of being, the positive final predicates which he gives to these other individuals, are always determinations or qualities drawn from his own nature—qualities in which he in truth only imagines and projects himself.[104]

This anthropomorphism we would find in every being if they knew how to think their species. As seen, the idea recur in Nietzsche's discussion of the 'mosquito' from above, as well as in Feuerbach's plant example: "If the plants had eyes, taste, and judgment, each plant would declare its own flower the most beautiful."[105] As well as the human is anthropocentric, as self-centered would be the mosquito and the plant, if they had evolved the capacity for self-consciousness.

However, in Feuerbach's dialectical Hegel-inspired thinking, when humans project their own nature into god, they necessarily see god as another being, and they naturally *repress* identity between themselves and their god-image. *They must be ignorant of identity*, because religion only convinces as long as worshippers are ignorant of the identity between themselves and their religious object. If or when they become aware, their religion disintegrates, because they now realize that what they believed was objectivity, is in fact subjective. Scandalously, they have been worshipping themselves.

To Feuerbach, the Christian god is a reflection of our purified nature. In god, we see ourselves as objective and, simultaneously, as another, namely god. If in Christian thinking God traditionally is endowed with attributes such as love and wisdom, it is because we, at least as far as our ideals are concerned, posit the values of love and knowledge as extraordinarily precious. Even if we in reality are neither loving nor wise, we implant these predicates in god, who is now infinitely and absolutely *benevolent, omnipotent*, and *omniscient*. "To the religious sentiment god is a real Father [...] to it he is a real, living, personal being, and therefore his attributes are also living and personal."[106]

Human self-alienation and self-reification from own anthropomorphic projections comes about because of the repression of identity between ideal human nature and the attributes of God. God is asserted as the absolute other over and against the humans, who in creating their god empty themselves for their best qualities, uploading them instead onto god. "Such as are a man's thought and dispositions, such is his God; so much worth as a man has, so much and no more has his God. Consciousness of God is self-consciousness; knowledge of God is self-knowledge. By his God thou knowest the man, and by the man his God; the two are identical."[107]

In this process God becomes the exclusive repository for ideal human qualities to the same extent as humans deprive themselves of them. If everything about God is seen in the positive, everything about the human is now seen in the negative: "to enrich God, man must become poor, that God may be all, man must be nothing."[108]

At the end of this process, the human has become an object of an object.

> Man—this is the mystery of religion—projects his being into objectivity, and then again makes himself an object; this projected image of himself he must convert into a subject; he thinks of himself as an object to himself, but as the object of an object, of another being than himself. Thus here, man is an object to God.[109]

The human has first objectified its in-itself unknown nature by projecting it into the god-metaphor, then subjected itself as object to the will of God-himself as absolute subject. The religious man no longer needs his own subjectivity, because, although he has emptied himself of qualities, he has found himself in God in a much more perfect manner, and, as Feuerbach notices, "where is the necessity of positing the same thing twice, of having it twice? What man withdraws from himself, what he renounces in himself, he only enjoys in an incomparably higher and fuller measure in God."[110]

In a schematic table, we may summarize the steps of the dialectical process as follows. First, we have a human unaware of its own nature, as it cannot see and discover itself in itself. Second, we have a human becoming indirectly aware of own 'nature' or 'qualities' qua projecting itself into the extraneous god-image. Third, we have a human alienated from itself because of the successful projection at the second stage, i.e., a human robbed from its 'nature,' which can now only be perceived in God.

Table 1 The replacement of 'human nature' with God as 'dead metaphor'

Self-unconscious human	Human projecting ideal qualities into God		Human "making himself poor" by seeing only ideal qualities in God	
Human	Human	God	Human	God
Ideal Human Nature	Ideal Human Nature ➚		~~Ideal Human Nature~~ ➚	

We notice that self-projection immediately is followed by self-alienation. The cost of winning a God is the loss of self. When we read Feuerbach, we notice his ambivalence about the value of this cost-benefit calculation, which we do not find in Nietzsche. In Feuerbach, the religious human wins itself in the perfect image of God, which makes up for the loss of incomprehensible human nature.[111] In Nietzsche, this 'win' rather appears like a double if not a triple lie, first the lie of the existence of a 'human nature' in the first place, second, the lie in projecting it into an abstract extraneous image of an absolute subject, thereupon enslaving oneself to that absolute subjectivity. In Nietzsche, self-projection followed by self-alienation is rather a lose-lose situation, i.e., a double self-deception where the human first falsely is supposed to inhabit 'ideal nature' and thereupon, equally falsely, is supposed to recover this 'false nature' in the god-image.

7. The Rationalizing Concept

1. Reason as Constructive Human Intelligence

The first part of Nietzsche's TL is composed of a total of ten paragraphs, the seventh being the brief and often-quoted truths are 'metaphors'/'illusions' passage as discussed, foreshadowing the subsequent eighth, ninth, and tenth paragraphs where Nietzsche elaborates on the nature of 'truth' as metaphor and illusion. It is here characteristic that we keep coming back to *concepts*, this last and final stage in our production of knowledge, but in a presentation where Nietzsche seemingly cannot make up his mind as whether to see concepts as perversions of human knowledge or springing from human genius. Concepts provide us with cold logical constructions build on a foundation of *nothing*, while *pretending* to assert truth; they are simultaneously *admired* for the logical consistency they bring to the world of knowledge and *dismissed* because of their deceptiveness.

According to Nietzsche's genealogical understanding of knowledge, concept-formation is the last stage in the human development toward rational thinking, both in the structural-cognitive sense as apparent in the model, *nerve-stimulus* → *image* → *sound/word* → *concept*, and in a historical-genealogical sense as they arrive into human existence at the latest stage.

Nietzsche introduced us to this genealogy already in the beginning of the essay in his account of human socialization. Now he reemphasizes that when socialization is internalized and imprinted as *conscience*, humans no longer accept ethical standpoints that may be "disrupted by sudden impressions." "[Man] now subjects his behavior as a "rational" being to the rule of abstractions; he no longer tolerates that his standpoints are disrupted by sudden impressions; he generalizes all these impressions first into colorless and cool concepts in order to then entrust them with the guidance of his life and action."[112] In this passage, 'concepts' have the function to elevate humans above animals by giving them the ability to organize the world into schemata.

> Everything that raises man above the animal depends upon this ability to transfer visual metaphors into a schema, that is, to transform an image into a concept. Because in the realm of these schemata something is possible, which never could have been accomplished in the visual first impressions, namely the construction of a pyramidal order of classes and gradations, the creation of a new world of laws, privileges, subordinations, boundaries, which now stands over and against the other visual world of first impressions as something more solid and universal, more familiar and human, and with this also more regulative and authoritative.[113]

Nietzsche takes the observation further in another of his early works, namely the second *Unzeitgemäße Betrachtungen* (UBII), where he describes the "happiness" of the "forgetful cattle," "fettered to the pale of the moment."[114] Animals remain bound to the narrow horizon of the present, as new impressions immediately cancel out the past impressions. They cannot hold on to the past and cannot remember "neither life nor death," while humans have lost this thoughtlessness thanks to their ability to form words (or concepts). They have learnt to master language, to communicate, remember, and think, and in this removed themselves from a life lived in the self-presence of the moment.[115] Before Nietzsche, Schopenhauer made a similar observation.

> [Animals] live in the present alone; [man] lives at the same time in the future and the past. They satisfy the need of the moment; he provides by the most ingenious preparations for his future. [...] They are given up entirely to the impression of the moment, to the effect of the motive of perception; he is determined by abstract concepts independent of the present moment. [...] The animal feels and perceives; man, in addition, *thinks* and *knows*; both *will*. [...] The animal learns to know death only when he dies, but man consciously draws every hour nearer his death.[116]

Whether we designate the linguistic form *word* or *concept*, its formation is a particular human capacity not shared by animals. Animals live exclusively in the moment, as every of their experienced instances is being perpetually replaced by new and ever-new instances, while the past glides back into indistinct darkness.

Notwithstanding the tenuous distinction between word and concept, it is clear that Nietzsche sees the evolution of our cognitive-linguistic abilities as a *rationalization-process* enabling us (for better or for worse) to replace 'images' with words and thereupon construct abstract edifices out of concepts.

> His construction must be like a spider's web, delicate enough to be carried along by the ripples of the waves, strong enough not to be blown apart by the wind. [...] Great conceptual construction shows the rigid regularity of a Roman columbarium, breathing the logical strictness and coolness that characterizes mathematics. [...] Just as the Romans and Etruscans divided heaven in rigid mathematical lines, and then exiled God to such a space segmented like a template, so every people has above themselves such a mathematically divided concept-heaven. [...] One is certainly allowed to admire the human being as a formidable genius of construction, succeeding in rising the tower of an endlessly complicated dome of concepts on a moving foundation, as if on running water. [...] As a genius of construction, the human raises itself far above the bees: they built from wax, which they gather in nature, but humans build from the far more delicate material of concepts, which they must first fabricate out of themselves. In this, they are very admirable—but not due to their drives for truth or for a pure knowledge of things.[117]

The human being accomplishing these abstract constructions is "admirable" is its rational capacity. By erecting its epistemic constructions out of *concepts*, its elementary but delicate building blocks, it becomes a "formidable genius of construction." In a number of comparisons between man and other of nature's builders, man surpasses them all. The spider and the bee build their constructions out of the delicate materials of silk and wax, but man is incomparable more delicate when building his constructions out of concepts, spun out of pure imagination.[118] This is "very admirable," but *what* they spin out of themselves is obviously less admirable. Man's constructions have the "rigid regularity of a Roman columbarium," they "breathe logical strictness and coolness," they "divide heaven in rigid mathematical lines," they create a "mathematically divided concept-heaven." However, even if man is "admirable" for these cool and rigid concept constructions, he is less admirable for the "drive for truth" expressed in this activity.[119]

2. Unreason as Imaginary Divine Intelligence

However impressive concept-constructions are, however ingenious man is as a rational builder, he always fails to discover and deliver 'truth'

(= 'thing-in-itself' = the 'enigmatic x'). As concept-builders out of concepts, our *reason* and *rationality* is not in question in Nietzsche—this is rather the part of human concept-construction that he admires. Still, we are seen as playing a game of dice with our reason and concepts, a game which is *in itself random*: "In this conceptual game of dice, *truth* means to use every dice according to its markings, to accurately count its spots, to form correct categories, and never violate the order of classes and the sequence of rankings."[120] However ingenious we have become, we are subjected to the chance cast of the dice, which we thereupon rationalize by "counting, classifying, ranking," etc. That is, human reason touches nothing deeper than its ability of organize the number of dots on the dice; i.e., it has no supernatural sense of order, no innate capacity to discover a rational order of things. Still, we have abilities to perceive 'dots,' to count them, and to classify and organize them according to certain rules.

Paradoxically, when humans as 'constructive geniuses' become 'irrational,' it is when they ignore, forget, or fail to realize that they are merely playing a game of dice. Unreason comes about thanks to this particular self-deception regarding *transcendental reason*, i.e., when humans become so engrossed in their own wondrous constructions that they see them as infused by a 'truth' of transcendental-objective origin. At that point, we are back to human pretension, vanity, and pride; we are back to the human being seduced into its delusional belief in truth as a discovery of a divinely inscribed order of things.

In this discussion of man's reason and unreason, Nietzsche's often changes his mood, his voice, his judgments or evaluations, during his explanations. He is wavering between respect/admiration and mockery/dismissal of this enterprising 'constructive genius.' He falls in and out of respect for man according to his adopted polemic perspective and context. This indecision as to whether describe man as a 'constructive' or 'pretentious' genius seems never to be resolved in his essay, and may not be resolvable exactly because the 'master-concept,' *Truth*, has lost its authority. We may suggest that if there is no longer any ground and foundation on which to validate states of affairs, man is the final (non-)'origin' of truth-claims. We consequently encounter the following problem, man as 'foundation' of 'truth' is tantamount to the admitted 'non-foundation' of 'truth,' because man seen as foundation of 'man-made truth' necessarily *degrades* Truth and *is* not Truth (= 'thing-in-itself' = the 'enigmatic x'). Nietzsche is caught in a tension where, on the one hand, man-made truth is false (according to classical theological-rationalist thinking), but on the other hand, truth-in-itself is false too (according to the thinking of the emerging biological and cognitive sciences). Man-made truth cannot qualify as 'truth' semantically, but truth-in-itself cannot qualify as 'truth' scientifically. If now man as constructive genius claims to produce truth, he is pretentious, but if he believes in objective truth, he is naïve. We notice that Nietzsche is not here asking us to adopt a position either true or false; he is entangled in a dichotomy, which he throughout his thinking attempts to resolve.

The final step in Nietzsche's thinking now follows in good logical order. When man creates 'truth' out of concepts, he merely re-creates himself. His concept-formations are, instead of objectively True (i.e., corresponding to things-in-themselves), *anthropomorphic*.[121]

Let us for illustration return to the concept of the 'mammal,' which is explained to be "anthropomorphic through and through," and which contains nothing that is "really and universally *true in itself* apart from man."

> If I create the definition of the mammal and then, after observing a camel, declare: "look, a mammal," then a truth is brought to light, but it is of limited value. I mean, it is anthropomorphic through and through and does not contain a single speck that apart from man would be really and universally "true in itself."[122]

Nietzsche is not here making the indefensible and nonsensical claim that the 'camel' is human or human-like, he is claiming that the linguistic *concept* organizing the individual camel into the family of 'mammals' is human. Thus, *the concept* is human. This stipulation makes his claim far safer to the point of making it self-evident. Human language is necessarily a human invention and our ways of classifying and organizing the world around us is therefore necessarily "anthropomorphic through and through." This characterization applies to all knowledge. The hardest of the hard sciences, too, must produce their rigorous conceptual languages from linguistic "metaphors" that are uniquely human.

However, as Nietzsche sees it, the researcher has a propensity to commit the error discussed above. The scientists are instinctively committed to objectivity and represses simultaneously the cognitive-linguistic form-giving power of their scientific languages. It is not when they apply human metaphors in their science they err, but when they fail to understand that this is what they do. On Nietzsche's bird's-eye view on knowledge, the researcher's primordial point of departure is man as the "measure of all things" (since s/he is a human equipped with human perception and language), even while spontaneously repressing own involvement in the creation of the scientific object. The scientists defend the belief that these created objects are "pure objects"; they forget or repress both the metaphoricity of perceptive images and of language, and take the end-product, the linguistically mediated perceptions, to be things-in-themselves.

> The researcher regards the entire world as tied up with the human being, as an infinitely broken reverberation of an arché-sound, the human, as a manifold replica of an arché-image, the human. His method is to hold man to be the measure of all things. In this assumption, however, he proceeds from the error to believe that he has these things immediately as pure objects in front of him. He forgets therefore the original pictorial metaphors as metaphors and takes them to be things in themselves.[123]

Nietzsche presents us to two different 'errors' emerging on two different stages of knowledge-formation. The first 'error' is the metaphorical representation of the world, and the second is to forget/repress this metaphoricity of our representations. The first error falsifies the world as thing-in-itself, but the second, more seriously, represses the representational character of our knowledge. Committing the second error, it becomes impossible to take back the 'objective' world as ours.

Still, as Nietzsche submits without self-contradiction, we commit the second error out of *pragmatic necessity*; i.e., because we cannot suspend our strong belief in reality as a 'thing-in-itself,' for example that a table is a table. Doubt about our real perceived world cannot be upheld in our lived actuality even if we according to abstract analysis indeed are "artistic-creative subjects" in our perceptions and verbalizations.

> Only by forgetting this primitive metaphor-world, only by making hard and rigid the mass of images that originally streamed like a stormy flood through the primary constitution of human imagination, only thanks to the unshakable belief that this sun, this window, this table possess truth in itself, in short, only because the human beings forgot themselves as subjects, and indeed as artistic-creative subjects, do they live somewhat tranquilly, securely, and consistently.[124]

We need to believe in the self-evidence of our common-sense perceptions, even if the advanced sciences of biology and psychology reveal to us a fluid world of relativity and perspectivism. Nietzsche and several of his peers do not see a self-contradiction in defending this view.

8. Biological Perspectivism

1. The World according to Homo Sapiens

We notice that the theoretical paradigm that informs Nietzsche and peers promotes a version of 'perspectivism,' which I will here label 'biological perspectivism.'

It refers to the obvious fact that different species sense the world with differently evolved perceptive apparatuses. Accordingly, it takes for granted that different species cannot experience the externality that we call 'world' in the same manner, and they cannot have identical perceptions of one self-identical world. They have different experiences of for example space, time, movement, dimension, and color, as well as different internal experiences of sensations such as pain, fear, or pleasure (if or when such sensations reach consciousness in various species). This biological view comes about thanks to the progress in the understanding of perception and mind, and it has the consequence that human perception of world no longer is regarded as privileged but must be seen as only *one possible interpretation* of the external and internal worlds as they impress themselves on the senses. As such, the human species sees the world according to its own *biological perspective*.

It is this biological perspectivism Nietzsche refers to in the following passage when he criticizes the notion of a "correct perception" as anthropocentrism reducing all externality to human perception.

> It is already difficult for man to acknowledge that the insect and the bird perceive an entirely different world than humans, and that the question which of the two world-perceptions is the correct one is quite meaningless, as it hereby already assumes the correct perception as measuring rod, that is, assumes a non-existing standard. In any case, it seems to me that "the correct perception"—i.e., the adequate expression of an object in the subject—is a self-contradictory absurdity.[125]

We read explicitly that the notion of a "correct perception" is nothing less than a "self-contradictory absurdity." It is anthropocentricism tacitly implying the *correspondence theory of truth*, since it postulates the "adequate expression of an object in the subject" (ibid.). In Nietzsche's biological perspectivism there is no privileged animal perception; the perceptions of insects, birds, or humans produce different possible worlds, none of which are more correct, accurate, and truthful than any other. We are thus back to the neo-Kantian idea of a 'world-in-itself' that remains inaccessible for-us thanks to our species-specific sense-apparatus and at best is a limitative concept asserted as hypothesis.[126] In the language of TL, we are caught up in our own "perceptive metaphors," as such, in our biological make-up falsifying the stubborn idea of *The World*.

In biological perspectivism, the thesis of *The World* is discredited, but not the thesis of *a world*, as Nietzsche realizes in a subsequent passage. In the broad biological context, animals produce different "world-perceptions," but every species remain per biological necessity faithful to its own perspective. The case in point is of course the human species that produce a perception of world that (*mutatis mutandis*) remains stable for the entire species. Our perception of world is therefore not thrown into absolute relativistic disarray, as Nietzsche emphasizes in the passage below, where he also dismisses 'subjectivism.'

> Against this, we must first of all say that if each of us had different sense-perceptions, if we could perceive now as a bird, now as a worm, now as a plant, or if one of us saw the same stimulus as red, another as blue, and a third ever heard it as a tone, then nobody would talk about such a lawfulness of nature, but instead comprehend it as an extremely subjective construction.[127]

On a superficial reading of the passages above, one may be tempted to see yet another example of a Nietzschean 'inconsistency' or 'incoherence.' In one passage, perspectivism is forcefully defended in pointing out how world-perceptions are species-specific; in the other passage, the notion is amended to the extent that Nietzsche defends our construction of natural laws against subjectivism. Is Nietzsche unable to make up his mind whether he wants to be a 'relativist' or an 'absolutist'?—Rather, Nietzsche is adhering to the biological paradigm to which he has committed himself. His fundamental claim stands; we see everything from our human perspective and are in this no different from other species (cf. above, if the mosquito, the worm, or the plant could think themselves as species, they would be as centric as humans are anthropocentric; cf. Part I, A.2: "Feuerbach and Nietzsche on Anthropocentrism"). Still, we produce world-perceptions *as species*, not as *individuals*. As species, we perceive colors visually, not acoustically; as species, we do not and cannot adopt the bird's perception of world; as species we form perceptive images that are uniform and able to be communicated between ourselves; cf. *Notebook 19*: "The formidable consensus of men about things proves the total uniformity of their perceptive apparatus."[128] [...] "To the plant the world is such and such—to us such and such. If we compare the two capacities of perception, we regard our conception of the world as more correct."[129]

If we according to Fr. Jameson's famous phrase were regarded as locked up in a 'prison house of language' in the late twentieth century's dominant postmodern paradigm,[130] under the inspiration of Nietzsche we are much more profoundly locked up in a 'prison house of perception.' Still, our physiology evolved to fit the entire human species in our perception of nature; therefore, conditionally upon our physiological limitations, we produce 'laws of nature' that are neither individual constructions nor transcendental objectivities. As species, we have evolved a cognitive apparatus able to "mirror" nature, and it is in this mirror we see nature, and as such, become the glue between *nature* and *law*.

These stipulations point toward a Nietzschean 'Naturalist Deconstruction' of *objective truth*, since Nietzsche and peers no longer believe in *True* perception of *The World*. Given biological perspectivism and relativism, it no longer makes sense to talk about correspondences between perception and objectivity.

Let us notice here that Nietzsche, about fifteen years later, in *Der Fröhlichen Wissenschaft* V (1889; *The Gay Science* [GS]), returns to the discussion of biological perspectivism when he claims that, "The human intellect cannot avoid seeing itself under its perspectival forms, and only in them. We cannot see around our own corner"[131] (cf. discussion of passage below).[132] It is nearly impossible to detect any essential conceptual difference between the early and this later view of biological perspectivism. If in TL, it is "human vanity" and "quite meaningless" to try to determine the correct world-perception, we are in GS declared to be beyond the ridiculous immodesty of allowing perspectives only from our point of view, our "corner." The later statement from GS is hardly more that an addendum to his earlier reflections.[133]

9. Nietzsche's Empiricist Neo-Kantianism

1. The Reversal of Thing and Predicate

Already Kant contended that substances remain unknown and that we can never reach deeper into nature than our predicates allow. Reason may compel us to seek the absolute nature of things, but due to the limitations of conceptual thinking, we can at best only reproduce predicates, however deeply we desire to peek into absolute essences. This is stated in for example Kant's *Prolegomena*.

> Pure reason requires us to seek for every predicate of a thing its own subject, and for this subject, which is itself necessarily nothing but a predicate, its subject, and so on indefinitely (or as far as we can reach). But hence it follows that we must not hold anything at which we arrive to a be an ultimate subject, and that substance itself never can be thought by our understanding, however deep we may penetrate, even if all nature were unveiled to us. For the specific nature of our understanding consists in thinking everything discursively, i.e., by concepts, and so by mere predicates, to which, therefore, the absolute subject must always be wanting.[134]

In this conception, Kant announces the finitude of human knowledge and the limitation of human understanding. We are always coming up against a wall of concepts. An 'unveiled nature' would be the thing-in-itself, and this will always escape us.

The idea is reiterated in Schopenhauer, who, elaborating on Kant's idea, concludes that we cannot hope finding a resting place for human reason in resorting to ultimate essences in the form of causes or substances (cf. *Die Welt als Wille und Vorstellung*, 1). This discussion is continued in Nietzsche as well, as he understands Kant's contention having the consequence that however many 'properties' we add to 'things,' we will never arrive to *the thing*, but only to *the relationships* between the properties. So-called 'substances' are not self-identical singularities, but determined only qua the relationships of their predicates.

We see this view elaborated already in *Notebook 19*, where Nietzsche is reflecting on the consequences of Kant's concept of the synthetic judgment. In one passage, he concludes that, "all laws of nature are only relations from x to y and z. We define laws of nature as the relations between xyz, from where again they are known to us only as relations to other xyz";[135] and in a longer passage, he follows up and explains.

> On the essence of definition: the pencil is an elongated, etc., body. A is B. That which is elongated is at the same time colored. Properties [*Eigenschaften*] only contain relation. A certain body is exactly made up of so and so many relationships. Relations can never be identical to essence [*Wesen*], they are only consequences of essences. The synthetic judgment describes a thing according to its effects [*Folgen*], that is, essence and effect become identical. [...] That is, *synthetic inferences are illogical* [*Synthetischen Schlüsse sind unlogisch*]. When we apply them, we presuppose the popular metaphysics, that is, one that sees effects as causes. [...] The concept, "pencil," is confused with the "thing" pencil. The "is" [*Das "ist"*] in the synthetic judgment is false, it contains a transference, where two different spheres are posited next to each other, between them equalization never happens.[136]

According to this passage, the fundamental form for the synthetic judgment, *A is B*, is false insofar as we assume identity between A as a body (or a subject) and B as a property (or a predicate). What we actually do in synthetic judgments of the type *A is B*, is simply to *add* properties associated with A; or more precisely expressed, we add up properties *as if* A; we produce the *idea* of a 'thing,' A, by means of the sequence, $B_1, B_2, .. B_n$. In our accumulation of an indefinite sequence of properties or predicates, $B_1, B_2, .. B_n$, we define A as substance or subject without ever 'reaching' it, or 'exhaustively defining' it. Instead, the relationships between the distinct elements in the sequence, $B_1, B_2, .. B_n$ are our best representative for the supposed substantial body.[137]

Therefore, it is to Nietzsche an error to confuse this sequence of elements as a 'body,' since it gives us the *idea of body* in the first place. The sequence of elements is our *first* encounter, and they form a relationship which we abbreviate into the self-identical body, A, which in the synthetic judgment, *A is B*, is reversed and falsely appears to be *deriving* its properties.

An important implication of the thinking is that the subject in the synthetic judgment is visible only in and through its predicates.[138] Our synthetic judgments are judgments on or about visible surfaces, and touch never anything deeper. This again implies that our judgments are tautological, because judgments are reiterating the already visible; their conclusions are self-evident, because they describe rather than explain. Knowledge therefore is *empty*, says Nietzsche (again *Notebook 19*): "Knowledge [*Das Erkennen*] has, in the strongest sense, only the form of a tautology, *and is empty*."[139] It is this tautological structure of knowledge, Nietzsche is describing in the well-known example from TL: "When somebody hides something behind a bush and then looks for it again at the same place and finds it there, there is in such seeking and finding not much to applaud. Yet, this is how we seek and find of 'truth' within our realm of reason [*Vernunft-Bezirkes*]."[140] Knowledge at best only *adds* a concept to the already perceived; it never discovers something uniquely new.

We now understand that the term 'A' in the synthetic judgment is equivalent to Nietzsche's 'metaphor' in TL since in the synthetic judgment it is creatively asserted as the derivation-point of the sum total of the sequence of 'B's. Now, as self-identical 'thing,' 'A' has become "hard and rigid," but as Nietzsche warns, "a metaphor's becoming hard and rigid does not reveal the necessity and the decisive verification of this metaphor."[141]

Nietzsche starts §10 of TL by testing his thesis by summarizing the strongest counter-argument that traditionally meets it.

> Every person, familiar with such considerations, must certainly have felt a deep mistrust against any such idealism whenever he clearly had convinced himself of the eternal consistency, omnipresence, and infallibility of the laws of nature. He has concluded that however far we penetrate into the heights of the telescopic and into the depths of the microscopic world, everything is certain, well-constructed, infinite, lawful, and complete; that science will successfully be excavating these chambers forever, to discover that everything is consistent and non-contradictory. How far this is from resembling a phantasm creation; because if this were what it was, it would have to suppose illusion and unreality to be anywhere.[142]

That was the classical view of the task of the sciences in the nineteenth century (as it largely still is). The sciences are penetrating into the "depth of things" and revealing a world that is "certain, well-constructed, infinite, lawful, and complete"; they "successfully excavate" a world existing in its eternal truth. The position is brought forward by Nietzsche as the most obvious counter-argument to his own position and must as such not be confused with *Nietzsche's position* (if or when it is, Nietzsche becomes completely incomprehensible and it appears as if he suddenly provides us with arguments against his consistent truth-criticism; as if he after all defends a theory of Truth in the classical and commonsensical sense).

It is this view of Nietzsche's *antipode* that is "far from resembling [his own] phantasm creation" that seems to "suppose illusion and unreality to be anywhere." Playing the devil's advocate, he is paraphrasing his opponents' strongest objection in order to refute it with his own supposedly stronger counter-argument entertained in the following passage.

> Against this [i.e., this view of his antipode], we must first of all say that if each of us had different sense perceptions, if we could perceive now as a bird, now as a worm [...] then nobody would talk about such a lawfulness of nature, but instead comprehend it as an extremely subjective construction.[143]

Thereupon Nietzsche draws his, at this point in our exposition, well-known conclusion that we do not know the in-itself, i.e., the laws and essences of nature, as he adds to this insight the relativistic view that we know only relationships (in this, he is anticipating Mach's relativism, as we shall discuss below; cf. Part II, B.3: "A Nietzsche-Machean Theory of Knowledge"[144]).

> So, what at all is the law of nature for us? It is not known by us in-itself, but only in its effects, that is, in its relations to other laws of nature, which again are known to us only as the sum-total of relations. In other words, all these relations refer always only to each other and are completely incomprehensible to us in their essence.[145]

From reading these passages in the context of the voices Nietzsche adopts, now imitating his opponent now defending his own position, we can conclude that Nietzsche remains consistent to his fundamental position, his post-Truth and post-Metaphysical Naturalism.

2. The Proto-Forms of Knowledge: Time and Space

In the last part of §10, we see that Nietzsche in introducing a relativistic view of the apparent world continues to defend the existence of some of the Kantian categories, although he in the spirit of Schopenhauer and other neo-Kantians reduces the Kantian scheme of twelve categories to two, namely time and space.

His conclusive view must be that we in our encounter with the apparent world only encounter relations, never essences, substances, causes, or laws; *still*, we bring to this indefinite manifold of relationships our two fundamental categories, space and time, in order to organize them in comprehensible sequences and numbers. Space makes it possible to perceive coexistence; time makes it possible to perceive succession; consequently, thanks to space, we perceive elements situated in relationships to one and other; thanks to time, we perceive these elements in sequences of movement or permanence. This arché-foundation of knowledge in the form of space and time accounts for the *thing-representation*: elements are identified as things in their relation to other elements (co-existence) and in the relation to change and becoming in a world that moves in time (succession); in time, they can have a past, a present, and a future. So-called 'things' comes into being as self-identical element-clusters thanks to our subjective categories in the form of space and time.

> Only that what we bring to the relations—time and space, that is, successive sequences and numbers—is really known to us in them. However, all the marvelous that we correctly admire about the laws of nature, that which requires our explanation and may seduce us into mistrusting idealism, is strictly and exclusively contained only within the mathematical rigor and indestructibility of our representations of time and space. These, however, we produce in and from ourselves with the same necessity with which the spider spins. If we are forced to comprehend all things only under these forms, then it is no longer astonishing that we essentially only comprehend all things according to these forms. [...] All lawfulness, which so impresses us in the movements of the stars and in the chemical processes, is fundamentally identical to the properties that we ourselves bring to things; so, we are in this impressed about ourselves. From this, it must of course follow that every artistic metaphorical construction, with which every sensation in us begins, already presupposes those forms and thus is executed according to them. Only thanks to the unmovable persistence of these arché-forms can we explain how it is possible build an edifice of concepts out of metaphors. It is namely an imitation of time-, space-, and number-relations on the foundation of metaphors.[146]

Nietzsche uses the spider-metaphor twice in TL (KSA 1, 882, and 886), and brings it back in *Morgenröte* (1881; *Daybreak*). In the passage above, we produce our representations "in and from ourselves with the same necessity with which the spider spins" (ibid.). In *Daybreak*, we are in our production of knowledge compared to "spiders in our webs":

> The habits of our senses have wrapped us in a tissue of lies and deceptions of sensations; these, in their turn, are the basis of all our judgments and our

'knowledge'—there is no means of escape, no crooked path or exit into the real world! We are like spiders in our webs [...] whatever we may catch in them will be something that our webs are able to catch!"[147]

'Our webs' are Nietzsche's poetic-metaphorical expression of our "arché-forms" (ibid.), i.e., his reduced scheme of categories, space and time, able to catch 'sensations' in their structure. In this activity our 'webs' are already forming sensations, partly because they have developed to catch only particular sensations, in this sense being selective and discriminate, and partly because they represent us with limited fragments of the world, not the entire universe of possible sensations.

Nietzsche's 'webs' provide us with the rules of transcendental subjectivity on which our worlds of knowledge are being produced, i.e., the subjective forms of time and space, giving us the ability to think sequence and number. This is Nietzsche's foundation on which perceptual and conceptual constructions are being built. Despite the reduced scheme of categories, where 'causality' is a later construction added to the primary experience of 'sequence' in the spirit of Hume, the thinking is Kantian as it repeats Kant's arguments for a 'transcendental idealism' as presented in the first edition of *Critique of Pure Reason*. It is on this ground we form natural laws, whose objectivity according to the new paradigm is seen as nested in transcendental subjectivity and not in the objective world of things. The objectivity of the internal has replaced the objectivity of the external. It is on this ground our 'metaphorical' constructions are being erected, partly as perceptive, partly as linguistic 'metaphors.' Let us again draw attention to Nietzsche's idiosyncratic use of the word 'metaphor.' As noted above (cf. Part I, A.6), we see that although Nietzsche talks about so-called 'artistic metaphorical constructions,' he is in the context referring to psychology and cognition, rather than to the disciplines of Rhetoric and Poetry. It is *sensations* that start as metaphors, cf., "every artistic metaphorical construction, *with which every sensation in us begins*, already presupposes those forms" (ibid.).

Nietzsche has learnt from Schopenhauer that we are not perceiving and apprehending an objective world, but a world pre-formed by our subjective categories, or as Schopenhauer has it, by our 'brain': "The objective world as we know it does not belong to the true being of things-in-themselves, but is its mere phenomenon, conditioned by those very forms that lie a priori in the human intellect (i.e., the brain); hence the world cannot contain anything but phenomena."[148]

Nietzsche has also learnt from Schopenhauer that an impression is not identical to a representation (or a phenomenon). The sense-impression is not already given to us as phenomenon, but undergoes a transformation after which is *becomes* a phenomenon (cf. Nietzsche's distinction between 'nerve-stimulus' and 'image'). An 'impression' is doing nothing but simply *im-pressing* itself on a sense organ; it is nothing but a "sensation in a sense-organ," as Schopenhauer puts it below.

> [An impression] is nothing more than a mere sensation in the sense-organ, and only by the application of the understanding (i.e., of the law of causality), and of the forms of perception, of space and time, does our intellect convert this mere sensation into a representation. This representation now exists as object in space and time, and cannot be distinguished from the latter (the object).[149]

First we receive impressions/sensations (Nietzsche's 'nerve-stimuli'), thereupon sensations are formatted within our so-called 'nets,' granted our fundamental spatial-temporal perception of world, and become first now representations or phenomena (Nietzsche's 'images'); in my vocabulary, 'thing-representations' (in contrast to 'word-representations').

3. Active versus Passive Receptivity in the Neo-Kantian Tradition

The premise that the spatio-temporal organization of world is given as subjective condition, is granted by virtually all the neo-Kantian participants in this paradigm.

Otto Liebmann offers the following discussion:

> The manifold of elements of experience (the matter of representation) given in space and time, can first become experience (or enter consciousness as a coherent world of apparent objects) when they are associated through certain syntheses (categories) of our intellect. As Hume correctly has noticed, we cannot create these syntheses from experience, since they are given to us merely as a multiplicity of successive and coexistent impressions of (inner or outer) sensations, but never supply us with their necessary connections. Therefore, the categories, such as space and time, are functions of the knowing subject, i.e., they are a priori necessary representations. [*Diese Synthesen können wir, wie Hume richtig bemerkt hat, nicht aus der Erfahrung geschöpft haben, da sie uns eben nur eine Vielheit von nach und nebeneinander gegebenen Eindrücken des (inneren und äußeren) Sinnes, niemals aber den nothwendigen Zusammenhang derselben liefert. Also sind die Kategorien, ebenso wie Raum und Zeit, Functionen des erkennenden Subjectes, d.h. nothwendige Vorstellungen a priori*]. Insofar as they can be thought only within space and time, they relate only to spatial and temporal objects, that is, they have validity only within our intellect. [...] 1) Our intellect can only know the in space and time given elements, associated by the categories, as object. 2) Everything given

in space and time, i.e., everything, onto which we can apply the categories, has only validity in relation to our intellect, and is independently from this, nothing.[150]

Writers of the neo-Kantian tradition all agree on criticizing the notion of a passively existing 'thing-in-itself,' with its strong connotations to the metaphysical concept of Truth in the form of a putatively self-present objectivity.

They 'deconstruct' this notion in agreement with Kant, seen as the precursor of the criticism and they applaud how this deconstruction is consistently presented in the first edition of *Critique of Pure Reason*. However, in almost equal measure, they regret Kant's amended version of this criticism in the second edition of the *Critique* and regard it as a major blunder. Several of Kant's commentators complain over the changes Kant introduces between his first and second edition of the *Critique*, first among them Schopenhauer in his appendix to WWV1, "Critique of the Kantian Philosophy."[151] Later writers like Liebmann,[152] K. Fischer in *Kritik der kantischen Philosophie*,[153] and Fr. Lange in his *Geschichte der Materialismus*, bd. 3,[154] express the same regret of this change of mind, which they believe they detect in Kant. As pointed out above, they are all writers that Nietzsche studied in the 1860s and 1870s, and they must have inspired him into committing himself to defending a phenomenal world while simultaneously rejecting the possibility of a self-present 'thing.'

To the new Kantians, Kant seems in the late edition to involve himself in a self-contradiction regarding the notion of the 'thing-in-itself.' They praise Kant of having done away with the dogmatic philosophy of Rationalism in his first edition, but are disparaged when Kant in the second re-introduces dogmatic philosophy's adherence to the 'thing-itself' as a necessary (substantial and causal) background for the formation of knowledge. They are impressed with Kant's transcendental idealism, seeing him here turning the epistemological center of gravity around from the objective to the subjective conditions for the production of knowledge, but are unimpressed with Kant's later restoration of that objectivity he seemed so persuasively to have abandoned in the first edition. They emphatically regard themselves as 'Kantians,' but as they often emphasize, according to the first edition of the *Critique*.

We find strong statements of the problem already in Schopenhauer's "Critique of the Kantian Philosophy" (cf. WWV1, appendix), where he spells out the inconsistency.

[Whenever Kant makes use of the thing-in-itself], he at once brings it in through the conclusion that the phenomenon, and hence the visible world, must have a ground or reason, an intelligible cause, which is not phenomenon, and which therefore does not belong to any possible experience. [But] this he does

> after having incessantly urged that the categories, and thus also the category of causality [...] were mere forms of the understanding serving to spell out the phenomena of the world of sense, beyond which, on the other hand, they had no significance at all, and so on. He therefore most strictly forbids their application to things beyond experience, and rightly explains, and at the same time overthrows, all previous dogmatism as resulting from a violation of this law. The incredible inconsistency Kant here committed was soon noticed, and used by his first opponents for attacks to which his philosophy could not offer any resistance. [...] The truth is that on the path of the representation we can never get beyond the representation. [...] If a thing-in-itself is to be assumed, it cannot be an object at all, which, however, he always assumes it to be; but such a thing-in-itself would have to lie in a sphere *toto genere* different from the representation (from knowing and being known).[155]

So Schopenhauer, Kant first tells us that *causality* is one of the categories, belonging as such to transcendental subjectivity constituting the empirical perception of thing-hood, but thereupon he sees the 'thing' as *cause* to the phenomenon. If the categories are restricted as forms of understanding, they can only be organizing a world of sense-impressions into a world for-us. Therefore, when Kant insists on the category of *cause* existing *before* this world of representations, he is guilty of an "incredible inconsistency."

In Kuno Fischer's *Critique of Kant*,[156] we find the following clear-minded and precise summary of the problem.

> Kant teaches in the first edition of the *Critique* that external objects (bodies) only have existence in virtue of our ideas, but apart from them they are nothing; in the second edition, on the other hand, that the perception of matter is only possible through a thing external to me, and not through the mere idea of such a thing. There he teaches that things external to us are mere ideas; here, on the other hand, that they are not mere ideas. There he teaches that things external to us have existence merely in virtue of our ideas, but that they are nothing independent of the latter; here, that they have existence, by no means in virtue of our ideas, but independently of them.[157]

Liebmann complains in *Kant und die Epigonen* that Kant is being inconsistent already in his choice of vocabulary.

> First, he labels the in time and space given manifold of data of inner and outer experiences, appearances [*Erscheinungen*].—How does he come about that? What justifies him in doing so? [...] In the label 'appearance' lies the idea that we need to presuppose something that appears, namely an empirical world.[158]

To Liebmann, Kant starts a downward slide into that dogmatism he attempts to deconstruct already in his choice of words; the concept of 'appearance' already postulates a thing-itself on Liebmann's account. As we will see, Nietzsche will reiterate this problem posed by the distinction between 'appearance' and 'thing' in his later work (cf. Part I, A.3: "A Surface without Abyss").

Fischer attempts to resolve the apparent inconsistency between Kant's first and second edition. Without giving up the essential transcendental idealism of Kant, Fischer explains the necessity of the concept of the thing itself:

> There must be something which causes the impressions we receive, something which underlies our sensibility, and there with the whole constitution of our knowing reason, something therefore which also underlies all phenomena and the entire sense-world. But precisely on this account it cannot itself be anything sensible, cannot be a phenomenon, cannot be an object of knowledge. This 'supersensible substratum' Kant calls Thing-in-itself, designating thereby that transcendental X which the *Critique of Pure Reason* introduces, and which it sees itself, on the grounds pointed out, obliged to introduce into its calculation. It is called thing-in-itself in distinction from all phenomena. If our reason were not sensuous, but divine, not receptive, but creative, then its ideas would be things themselves, then there would be no difference between phenomena and things-in-themselves. Since, however, it is sensuous, space and time are the fundamental forms of its perception, its objects of knowledge are phenomena, and these merely ideas, hence not things-in-themselves. Consequently, in the Critical investigation of reason, we must distinguish between phenomena and things-in-themselves with the utmost precision, regarding every attempt to unite the two as the cause of irremediable confusion.[159]

On Fischer's analysis, we must as such accept the existence of a thing-itself. Our reason demands that there must be something that precedes the impressions we receive as sensuous matter; that is, we must demand a world of matter underlying sensuous matter. Still, Fischer maintains that this world of matter cannot itself be phenomenon, it cannot itself be perceived, and it is this unperceivable and thus incomprehensible world that is identical to the thing-in-itself, i.e., identical to Kant's transcendental X, and to Nietzsche's 'inaccessible and enigmatic X.' In this, it must be radically different from all phenomena, because if it was not, we would perceive thing-in-themselves, implying (besides being contrary to all Kantian teaching) that there is ultimately no difference between phenomena and things-in-themselves. In that case, our reason would no longer be receptive and we would be equipped with divine reason giving us direct insight into 'things.' It is Kant's realization of the rupture, the *original difference*, between the *thing-in-itself* and the *thing-representation* that Fischer regards as his great revolution of epistemological thinking. The enigmatic X as self-present there-being is asserted while simultaneously any access to the enigmatic X is denied. The dogmatic *correspondence theory of truth* is therefore rejected, since we cannot form knowledge of that which we cannot possibly know.

As we will see below (cf. Part II, A.2: "Nietzsche's Critiques of the In-Itself in his Middle Period"), several of Nietzsche's most virulent 'anti-Kantian' aphorisms in later work are addressing *Kant of the second edition of the Critique*; apparently, as it seems to undersigned, without Nietzsche's full recognition of the differences between Kant of the first and Kant of the second edition of *Critique*. It seems as if Nietzsche's *'anti-Kant'* applies to Kant as commonly criticized for the revised second edition of the *Critique*, but not to the essential Kantian project as introduced in the first edition. I therefore tend to agree with Hans Vaihinger, that Nietzsche is far more profoundly inspired by Kant than he likes to admit.

B: PART II OF *TRUTH AND LIES*

1. Regressions to Romantic Arts-Metaphysics

1. The Distinction between Authentic and Inauthentic Conceptualizations

Nietzsche divides his essay into fourteen paragraphs, organized in two parts of unequal length in approximately the ratio of three to one—the first ten paragraphs constituting Part I and the last four constituting Part II. Nietzsche does not explain the reason for the division and it is not obvious that his second part is initiating a new phase in his investigations. This division may possibly be an outcome of a random selection of two different sets of notes being organized into a first and a second part.

In Part II, starting with §11, we seem to be harking back to unresolved issues regarding the discussion of concept. We notice that Nietzsche is suddenly more insistent on describing the concept as an *inauthentic* 'metaphor' in distinction to artistic uses of language as providing us with words as *authentic* 'metaphors.' The vague and unresolved difference between 'word' and 'concept' from the first part of the essay (cf. Part I, A.5: "Word and/or/versus Concept?") seems here to be clarified as a distinction between an authentic and inauthentic conceptualization of the world. In Part II, Nietzsche will argue that originally, spoken language rendered concepts as word-forms (word-representations), as spoken language were referring directly to a world of thing-representations. This original language-use made up some kind of *lebendige sprache* that was reflecting immediate and spontaneously given sense-impressions. With time, so Nietzsche's new narrative, this authentic concept-formation was taken over by the scientists, and originally positive concept-metaphors formed in spoken language turned into negative forms when applied in the sciences. Nietzsche will suggest a master-distinction between *an authentic linguistic concept formation* and *an inauthentic scientific concept formation*.[160]

This master-distinction was already introduced in the discussions above on Schopenhauer's influence. We recall that Schopenhauer defined the 'word' as a "representation of a representation" (one step removed from the 'apparent world') while a 'concept' was a "representation of representation of a representation" (two steps removed from the 'apparent world'). Concepts were consequently less authentic than words, given their additional distance to image-representations, i.e., appearances.

Nietzsche is never more eloquent than in this last part of his essay. His disapproval of scientific concepts rests on uncertain *logical* foundation, but this weakness is compensated by his *rhetorical* insistence on a looming problem.

> As we have seen, it is originally language that works on the construction of concepts, in later ages the work is taken over by the sciences. Just as the bees simultaneously build the cells and fill them with honey, so the sciences work constantly on this great columbarium of concepts, this graveyard for sense-impressions, when it continues to build still new and higher stories and reinforcements, cleaning and renovating the old cells, as it attempts to fill out this enormous towering framework and arrange within it the entire empirical world, i.e., the anthropomorphic world. If the man of action binds his life to reason and its concepts in order not to be carried away and lose himself, the researcher builds his hut close to the tower of science so it can assist him and give him protection beneath its already existing bulwark. And support he needs, because there are terrible powers that constantly imposes themselves upon him and confront scientific 'Truth' with quite different kinds of 'truths' displaying the most varied inscriptions on their shields.[161]

The concept-formation of scientists and researchers is explicitly described as negative, as they create a "great columbarium of concepts," a "graveyard for sense-impressions." A columbarium is a structure of underground vaults lined with recesses for urns preserving the ashes of the cremated corpse. Concepts are therefore likened to such urns containing only the ashes of something that was once alive, which in the metaphor is the 'sense-impression,' and researchers are consequently creating a 'wrong' kind of metaphor, which is even, by implication, a dangerous and deadly kind of metaphor, since it is exterminating the sense-impressions.

Earlier in the essay, Nietzsche had a reference to the *columbarium* as an image of conceptual constructions already in §8. There, he talked about the "Roman columbarium" as "breathing the logical strictness and coolness that characterizes mathematics" into the world. There, we were allowed to "admire the human being as a formidable genius of construction, succeeding in rising the tower of an endlessly complicated dome of concepts on a moving foundation, as if on running water."[162] Now, this admiration has faded away. The description of concept-formation as a columbarium or a graveyard for dead 'sense-impressions' emphasizes the menace of conceptual and scientific languages. Now, the scientific concept is explicitly a *dead metaphor*, and it is as such it "arranges the entire empirical world" (i.e., the world of sense-impressions) into a rigid framework that is as artificial and unnatural as it is ponderous and inept.

Moreover, continuing the discussion of the 'false' concept in the passage, Nietzsche feels that he needs a distinction between two types of 'men of reason.' His first (true) man of reason is the "man of action" who "binds his life to reason and its concepts in order not to be carried away"; his second (false) man of reason is the "researcher" who builds his hut close "to the tower of science so it can assist him and give him protection." Both of the two types are apparently 'men of reason' and both do they use concepts in their respective projects, and we may therefore ask, what is the supposed difference between them? —The distinction comes across as tenuous; arbitrarily asserted without much justification, since both the 'true' and 'false' man of reason strive to be under some degree of protection by reason. If the researcher is dismissed, it is only because he needs protection *to a higher degree* than the 'man of action.'

In Part I, Nietzsche admires researchers for their capacity to conceptualize, i.e., to create conceptual metaphors; but in the Part II, he denounces them because they, engaging this capacity, erroneously confuse conceptual *construction* with transcendental *existence*. Between Part I and Part II, Nietzsche has changed his mind regarding the usefulness of the conceptual language of science and research. The researcher, from being the progressive naturalist in the first part, changes into a regressive dogmatist in the second. From creating conceptual 'metaphors' in the first part, the researcher creates 'dead metaphors' ('coins having lost their stamp,' etc.) in the second, establishing as such a society's dogmatic belief-system. Scientists using conceptual language may of course adopt any of these two suggested positions since *in any case* they erect their constructions, which thereupon they *may* or *may not* believe are *discovered Truths* in the transcendental, metaphysical, and dogmatic sense.

When in the subsequent sentence we are told that the researcher's scientific 'Truths' always are threatened by "quite different kinds of 'truths' displaying the most varied inscriptions on their shields," we again need to ponder what different kinds of truths Nietzsche may be alluding to in this context. Here the researcher is contrasted to a more intuitive human type, producing "different kinds of truths" of a quite different order, as Nietzsche here is alluding to new truth-requirements we have not encountered elsewhere in the essay since they are identical neither to the scientific nor to the pragmatic notion of truth mentioned early in the essay (cf. Part I, A.3: "Genealogy of the Pragmatic Notion of Truth"). By contrast, these "different kinds of truth" require *insight, intuition, and inspiration* in the creative agent in order to be received and communicated. It will become still clearer that they are inherited from the Romantic paradigm, most likely under the influence of Schopenhauer and Wagner, but introduced earlier in the century by a number of romantic writers, notably by Friedrich Schiller and the brothers Schlegel.[163]

The 'different kinds of truth' to which Nietzsche is appealing are posed in order to oppose the absolutistic truths of the sciences. In his last paragraphs, this becomes evident. The researchers and scientists build their constructions, their columbaria, their rigid fortresses in order to delimit the colorful world of the senses, whether this world is presented in perception, in dreams, or in that delightful mixture occupying the realms of myth, art, and poetry. If in Part I conceptual constructions were 'metaphors' like any other human construction, in Part II, they are in addition seen as standardizing, dogmatic, restrictive, delimiting, controlling, and autocratic constructions in an evaluation that is biased against them.[164]

2. Mobilizing the Metaphor-Drive of Intuitive Man against Intellectual Man

As Nietzsche continues the next paragraph, he promises that the scientists will not and cannot succeed in asserting their rigid metaphorical constructions, because the human being has an inexhaustible '*drive* to form metaphors' and *as such* resists absolutistic formalizations.

> That drive to form metaphors, that fundamental human drive, which one cannot ignore for even an instant because one would then discard the human being itself, is in fact neither defeated nor tamed when it, from its transient creations, the concepts, builds a regular and rigid new world as its fortress. It seeks a new realm for its activity, a new riverbed, and finds it in mythology, and generally in art. This drive is constantly confusing the classifications and cubicles of the concept by which new transferences, metaphors, and metonymies are suggested; it constantly manifests the desire to refashion the present world of the waking human being, which is so colorful, irregular, causally incoherent, alluring, and forever new, as if it were a dream-world. In and for themselves the waking human beings are only sure that they are awake thanks to of the rigid and regular net of concepts, and are therefore sometimes impelled to believe that they dream, if once this net of concepts happens to be torn apart by art.[165]

This *metaphor-drive* is intrinsic in the human being and is curtailed only if we do away with the human being itself.[166] The researchers may build their regular and rigid fortresses, but thanks to myth, art, and poetry, the world is metaphorized in far more intuitive languages.

Scientific and artistic languages are opposed approximately along the line of waking and dreaming life, i.e., between processing perceptive images from waken life and hallucinatory images from dream and fantasy life. The sciences ensure our experiences of reality by placing us within the rigid schemata of concepts, but art occasionally tears apart this net and introduces us to a world of dream, fantasy, and myth. In art and myth there is no rigid distinction between reality and dream, Nietzsche suggests, referring to a Pascal example: "'If a worker could be sure that he for a full twelve hours every night was dreaming that he was a King, then I believe,' says Pascal, 'that he would be as happy as a King who for twelve hours every night dreamt that he was a worker.'"[167] The *consistent dream* would be as real as reality itself, the worker would turn king and the king would turn worker if they consistently dreamt themselves into these respective roles. The example argues that the line between reality and dream is blurred, and Nietzsche reiterates the Romantic creed that in embracing the power of myth, fantasy, and dream we might transpose ourselves to a world of greater spontaneity, immediacy, and illumination. Nietzsche suggests that the ancient Greeks had the ability to blur the division between dream and reality when he appreciatively refers back to the "honest Athenian" still able to see the "goddess Athena riding her beautiful chariot [...] through the market places of Athens."[168]

Nietzsche subsequent §13 emphasizes again that metaphorical construction in myth and poetry is a delight. As in the previous discussions (cf. Part I, A.3), he reiterates that deception without doing harm is acceptable to society; *a fortiori*, the mind's drive to lying is stronger than its drive to truth. The pleasure of pretense is one of the characteristics of Nietzsche's poetic human.

> Humans have an indestructible penchant for letting themselves be deceived and are like spellbound by happiness when the rhapsodist tells them epic fairy tales as if they were true, or when the actor on the stage plays the king more royally than he actually is. The intellect, this master of pretense, is free and relieved from its other slave-duties as long as it can deceive without harming, and celebrates then its Saturnalia. Never is it more sensual, more opulent, more proud, more adroit and bold.[169]

Adopting this poetic *modus vivendi*, humans liberate themselves from "the boundary stones of abstraction"; reason's metaphors are smashed into a "chaotic mess"; the emancipated intellect shuns the "ghostly schemata of abstractions," and begins speaking in "forbidden metaphors and unheard-of conceptual combinations" in order to "match creatively the impression of the powerful present intuition."

> With creative pleasure, it throws metaphors into chaos and displaces the boundary stones of abstraction. [...] Every enormous timber and woodwork of the concept, onto which the needy human clings throughout life, is for the emancipated intellect merely a platform and plaything for its audacious magic tricks. And when it smashes it, throws it into a chaotic mess, ironically to put it together again, pairing the most foreign and dividing the most familiar things, then it reveals that it does not need this deficient substitute, and that it will not be guided by concepts, but by intuitions. No straight pathway leads from these intuitions to the land of the ghostly schemata, the abstractions; no word is created for them; man falls silent when he sees them. Or else, man speaks purely in forbidden metaphors and unheard-of conceptual combinations, for at least, in the shattering and mockery of the old conceptual boundaries, to match creatively the impression of the powerful present intuition.[170]

It is no wonder that Nietzsche's essay became exemplary inspiration for deconstructive or rhetorically inclined readers, such as S. Kofman and P. de Man.[171] Nietzsche's poetically emancipated humans are explicitly deconstructionists of reason, and his appeal to speak in "forbidden metaphors and unheard-of conceptual combinations," may well be seen as inspiration of the deconstructive style applied to theoretical discussion a century later.[172]

The victory of poetry over science is further established in the final paragraph (§14), where we are reintroduced to the two types of humans, now as an opposition between one human who 'fears intuition' and another who 'disdains abstraction,' where one is 'inartistic' and the other is 'irrational.' The two types may exist side by side competing in asserting the 'rule of life,' but in rare, favorable circumstances, the intuitive humans being assert their rule, and society becomes like transfigured into poetry itself. Man transforms into an "over-joyful hero" and the world is transfigured into art, as if the social community is able to dispense with utilitarian needs and transform simple utensils into art.[173] In this transfiguration of the social universe, the jug of clay has neither use-value nor exchange-value, but assumes a particular poetic 'art-value,' insofar as it reflects the "sublime happiness," the "cloudless Olympian sky" of the naïve Greeks, as if they were mocking the seriousness of necessity and need.

> There are ages, in which the rational and the intuitive human being exist side by side, one in fear of intuition, the other with disdain for abstraction—the latter being just as irrational as the former is being inartistic. Both have a desire

to rule over life; one, because he through precaution, wisdom, and regularity knows how to meet basic needs; the other, because he as an 'over joyful hero' ignores these needs and only counts as real the life represented as appearance and beauty. Where once upon a time the intuitive human being, like for example in ancient Greece, wields his weapons more powerfully and victoriously than his opponent, a culture may in favorable circumstances emerge establishing the rule of art over life: i.e., the pretense, the denial of necessity, the brilliance of the metaphorical perspective, and generally, the immediacy of the illusions that accompanies all expressions of this life. Neither the house, nor the gait, nor the garment, nor the clay jug, reveals that they were created out of need. It seems as if they all want to express a sublime happiness and a cloudless Olympian sky, as if they play with seriousness.[174]

Nietzsche ends his essay with a confirmation of the distinction between 'intuitive man' and 'intellectual man' by adding a new facet to the distinction, the ability to express or not express 'feeling.' The 'intuitive man' is emotional and suffers both more frequently and intensely than 'intellectual man.'

Whereas the human guided by concepts and abstractions only prevents misfortune, without being able to squeeze happiness out of the abstractions while striving toward the highest possible freedom from pain, the intuitive human is rewarded with illumination, cheerfulness, and redemption continuously streaming toward him. Obviously, he suffers more intensely when he suffers; yes, he suffers far more frequently, since he does not know how to learn from experience and always stumbles into the same hole twice. In his suffering, he is as irrational as in his happiness; he cries out loudly and is beyond consolation. How different it is with the stoic man, who, when effected by the same misfortunes, learns from experience how to control himself thanks to concepts. He, who otherwise seeks sincerity, truth, freedom from illusions, and protection from enchanting intrusions, executes now in his misfortune a masterful deception, just as the other type of man did in his happiness. His human face is not elastic and flexible, but is rather like a mask of dignified monotonous features. He never shouts and does not even change his tone of voice when a real thundercloud pours down on him; he only wraps himself up in his overcoat and walks with measured steps into the rain.[175]

Intuitive man cannot suppress and hide emotions, while *intellectual man* becomes a master of self-control and dissimulation; his entire existence relies on concealment, deception, and control. At the end of the paragraph, his face is described as a mask of inflexible and monotonous features. Again, the connotations to death are obvious in this image where a face that is alive, expressive, and cheerful in the "over-joyful hero" has congealed into a death-mask of dignity in intellectual man. Nietzsche conjures up a final image of this 'man of reason' in the ominous dark figure wrapped up in his overcoat as he walks out in the rain in pursuit of his sinister business. As if taken out of a Victorian novel, this unmovable shady figure patrols a dark world of rain-soaked streets, virtually the opposite of the 'cloudless Olympian sky' of the Hellenic world.

This final image of the intellectual type may be seen as repeating the position of *Socrates* in *Die geburt der Tragödie* (1871; *The Birth of Tragedy*) and/or anticipating Nietzsche's *Priest* as developed in for example the third part of *Genealogie der Moral*.[176] The image offers a profoundly negative image of intellectuality. It seems that Nietzsche in this image has started profiling the social character-type responsible for producing resentment, revengefulness, and envy. The later 'priest' is also wrapped up in his own inscrutability, exercising self-control dangerously turned into control of the populaces he dupes into embracing his destructive ideological-religious agendas.[177]

3. Nietzsche and 'The Romantic School'

In distinctions such as *intuitive* and *intellectual* man, we are back to the Romantic Schools arguing for a return to the immediacy of the 'naïve' or 'objective' world of the ancient Greeks, against the alienating 'sentimental' or 'mannered' European culture. The distinction between the 'naïve' and the 'sentimental' was originally suggested by Frederick Schiller, later elaborated into the 'objective' vs. 'mannered' opposition by Frederick and William Schlegel, and finally into the better-known 'classic' vs. 'romantic' opposition seemingly suggested by Schiller and Goethe in unison.[178] They saw the naïveté of the Greeks as superior to the sentimental decline of poetry in Western Europe.

The idea that Ancient Greece established "the rule of art over life," we find elaborated in the *Romantic School* by key writers such as Fr. Schiller and Fr. Schlegel. The 'naïve' Greeks provide the Ideal that we as contemporary humans ought to recover; cf., Schiller's memorable phrase, "They are what we were; they are what we shall once again become [*Sie sind, was wir waren; sie sind, was wir wieder werden sollen*]."[179]

> We were nature just as they, and our culture, by means of reason and freedom, should lead us back to nature. [*Wir waren Natur wie sie, und unsere Kultur soll uns, auf dem Wege der Vernunft und der Freiheit, zur Natur zurückführen*]. They are, therefore, not only the representation of our lost childhood, which eternally remains most dear to us, so that they fill us with a certain melancholy. But they are also representations of our highest fulfillment in the ideal.[180]

Our alienated and modern present has become 'un-natural,' and is in need of a poetic transfiguration taking us back to the 'natural.' We are promised that we are only temporarily alienated from our predetermined destiny as humans, as a poeticized culture will eventually return us to nature. What we once were is what we presently seek in form of a 'naïveté' that is already exemplified in children and in nature surrounding us. The naïve artists have now the responsibility to recover this lost accord, and in order to succeed, they must themselves personify nature. The naïve artist *is*, while the sentimental artist only *strives* for, nature: "Poets will either *be* nature, or they will *seek* lost nature [*Der Dichter . . . ist entweder Natur, oder er wird sie suchen*]. The former is the naive, the latter the sentimental poet."[181]

True genius is 'naïve,' conceiving art not by employing accepted rules and principles of composition, but by 'flashes of insight and feeling' [*Einfällen und Gefühlen*].

> Only its naiveté makes for its genius. [...] Unacquainted with the rules, those crutches for weakness and taskmasters of awkwardness, led only by nature or by instinct, its guardian angel, it goes calmly and surely through all the snares of false taste in which, if it is not shrewd enough to avoid them from afar, the non-genius must inevitably be entrapped. [...] The genius must solve the most complex tasks with unpretentious simplicity and facility. [...] And only thus does genius identify itself as such, by triumphing over the complications of art by simplicity. [Genius] proceeds not by the accepted principles, but by flashes of insight and feeling; but its insights are the inspirations of a god, its feelings are laws for all ages and for all races of men. [*Es verfährt nicht nach erkannten Prinzipien, sondern nach Einfällen und Gefühlen; aber seine Einfälle sind Eingebungen eines Gottes (alles, was die gesunde Natur tut, ist göttlich), seine Gefühle sind Gesetze für alle Zeiten und für alle Geschlechter der Menschen*].[182]

In this new conception, creativity is never *work*. Genius is conceived as spontaneous, simple, innocent, un-reflective, and unaware about its own activity. Ingenious artists 'see' into the depth of the world, where suddenly its laws stand illuminated. The work is conceived, or more accurately, conceives itself in such brief and intense moments of insight; not from painstakingly employed rules and principles and not from the knowledge of the dogmas of taste.

However, as Schiller contends, poets of the former 'naïve' kind are becoming extinct in present times, "Poets of this naive category are no longer at home in an artificial age, they are indeed scarcely even possible,"[183] therefore, this persistent yearning for repairing an original loss in Romantic thinking. The 'natural' is absent, and the feeling for nature is only present as the desire for health in the sick, "like the feeling of an invalid for health."[184]

The basic distinctions between realistic/idealistic or naive/sentimental also finds expression in Fr. Schlegel's early work: *Über das Studium der Griechischen Poesie*,[185] eventually morphing into a distinction between objective/interested or beautiful/mannered poetry. Objective poetry is "truly beautiful" [*wahrhaft schöne*], while mannered poetry is "merely interesting" [*bloß interessanten*].

In Fr. Schlegel, too, the 'truly beautiful' is only realized in Greek art and poetry as organic unity of the work, insofar as the "beautiful construction is not disturbed by the slightest deficiency or by the least excess."[186] In contrast to the perfect classical Greek art, contemporary 'romantic' poetry, originating in the medieval age and developing up to Schlegel's time, is a futile attempt to attain completeness. Modern poetry is deficient and can only strive to attain what it does not have: "It catches the eye that *modern poetry strives towards a goal that it has either not yet attained*, or that its strive is completely without definite aim, its education without clear direction, the totality of its history without law-governed coherence, the totality without unity."[187] What characterizes modern poetry is the *"the restless insatiate striving toward the new, the piquant, and the striking,* in which the longing remains ungratified."[188] and what confirms the artificiality of the modern aesthetics is the "*dominance of the individual, the characteristic and the philosophical* in the totality of modern poetry."[189] "The objective poetry has no interest in and makes no demands on reality. It only strives towards a *play* that is as worthy as the most sacred sincerity, towards an *appearance* that is as universal and legislative as the most unconditional truth."[190] Schlegel's *Schönen Kunst*, the genuine and authentic work of art, is determined as play without a definite purpose. "The specific characteristics of beautiful art is the free play without definite purpose [*Der spezifische Character der schönen Kunst ist freies Spiel ohne bestimmten Zweck*], that of representative art is the ideal of the representation."[191]

'Interested,' 'representative' art of the contemporaries is the opposite of Kant's 'disinterested' art, but only ancient Greek art fulfills the prescription of art to provide 'disinterested pleasure.' The modern 'interested' art only pursues inauthentic forms of liking. This is art with a purpose and without universality. Only art that is 'purposive without purpose,' 'universal,' 'disinterested,' and 'necessary' qualifies as objective and universal art.

> Only the universal, the permanent, and the necessary—the objective can fill out this big gap; only the beautiful can alleviate this burning yearn. *The beautiful* [...] is the universal object of a disinterested pleasure, which is independent of the pressure of demands and rules, it is free and therefore necessary, completely without purpose and therefore unconditional purposeful [*Das Schöne [...] ist*

der allgemeingültige Gegenstand eines uninteressierten Wohlgefallens, welches von dem Zwange des Bedürfnisses und des Gesetzes gleich unabhängig, frei und dennoch notwendig, ganz zwecklos und dennoch unbedingt zweckmäßig ist].[192]

In another of his essays, the programmatic *Gespräch über die Poesie*, Fr. Schlegel talks about creating a new foundation for poetry and the poet, something poets can share as a basis for their poetic work: "Our poetry, I maintain, lacks a focal point, such as mythology was for the ancients; and one could summarize all the essentials in which modern poetry is inferior to the ancient in these words: We have no mythology."[193] An aesthetic society needs a new mythology able to reflect nature in its essence. A poetry able to reflect nature gives the work of art organic unity. The poet need not pursue laws or rules in order to achieve organic unity, but would indeed abandon the laws "of rationally thinking reason" and instead permit "the beautiful confusion of imagination, the original chaos of human nature." The poet would submit him or herself to an instinctive representation of unity and let unity grow organically out of the chaos as initially conceived. Provided that artists surrender themselves to the new ideals and to their own enthusiasm, nature will pervade poetry and make it powerful and homogeneous.

In Schlegel's romantic criticism, the ultimate ideal of art is seen as unachievable and poetry is interpreted as an unending process of becoming. The ideal of the perfect work of art may have been realized in the past, in the golden ages of the Greeks, but this ideal is lost in modern times. Therefore, after the Greeks, art remains *infinitely perfectible*, but therefore also *infinitely imperfect, infinitely fragmentary*. It can never attain its maximum. It perpetually strives towards the fulfillment of the lost ideal, but it strives in vain: "Art is infinitely perfectible, and to attain an absolute maximum is not possible in its continuous development; one can only attain a conditional relative maximum, an insurmountable fix proximal."[194] Romantic poetry is a poetry infinitely striving, always becoming, but never achieving its ideals,[195]

4. The Young Nietzsche's Romantic-Aesthetic Program

The notes Nietzsche wrote in preparation for and often worked into TL, we find mostly in his notebooks from 1872 and 1873.[196] They are remarkable in several ways.

For one thing, they show us a Nietzsche early in his career conflicted about his newly published *The Birth of Tragedy* and preparing himself to take his thinking in an entirely different direction. He oscillates between supporting a 'romantic-aesthetic' paradigm and a 'scientific-naturalist,' as he over a relatively brief span of years is progressing from the romantic to the naturalist paradigm that eventually becomes his final stance. It is not a shift that has a precise breaking-point, but is manifested rather as a process where Nietzsche gradually becomes more and more uncomfortable with his identification with the Schopenhauer-Wagnerian aesthetics he supported in BT.

As suggested above, although TL1 introduces the new progressive Naturalist paradigm into Nietzsche's discourse, TL2 refers to the Romantic aesthetic theory introduced by Schiller and the Schlegel brothers, and continued in the arts-metaphysics of Schopenhauer and Wagner. Life is depicted as tragic and only in transfigurations through art, qua the work of the intuitive genius, is it worthwhile. We encounter identical views expressed in Nietzsche's *The Birth of Tragedy*, in some of the notebooks from the early 1870s (besides in TL2). Life is tragic, but the Ancient Greeks show us the way toward redemption; instead of surrendering to pessimism, they transform human life through the medium of art and affirm the world as an aesthetic phenomenon. The Greeks provide the model-example of a society having established "the rule of art over life," and Nietzsche reiterates the appeal to the revival of a culture that aspires to assert aesthetics over and above necessity, i.e., privileging beauty over pragmatics and utility.

In his now adopted and defended Romanticism, the young Nietzsche is not shying away from defending quasi-religious truth-requirements, for example qua his conviction that genuine art is created by true genius and stemming from an overflow of intuition, insight, and illumination. On that background, it follows automatically that 'intellectual man' is downgraded, and spontaneous, intuitive, emotional, and feeling man is upgraded. Now (in TL2) Nietzsche thinks it is positive that artistic man, "suffers more intensely [...] suffers far more frequently [...] and cries out loudly [...] beyond consolation (ibid.)." The naïve, spontaneous, and childlike man relies on myth, dreams, and intuitions and his 'words' are springing from these realms, to which they (somehow) correspond. In the young Nietzsche from BT, the early notebooks, and TL2, we are back to the celebration of the Greeks, to the aesthetical-political project of building a world where beauty rules society and life, where the child is the model for aesthetic genius: "The playful construction and destruction of the individual world [*der Individualwelt*] is flowing from a primal pleasure [*Urlust*] [...], in a way similar to how the world-creating child moves stones from here to there and built sand heaps only to destroy them again."[197] This appeal to the innocence of the child as model for artistic creation, is typical in much Romanticism and it may seem pleasant and harmless (albeit fanciful and naïve), but in the young Nietzsche innocence is belied by the draconian social-political measures he seems ready to implement in order to create an 'aesthetic society.'—In early notes, he goes as far as suggesting the creation of a totalitarian slave-society in which the labor of the working masses releases the artistic elite to create masterful art.[198]

Moreover, we notice that young Nietzsche involuntarily proposes a *de facto 'correspondence theory of truth'* in the sense that *words* are supposed to express intuitions and feelings. In TL, we find a never-addressed contradiction between this proposal of a *romantic correspondence theory of truth*, where words correspond to feelings in TL2, and a naturalist *anti-correspondence theory of truth* in TL1, where 'words' *do not correspond* to their supposed references, but belong in an autonomous linguistic domain as a result of vague *transferences*. The ambivalent evaluation of the learned or scientific man is an upshot of this self-contradiction. In TL1, he positively 'built' a world out of arbitrary concepts and their schematic relationships, in TL2, he is devalued because of his dependence on alienating concepts.

Famously in BT, Nietzsche suggests two ways of overcoming lamentable existence and transforming it into art, respectively according to the figures of the Dionysian and the Apollonian, the former symbolizing a life in chaos and becoming, the breakdown of individuation, while the latter symbolizes measure and restraint, representing the principle of individuation. If Dionysus triumphantly affirms and embraces existence in all its darkness and horror, Apollo draws an aesthetic veil over reality, creating an ideal world of form and beauty. As such, art transforms tragic existence into an aesthetic phenomenon, not by denying its existence, but by exhibiting existence as aesthetic form, in order to affirm it. True culture is seen as a unity of the forces of life, the Dionysian element, and the implementation of form and beauty, the Apollonian element. In *The Birth of Tragedy*, we furthermore encounter the enemy of this supreme achievement of Greek culture, this happy unification of the chaotic and formative principle, this fusion of Dionysian and Apollonian elements, namely in the principle of 'Socrates' as the principle of rationalism and intellectualism.

In TL2, Nietzsche rehearses these themes from his recently published *The Birth of Tragedy*. Although TL1 seems to dismiss romanticism and the impossible project of integrating romantic aesthetics in naturalist epistemology, Nietzsche regresses in TL2 to BT in what seems to be an attempt to integrate the positions of Dionysus, Apollo, and Socrates into the Naturalist thinking according to the following contrived analogies: (1) The 'Dionysian' world of becoming that is chaotic becomes equivalent to the life-giving sensuous impressions; (2) the 'Apollonian' addition of form to the chaotic life-forces, becomes equivalent to the form-giving *word* as the first 'authentic' conceptualization of world; and finally (3) the 'Socratic' intellectuality and rationality becomes equivalent to the 'unauthentic' scientific concept as devalued and rejected in the final passages of TL2. In this artificial parallelism, it is as if we encounter a young Nietzsche engaged in the ill-conceived project of *reconciling*, as it were, Richard Wagner and Friedrich Lange.

5. Nietzsche's Later Self-Criticisms

It is a consolation that Nietzsche does not continue to pursue this romantic-aesthetic project for long. The theories from BT, seeping into TL2, Nietzsche will be criticizing in his later thinking, and criticizing himself for having followed so readily and uncritically. This self-criticism starts surprisingly early. A. Nehamas points out that Nietzsche represses critical notes on Schopenhauer's aesthetics already while working on BT, and suggests that Nietzsche writes BT largely under the influence of Wagner and as an attempt to accommodate Wagner and protect their shared admiration of Schopenhauer. Nietzsche therefore chooses in BT to stay faithful to Wagner and his circle despite his beginning doubts about central issues of the aesthetic paradigm, prominently the status of Schopenhauer's so-called 'Will' (which Nietzsche in the early notes sees as another *representation*):

> It is impossible not to wonder why Nietzsche avoids all criticism of Schopenhauer on this issue [of the Will] and why the work [BT] seems almost designed to give the overwhelming impression that it follows faithfully in his footsteps. We might, in fact, begin to suspect that Nietzsche may have made a strategic decision to proceed in a way that would not alienate the work's first and ideal reader—Wagner, to whom the work is dedicated and whose friendship with Nietzsche was cemented on their mutual admiration for the philosopher of metaphysical pessimism.[199]

The self-criticism becomes explicit in the notebooks from the early to the mid-1870s, during the preparations for *Human, All Too Human*, as Nietzsche here describes HH "as an atonement" for BT, and criticizes BT for the view, cf. Nehamas:

> that the world has an 'author' (30 [51]) or an 'artist-creator' (30 [68]) who provides it with an aesthetic justification, and he even expresses considerable skepticism regarding his understanding of Greek philosophy. [...] His self-criticism is relentless and sweeping, clearing the ground for the immense project he is beginning to set for himself and which he will pursue until the end of his life: how to find a way to live and thrive in a world that provides no absolute foundation for value, imposes no requirements and offers no pre-established paths for anyone to follow.[200]

The self-criticism is explicit also in a foreword he writes about fifteen years later to his second edition to BT (1886). In this "Attempt at a Self-criticism," he objects to himself that BT, under the pretense of promoting the Hellenic mentality, was itself hopelessly interwoven with romantic thinking, interrogating himself as author of BT:

> But what, my good man, is romanticism if it is not your book [BT]? Can the profound hatred of the 'contemporary age,' 'reality,' and 'modern ideas' be taken further than it is in your artist's metaphysics, which would rather believe in nothing, in the devil, than in the now? [...] Is your pessimistic book not itself a piece of anti-Hellenism and romanticism; is it not itself something as intoxicating as it is befogging, a narcotic at any rate?[201]

And in one of his later notebooks from 1885, Nietzsche has the following commentary on his youthful misstep: "In my youth I was unlucky: a very ambiguous man crossed my path. When I recognized him for what he is, namely a great actor who has no authentic relationship to anything (not even to music), I was so sickened and disgusted that I believed all famous people had been actors."[202]

C: HUMAN KNOWLEDGE FROM *TRUTH AND LIES* TO *HUMAN, ALL TOO HUMAN*

1. 'Vanity' as the Specifically Human 'Thing-in-Itself'

Already the title of Nietzsche's work, *Human, all too Human* [HH],[203] indicates that Nietzsche is discussing a human quality, which we supposedly possess in excess and would be better off without. As we read the work, we learn that 'vanity' is the quality he dismisses as 'all too human.' In an aphorism with the label, "*The Human Thing-in-Itself*," Nietzsche explicitly declares that "the most vulnerable and yet most unconquerable of things is *human vanity*: nay, through being wounded its strength increases and can grow to giant proportions."[204] It is one of the few times, Nietzsche refers to a 'thing-in-itself' in the work, which he addressed several times in TL and he returns to examine in later work like *The Gay Science* and *Beyond Good and Evil*. In these works, he discusses the Kantian 'thing' in line with the critical epistemological examinations we find among his peers (Fr. Lange, K. Fischer, O. Liebmann, A. Spir, E. Mach, and others). However, none of these writers have, to my knowledge, a notion of a 'human thing-in-itself' as 'vanity.'

To address the 'human thing-in-itself' as *vanity* may be rhetorical hyperbole; nonetheless, it underscores the importance of the relation Nietzsche sees between epistemology and human psychology. Already in TL, our self-evaluations were regarded as 'all too human,' and our so-called 'truth' was merely that which we in our vanity hold to be true with ourselves as the only measurers.[205] We notice that Nietzsche in HH is repeating and rephrasing discussions he had in the first passages of TL, where human beings were blasted for this stubborn narcissistic sense of self-importance, as inane and erroneous as the self-importance of a "mosquito" conceiving itself as "the flying center of the world," if it could think.

In HH, we return to the passage introducing TL about the insignificance of the human seen in the context of infinite space. This passage is apparently rephrased and reused:

> Our uniqueness in the world! Oh, what an improbable thing it is! Astronomers, who occasionally acquire a horizon outside our world, give us to understand that the drop of life on the earth is without significance for the total character of the mighty ocean of birth and decay; that countless stars present conditions for the generation of life similar to those of the earth. [...] Possibly the ant in the forest is quite as firmly convinced that it is the aim and purpose of the existence of the forest, as we are convinced in our imaginations (almost unconsciously) that the destruction of mankind involves the destruction of the world.[206]

In HH, Nietzsche's anthropocentrism is called *vanity*. These are only two different labels for that inevitable personalization of the world we perform when we try to know it. As in Feuerbach (and later in Lange, Du Bois Reymond, Mach, and Vaihinger), it is to Nietzsche not possible to see the world apart from the perspective of one's personalization of it (cf. Part I, A.6: "Feuerbach and Nietzsche on Anthropocentrism"). We cannot go outside ourselves, go outside of our own perceptions; cannot see around our own 'corner'; cannot see an object 'impersonally': "Nothing is harder for a man than to conceive of an object impersonally, I mean to see in it an object and not a person. One may even ask whether it is possible for him to dispense for a single moment with the machinery of his instinct to create and construct a personality."[207]

'Vanity' is to Nietzsche a human characteristic bringing about this 'personalization' of a world that is in-itself indifferent to human investments of meaning and value. In particular, it is paradoxical that 'vanity' bolster the inclination in humans to *forget and repress* 'personalization,' in order to thereupon assert 'personalized' knowledge as objective reality as such—as if we *describe* objective reality while we, in fact, only *encounter* an objectivity we ourselves form in the first place.

Nietzsche's 'vanity' is *epistemological vanity*. It is to Nietzsche in equal measure appalling and laughable, and he does his best to give us the most pregnant expressions of his disapproval. In an aphorism with the label, *"Man as the Comical Actor of the World*," we are told that if God created the world, man was at best created only as God's monkey, an entertainment and boon God needed in order to endure the boredom of his "rather tedious eternities."

> *Man as the Comical Actor of the World.* [...] If a God created the world, he created man to be his ape, as a perpetual source of amusement in the midst of his rather tedious eternities. [...] God in his boredom uses pain for the tickling of his favorite animal, in order to enjoy his proudly tragic gestures and expressions of suffering, and, in general, the intellectual inventiveness of the vainest of his creatures—as inventor of this inventor.[208]

2. Will to Truth as Will to Immortality

When Nietzsche in HH turns to the question of 'truth,' we find as in TL that truth is first understood as socially and pragmatically useful. We encounter the same genealogy. It is clear that Nietzsche is reusing the discussions of the origin of truth introduced in TL (cf. our discussion in Part I, A.3: "Genealogy of the Pragmatic Notion of Truth").

'Truth' is appearing first as 'honesty' being practiced in social contexts because it is more reputable to tell the truth than telling the untrue. Man is first practicing honesty "in intercourse with real persons." But this real interaction, this practical value of truth, is eventually abstracted into interaction between different "thought-personalities" competing between themselves to tell the truth. "Thought-personalities" are necessarily situated in the mind of a single ego, so they are no longer 'real persons,' but abstract entities (or perhaps rather internal 'voices') advocating their disparate interests within the single ego. "Thought-personalities" are as such competing against each other; they are within the mind carrying on a 'will to power' game for the purpose of survival of the fittest. As we read Nietzsche's passage, we are able to infer what it is to be fit as 'thought-personality':

> [Man] practices honesty in intercourse with real persons: now from habit, heredity, and training, originally because the true, like the fair and the just, is more expedient and more reputable than the untrue. For in the realm of thought it is difficult to assume a power and glory that are built on error or on falsehood. The feeling that such an edifice might at some time collapse is humiliating to the self-esteem of the architect—he is ashamed of the fragility of the material, and, as he considers himself more important than the rest of the world, he would fain construct nothing that is less durable than the rest of the world. In his longing for truth he embraces the belief in a personal immortality, the most arrogant and defiant idea that exists. [...] His work has become his "ego," he transforms himself into the Imperishable with its universal challenge. It is his immeasurable

pride that will only employ the best and hardest stones for the work—truths, or what he holds for such.[209]

We see that Nietzsche accepts without further ado that truth is pursued between humans out of social necessity. Thereupon, he contends that it is internalized by 'thought-personalities' as a requirement when they voice their opinions within the single ego. At this point, he sees the truth-requirement becoming more dubious. Now ensues, within the single ego, a power-struggle between opinions (voices or thought-personalities), because some opinions are fleeting and flimsy, while the ego attempts to erect an 'edifice' of truths that is as solid as possible. The telos of the power struggle between 'thought personalities' is therefore defined as the erection of the most durable 'edifice.' The *will to power* among thought-personalities is *to will* the most solid, sturdy, resilient, stable, durable, permanent, universal edifice; or, to capture it all in a single phrase, *it is to will immortality* (cf. "in his longing for truth he embraces the belief in a personal immortality, the most arrogant and defiant idea that exists").

At this point, Nietzsche's self-evident pragmatically necessary truth-requirements have turned into a perverted image of themselves. The most 'fit' thought-personality is the one best equipped to establish a universal and immortal truth-ideal, which is again the vainest and most arrogant of ideals. *Will to power as truth* is essentially *will to power as immortality*. It is these false edifices, these concept-constructions, Nietzsche criticized in the second part of his TL, and now continues to criticize in HH, *if or when* they are not complemented with an enlightened consciousness comprehending that they are merely human personalizations.

Part II
Nietzsche's Positivist-Pragmatic Paradigm

A: NIETZSCHE'S LATER THEORIES OF TRUTH AND KNOWLEDGE

1. Nietzsche's Critiques of the In-Itself as *Cause* in the Middle Work

1. Associations to Hume

In his work from the mid-1880s,[1] Nietzsche is reiterating his criticism of knowledge as supposed objectivity, as he sees it as merely simplifying and humanizing an in-itself indifferent world; he reiterates how the subjective element in the construction of knowledge has been ignored.[2] As we notice, it is not *humanization* but *repressed humanization* that bothers Nietzsche. His criticism is targeting the lack of acceptance of us having a hand in the creation of knowledge and our inclination to comprehend ourselves as discoverers of purely objective knowledge. From being active epistemological agents we become passive epistemological patients. He is as such criticizing today's 'correspondence theory of knowledge,' knowledge as supposedly corresponding to and reflecting the externally real as a 'thing-in-itself,' which Nietzsche and his peers hold to be beyond human perception and cognition; he seems to be defending a position that approximates today's epistemological *constructivism*.[3]

Nietzsche's criticism of the notion of *cause* as objectively given serves as his best example of how our personifications of the world are repressed and thereupon re-asserted as discovery of objectivity. In his discussions of causality, Nietzsche acknowledges the analyses carried out by Hume: "Hume is fundamentally right, habit [...] makes us expect that a certain often perceived succession follows from another: nothing else."[4] Hume's criticism is repeated in passages like the following:

> From [observing] a necessary sequence of events, it does not follow there is a causal relationship between them (that is that they have a capacity to effect in leaps from 1 to 2, to 3, to 4, to 5) *there is neither causes nor effect*.[5]

> The *predictability of an event* does not come about because a rule has been followed or a necessity has been obeyed or that we have projected a law of causality into every event; it comes about thanks to the *recurrence of identical cases*.[6]

> Cause and effect—a dangerous concept as long as one thinks of *something* that *causes,* and of something that is *affected.*[7]

> Two successive states, the one cause, the other effect: this is false. The first state has nothing to effect, the second has not been effected.[8]

Hume's analysis becomes a steppingstone for his own psychologically and linguistically expanded analysis. Initially, he accepts Hume's premise that the cause-effect relation comes about from experiencing the repetition of sequences of the form *AB*. After we have been accustomed to experience the succession *AB*, whenever we see *A*, we expect *B*, and vice versa. We start to interpret the succession *AB* as a cause-effect relationship, separated in the active agent *A* and the passive patient *B*, with a universal and objective (a priori) nexus binding the two terms together.

To Hume, as to Nietzsche, this combination of cause and effect is contingent and associative, implying that we cannot *logically* derive one concept from the other. When nonetheless the two concepts are combined, the binding comes about because of empirical association or *experience*. So Hume: "What is the foundation of all our reasonings and conclusions concerning that relation [of cause and effect]? It may be replied in one word. *Experience*."[9] In the repeated experience of a sequence, *A* and *B*, we form the idea that there exist a *necessary* connection between the entities and that *A* possesses a *power* or *force* by which it occasions a change in *B*. As such, succession is re-constructed and interpreted as objective, while it is actually only empirical. In Hume's vocabulary, the causality-relation is established *a posteriori* and not *a priori*. Causation, said Hume, is "in the mind, not in the object."[10] Experience could only be experience of an appearance, and an appearance was therefore never a *proof* of anything other than its own existence.

When Nietzsche criticizes the cause-effect duality in *The Gay Science* (GS), it is his point that the isolation of an *A* and a *B* in a super-abundant continuum of events is an extreme simplification that does not correspond to anything in his 'world of becoming':

> *Cause and effect*: such a duality probably never exists; in truth we are confronted by a continuum out of which we isolate a couple of pieces, just as we perceive motion only as isolated points and then infer it without ever actually seeing it.[11]

Changes in so-called 'reality' happen too rapidly and frequently to be registered by our inadequate cognitive apparatus.

2. Causes Interpreted as Deeds

Despite Nietzsche's fundamental agreement with Hume, he radicalizes his critique by adding three distinct explanations to Hume's explanation of *cause*. (1) He adds to Hume's analysis a fundamental *biological-psychological* motive according to which we as species always interpret appearances *as if* following from a *will* or an *intention*. (2) He adds to this biological-psychological explanation a *linguistic explanation* of causality, insofar as the causality-relation is subconsciously constructed upon the matrix of our grammar. Finally, (3) he adds a 'fear-factor' as motivation for invention of causes, insofar as 'causes' introduce simple explanations of complex, incomprehensible, and unfamiliar phenomena—an introduction of simplicity that to Nietzsche (here inheriting R. Avenarius[12]) 'calms us down.' So, "Hume is right," as Nietzsche readily admits, thereupon taking his analysis two or three steps further.

To Nietzsche, we want to see *will* in things, and the cause becomes therefore the representative for a deep-rooted desire to impose *wills, intentions,* and thus *meaning* on a world that is essentially meaningless. Inventing the cause, we animate a world in-itself inanimate:

> Man believes himself to be a cause, a doer. —Everything that happens relates as predicate to a subject. Every judgment presupposes the whole deep belief in subject and predicate or in cause and effect; and the latter belief (that is, the claim that every effect is an activity, and that to an activity one must presuppose an actor) is even only a special case of the former. So the fundamental belief remains: there exist subjects. I observe something, and look *for a reason* for it: this means originally, I am looking *for an intention*; first and foremost for someone with an intention, i.e., for a subject, for an actor. […] This is our oldest habit.[13]

To seek intentions in activities "is our oldest habit," and Nietzsche's humans are thus under the spell of a habit *older* than Hume's: "What gives us extraordinary belief in causality is not just the habit of seeing a repetition of events, but *our inability to interpret* an event as anything but an event from *intentions*."[14] We scan the world and search for *someone* who *has* intentions and *does* something intentionally. Frequently occurring sequences are reinterpreted as *intentional activity* projected into nature, i.e., as 'causal activity' subconsciously interpreted as having a design: "Briefly: The psychological need for a belief in causality derives from the *inability to imagine that something can happen without intentions*."[15] We are thus engaged in a false reinterpretation of nature, because the cause supposedly instantiates rules and necessities that in a fluctuating process-world have no existence as such.

Like 'action' implies a split between an actor and an act, a doer and a deed, the causality-relation implies a split between a cause and an effect. When causes are added to appearances, nature is being *humanized*. The tacit assumption is that like human beings act in culture, causes act in nature. By adding this *human will to see itself* in an in-itself indifferent nature, Nietzsche has added an 'older habit' to Hume's 'habit,' implying that humans are no longer seen as mere *passive recipients* of impressions, but are active in *constructing* causal sequences.

We notice that Nietzsche—like several of his predecessors such as Kant, Schopenhauer, and Drossbach—suggests a 'cause' for the (Humean) *cause*, but that Nietzsche's 'cause' rules out Kant's transcendental categories as well as Schopenhauer and Drossbach's objective 'forces.' He instead ponders what *psychological human characteristics* makes it *compelling* to think the concept of a 'cause.' In this, he rejects Kant's transcendental principle and thinks the 'cause' in biological, psychological, and linguistic terms. If our causality-judgment has a 'cause,' or better, has *a condition of its possibility*, it is rooted in our *deep history*, i.e., in our biological, psychological, and linguistic genealogies.

> *On "Causality."* [...] Actually, the notion of cause and effect derives, examined psychologically, only from a way of thinking, which always and everywhere believes in will.[16]

> 'There is no change without cause [*Grund*]'—this [view] always presupposes a something, which remains stable and steady behind the changes. "Cause" and "effect," examined psychologically, [...] implies that an event is divided into agent and patient. The belief is that *the doer* remains in place; *as if when all doing was subtracted from the doer, he would himself be left.*[17]

Nietzsche's theory of knowledge is therefore anti-transcendental, anti-representational, anti-theological, and anti-foundational (what I translate into his *positive* association with 'Pragmatism,' 'Phenomenalism,' and 'Positivism'). He aspires to explain how *we deal with the chaotic and random as our condition*, i.e., how and by what means and motivations we have attempted to bring this chaos under control. In Nietzsche's anti-foundational naturalism, we do not 'know,' we only 'schematize': "Not 'to know' but to schematize—to impose upon chaos as much regularity and form as our practical needs require."[18]

3. The Cause-Effect Relation as Imitation of Subject-Predicate Logic

Psychologically, we *want* to see a will in nature and we consequently impose upon appearances a will *as if it is a cause*. Hence, Nietzsche takes for granted that we have *epistemological desires*, although they are biological-psychological (notice, they are species-specific, not individual; narcissistic, not sexual). However, in order to *establish a relation* between doer and deed, actor and action, cause and effect, we use according to Nietzsche another resource, namely language. It is language with its subject-predicate logic that prompts us to split an apparent world into a twofold; i.e., cause and effect. As *structure* and *binary*, the falsely invented cause-effect duality is motivated by the grammatical subject-predicate form, which we find in most languages and in all Indo-European languages. In this sense, language gives *voice* to nature.

This thinking is repeatedly addressed in notes and work from Nietzsche's middle period.

> That we have a right to *distinguish* between subject and predicate, between cause and effect— that is our strongest belief; in fact, at bottom even the belief in cause and effect itself, in *conditio* and *conditionatum*, is merely an individual case of the first and general belief, our primeval belief in subject and predicate.[19]

> It is grammar which misleads us into thinking that, apart from the (changing) qualities, effects, or 'powers' of a 'thing,' there is some permanent, unchanging and unknown, seat or bearer of these properties in which an object's qualities inhere and from which its powers emanate. [...] Only under the seduction of language, [...] which understands and misunderstands all effecting as conditioned by something that effects, by a 'subject,' can it appear otherwise.[20]

One of Nietzsche's best and best-known examples on this splitting of the apparent world in cause and effect comes from *The Genealogy of Morals* (GM), where he illustrates the idea by means of an example to which he refers also in BGE and the *Nachlaß* material: 'lightning flashes' [*der Blitz leuchtet*].[21]

In GM, Nietzsche is engaged in a discussion of how the strong cannot and should not be separated from his strength. Evidently, he believes that the schematic example *der Blitz leuchtet* serves as an adequate illustration of his assertion.

> Exactly like the people separate the lightning from its flash, and makes the latter a deed, an effect of a subject they call lightning, so people-morality also separates strength from the expressions of strength, as if behind the strong there were some indifferent substratum, which had the freedom to express itself as strength or not. But there exists no such substratum; there is no 'Being' behind the deed, the effect, the becoming. 'The doer' is simply creatively added [*hinzugedichtet*] to the deed—the deed is everything. People essentially double the deed when they make the lightning flash (*der Blitz leuchtet*); it is a deed-deed; it posits the same occurrence first as cause and then again as its effect. The scientists are no better, when they say 'the force moves, the force causes,' etc.[22]

Several commentators of Nietzsche's GM, I, 13 address this example focusing on its *ethical* implications, but rarer on its epistemological. One seems to agree that Nietzsche must mean that the 'strong' in expressing his strength is not guilty of being 'evil,' i.e., that the 'strong' does not have the 'freedom' to choose or not to choose to express his strength—like the predator is not 'evil' because it kills its prey. This raises the classical discussion of 'free will' and 'agency,' which is not my concern in the present work.[23] I will rather discuss the linguistic aspect of the example, i.e., how our beliefs in 'double-deeds' (i.e., cause-effect relations of the form *AB*) are caused by the 'seduction of language,' and how apparently innocuous statements like 'lightning flashes,' 'I think,' or 'forces move' are grammatically motivated 'double-deeds' giving rise to erroneous cause-effect relations (even to metaphysics itself).

I will start suggesting that Nietzsche's example is extremely simple and that we only need to see *the sentence-fragment itself* in order to see a doubling. When Nietzsche is talking about *lightning* and *flashing*, he is arguing that this is one thing, which constructed as a sentence *seduces us* into believing that the same thing is two different things, *lightning* (and) *flashing*. Our grammar construct sentences as noun-verb relationships; it cannot express an event as event, but only as separated into two events as reported in language. According to this 'seduction,' one event seems to be acting and another responding to the action. On Nietzsche's argument, when 'lightning flashes' in a world of appearances, it 'does' a single thing as it produces the characteristic flash on the dark sky. This means that we *de facto* experience only one 'event,' the flash, as this is what *shows itself* in our apparent world. However, our language does not report this single event as one. We do not point to the sky and say 'flash,' but rather 'lighting flashes,' and add as such a 'depth' to a world where there *is* only the 'flash.' As such, our *language seduces our minds* into believing that there is lightning before there is flashing, and it is as such our language with its subject-predicate logic that motivates the emergence of a cause-effect relation from our otherwise metaphysically flat world. Language introduces the same thing first as subject and then as predicate, and it introduces as such into the flicker an actor-action or a doer-deed relationship. In Nietzsche's words, the flash is transformed into a "double-deed" or a "deed-deed." Tacitly, language introduces an actor for the flash. First *after* language, are we able to ask, 'what is doing the flashing,' and then adequately answer, 'lightning is.'

With an eye to Kant, we may illustrate Nietzsche's point by an example even more simple than his own: 'the sun shines.' This is also a 'doer-deed' construction, in which the sentence itself adds a 'doer' to a 'deed.' Imbedded in our Indo-European languages, we are 'seduced' into believing that the sun is *doing* shining as *deed*. Employing this example, it is not my absurd argument that the sun does *not* shine, or even worse, that the 'sun' is not *there* to shine. We make no extravagant claims regarding the existence of the sun; no claims about the sun being an 'idea' or a figment of our mind. In this reading of Nietzsche, we only claim that the sun is 'not there' as *doer*, i.e., as constructed upon the matrix of the grammatical subject. In a metaphysically flat world 'sun' and 'shining' is the same undifferentiated appearance; nothing is before and nothing after. For example, we must assume that animals live in a metaphysically flat world experiencing no distinction between the sun and its shining, and we must assume that if we travel far enough back to our prehistoric ancestors, they too were unconscious of such a distinction. We may therefore legitimately ask ourselves, 'what happened'? And the simple answer is that *language happened.*[24]

Let us recall that Kant in his example on sunshine needed two clauses to establish a causal relationship, namely 'the sun shines' and 'the stone grows warm.' In Nietzsche, the first clause is sufficient to get an elementary sense of causality. Analogously, Descartes needed two clauses in order to establish a causal relationship between his 'I think' and 'therefore I am'; Nietzsche sees the application of false causality already in the 'I think.' Language enables us to make a primordial differentiation between actor and action, doer and deed, cause and effect, before and after, qua its grammatical structure. This differentiation is thereupon projected into nature. Nietzsche's simple but profound argument is that linguistic convention has an unconscious (indeed a *metaphysical*) effect upon humans, since the sun is now construed as an actor that *does* something, namely shining. In our pre-consciously *language-constructed* metaphysics, it is *as if* the sun has intention, and in this simple but profound manner, our world is 'humanized.'

I mentioned earlier that Nietzsche already in his notebooks from the early 1870s anticipated epistemological positions he would elaborate in much later thinking. The linguistically formed cause-effect relation is an example of an idea he already proposes in *Notebook 19*. Here he says in a note:

> First the word for the action comes into being, and from there the word for the property. This relationship, transferred to all things, is causality. First 'seeing,' then 'sight.' That which 'sees' is regarded as the cause of 'seeing.' [...] A primal phenomenon is relating a stimulus perceived by the eye to the eye, i.e., relating an excitation of a sense to the sense itself.[25]

This early note from 1872 is at least as profound and dense as the aphorisms that Nietzsche writes at a much later stage. In this note, Nietzsche is questioning the 'doer-deed' relationship applied the simple act of seeing, where the eye becomes the actor for the action as *that which sees* preceding the 'sight' as the *being seen*.

Let us briefly notice that in the context of the nineteenth century's science discussions, Nietzsche's proposal is far from esoteric. The idea of a world being 'humanized' by means of language (in this 'simplified,' 'falsified,' and 'interpreted') is in its contemporary intellectual context often rehearsed. As we shall see below, physiologist Du Bois-Reymond, expresses the idea of 'humanization of nature,' when he says that we have an "irresistible tendency to *personification* of that which is impressed upon us."[26] Lange agrees, when in *Geschichte des Materialismus*,[27] he argues that scientists always deal with something, which essentially has no representation in-and-of-itself, and which necessarily must be *personalized* or *pictured* in concepts in order to be represented in thought; the concept personalizes this in-itself. Significantly, when Lange proceeds to explain the *mechanism* behind this personification-process, he resorts precisely to *subject-predicate* logic: "Our 'tendency to personification,' or, if we use Kant's phrase, what comes to the same thing, the *category of substance*, compels us always to conceive one of these ideas as subject, the other as predicate."[28] We find references to subject-predicate logic in Eduard von Hartmann's *Philosophie des Unbewußten* as well in observations like the following: "The notion of the judgment is unquestionably abstracted from the grammatical sentence by the omission of the verbal form. The categories of substance and accident are derived in the same way from subject and predicate; the discovery of a corresponding natural antitheses of substantive and verb is still an unsolved, perhaps a very fruitful philosophical problem."[29] Finally, E. Mach[30] takes the thinking in the same direction as Nietzsche when he suggests that the conception of cause has been created thanks to analogical thinking, and that the analogy is the *human will*. Movements in nature are projected back to movements in humans and are explained as analogical to *purposeful action*. As such, the cause-effect relation is an 'anthropomorphism' (in Mach and Nietzsche's identical vocabulary). Mach explains: "As soon as [the savage] perceives unexpected but striking movements in nature, he instinctively interprets these movements on the analogy of his own. [...] Gradually, the similarities and differences between physical and biological processes stand out alternately with even greater clearness against the background of the fundamental scheme of volitional action."[31]

Nineteenth-century scientists and philosophers of science, like Helmholtz, Bois-Reymond, Lange, Avenarius, and Mach, are still steeped in, but increasingly transgressing, Kantian thinking. The world itself is an inconceivable continuum that can only be represented symbolically in 'pictures,' 'symbols,' or 'signs' of our own making. Only given this 'personification' of the world, are we able to *talk about* a 'thing.' However, what lays hidden behind our simple and simplifying schematizations remains a mystery, which gradually, as the paradigm evolves, is not even worthwhile addressing. Nietzsche is expressing that idea in his late notes, when he says: "The presuppositions of Mechanism, the stuff, the atom, pressure, impact, and weight are not 'facts as such' [*Thatsachen an sich*], but rather interpretations helped by *psychological fictions*."[32]

4. The 'Fear-Factor': How Knowledge Is Created Out of Fear of the New

Let us assume that if Nietzsche's *homo sapiens* in principle desires to see itself imbedded in the world as its origin and fundamental principle, the *negation* of this desire must fill it with fear.

Desires and fears are commonly interlocked as a single motivation for seeking pleasure in the nineteenth-century paradigm. This is the traditional way of thinking pain and pleasure in several of Nietzsche's contemporaries with interest in human psychology. In his definition of the 'greatest happiness principle,' J. Stuart Mill takes for granted that "actions are right in proportion as they tend to promote happiness, wrong as they tend to produce the reverse happiness. By happiness is intended pleasure, and the absence of pain; by unhappiness, pain, and the privation of pleasure."[33]

However, to take this thinking into the field of theory of knowledge seems to be novel, as it implies that knowledge is producing pleasure and non-knowledge pain. Nietzsche is most obviously inspired by R. Avenarius in such propositions (cf. discussion Part II, B.4: "The Biological Theory of Knowledge in Vaihinger, Avenarius, and Nietzsche"). To Nietzsche, our 'desires' to invent causes are emerging out of fear for the new and strange. When we search for and eventually 'find' causes, we merely replace and suspend the new and strange with the old and familiar. We invent or rather re-invent a familiarity in the new and strange that is "soothing," "calming," "gratifying," and moreover gives us "a feeling of power."

> To trace something unknown back to something known is alleviating, soothing, gratifying and gives moreover a feeling of power. Danger, disquiet, anxiety attend the unknown—the first instinct is to eliminate these distressing states. First principle: any explanation is better than none.[34]

The same idea is expressed in the later notebooks:

> What is "knowledge" ["*erkennen*"]? To lead something strange back to something well-known and familiar. First principle: that which we have *gotten used to*, counts no longer as enigma, as problem. [...] Therefore, the first instinct in the knowing subject *is to seek a rule*: while obviously, with the ascertainment of the rule, nothing has been "known"—hence the superstition of the physicists: that which they have halted, that is, where the regularity of the phenomena allows the application of an abbreviating/reductive [*abkürzenden*] formula, that

they believe *is known* [*Erkennt*]. They feel 'secure'; but behind this intellectual security stands the appeasement of their fear: *they want the rule*, because it disrobes the world of fearfulness.³⁵

The invention of causes has this deep-rooted psychological motivation, when they reduce a world of surfaces and chaos to something simple and familiar.

> There is no causality-sense, as Kant believed. [...] As soon as something new is referred back to something old, we are calmed down. The so-called causality-instinct is only the fear of the strange and an attempt to uncover therein something familiar. A search not for causes but rather for the familiar.³⁶

To *see* necessity in successive events is not the work of a higher intellectual faculty like Kant and Schopenhauer believed, but on the contrary an animal instinct. Out of fear of the unknown, we seek as species the known and familiar as we reduce complexities to the fewest possible principles: one cause is better than many, and a known cause is better than an unknown.

5. The Naturalist Deconstruction of 'Causality' and the 'Synthetic A Priori'

In a note from 1885, called *Anti-Kant*, Nietzsche outlines his criticism of the Kantian faculties: "*Anti-Kant.* [...] Hume explained the causality-sense by habit. Kant, with great composure, said instead, 'it is a faculty [*Vermögen*].' The entire world was happy, especially because it also exposed a moral faculty."³⁷ (The note might also have been labeled 'Anti-Schopenhauer,' since Schopenhauer's 'causality' as a 'form of the understanding' is no less a faculty than is Kant's.)

In a well-known aphorism from *Beyond Good and Evil* (BGE), Nietzsche accuses Kant for providing a redundant answer to his guiding question, "how are synthetic a priori judgments possible," insofar as Kant refers us to his table of categories seen as faculties able to turn synthetic judgments into a priori judgments. Kant intends to revise Hume, who maintained that synthetic judgments were *a posteriori*, by positing his 'categories' supposed to give them a priori truth-value. This Kantian invention of a *synthetic* a priori, Nietzsche sees as question-begging: If Kant asks by what means, abilities, capacities, or faculties [*Vermögen*] synthetic judgments are possible, and essentially answers, by means of certain means, abilities, capabilities, or faculties, his answer has only repeated the question. Nietzsche's mockery of the answer is immortalized in the following paraphrase of Kant:

> How are synthetic judgments a priori *possible*? Kant asked himself,—and what, really, did he answer? *By means of a faculty* [*Vermöge eines Vermögens*]: but unfortunately not in a few words, but so circumspectly, venerably, and with such an expenditure of German profundity and flourishes that one overlooked

the comical *niaiserie allemande* involved is such an answer. [...] By means of a faculty [*Vermöge eines Vermögens*]—he had said, at least meant. But is that— an answer? An explanation? Or is it not rather a repetition of the question.³⁸

Kant explains nothing when he gives 'our faculties' as a reason for our sense of causality. The answer becomes particularly trivial if we translate *vermögen* with 'ability' (the German *vermögen*, as transitive verb, is normally translated as *capability* or *ability*, while *Vermögen*, as substantive neutrum, is translated as *property* or *faculty*); if we have a sense of causality, then obviously, we have an *ability* to have such a sense. Nietzsche's mock-paraphrase of Kant's, *Vermöge eines Vermögens*, underscores the repetitions and circular pattern in Kant's argument. To render Nietzsche's mock-paraphrase on short form: "By means of what ability/faculty do we know synthetic a priori judgments?—By means of the abilities following from that faculty!"

To drive home his point and make the travesty apparent to everybody (and to great amusement for Nietzsche's readers ever after), Nietzsche compares Kant's complex argument for the categories to the following scene from Moliere's *Le Malade imaginaire*:³⁹ an examiner asks a medical student why opium makes people sleepy; the student thinks long and hard on the question before he answers ponderously: *quia est in eo virtus dormitiva, cujus est natura sensus assoupire*. Opium makes people sleepy 'because it contains a certain dormant faculty that has the property of making the senses sleepy' (therefore, 'by the ability of a faculty')—and the examiner passes the student in admiration of this display of profundity. Similarly, in his solution to his problem (why a *vermögen*, because of a *Vermögen*), Kant has seduced himself and his audiences into believing that he has uncovered something profound, while his notion of an ability/faculty is "not even superficial"; it is already represented as surface manifestation of the phenomenon he investigates. By analogy to the humorous example, Kant's answer has the same structure and belongs as such 'to comedy,' as Nietzsche puts it. The *synthetic a priori* becomes Kant's sleeping pill. In its appeal to a faculty, it contains a *virtus dormitiva* that dulls the senses.

We may recall that Kant famously talked about the 'synthetic a priori' as a "condition of the possibility for experience" [*Bedingung der Möglichkeit von Erfahrung*], meaning that our always possible experiences have conditions that are necessary. This 'condition of the possibility' referred to a priori *conditions* of possible experience, thus *necessary conditions for experience*. They possessed rigorous necessity [*strenge nodvendighet*] and would no longer be *a priori* without this *strenge nodvendighet*. As Kant tells us, "experience [i.e., 'synthetic judgments'] teaches us that something is so and so, but *not* that it could not be any different."⁴⁰ To achieve *certainty*, we need to add the formal a priori conditions for experience in the form of the categories (e.g., space, time, and causality). As such, categories are not meant to constitute *norms* or *ideals* for perception. 'Space' is not a convention, a norm, or an ideal we look to be fulfilled in our perceptions, but a *necessary* condition insofar as we *have* spatial perception; ditto 'time' and 'cause.' If the category 'space' in Kant is an explanation of spatial perception, Nietzsche is consequently objecting to this as 'explanation,' because he thinks it is empty and vacuous. The *category 'space'* does not add more information to the *fact* that we have 'spatial perception.' However, since this is one of our conditions of knowledge, we add nothing to this constitutional given by adding a 'space-category.' In this sense, *synthetic a priori judgments* of space-, time-, and especially cause-categories become sleeping-pills we add to our thinking at the point where we like to put our thinking to rest.

6. Nietzsche's Irony: The Analysis of Kant's "Vermögen" as a 'Paralogism'

It is a high point of irony that Nietzsche in his critical discussion reveals a *paralogism* perpetrated by Kant, the ingenious examiner of the paralogism. Kant's *vermögen*, as an ability to sense causality, becomes a *Vermögen* understood as category, principle, and faculty; *vermögen* with a lowercase 'v' slides tacitly into *Vermögen* with a uppercase 'V.' Kant is thus committing a categorical mistake similar to Descartes's category-mistake regarding the *cogito*, introduced by Kant in the chapter, 'Paralogisms of Pure Reason' from *Critique of Pure Reason*.[41] In Kant's acute exposition of that 'paralogism,' it had two important aspects: (1) it employed an ambiguous middle term in the first and second premises of a syllogism, and (2) it confused the empirical and the transcendental.[42] His own *vermögen/Vermögen* (so Nietzsche) has the same double-aspect.

If in the *syllogism*, the first and second premise share a Middle term (M), the *paralogism* pretends to but does not share that Middle term (M), as it displaces (M) in the first premise with (M') in the second; hence, no conclusion can follow. In the paralogism, M' in the second premise indicates a term, which on appearances is identical to M in the first, but disguises a fundamental difference. The paralogism disguises itself as a syllogism, as a proper argument, but the middle term M discussed in the first and the second premise are two different things.

Table 2 Syllogism versus Paralogism

Syllogism	versus Paralogism
S is M	S is M
M is P	M' is P
---------	---------
S is P	S is P

In Kant's fundamental argument, the ambiguous middle term is ability/faculty, *vermögen*. In the first premise, it is an empirical-pragmatic ability, but in the second, it is a transcendental and generalized faculty. In the first premise, we have abilities plain and simple, in the second, we have a transcendental-logically explanation of that ability. We can consequently construct Kant's (and Schopenhauer's) paralogism in summary form of a table:

Table 3 Kant's Paralogism of Vermögen According to Nietzsche

Kant's paralogism of *Vermögen*

S is M: Our experience of causality is a vermögen (i.e., ability)
M' is P: *Vermögen* (as faculty) is a transcendental principle

S is P: We owe our experience of causality to a transcendental faculty (*Vermögen*).

Drawing attention to this redundancy in Kant's explanation, Nietzsche can now re-phrase Kant's famous question, "How are synthetic a priori judgments possible," into the psychological, even psychoanalytical, question probing what theoretical desires motivate a search for *a priori* judgments in the first place, "Why are synthetic a priori judgments *necessary*?" (ibid.).

2. 'Chronological Reversal' of Cause and Effect

1. Chronological Reversal as Humanization of Nature

Nietzsche has added to Hume's skepticism regarding the objectivity of the cause-effect relation a psychological-linguistic explanation of *why* this type of explanation is *psychologically attractive*. We familiarize the world around us by projecting *human action* and *human grammar* into nature. Subconsciously we infer that if we can act, nature can act too; if we can will an action, nature can will an action too; if we can have intentions, nature can have intentions too; if we have a language expressing subjects and predicates, nature can have such a language too;—as stated in TI:

> Man projected his three 'inner facts,' that in which he believed more firmly than in anything else, will, spirit, ego, outside himself—he derived the concept 'being' only from the concept 'ego,' he posited 'things' as possessing being according to his own image, according to his concept of the ego as cause. What

surprise that he later only rediscovered in things *what he had put into them*. The thing itself, to say it again, the concept 'thing' is merely a reflection of the belief in the ego as cause.[43]

Notice here the similarity between this late assessment from 1888 and Nietzsche's much earlier passage from *On Truth and Lies* in 1872 where Nietzsche anticipated this 'hermeneutical circle.' Here he described the irony of looking for and finding something one had oneself been hiding: "When somebody hides something behind a bush and then looks for it again at the same place and finds it there, there is in such seeking and finding not much to applaud. Yet, this is how we seek and find of 'truth' within our realm of reason [*Vernunft-Bezirkes*]."[44]

Whether early or late in his writings, we humanize nature. We use that which is nearest to us as *explanatory matrix*, namely our 'wills' and the subject-predicate logic of language, becoming a toolbox by which we form and manipulate nature into our image. From gazing into a world of meaningless appearances, we produce a meaningful world of causes and intentions. We must here warn against a misinterpretation, because it is in Nietzsche not the implication that *nature is language* (*not* the implication that *the world is a text, writing*, etc.); nor does he imply that we cannot *perceive* a language-independent world, which for any naturalist would be a nonsensical claim making it utterly inexplicable how our relatives in the animal kingdom can sense, live in, and survive in their language-independent natural environments. It is only the claim that we in our *explanations* turn nature into *language*.

In his more detailed discussion of how we achieve this particular effect, Nietzsche often refers to a process he labels 'chronological reversal' or 'time-reversal,' applied to both the case of sensation and the case of causation. In the first case, he notices a 'time-reversal' between the moment of an impression (the reception of a sense-data) and its conscious materialization as perception (that which we see with awareness). We are back to Schopenhauer's distinction between 'raw sensations' and conscious perceptions, a basic distinction that was shared by numerous neo-Kantian philosophers and physiologists of the nineteenth century.[45] In the first case, Nietzsche's 'time-reversal' concerns the following observation: perception is always by the subject felt as *spontaneous and immediate presence*; however, properly speaking, the perception is the result of a *work*, namely the mind's processing of sense-data. The experience of a self-present world emerges therefore only *after-the-fact* of the generation of a perceptive image, i.e., after the conclusion of processes that the sense-impression must undergo before it materializes as perception. At the exact moment for inscription of the sense-data, there is no awareness, because the impression, as Nietzsche puts it, "needs time before it is finished":

The reversal of time: we believe in the outer-world as causing an effect on us, but we have already initially changed the actual and unconsciously progressing effect *into outer-world*. That, which stands opposed to us, is already our work, which now effects us retrogressively [*zurückwirkt*]. It needs time, before it is finished: but this time is so small [*diese Zeit is so klein*].[46]

The time may be "small"; still the brain needs time for processing sense-impressions. After the sense-impression is processed, it 'returns' as perception, as the subject in this moment starts consciously to see the outer world. The impression has taken a round-trip (so to speak) from the eye to the brain back to the eye. Because of the necessity of this detour, the 'outer world' is "our work."

We notice with Nietzsche that already in *perception*, we *humanize* an 'outer world.' The humanization is necessarily species-specific insofar as it is as biological *species* we see *a world*. Hence, we do not see *the world* as (i) a 'neutral,' 'objective' divinely privileged species, neither as (ii) some other species, and neither as (iii) separate individuals in which case we would live in different worlds preventing us from sharing observations. When we produce knowledge of this *our-world*, we do so as a biological species with our particular evolved abilities to see and understand; i.e., from our species-specific *perspective*.[47] Nietzsche thus takes for granted that we see the world only from our evolved vantage point as species, not from outside of our biology, nor with a neutral gaze at the world from nowhere. On this biological-pragmatic argument, which was rehearsed already in TL, we have no access to the world 'in-itself.' We do not see an extra-perspectival 'objective,' 'real,' or 'true' world residing 'as it is' before-the-fact of the *perspective perceptive interpretations* we give it.[48]

Likewise, in his second case, our *knowledge* of the world is 'our work,' an *after-the-fact* addition of causes to an appearing world in order to give it a measure of order and simplicity. It is as if Nietzsche in this distinction between a 'perceptive' and a 'cognitive' time-reversal has inherited the distinction between 'forms of sensibility' and 'forms of understanding' already essential in Kant and Schopenhauer, but giving these 'forms' new definitions that (importantly) move them from the domain of the transcendental to the domain of the biological.

In any case, also causes are an after-the-fact interpretation thanks to time-reversal:

The error of imaginary causes.—To start with dreams: we have a certain sensation, for example after a distant cannon shot, for which we retrospectively supply a cause [*nachträglich ein Ursache untergeschoben*] [...] The sensation remains in the meantime in a kind of resonance: it is as if it waits until our causality-drive [*Ursachentrieb*] allows it to come into the foreground,—from now on no longer as accidental, but rather as "meaning" [*Sinn*]. The cannon shot presents itself in a *causal* manner, in what appears as a reversal of time [*Umkehrung der Zeit*]. What comes later, the motivation is experienced first [...], the shot follows. What has happened? The ideas that were created by a certain physical condition were mistaken for the cause of that condition. —In fact, we do the same thing when we are awake. Most of our general feelings [...] excite our causality-drive: we want there to be a *reason* why we feel *this or that*, — why we are feeling good or bad. It is never enough just to establish the fact that we are in a particular state [...], we only become *conscious* of it, when we have assigned it a kind of motivation. The memory that unconsciously is activated in such cases leads back to earlier states of the same type and the associated causal interpretation,—not their causality.[49]

Like in dreams we at the outset seek the cause for a canon shot and first subsequently hear the shot (therefore a reversal of time [*Zeit-Umkehrung*] has occurred: *this time-reversal [Zeitumkehrung] always occurs*, also in waken life. The 'cause' is imagined *after the 'deed'*; what I mean is that *our means and purposes* are consequences of a process?)[50]

Generalizing Nietzsche's example, we *seek* a cause for an event, and first then do we *find* it; we first see the 'deed,' and then do we imagine the 'doer' or the cause.[51] The process he is attempting to describe must have four steps. We first perceive an event, then we seek a cause, then we imagine a cause, then we find a cause and construe the event as 'deed.' The 'anthropic circle' or the 'humanization of nature' is naming this inversion where a simplifying cause is added to an appearance as one of its possibilities.[52]

Attempting to capture the thinking in a model, the circular movement is evident:[53]

Table 4 Time-Reversal as Humanization of Nature

Stage 1: Appearances as instances: We gaze into a superficial *a posteriori* world of disorganized appearances and events.

> *Stage 2*: Appearances need 'motive'. We doubt the gaze, the superficiality and nothingness of the world. We *need*, we *look* and *ask for* 'wills' in nature; i.e., we ask for our familiar selves mirrored in nature.
>
> *Stage 3*: Appearances need 'structure'. We divine that for actions and movements to exist, actors and movers must exist. We apply subject-predicate logic as our best precedent matrix for the thinking. The world is *logicized* and *linguisticized*.

Stage 4: Appearances are (pseudo-) understood. The psychological-linguistic *subject-will* construction is as cause understood as preceding the *a posteriori* world of appearances from *stage 1*. In this last step, nature is humanized: subject, intention, will, meaning, truth, and finally 'God' are restored as (pseudo-) explanations of the world.

The figure illustrates a 'time reversal' of positions, where the first is turned into the last, and the last turned into the first. The figure thus means to express that in our logical reconstructions of appearances, we conceive the explanatory concept to be chronologically *first*, and the observation it explains, *last*, as if its product. However, in Nietzsche's anthropic circle, the process goes the other way around: the observation is always *first*, and it prompts an explanation that is *last* as a *delayed effect* of the observation. Nietzsche's circle of interpretation indicates that the proposed explanation can never explain *more* than what is already apparent. In the last analysis, human explanation/interpretation is confined to appearances.

2. De Man's Reading of Nietzsche's Chronological Reversal as Rhetoric

Nietzsche's 'Chronological Reversal' was introduced into deconstructive commentary thanks to Paul de Man's exposition of a pertinent passage from *The Will to Power* (WP) on the issue.[54] Under the label, *The phenomenalism of the 'inner world,'* Nietzsche states:

> The phenomenalism of the 'inner world.' [...] The chronological inversion *[die Chronologische Umdrehung]*, so that the cause enters consciousness later than the effect. // we have learned that pain is projected to a part of the body without being situated there // we have learned that sense impressions naively supposed to be conditioned by the outer world [*Außenwelt*] are, on the contrary, conditioned by the inner world [*Innenwelt*]; that we are always unconscious of the real activity of the outer world [...] The fragment of the outer world of which we are conscious is born after an effect [*nachgeboren nach der Wirkung*] from the outside has impressed [*geübt*] itself upon us, and is subsequently projected [*Nachträglich Projiziert*] as its 'cause.' [...] 'Inner experience' *["innere Erfahrung"]* enters our consciousness only after it has found a language the individual *understands* . . . i.e., a translation of a condition into a condition *more familiar [bekanntere]* to him—'to understand' means merely: to be able to express something new in the language of something old and familiar.[55]

Nietzsche joins here the classical epistemological discussion of the subject-object or mind-world problem, as he is challenging a simplified Empiricist solution to this problem, namely the idea that our sensations travel in a straight line from the outside to the inside where they settle as 'ideas.' According to this, as it would seem, Lockean model (cf. Part I, A.4: 'What is a Word?'), one presupposes that (i) sense-material travels from outside to inside along a linear trajectory; that (ii) senses are entrances for material that eventually will fill up the psyche; that (iii) the linear trajectory firmly establishes a causal relationship between outside and inside, such that the outside is 'cause' and the inside is 'effect'; finally, (iv) that there is one-to-one relationships between inside images and outside objects.

That Nietzsche is challenging this model cannot be a matter of contention, since this is explicitly stated, "we have learned that sense-impressions naively supposed to be conditioned by the outer world [*Außenwelt*] are, on the contrary, conditioned by the inner world [*Innenwelt*]" (ibid.). This is seen by de Man as well. However, he ignores that Nietzsche carries out his critique in the context of the neo-Kantian and psycho-physiological paradigm. Nietzsche reverses the traditional Empiricist position in distinction to Kant's so-called Copernican Revolution, claiming that perception and cognition are formed by an 'inner world' thanks to the 'categories,' and in distinction to the scientifically upgraded Copernican Revolution according to the psycho-physiologists beginning to understand the secrets of human perception. When Nietzsche reiterates that "we have learned," he includes himself in that 'we,' because he is associated with the Kantian/neo-Kantian project. If we perceive *things* thanks to the formative power of our 'inner world,' the apparent world is truly dependent on a human component. Such references to biology, perception, or cognition are as absent in de Man as in Derrida, and it is unsurprising that de Man displaces Nietzsche's discussion to another field, better situated within the deconstructive comfort-zone, namely rhetoric.[56]

De Man sees now Nietzsche applying the rhetorical figures of *metalepsis* and *antithesis* in his reversal of the priority of cause and effect, outer and inner. Cause and effect, outer and inner, consist of two positions organized hierarchically, and Nietzsche's application of *metalepsis* onto the *antithesis* reverses the classical hierarchical order. This is in de Man's analysis seen as the first step in Nietzsche's deconstruction of the cause-effect relation. If this relation traditionally is organized as follows, *cause* → *effect* equivalent to the distinction *outer* → *inner,* de Man understands Nietzsche as reversing the relationship into its opposite, *effect* → *cause* equivalent to *inner* → *outer.*

> Nietzsche's argument starts out from a binary polarity of classical banality in the history of Metaphysics: the opposition of subject to object based on the spatial model of an 'inside' to an 'outside' world. [...] But the working hypothesis of the polarity becomes soon itself target of the analysis. This occurs first of all by showing that the priority status of the two poles can be reversed. The outer, objective event in the world was supposed to determine the inner, conscious event as cause determines effect. [...] The outer, objective event in the world was supposed to determine the inner, conscious event as cause determines effect. It turns out however that what was assumed to be the objective, external cause is itself the result of an internal effect.[57]

However, de Man must take his deconstructive analysis a step further, because reversing a hierarchically organized binary into its opposite, leaves us with another no less hierarchical and no less dogmatic binary. If Nietzsche reverses *outer → inner* into its opposite, *inner → outer*, he is merely affirming dogmatic Idealism, which would emerge as the most radical effect of deconstruction; certainly a non-starter for radical thinking since the position has been around for millennia. As his more radical claim, de Man instead suggests an *infinite interchangeability* of the two positions, inner and outer.

> The two sets of polarities, inside/outside and cause/effect, which seemed to made up a closed and coherent system (outside causes producing inside effect) has now been scrambled into an arbitrary, open system in which the attributes of causality and of location can be deceptively exchanged, substituted for each other at will. As a consequence, our confidence in the original, binary model that was used as a starting point is bound to be shaken.[58]

In other words, it is the alleged oscillation forth and back of positions in the opposition, which to de Man represents the true critical potential in Nietzsche. This radicalization of the deconstructive reading of the binary is meant to destabilize the traditional inventory of oppositions in Western Thinking, as Nietzsche is credited for having realized this radical indetermination or indecidability of positions.

It is a dubious analysis, however, because if it was Nietzsche's intention to "exchange" or "substitute at will" the two positions 'inner' and 'outer,' in this making them "arbitrarily interchangeable," he would to undersigned defend a position even more indigestible than dogmatic Idealism, namely the 'position' of having no position at all. "Arbitrary interchangeability" of classical epistemological oppositions translates into deconstruction's concept of 'play,' but is Nietzsche *playing philosophy* in that simple sense?

If we, in an un-deconstructive manner, try to *make sense* of Nietzsche, we may start by suggesting that Nietzsche's 'chronological reversal' does not apply to *receptivity* but only to the 'inner world' of *interpretation*; we may consequently propose a distinction between a *time for receptivity* and a *time for interpretation*.

Thus, the 'chronological reversal' applies to the time it takes for the mind to make itself conscious of a fragment of the outer world it has received as impression. We still have an *intact chronological sequence* of something moving from outer to inner in the process of first being received and then being perceived. However, the *chronology of causality* has broken down and reversed thanks to the cognitive delay with which the mind understands impressions to be 'causes.' When Nietzsche emphasizes that *perception* of the exterior is effected 'from within,' it implies that we have evolved a mental apparatus by which we select, process, and simplify information received from without. This processing takes time, but still, it does not contradict the fact that we *receive* before we *perceive*.

In this, Nietzsche is not defending philosophy as a 'play' of arbitrarily interchangeable positions; he cannot be questioning *that* we receive information or data. In TL, as we recall, he even sequenced this process as proceeding from *stimuli* to *images* to *concepts* (cf. Part I, A.4: "Nerve-Stimuli, Images, and Sounds"). He takes for granted that we must receive a material before we can interpret this material and project it back onto the empirical world *as if a cause*. The latter part is an *interpretation-process* properly speaking, which still *takes time*, rather than *reversing time*. The *outer* as data must *exist* before the *inner* as processed data, but the outer can never be *interpreted* before the *inner*. Hence, it must still be the case (also to Nietzsche) that *time can only move in one direction*, namely from the past, through the present, toward the future. Both receptivity and interpretation are subjected to this indispensable *arrow of time*.

However, as Nietzsche acutely observes, in the *interpretation-process*, i.e., in our rationalizations of the external, the arrow of time seems to be bended back upon itself because the mind posits the external as 'cause' *as if* this 'cause' is pure objectivity while it is our construction. This must be the meaning of the sentence in the passage above: "The fragment of the outer world of which we are conscious is born after an effect from outside has impressed itself upon us, and is subsequently projected as its *cause*" (ibid.); i.e., at *time 1*, something impresses itself upon us; at *time 2*, it is processed in the brain; at *time 3*, it is interpreted as an outside cause. Ergo, the becoming conscious of an outside proceeds along a traditional linear time-line advancing from *1* to *2* to *3*.

Our evolved physiology enables our reception of material and our psychology enables us to perceive *consciously* this material according to a general hermeneutics for which our mind is responsible. One process is as necessary as the other, but the last process provides us with the notion of *cause*, implying that *causes are interpreted perceptions of the 'outside.'* It is as if raw stimuli have been taken a *round-trip* from outer to inner and back, before they are fully interpreted and consciously perceived. In formulaic language, *some unknown 's' is transformed into some known 'p'* (let 's' designate 'sense-impression' and 'p' perception). The unknown 's' and the known 'p' is essentially the same thing, just in different stages of processing, the anonymous 's' representing an abundance of raw data, while the defined 'p' represents the selection, simplification, and determination of this mass of data. This process helps us to *characterize* a sensation that is at first *uncharacterized*. In this sense, impressions are always 'new,' while the '*interpreting explanation*' is always 'old and familiar,' as Nietzsche acutely observes in the passage: "'to understand' means merely: to be able to express something new in the language of something old and familiar" (ibid.).

This reconstruction of the passage is essentially different from de Man's because it suspends any postulate about 'arbitrary interchangeability' between two binary terms that are purely formal.

3. A Surface without Abyss

1. Nietzsche's Development of His Epistemological Positions

In Lange's *Naturalist* interpretation, the thing-in-itself is conceived as a *Grenzbegriff*,[59] indicating an unknown and indeterminable realm not accessible to us given our *species-specific* perceptive-cognitive limitations. The emergence of evolutionary biology and psycho-physiology is in Lange supporting this 'naturalized' version of the 'thing-in-itself.' Accordingly, we may conceive the 'thing' as that which is below Fechner's "thresholds";[60] that which we are incapable of perceiving below our threshold (beyond a certain limit) is conceived as the 'thing.'

In Mach's *Positivist* interpretation, the concept of the 'thing' is suspended and replaced with a sensation-chaos of elements. Contemplating the 'thing-in-itself' is not worth our while, since we have access only to this assemble of elements, relations, and perspectives. The 'thing' is at best an after-the-fact *objectification* of a "sensation-chaos," the result of a spontaneous cognitive processing, abstraction, and abbreviation of complexes of relations and sense-data, which we necessarily receive before we start to *perceive* properly speaking.[61]

It is clear that in any of these two interpretations (whether 'Naturalist' or 'Positivist') the 'thing itself' is a concept of an *impossible something*. It is in any case that which in dogmatic philosophy is *falsely* regarded as 'true' contrary to that which is 'apparent.' (We return to the intellectual context of these positions in more detail below, cf. Part II, B: "Nietzsche and Critical Positivism").

In the argument here defended, Nietzsche adheres to both of these two interpretations, the tendency being that the first interpretation is prevalent in the early writings, and the second in the later writings. If or when we perceive a *change* in Nietzsche's understanding of the 'thing-in-itself' from early to late writings, the change consists merely in the replacement of the neo-Kantian Naturalist view with an increasingly Positivist view of the in-itself. In the context of the discussion of the supposed difference between Nietzsche's early and late theories of truth, he seems to be progressing from 'epistemological agnosticism' in the early essay to 'epistemological positivism' in the later work.

M. Clark has performed what is supposed to be a rescuing reading of Nietzsche's theory of truth according to which Nietzsche had a 'falsification-thesis' in the early work, which he supposedly abandons in his 'mature' writings, ending up re-confirming the correspondence theory of truth and the 'thing itself.' In his mature writings, Clark notices that Nietzsche gives up the idea of a thing-itself, and she concludes, "Given the rejection of the thing-in-itself, Nietzsche should now give up the [falsification] thesis since if there are only representations, to what could they fail to correspond? What is left to be falsified?" (Clark, 1990, ibid., p. 120). The answer to the rhetorical question is, as far as I am concerned, 'nothing,' what I see as being Nietzsche's point: If the thing-in-itself is a thing-of-nothing, what is left to be falsified? In good, logical consequence, *nothing*! However, my conclusion is not Clark's conclusion. Her answer is approximately that if 'nothing' is being falsified, there is no falsification, and everything is restored as 'transparent'! She concludes that with his rejection of the falsification-thesis, Nietzsche is finally arriving to a confirmation of a world existing independently of our sensations of them, a world of distinct pre-given objects. (cf., Clark, ibid., p. 123). If Nietzsche states that 'senses do not lie' (cf. discussion Part II, A.4.3: "Senses Do Not Falsify"), he is apparently saying that 'senses tell us the truth,' in this restoring the world of objects and the truth as things-in-themselves (i.e., restoring classical truth-metaphysics according to my equation, *In-Itself = Truth*). This suggestion has again the implication that there has to be an extreme discontinuity between the young and late Nietzsche, as often argued by Clark.

On my argument, Nietzsche does not have this radical development. He may in TL defend the idea of a 'thing-in-itself' being 'falsified,' but already as early as 1872/1873, he understands that this notion is inadequate, because the 'thing-itself' necessarily has to be rendered as unknown and inaccessible, cf., the "enigmatic X." So-called 'illusions,' 'lies,' 'errors,' or 'falsifications' come about only given the false but *necessary provisional acceptance* of a *background that is true*, namely as the metaphysical hypothesis of a true thing-world. He does not subscribe to this hypothesis, but is addressing it as a conceptual comparison-background required in order to propose a counter-argument. In any case, in later writings he ends up attempting to suspend all talk about 'things-in-themselves,' exactly because of this logical-semantic problem. If in the early work, the 'thing' is addressed as an inaccessible and enigmatic 'x,' in the late work, the 'thing-itself' is dismissed as a fantasy of an unconditioned, relation-less, context-less, and subject-less 'in-itself.'

Hence I see the following modified 'development' from early to late writings: If in early writings, Nietzsche may leave open the possibility of the existence of the 'enigmatic x,' in late writings this hypothetical possibility-being of 'x' is rejected when he reiterates that there is no things-in-itself, i.e., no *unique, unitary, and pre-given object*. If we want to see this development of his positions as a *change*, it is on my argument a change to a more radical "Truth-denying" position. (More about these positions in Part II, B: "Nietzsche and Critical Positivism.")

That Nietzsche mature anti-objectivist position becomes a radical rejection of the in-itself, we see in numerous passages from the later work:

> The properties of a thing are effects of other things: if one thinks the other 'things' away, then a thing has no properties; that is, there is no thing without other things [*es giebt kein Ding ohne andere Dinge*]; that is, there is no 'thing-in-itself.'[62]

> A "thing-in-itself" is as wrong as a "sense [*Sinn*] in itself," a "meaning [*Bedeutung*] in itself." There is no state of affairs [*Thatbestand*] in itself; a sense must always first have been added [*hineingelegt*], before a state of affairs can come into existence.[63]

> One wants to know what things-in-themselves are made up off: but see, there are no things-in-themselves! Let us suppose nonetheless, that there could be an "in-itself," an unconditioned; still, it could not be known [*Erkannt*]! Something unconditioned cannot be known, otherwise it would not be unconditioned! To know is always to 'pose-something-into-a-relationship-to-something.'[64]

> That things have a constitution [*Beschaffenheit*] in-themselves, completely independent of interpretation and subjectivity, is a quite superfluous hypothesis: it would presuppose, that interpretation and subject-being [*Subjektiv-sein*] would be inessential, that a thing outside all relations would still be a thing.[65]

> The "Thing-in-itself" is self-contradictory. If I think away all 'properties,' all 'activities' of a thing, then there is no thing left.[66]

> The concept of 'truth' *is absurd* [...] The whole realm of 'true,' 'false' refers only to relations between entities, not the 'in-itself.' [...] *Nonsense*: There is no 'entity-in-itself,' it is only relations that constitute entities, and neither can there be a 'knowledge-in-itself.'[67]

I my analysis, the rejection of the notion of the thing-in-itself is logically linked to the emphasis on a perspectival-phenomenal world of relationships. So, again in disagreement with Clark's suggestion that Nietzsche reinvents *objectivism* and *realism*, I can only see that his epistemology unapologetically is developing into *relativism* and *perspectivism*.⁶⁸

2. Attempts to Un-Think the 'True World' in Twilight of the Idols

Nietzsche criticizes the 'thing-in-itself' and the 'true-apparent distinction' throughout his work, where the in-itself usually is synonymous with his concept of Truth in the metaphysical sense. Hence, the *In-Itself* is equal to *Truth*, and that equation is opposed to *appearances*, according to the following formalization:

(*In-itself* = *Truth*) vs. *appearances*.

The *pragmatic* concept of truth (cf. Part I, A.3) is not an object for this criticism precisely because it does not refer back to 'things-in-themselves.' Nietzsche is not questioning our capacity to perceive an apparent world and to express state of affairs. His theory of truth never becomes whimsical or counter-intuitive. His legitimate concern is truth-in-itself equal to the thing-in-itself as illusion and absurdity, as a *metaphysical lie* perpetrated by Western-Christian thinking. In this context, Truth is a 'lie,' an 'illusion,' and a 'falsification.' His seemingly paradoxical position concerning the question of truth cannot produce a contradiction in terms, because he does not assert that *truth* in all its forms is false, but only that *a specific concept of truth* is false.

If the '*In-itself* = *Truth*' is an illusion or a falsification, Nietzsche's 'appearances' are that which is left in the presentation of the world. However, a one-sided emphasis on 'appearances' catches Nietzsche and peers in a conundrum because the semantic content of the term 'appearance' connotes a binary relation between *representation and represented*. The term itself seduces us into believing in a 'thing' or an 'object' as that which *appears*. We saw that already Otto Liebmann was struggling with this problem in criticizing Kant's terminology (cf. Part I, A.9: "Nietzsche's Empiricist Neo-Kantianism"), and Nietzsche too is discerning it already in *TL* when he writes, "The word 'appearance' contains many seductions, why I try to avoid it as much as possible: because it is not true that the essence of things 'appears' in the empirical world."⁶⁹

In *TI*, Nietzsche continues his endeavors to *articulate* and *think* a notion of 'appearance' detached from its logical opposite. His famous and often-cited aphorism, "*Wie die 'wahre Welt' endlich zur Fabel Wurde*," with the subtitle "*Geschichte eines Errtums*," serves as a summary of his still more radical attempts to detach appearances from the supposed 'in-itself.' As the title of the aphorism indicates, the *'wahre Welt'* is synonymous with the thing-in-itself; i.e., the equation, *In-itself = Truth*, applies.

The well-known aphorism attempts in six sketches to give us a brief history of how this belief has become fable, mythology, and superstition in the development of metaphysics.[70] We ignore the two first pre-Kantian positions introducing the aphorism and start with Nietzsche's position '3' corresponding to Kant's putative position: "3. The true world, unattainable, unprovable, unutterable, but still thought of as a consolation, an obligation, an imperative [*Die wahre Welt, unerreichbar, unbeweisbar, unversprechbar, aber schon als gedacht ein Trost, eine Verpflichtung, ein Imperativ*]. (Basically the old sun but through fog and skepticism; the idea become elusive, pale, Nordic, Königsbergian)."[71] Position '3' re-asserts, in Nietzsche's interpretation, the Kantian thing-in-itself, while his three pursuant positions are attempts to articulate the critical implications of something being "unreachable" and "unknowable."

> 4. The true world—unattainable? At any rate, unattained. And as unattained also unknown. Consequently, not consoling, redeeming, obligating: how could something unknown be an obligation? [*Die wahre Welt—unerreichbar? Jedenfalls unerreicht. Und als unerreicht auch unbekannt. Folglich auch nicht tröstend, erlösend, verpflichtend: wozu könnte uns etwas Unbekanntes verpflichten?*]. (Grey morning. First yawn of reason. Cockcrow of positivism).

> 5. The 'true world'—an idea that is of no further use, not even as an obligation,—a useless, superfluous idea, consequently a refuted idea: let us get rid of it! [*Die "wahre Welt"—eine Idee, die zu Nichts mehr nütz ist, nicht einmal mehr verpflichtend,—eine unnütz, eine überflüssig gewordene Idee, folglich eine widerlegte Idee: schaffen wir sie ab!*]. (Bright day; breakfast; return of good sense and cheerfulness; Plato blushes in shame; pandemonium of all free spirits).

> 6. We have got rid of the true world: which world is left? Perhaps the apparent one?—But no! With the true world, we got rid of the apparent world as well! [*Die wahre Welt haben wir abgeschafft: welche Welt blieb übrig? die scheinbare vielleicht? ... Aber nein! mit der wahren Welt haben wir auch die scheinbare abgeschafft!*]. (Noon; moment of shortest shadow; end of longest error; high point of humanity; INCIPIT ZARATHUSTRA).[72]

Positions '4' and '5' may be seen as logically co-dependent,[73] and '6' may be seen as the most radical consequence of the two previous positions. From '4' over '5' to '6,' it seems as if the deconstruction of the Kantian 'thing' is carried out in still more uncompromising language.[74] If position '4' states that the "true world" is unreachable and unknowable, the following position

'5' articulates the pragmatic recognition that the 'true' world is useless baggage we can discard. After this realization, Nietzsche suggests the seemingly puzzling position '6' suggesting that the apparent world is useless too. This conclusion may immediately appear as counter-intuitive given that without a 'true' world, we are inclined to believe that we are left with an 'apparent' as the only meaningful alternative—arguably be the most *logical* conclusion if we imagine that we subtract 'true' from 'true and apparent' like in an equation of the form: *(true + apparent) − true = apparent*. Accordingly, we should be left with precisely the 'apparent world.' Instead, Nietzsche insists that we now "got rid of the apparent world as well," as if he has abandoned both transcendental and empirical world, as if we live in a fictional realm of imagination, dream, or literature; as if he here suggests that particularly extreme form for Idealism that by some of his detractors has been dismissively described as 'Nietzscheanism.'[75]

We are on surer ground if we interpret Nietzsche's 'we got rid of the apparent world' in *structural* terms. Then, the implication is that when we abandon the *concept* of a 'true' world, we immediately annihilate the *hierarchical opposition* between 'true' and 'apparent' according to which 'true' is appreciated and 'apparent' depreciated. If there is no 'true' world, the background on which appearances emerge as appearances disappears and the philosophical dichotomy *true versus apparent* collapses. He anticipates as such the linguistic point of view where the law of binary opposition dictates that nothing can reside in one term. Nietzsche is as such trying to un-think *binary logic*, according to which the opposition *A versus B* is translated into the opposition *A versus non-A*, making *A* and *non-A* co-dependent in their complementariness, *linking* the two positions. On this exposition, Nietzsche correctly concludes that if we erase one of the positions, we erase the *link* as such. When we retract one term in the opposition, both terms lose value, because they are asserted only through their reciprocal difference; *A* is powerless to designate anything without the help of *non-A*, and vice versa. This is the hard rule for the *binary opposition* or what Nietzsche calls *antithesis*, and it is *as 'antithesis'* he understands the opposition 'truth-appearance.'

That this structural reading applies is explicit in several passages from his later notes, where Nietzsche addresses the 'anti-thesis' or the 'distinction':

> Let's abolish the 'thing-in-itself' and with it one of the least clear concepts, that of 'appearance'! This whole antithesis, like the older one of 'matter and spirit,' has been proven unusable.[76]

> It matters little to me whether someone says today [...] 'The essence of things is unknown to me,' or whether another [...] says: 'The essence of things is

to a large extent unknown to me.' [...] As if the distinction they both assume were justified: the distinction between an 'essence of things' and a world of appearances.[77]

> The antithesis of 'thing-in-itself' and 'appearance' is untenable; with this, however, the concept 'appearance' collapses too.[78]

If in erasing the concept 'truth' we simultaneous erase the concept with which it is linked, 'appearance,' it makes now as little sense to assert a 'true world' as it does to assert an 'apparent.' Without its opposite 'truth,' 'appearance' is without value—*therefore*, Nietzsche's correct conclusion, "the concept 'appearance' collapses too." Nietzsche's question is cogent, "what world is left? Perhaps the apparent one?" and his answer in the negative is consistent, "But no!" since this 'no' has to follow with logical and structural necessity.

We may put it differently. If appearances do not refer to anything, they have *lost their sign-function*, they are no longer perceptive signs for a more true double. His point is that *appearances cannot be signs* for an objective order antedating them, i.e., they cannot be signs for a prearranged *True* world.[79]

3. Senses Do Not Falsify

From another perspective, Nietzsche's 'no' to an apparent world changes eventually into a 'yes,' because without a 'true' world, the apparent or rather *super-apparent* world becomes the 'only world,' implying that it *is not* and *cannot be* a 'falsification.' If the 'thing-in-itself' is erased in Nietzsche's conceptual universe, there is nothing left for an 'appearance' to 'falsify.' If we encounter, perceive, or experience only one world, it makes no sense to declare this one world a 'falsification' or a 'lie' (falsifying *what*, lying about *what*? —remember we just erased the 'what').

Another famous passage from TI addresses precisely this issue.

> When the rest of the philosophic folk rejected the testimony [*Zeugniss*] of the senses because they showed multiplicity and change, [Heraclitus] rejected their testimony because they showed things as if they had permanence and unity. Heraclitus too did the senses an injustice. They lie neither in the way the Eleatics believed nor as he believed—they do not lie at all [*sie lügen überhaupt nicht*]. What we *make of* their testimony, that alone introduces lies; for example, the lie of unity, the lie of thinghood, of substance, of permanence. 'Reason' makes us falsify the testimony of the senses [*Was wir aus ihrem Zeugniss machen, das legt erst die Lüge hinein, zum Beispiel die Lüge der Einheit, die Lüge der Dinglichkeit, der Substanz, Der Dauer [...] Die 'Vernunft' ist die Ursache,*

dass wir das Zeugniss der Sinne fälschen]. The senses are not lying when they show becoming, passing away, and change . . . Heraclitus will always be right in thinking that being is an empty fiction. The 'apparent' world is the only one; the 'true world' is only added as a lie. [*Die 'Scheinbare' Welt ist die Einzige; die 'wahre Welt' ist nur hinzugelogen*].[80]

On a superficial reading, the passage seems ambiguous, perhaps even self-contradictory, as Nietzsche seems to express opposing views on the same subject-matter: Senses 'do not lie' in one sentence and then again they do in another.

We first notice that Nietzsche is *objecting to* Heraclitus who criticizes 'senses' for showing us a unified, permanent world, where there is only a flux. Nietzsche usually has high regards for Heraclitus, but now he protests, "senses do not lie at all," because *they are* the flux, the chaos that Heraclitus otherwise defends. In other words, senses do *not* show us a permanent unified world, and are as such not *responsible* for 'lying.' They *are* themselves the chaos which no longer have a background (i.e., a 'thing-in-itself' world) against which they can be judged either 'true' or 'false.'

Senses are here the same as *sense-impressions* or *sense-data*, with us in the receiving end of these impressions. Since we do not and cannot *receive* something differently from how we receive it, nor have any influence on what and how we receive what we receive, we can no longer talk about receiving data some of which do lie and some that do not—and that seems to be what Nietzsche has in mind. Since, furthermore, impressions or data are our primary encounter with the world, we also cannot conclude that they are *about something* that is not a lie, because that would falsely imply that we could encounter this other something. However, as Nietzsche says elsewhere, we have no 'organs' for knowing such *another something*: "We simply have no organ for *knowing*, for 'truth': we 'know' (or believe or imagine we do) exactly as much as may be *useful* to the human herd, to the species."[81]

Nietzsche's 'senses,' i.e., sense-impressions/sense-data, are now redefined as a 'chaos.' Such a chaos is without reference to *something-other* since *chaos is chaos* and cannot refer back to *order*. Logically speaking, if Nietzsche is reducing everything to sense-appearances, he has abandoned the logical possibility for *falsifying a ground*. If sense-appearances are our first encounter with 'the world,' there is no ground for that ground and we cannot sneak a peek into something even more primordial; there is as such no first ground that sense-appearances could be 'falsifying.' In this sense, Clark's reading is *correct*, but her conclusion *incorrect*, as I see it: Nietzsche does not here restore his everywhere reiterated criticism of the 'thing-in-itself,' he rather deals the in-itself its final death-blow.

As we continue reading the passage, it is clear that Nietzsche is talking about falsification happening on another level. Senses (i.e., sense-impressions/-data) do not lie, but what we *make of them* do (*was wir aus ihrem Zeugniss machen, das legt erst die Lüge hinein*); we notice that Nietzsche emphasizes 'machen.' So, *sense-receptions* may not lie, but our *processing* of them lie, falsify, or interpret. We live as such a lie in which we have constructed a simple and self-given world 'out there' (a world of 'objects') from our original sensational chaos, a lie created by our perceptive-cognitive apparatus, which Nietzsche in the passage calls our 'reason' [*Vernunft*] (*"Die 'Vernunft' ist die Ursache, dass wir das Zeugniss der Sinne fälschen*).*"*[82] This so-called 'reason' (*Vernunft*), we may be inclined to think as of linguistic nature,[83] but in the passage, Nietzsche talks about a *perceptive reason* that we must regard as pre-linguistic, since it is (as the spontaneous abbreviation and simplification of the chaotic sense-data world) accountable for a cognitive-perceptive ordering of the universe that is shared by all higher animals; specifically, we read that this ordering achieves, *"die Lüge der Einheit, die Lüge der Dinglichkeit, der Substanz, Der Dauer."*[84]

The outcome of this processing of data is obviously that in our perception of objects, they verily appear as whole, unified, and distinct. Still, this perception of a world of objects is now, in Nietzsche's language, our 'lie' and 'falsification.' It is dramatic language, and possibly overly dramatic, because it implies only that we, qua our cognitive and linguistic capabilities, are introducing an order into our sense-data world that has no match in that world itself. Nietzsche's view is here identical to Mach and Vaihinger's, often expressed in similar vocabulary, since Mach and Vaihinger talk about the distinct, independent, and self-identical object as a *fiction*.[85]

When Nietzsche in notes from 1887 and 88 attempts to give a psychological explanation of 'entities,' he sees them as deriving from our own false sense of self-identity projected into the world as the identity of the 'thing' and/or of the 'atom.' From this false sense of self emerge our false beliefs in individuals and singularities as such:

> It is only according to the model of the subject that we have invented the *thingness* [*Dinglichkeit*] and projected it unto the medley of sensations. If we no longer believe in the *effective* subject, then belief also disappears in *effective* things, in interaction, cause and effect between those phenomena that we call things. Equally disappears, of course, the world of *effective atoms:* the assumption of which always depended on the supposition that there has to be subjects.[86]

We need unities, in order to calculate, but this does not imply that such unities exist in themselves.

> We have borrowed the notion of unity from our "ego" concept [*"Ich"begriff*],—our oldest article of faith. If we had not regarded ourselves as unities, we would also never have formed the concept of "thing." Nowadays, rather lately, we have been abundantly convinced that our conception of an ego-concept [*Ich-Begriff*] does not confirm a real unity.[87]

One assumes this important "fable," "fiction," or "article of faith" of the unity of 'self' for the sake of self-preservation. In order to survive, humans necessarily simplify a world too complex and chaotic in its immediate display, the most rudimentary mechanism for simplification being the false notion of self (cf.: "It is only according to the model of the subject that we have invented *thing-ness*," ibid.).

4. Nietzsche's Struggle with Structural Linguistic Language-Constraints

A final comment on Nietzsche's 'position 6' from GD. We are seeing how the old opposition apparent-true is collapsing; however, this collapse or 'deconstruction' does not come about easily for Nietzsche; he remains *constrained by* binary thinking because he in several instances in the late notes will be recycling the term 'apparent' in *new oppositions*, in *new binaries*, albeit always in order to make the point that it does not stand in opposition to 'true.' He continues to call the world we inhabit *apparent*—just not in opposition to *true*; thus, we notice that he goes on constructing other and different oppositions between for example, (1) 'appearance' and 'nothing,' or (2) 'appearance' and 'appearance,' or (3) 'appearance' and 'incomprehensible.'

Add 1: "The antithesis of the apparent world and the true world is reduced to the antithesis 'world' and 'nothing'"[88] In Nietzsche's new opposition, the concept 'apparent' changes value since it stands no longer opposed to 'true,' but to nothing. Instead of an 'apparent world' in contrast to a 'true world,' we have asserted a kind of new super-apparent world without any conceivable opposite. A new 'super-apparent' world is a world with no double and nothing hidden. *Add 2:* "The "true world," as one has always conceived it so far—this is always only the apparent world yet again [*noch einmal*]."[89] Nietzsche here suggests a new opposition where the opposite to the apparent world is not the thing-in-itself, but another apparent world, another but same surface-world, i.e., a repetition of the same surface-world. In this new conceptual opposition, apparent is opposed to apparent, i.e., to itself as the same; again, it designates a world with no double and nothing hidden. *Add 3:* "The opposition to this phenomena-world is not 'the true world,' but rather the world as a formless-inexpressible chaos of sensations [*die formlos-unformulirbare Welt des Sensationen Chaos*]—consequently, another kind of phenomena-world, for us 'incomprehensible' [*'unerkennbar'*]."⁹⁰ Here, the other apparent world from the preceding passage, is by Nietzsche qualified as chaotic, complex, and for us incomprehensible. He is arguing for two phenomenal worlds, one is for us apparent and the other is still apparent, but is for us 'incomprehensible.' Here he seems to slide back into position '5' from GD. There is the chaos of the incomprehensible, but we have no sign for and no representation of the incomprehensible, in which case the incomprehensible would have been comprehensible.

In the three cases, Nietzsche's overriding principle is that the world is a single surface only (cf. GD, *Die "scheinbare" Welt ist die einzige*⁹¹). When he continues to refer to oppositional language, it is because he cannot find a way to express himself without the binary,⁹² the binary opposition becomes his paradoxical linguistic tool when talking about that one and only *"scheinbare" Welt*. With an analogy (which is appropriately as impossible as is Nietzsche's linguistic dilemma) we might say that he envisions the world like the surface of a piece of paper, but without a backside (as a coin without flipside, a recto without verso). However, albeit we can express the idea, it is paradoxical and impossible to defend in the classical logic in which we are imbedded.

In a flat metaphysical universe, all theoretical explanation must necessarily refer back to this single surface-reality. We can no longer entertain notions of a hypothetical extra-real or supernatural world, because the new 'super-apparent' world implies a world of impenetrable surfaces only. A super-apparent world is so to speak *rock-solid*. It offers us no 'openings' through which we can escape or sneak a peek into some other extra-real or super-natural world. Metaphysically speaking, we live in (or on) this two-dimensional flatland blending seamlessly into this flatland ourselves (since our selves are as metaphysically 'flat' as the world surrounding us).

This is the material and real world as the opposite of a fictive or narrative world; it is a naked world to which we at best *attach* narratives, but it is not itself a narrative. This 'new' phenomena-world is itself *not fictional*, it is quite to the contrary the world as exposed in our sensations, and Nietzsche is not on this account an ontological fictionalist, but is on the contrary fighting the *concept* of a so-called 'True' world as 'fictional.' H. Vaihinger drew the same conclusions about the same time as Nietzsche, when he in the 1870s started working on a treatise that would later be published as *The Philosophy 'As If'* (cf. Part II, B.4: "The Fictional Concept in Vaihinger and Nietzsche"). The metaphysical narrative of a 'true' world is supposed to give our flatland a third dimension, which is not permitted in Nietzsche's epistemology; this is the *lie* we add to our two-dimensional flatland (cf. GD, *"das Sein [ist] eine leere Fiktion [...] die "wahre Welt" ist nur hinzugelogen"*⁹³). The discussion is strongly reminiscent of Mach and Vaihinger's 'critical positivism' as a monistic principle opposed to traditional dualism (cf. Part II, B).⁹⁴

4. Three Pillars of Nietzschean Positivism: Phenomenalism Perspectivism Relativism

For the proponents of the correspondence theory of truth our 'best sciences' correspond to an objectivity that is 'discovered.' Scientific laws are generally applicable because they allegedly correspond to 'truth,' implying the equation, *Thing-In-Itself = Truth*.

The Nietzschean proposal replaces the equation *Thing-In-Itself = Truth* with a perceptive-cognitive apparatus interpreting the world first in perception, thereupon in languages, and lastly in formal languages. When the 'thing-in-itself' is removed, 'correspondence' is necessarily removed, and scientific 'discoveries' are no longer discoveries in the sense that they 'reveal' or 'match' a 'thing.' They now emerge as condensed economic expressions for certain relationships in a universe of indefinitely many possible relationships.

The consequence of the theory is that we have asserted a "new infinite" as Nietzsche says in an aphorism from GS:

> *Our new "Infinite."* How far the perspectival character of existence [*Dasein*] extends, whether it has another character, or whether existence without interpretation, without 'meaning' or even 'non-meaning,' exists; in other words, if not all being [*Dasein*] essentially is *interpreting* [*Auslegendes*] being, that cannot be determined even by the most diligent and extremely-conscientious analysis [...]. We cannot look around our own corner. It is hopeless curiosity to want to know what other kinds of intellect and perspectives there might be. [...] But I think that today we are at least far removed from the ridiculous immodesty to decree from our angle that one can only have perspectives from this angle. The world has become 'infinite' again, insofar as we cannot reject the possibility that it in itself *includes infinite interpretations*.[95]

In the passage, we are explicitly seen as situated in a natural-biological world, in which we have evolved our specific perceptive-cognitive capabilities, which therefore cannot be suspended at will. In the passage, it is explicitly a "ridiculous immodesty [to decree] from our angle that perspectives are permitted only from this angle." Appearances are now constituting our 'new infinite,' because they are never seen as the same, and they can never be finally explained by any artificially, i.e., metaphysically, invented anchoring point like God, Truth, Thing, Object, Substance, or Cause. Our world is envisioned as a surface continuing forever; in this sense, 'eternally recurring as the same.'

This surface-world is also a *Relations-Welt* on which elements are interrelated and interconnected, but from "our angle." In a passage below from the late notes (1888), Nietzsche attempts to express his *Relations-Welt* as a world of functional relationships between "points."

> The world, apart from our condition of living in it, the world that we have not reduced to our being, our logic, and psychological prejudices does *not* exist as a world 'in-itself' it is essentially a world of relationships [*Relations-Welt*]: it has, under certain conditions, a *different look* [*Gesicht*] from each and every point [*Punkt*]; its being [*Sein*] is essentially different in every point; it presses upon every point, every point resists it. [...] Our particular case is interesting enough: we have produced a conception in order to be able to live in a world, in order to perceive just enough to *endure it*.[96]

"Points" press upon and resist each other, and this play of pressures and resistances must constitute the relations. Notice that Nietzsche here avoids talking about cause-effect relationships; a 'point' is any position in a relationship-net he calls 'world'; a 'point' must be the abstract idea of a location from where something has a relation to something else. There is thus no *absolute* location, no absolute 'eye' *seeing*, and no absolute 'cause' *effecting*. As little as Mach's elements exist alone, Nietzsche's 'points' do. If we imagine a point as an intersection in the net, it has obviously no longer location, nor existence, if we take away the 'net.'[97]

This Nietzschean *Relations-welt* seems to be in itself relative; not merely *made* relative by *us*, for example as in the familiar example where individuals walk around looking at pre-given objects from different angles.[98] It may be rather the other way around, instead of a 'world' being an objective in-itself with us relativizing this in-itself, the world is itself relative, while *we objectify* this relative world out of biological necessity. *We create* unity out of the given fragmentary element-world:

> A calculable world of *identical* cases must first be created from *appearances*. [...] 'Appearance' is an arranged and simplified world, at which our *practical* instincts have been at work: it is perfectly true for us; namely insofar as we *live*, are able to live in it.[99]

Given our species-specific 'falsification' of the world, there is no *the* world, there is only *our* world; i.e., the world given to us from our biological *perspective* (cf., "we are adapted to a perspectival way of seeing [...] as creatures of our species must in order to preserve their existence."[100]) We have suggested that this 'biological species-specific perspective' expresses the most general sense of Nietzsche's notion of 'perspectivism'; as species, *homo sapiens*, we have, in order to orient ourselves and act in the world, evolved a certain perspective from which (and *how*) to sense, which is uniquely *ours* (cf. Part I, A.3: "Biological Perspectivism").

In aphorism 354 from GS, Nietzsche addresses several issues such as language, communication, consciousness, and thinking. In this aphorism, he explicitly labels his epistemological position, "phenomenalism *and* perspectivism":

> *Of 'the Genius of the Species.'* [...] All our actions are essentially incomparably personal, unique, and boundlessly individual. Of that there is no doubt, but as soon as we translate them into consciousness, *they seem no longer to be so*. This is the true phenomenalism and perspectivism, as *I* understand it [*Dies ist der eigentliche Phänomenalismus und Perspektivismus, wie ich ihn verstehe*]. The nature of *animal consciousness* entails that the world, that we are able to become conscious about, is only a surface- and sign-world; a generalized and trivialized world. Everything that becomes conscious, becomes with this flat, thin, relatively stupid, general, sign, herd-mark; all becoming conscious implies an enormous and thorough degeneration, falsification, superficialization, and generalization. [...] We simply have no organ for knowledge, for 'Truth.' We 'know' (or believe or imagine) exactly as much as it is in the interest for the human herd [*Menschen-Heerde*], the species, to create as useful.[101]

When in the passage 'perspectivism' and 'phenomenalism' are used synonymously as concepts for the one and same position, it must be legitimate to conclude that *Perspectivism is Phenomenalism* in Nietzsche's theorizing. They both entail *Relativism*, because the position implies that we as species know only the world in its surface-manifestation, as 'points' in an infinitely expanding net, and only insofar as we make this surface knowable in (perceptive and linguistic) signs, i.e., to the extend we become perceptively and conceptually conscious of this surface-world. This 'becoming conscious' designates simultaneously a generalization and a falsification of the world, but not in the sense that we should expect a 'true' world lying hidden behind the sign-world, i.e., a 'true' world the sign *represents and refers* to as an in-itself saved from falsification.

If we see the outlines of a face in a cloud-formation, it is because of our interpretation of this formation, not because the 'face' refers to a face hidden in the clouds. The cloud-formation is in this example our chaos, forming, reforming, and deforming itself as world of 'infinite becoming'; our pattern-recognition in this world of chaos is an activity attributable to human ingenuity and need to see *the familiar*.

Nietzsche again debunks the epistemic desire for absolute knowledge; we have 'no organ' for knowing in this metaphysical sense; we only 'know' (scare quotes again) according to our species-specific biological needs.

5. 'Long Live Science' as the 'Best Possible' Falsification

1. Objective Relativism

The replacement of an objective world composed of independent objects with a world of relationship, entails in Nietzsche as well as in Mach not the entire disappearance of 'constancy,' but rather the replacement of the constancy of substances with the constancy of relationships. Compare to Mach:

> Really unconditioned constancy does not exist. [...] We attain to the idea of absolute constancy only as we overlook or underrate conditions, or as we regard them as always given, or as we deliberately disregard them. There is only one sort of constancy, which embraces all the cases that occur, namely, constancy of connection or of relation. Substance or matter is not anything unconditionally constant. What we call matter is a combination of the elements or sensations according to certain laws. [...] [We] take as constant a fixed law of connexion among elements, which in themselves seem extremely unstable.[102]

In this 'objective theory of relativity,' the world itself is not constant and substances are not permanent. We may therefore suggest that Nietzsche and Mach's epistemology proposes a "Objective Relativism." Constancy and permanency are in Mach as in Nietzsche human additions to a fluctuating world. Thanks to simplification of multiplicity, detail, and nuance, we impose upon the world constancy, regularity, and order.

In Mach, so-called 'objects' are constituted from 'sensational elements' forming patterns we pragmatically understand as 'objects.' It is a conceptual abbreviation to talk about a world of *objects*, of *things*, of *bodies*, or of *facts*. Therefore, in Mach (as in Nietzsche), the classical value-hierarchy between 'things' and 'appearances' is deconstructed and turned on its head. We no longer assume that *objects* are original and *appearances* are copies of the original. We do not assume that appearances are anchored in 'objects' or 'facts'; they are *presentations in* a world of elements, relations, and perspectives, *not representations of* a world of *things*. In this conceptual context, a 'fact' is an abstraction, the reduced/simplified result of something else and more chaotic, such as a flicker of impressions or a multitude of data selected according to certain interests. In the reproduction of facts in thought, we never reproduce the facts in full, but only that side of them which is important to us, moved to this directly or indirectly by a practical interest. Our reproductions are invariably abstractions.

2. The Nobility of the Scientist

Nietzsche's late thinking does not come across as a dismissal of the importance of scientific inquiry. It appears rather as a psychological analysis of how the empirical sciences proceed when they research a topic. Scientists, insofar as they are anti-dogmatic and anti-metaphysical, refuse to resort to a higher divine intelligence for explanation. They start by observing a phenomenon (selected from the chaotic abundance of possibilities because it is regarded as useful for us to know), and they tend to expect the phenomenon to be an effect deriving from possible causes. After a period of experimentation, hypothesizing, and theoretical re-adjustments, they 'situate' a cause that they are compelled to understand as preceding the phenomenon. As such interpreted, Nietzsche's 'anthropic circle' describes the *logos* and *ethos* of proper empirical research.

Scientists must interpret and humanize the world in the sense discussed above like anyone else, but we notice that the later Nietzsche significantly describes the sciences as providing us with the *most accurate, most faithful* humanization of the world. So, in GS:

> It is sufficient to regard science as the *best possible and most faithful* [or 'accurate': *getreue*] humanization [*Anmenschlichnung*] of the things. We always learn to describe ourselves ever more accurately by describing things and their successions.[103]

Also in GS, he praises the scientists in unambiguous terms; again, the focus is on the psychological attempt to understand the scientific mindset:

> Now this 'severity of science' has something in common with the form and decorum of the very best society: it frightens the uninitiated. But someone accustomed to it wants to live nowhere else than in this bright, transparent, strongly electric air - in this *masculine* air. [...] In *this* severe and clear element he has his full strength: here he can fly! Why descend into those murky waters where one has to swim and wade and sully one's wings?[104]

Later in GS, Nietzsche explicitly declares, "Long live physics!"[105]

Certainly, Nietzsche must for the sake of consistency believe that scientists 'humanize' nature in their scientific explanations. If he is right in his explanation of 'causes,' then even scientists must be guided by a fundamental psychological drive to appease their fear of the unknown and made the strange known. He must continue to insist on the so-called 'fear-factor' as one of the driving motives in the production of knowledge.

> The first instinct in the knowing subject is *to seek a rule*: while obviously, with the ascertainment of the rule, nothing has been "known"—hence the superstition of the physicists: that which they have halted, that is, where the regularity of the phenomena allows the application of an abbreviating [or reductive; *abkürzenden*] formula, that *they believe is known* [*Erkennt*]. They feel 'secure'; but

behind this intellectual security stand the appeasement of their fear: *they want the rule*, because it disrobes the world of fearfulness. *The fear of the unpredictable is the background-instinct* of science.[106]

Nietzsche cannot consistently jettison his fundamental belief that we 'humanize' out of fear of the unknown, but he can applaud this humanization in the sciences. With their scientific imagination and creativity, scientists find metaphors for processes, which are thoroughly language-independent; the so-called 'background-instinct of science' therefore does not imply a criticism of the sciences and their task. It only indicates Nietzsche's realization that we as humans cannot suspend our profound self-involvement in our production of knowledge. He must take for granted that we cannot communicate, or even understand, the language-independent, but we can simplify and create economic expressions for relations and sequences often perceived. Scientific formulae are such economic expressions, mathematical metaphors, for complex processes. They are approximations serving our practical need to organize and control our environment.

Thus, his critical discussion of causality cannot be seen as a denunciation of scientific thinking as such—as little as we would want to accuse Lange, Avenarius, and Mach for denouncing scientific thinking. However, they do all criticize *traditional metaphysical* conceptions of science, for example the traditional understanding of truth, substance, and causality found in classical and pre-modern theories of knowledge.

B: NIETZSCHE AND CRITICAL POSITIVISM

1. From Materialism to Agnosticism

1. Laplace's 'Universal Mind' vs Du Bois-Reymond's 'Ignorabimus'

In the nineteenth century's neo- and post-Kantian intellectual climate, we find a long and sustained discussion of knowledge, trying to come to terms with Kant's notion of the "thing-in-itself." Everybody agrees that the old theological metaphysics is dead, i.e., that knowledge has no spiritual foundation, but one still hopes to establish a foundational principle with the same authority, namely a principle that can guarantee the objectivity of the sciences and the scientific laws. In the emerging materialism of the late eighteenth and early nineteenth centuries, the Kantian 'thing-in-itself' still has a role to play as the placeholder for matter, forces, substances, and causes.[107] In the materialism defending these entities, often referred to as 'mechanical materialism' (in Lange, often dismissed as 'naïve materialism'), natures smallest constituents are 'corpuscular atoms' and their associated central forces. It is in its days a radical explanation of the universe insofar as one has suspended the reference to spiritual causes.

If we heuristically distinguish between 'literal' and 'metaphorical' interpretations of the 'thing-in-itself,' 'mechanical materialism' espouses a 'literal' interpretation of the 'thing,' since corpuscular atoms are conceived as unitary, substantial, and foundational entities supposedly existing independently of the perceiving being. The 'thing' is as such a *hidden some-thing*; it is *as if* a lump of matter *actually* existing albeit not accessible for-us. As both *in-itself and hidden*, it is assumed to be *present in its hiding*, and is therefore conceived as a material and substantial actual cause of appearances. In this sense it represents 'truth' antedating appearances. A seen above (cf. Part I, A.9: "Nietzsche's Empiricist Neo-Kantianism"), this interpretation of the 'thing-in-itself' is later rejected by several contemporary neo-Kantians, because a thing-in-itself seen as *cause* and *substance*, cannot be allowed in the Kantian philosopher insofar as both of these two determinations are described as *categories*. *If* the thing is *cause*, it contradicts Kant who emphasized that *causality* is a category applicable only in the apparent world; *if* the thing is *substance*, it also contradicts Kant, who emphasized that *substance* is a category applicable only in the apparent world.[108]

Partly because of such logical inconsistencies, the construction and the principles it harbors is throughout the century seen by leading theoreticians to be mired in problems and paradoxes, as they start to question *any* material concept of an 'in-itself' (including the in-itself of atoms, energies, forces, and causes). Figures such as A. Comte, E. du Bois-Reymond, H. von Helmholtz, and Fr. A. Lange see the shortcomings of mechanical materialism, and suggest that profound questions about ultimate foundations do not have an answer. Perhaps, they suggest, we should resign ourselves to the idea that we can and shall never know the ultimate principles, i.e., that we are and shall forever stay ignorant. They conclude to what I will call 'epistemological agnosticism' (in distinction to but foreshadowing the subsequently developing 'epistemological positivism'). They object to the idea of an 'in-itself' because it as construction promotes something which per definition and deduction is inaccessible. Mobilizing different arguments, they see this as inconsistent, paradoxical, if not outright absurd. The very distinction between world and thinking, world and mind, world and subject seems problematic because *the dualism as such* postulates an inaccessible 'real' world that remains unknown as independent of our thinking.[109]

In their reformulation of the inaccessible 'thing,' they tend to adopt a 'metaphorical' interpretation of the 'thing,' which is as such seen as merely an expression of the unknown as such. It is conceptualized as a *limit-concept*

[*Grenzbegriff*], cf. Fr. Lange, i.e., the limit we cannot transgress given our species-specific perceptive apparatus. On this interpretation, Kant's suggestion of an inaccessible 'in-itself' is rehabilitated as foreshadowing scientific advances and he is applauded because he has anticipated an insight consolidated by psycho-physiology, namely that we have no direct access to 'things.' When he in the second edition of *Critique of Pure Reason* seems to rehabilitate the 'in-itself,' he is in the same measure criticized by the same neo-Kantians applauding his first edition (cf. discussion Part I, A.9: "Nietzsche's Empiricist Neo-Kantianism").

We find this discussion present already in A. Comte in his *A System of Positive Philosophy* (1842),[110] and echoed by J. Stuart Mill in both his *Auguste Comte and Positivism* (1865/1907)[111] and his *Examination of Sir William Hamilton's Philosophy* (1865).[112] Comte argues that we can have knowledge only of phenomena and that this knowledge is relative, not absolute. We know nothing of essences, but know only "facts" and the "relations" of these facts to one another by means of succession and similitude (Nietzsche will later dispute Comte's notion of 'facts,' albeit not his notion of 'relations'). Only in the relations between Comte's 'facts,' we see their objectivity secured since relationships remain constant in the way they are organized in sequences of what is antecedent and what is consequent. However, their essential nature, their substance or ultimate causes are unknown to us. Comte suggests his positive philosophy in juxtaposition to two other modes of thought that he sees preceding Positivism, the so-called Theological and the so-called Metaphysical, in his famous sketch of the development of knowledge into its final Positive state.

> In the *theological state*, the human mind, seeking the essential nature of beings, the first and final causes (the origin and purpose) of all effects, in short, Absolute knowledge supposes all phenomena to be produced by the immediate action of supernatural beings. In the *metaphysical state*, which is only a modification of the first, the mind supposes, instead of supernatural beings, abstract forces, veritable entities (that is, personified abstractions) inherent in all beings, and capable of producing all phenomena. What is called the explanation of phenomena is, in this stage, a mere reference of each to its proper entity. In the final, the *positive state*, the mind has given over the vain search after Absolute notions, the origin and destination of the universe, and the causes of phenomena, and applies itself to the study of their laws, that is, their invariable relations of succession and resemblance. Seasoning and observation, duly combined, are the means of this knowledge. What is now understood when we speak of an explanation of facts is simply the establishment of a connection between single phenomena and some general facts, the number of which continually diminishes with the progress of science.[113]

In the theological state, nature is seen as animated by the presence of the divine, while in the metaphysical, one has abandoned the idea of a spiritual animation of the world while still asserting the existence of certain powers or forces as the true nature residing in things or objects. This 'metaphysical' position, as described by Comte, may describe also the 'mechanical materialism' outlined above. Here forces are impersonal but are still assumed to be acting in nature in a manner that is analogous to the action of a divine spirit. Finally, in Comte's 'positive' phase, we have accepted the insight that such forces are inscrutable and resigned ourselves to our fundamental ignorance about the real nature of things (equivalent to the position termed 'epistemological agnosticism' above, and anticipating Du Bois-Reymond's position described below). Positive scientific knowledge is established by observing relationships of phenomena, as Comte emphasizes adopting a position that becomes immensely influential in the nineteenth century and will be further discussed in Epistemological Positivism emerging at the turn of the century.[114]

Emil du Bois-Reymond continues the discussion in his two influential essays, *Über die Grenzen des Naturerkennens* (1872) and *Die Sieben Welträthsel* (1880).[115] Du Bois-Reymond articulates here the problem in a way that will continue to reverberate into the twentieth century. If the 'thing-in-itself' is an unknown, our knowledge of the ultimate nature of the world will remain an enigma. This is in his later essay rendered as the so-called 'world-riddle.'

Du Bois-Reymond reacts in his essays to a version of mechanical materialism outlined above where atoms are substantial particles endowed with forces, as he is polemically referring to the prominent natural scientist Pierre-Simon Laplace, who had suggested that we might explain all natural processes, including our perception, experience, and consciousness, in terms of movements of atoms and their central forces. Moreover, Laplace would assume that all change happens according to the energy conservation law and the sum-total of potential and kinetic energy therefore remained constant. Granted that the number of atoms must be finite in a finite universe, Laplace suggested that we hypothetically should be able to explain all processes in nature if only we knew the first initial condition and if we had a universal mind understanding the position of atoms at any single moment. In that case, we would then be able to reconstruct all preceding moments and all subsequent moments by derivation or deduction. In the words of Laplace,

> A mind, which at a given instant should know all the forces acting in Nature [...] providing its power were sufficiently vast to analyze all these data, could embrace in one formula the movements of the largest bodies in the universe, and

those of the smallest atom; nothing would be uncertain to such a mind, and the future, like the past, would be present to its eyes. The human intellect offers, in the perfection to which it has brought astronomy, a faint idea of what such a mind would be.[116]

Du Bois summarizes the influential thesis in the following passage: "As the changes of the physical world are reduced to a constant sum of potential and kinetic energy, which is inseparable from a constant quantity of matter, there remains in these changes themselves nothing further that needs explanation."[117]

It is this 'theory of everything' that Du Bois-Reymond critically discusses. Laplace is obviously making a hypothetical proposal and he does not believe that we anytime soon have access to such a universal super-computer, as it were. Still, the hypothesis expresses the optimistic scientific view that we may in principle be able understand everything. It represents the dream of a unified theory explaining everything by reducing it to a single differential equation that can be applied to any case. Laplace's universal mind would theoretically not only know all acting forces in exterior nature, it would include knowledge of the trajectories of sense-impressions moving from the outside, to the retina, to the brain, and here causing conscious thought, which would now be illuminated and "understood" by the mechanical view as well.

German philosopher, Maximilian Drossbach, adopted the idea in two works where he attempted to resolve the epistemological mind/world dualism by means of this theory of moving atoms enforcing themselves upon the mind with different degrees of 'force,' therefore received differently, ultimately giving rise to our experience of a richly differentiated world. According to the model, forces with different degrees of strength are transporting the outer world into the inner world of the mind along a linear trajectory, and secure as such a causal correspondence between outer and inner.[118]

As a physiologist, Du Bois begs to disagree with this new materialism and raises two critical objections. First, he sees a problem in the conceptual efficiency of Laplace's explanation, and secondly, he objects that a theory of atoms and their central forces cannot explain qualitative sense-impressions.

Add 1. Laplace assumes that the atom is indivisible and that it constitutes the smallest possible substance. This is in the debate referred to as the 'corpuscular atom' (or as Nietzsche later mocks the idea, the "clump atom"[119]). This substantial and indivisible atom is in itself unexplained and cannot be explained any further within the theory, partly because it does not allow the existence of any smaller mass, and partly because it merely transfers to the infinitesimally small our most habitual experiences of an embodied world.

> But we make no advance whatever toward an understanding of things, since we, in fact, carry over into the region of the minute and the invisible the concepts we obtain in the region of the gross and the visible. Thus it is that we acquire the notion of the physical atom. If now we arbitrarily stop the process of dividing at some point where we are supposed to have reached philosophical atom, that are indivisible, perfectly hard, and furthermore per se inefficient, being merely the carriers of the central forces, we are expecting that a matter which we think of under the concept of matter as known to us should, without the aid of a new principle of explication, develop new primordial properties, to explain the nature of bodies.[120]

Du Bois argues that our perceptive image of a body is translated to the infinitesimally small in the concept of a corpuscular atom. We transfer back to the theory of atoms our experience of an embodied world and construct on this basis the corpuscular and indivisible atom. If now we use the atom as an explanation of physiological processes, we have achieved nothing, because we are using our pre-formed knowledge of bodies transferred onto the infinitesimally small as matrix for explanation. We have only randomly stopped the division of matter at the indivisible and invisible atom, and thereby claimed that our new extremely small substance explains everything. The explanatory power of the atomic theory can give intellectual satisfaction only as long as we are able to *repress* the fact that our corpuscular atom is drawn from our most familiar and habitual appearances.

> The conception of the world as consisting of minute parts that have always existed, and that are indestructible, and whose central forces produce all motion, is only a sort of substitute for an explanation. As has been remarked, it reduces all changes in the physical world to a constant sum of forces and a constant quantity of matter, and thus leaves in the changes themselves nothing that requires explanation. Given the existence of this constant, we can, in our joy for this new insight, be content for a little while; but soon we long to penetrate deeper and to comprehend it in its own substance.[121]

Add 2. Du Bois's thereupon objects that qualitative sense-impressions cannot be explained by a theory of atoms and their central forces. Even simple mental facts that we share with animals, such as sense-perceptions and pleasure/pain sensations, cannot be explained by the matter and force of atoms because they are concepts describing only inert mass and movement. The inert mass itself is passive and can inspire nothing in the brain, leaving only the central forces as an account of movement. However, our brains cannot pick up these movements. Consequently, even if we were equipped with Laplace's astronomical knowledge of all moving masses in the mind, it could not help us understanding our most simple experiences. Du Bois-Reymond asks rhetorically, "What conceivable connection subsists between definite movement of definite atoms in my brain, one the one hand, and on the other hand such primordial, indefinable, undeniable facts as these: 'I feel pain or pleasure; I experience a sweet taste, or smell a rose, or hear an organ, or see something red.'"[122] The possible alternative explanation, rhetorically suggested but immediately ruled out, had to be that the various atoms, like small monads, had a consciousness of their own, and somehow could collaborate in forming the mind's consciousness.

> It would be profoundly interesting if we, with the mind's eye, [...] could say what play of the carbon, hydrogen, nitrogen, oxygen, phosphorus, and other atoms, corresponds to the pleasure we experience on hearing musical sounds. [...] Still. as regards mental operations themselves, it is clear that, even with astronomical knowledge of the mind-organ, they would be as unintelligible as they are now. Were we possessed of such knowledge, they would still remain perfectly unintelligible. Astronomical knowledge of the brain [...] discloses to us nothing but matter in motion. [...] Motion can only produce motion, or be converted back into potential energy. Potential energy can only produce time, maintain static equilibrium, or exert pressure or traction. The sum of energy, however, remains the same. Beyond this law nothing can go in the physical world, nor can anything fall short of it; the mechanical cause passes completely into the mechanical effect. Hence the mental phenomena, [...] are so far as our understanding is concerned, void of sufficient basis. [...] What conceivable connection subsists between definite movement of definite atoms in my brain, one the one hand, and on the other hand such primordial, indefinable, undeniable facts as these: "I feel pain or pleasure; I experience a sweet taste, or smell a rose, or hear an organ, or see something red." And the immediately-consequent certainty, "therefore I exist?" It is absolutely and forever inconceivable that a number of carbon, hydrogen, nitrogen, oxygen, etc., atoms should not be indifferent as to their own position and motion past present or future. It is utterly inconceivable how consciousness should result from their joint action. If their respective positions and their motion were not indifferent to them, they would have to be regarded as each possessed of a consciousness of its own, and as so many monads. But this would not explain consciousness in general, nor would it in the least assist us in understanding the unitary consciousness of the individual.[123]

Du Bois concludes on this discussion that not only do we not known the nature of the two metaphysical entities, matter and force, in which we place such confidence in eventually providing us with final answers to the 'world-riddle.' Not only are we ignorant (*Ignoramus*), but the riddle is of a nature that will prevent us from *ever* knowing, we shall stay forever ignorant (*Ignorabimus*). Du Bois therefore ends his essay with one word, *IGNORABIMUS*, emphasized and capitalized, summarizing his epistemological position.

With regard to the enigma of the physical world the investigator of Nature has long been wont to utter his "*Ignoramus*" with manly resignation. As he looks back on the victorious career over which he has passed, he is upheld by the quiet consciousness that wherein he now is ignorant, he may at least under certain conditions be enlightened that he yet will know. But as regards the enigma what matter and force are, and how they are to be conceived, he must resign himself once for all to the far more difficult confession: "IGNORABIMUS"![124]

The conclusion shocked the enlightened scientific community. 'Ignorant' yes, but 'forever ignorant,' seemed like a significant step back from early nineteenth-century scientific optimism.[125]

Lange is generalizing this conclusion of Du Bois when he says:

If our notions do not regulate themselves according to things, but things according to our notions, it follows immediately from this that the objects of experience altogether are only our objects; that the whole objective world is, in a word, not absolute objectivity, but only objectivity for man and any similarly organized beings, while behind the phenomenal world, the absolute nature of things, the 'thing-in-itself,' is veiled in impenetrable darkness.[126]

This provisional conclusion of the contemporary epistemological debate, "we shall never know," "the world is and will remain a riddle," forever "veiled in impenetrable darkness," I label here *epistemological agnosticism*. I argue that it is eventually replaced with the more radical *epistemological positivism* (which will be introduced under a number of different labels such as *phenomenalism, emperio-criticism, fictionalism,* or *constructivism*). Applied to Nietzsche, we may understand him defending these two positions in various stages of his work: In TL (*mutatis mutandis*) he defends *epistemological agnosticism* declaring our ignorance of the thing-in-itself, and ends in later writings defending *epistemological positivism* rejecting the relevance of the thing-in-itself altogether.

2. Different Interpretations of the In-Itself in Helmholtz, Spir, and Ueberweg

Helmholtz agrees that we live in a world of representations, of so-called "sensible signs," which the subject eventually will learn to distinguish as signifying particular objects thanks to repeated associations achieved through learning-processes. Perceptions are therefore to Helmholtz *signs* but *not images*, as he understands signs to be *arbitrary representations* of the object, while images are *true reflections* of the object (as such, *corresponding* to the object).

Insofar as the quality of our sensation gives us information about the peculiarity of the external influence stimulating it, it can pass for a sign—but not for an image. [...] A sign, however, need not have any type of similarity with what it is a sign for. The relations between the two are so restricted that the same subject, taking effect under equal circumstances, produces the same sign, and hence unequal signs always correspond to unequal effects.[127]

Helmholtz still believes, however, that perceptive signs are produced by external causes, and confirms in this sense the existence of an exteriority outside our subjectivity and its categories. This view makes Helmholtz a less radical neo-Kantian than for example Schopenhauer, Liebmann, and Fischer (cf. discussion Part I, A.9: "Nietzsche's Empiricist Neo-Kantianism"), who argued that referring to the outside, the exteriority, as *causing* the inside, the interiority, was misunderstood Kantianism confusing the *category 'cause'* for a *material cause*.

In *Physiologische Optik*,[128] Helmholtz had emphasized the representational aspect of the new 'naturalistic materialism,' with affinities to 'Phenomenalism,' 'Positivism,' and 'Pragmatism.' The 'represented' and the 'representing' is still, as in Nietzsche's TL, belonging to two entirely different worlds; representation being only 'symbols' of things.

> I believe that there can be no other sense in talking about a truth of our representations except a *practical*. Our representations of things *can* simply not be anything else but symbols, naturally given signs for things, which we only use as regulations for our movements and activities. [...] Any other comparison between representations and things is not given in reality—in this agree all schools—another form of comparison is not even thinkable and has no meaning. [...] To ask whether the representation which I have of this table, its form, stability, color, etc., has in-and-for-itself, apart from the practical use that I can make from this representation [...] makes as much sense as to ask if a certain tone is red, yellow, or blue. [...] Representation and represented belong quite obviously to two completely different worlds.[129]

Helmholtz agrees that we cannot know the "true essence of things,"[130] but he rejects subjective idealism and defends a physiologically amended materialism, a so-called "Empirical Theory" where "the actual sensible 'sign,' whether it be simple or complex, is recognized as the sign of that which it signifies."[131] The sensible sign is *arbitrary* relative to that which it signifies, but eventually this arbitrariness *does not matter* and has *no practical consequences*, because it inevitably ends up being associated with an 'object,' or rather, with that 'possibility' of an external object that we cannot access in undistorted perception. Our widely acknowledged imperfect vision therefore also *does not matter and has no practical consequences*, because despite the poor quality of our sense-apparatus, it will in perception render the object as repaired (e.g., represent the object standing upright and not on its head, or erase the blind spot in our visual field). The upshot is that the perceiving human being is at no point troubled with retinal images being inverted or double, because it has learnt that "the signification of the local signs which belong to our sensation of sight, so as to be able to recognize the actual relations which they denote."[132] Less than half a century later, another major scientist of the period, Ferdinand de Saussure, suggests that the *linguistic sign* is arbitrary like the *sensible sign* is arbitrary in Helmholtz. Again, we notice that *the paradigm as such* is replacing the classical substantive, causal, and permanent world with a relative, arbitrary, and dynamic.

Another important participant in this debate, also diligently referenced in Lange's *Geschichte*, is Friedrich Ueberweg, who in his *System der Logik*[133] acknowledges that 'understanding' is *a function* of a perceptive-cognitive apparatus, and suggests a formula expressing the new naturalist-biological-physiological materialism. Like Helmholtz and Lange, Ueberweg, too, is caught up in the ambivalence of the new physiological position, and concludes that it is no longer possible to declare oneself either a pure Idealist or a pure Materialist: "The thesis that the world of phenomena accommodates itself to things in themselves; and the antithesis it accommodates itself to the organs of sense—are both one sided and half true."[134]

On the one hand, Ueberweg acknowledges that the constitution of the world of phenomena is conditioned, at least in part, by the subjective nature of our sense: "Sense may be different in other beings, and so may produce other kinds of worlds of sense-phenomena. What actually exists as such, as it is in itself independent of any way of apprehending it, or the thing-in-itself, is different from all of these."[135] This rephrases the idea of 'biological perspectivism' we introduced above (cf. Part I, A.8" "Biological Perspectivism"). On the other hand, Ueberweg refuses to surrender to the skeptical position that cancels the external world because, however inaccessible the world as such may be, the 'causal relation' between the exteriority and the interiority is sufficient reason for the confidence we have in our representations: "The skeptical thought which asserts that our knowledge of the outer world is impossible, or at least unreliable, because it cannot be compared with its objects, is finally overcome by this, that the consideration of the causal relation gives a sufficient equivalent for the immediate comparison which is wanting."[136]

In order to substantiate the argument for this dualist approach, Ueberweg cites two attempts to formalize the problem offered by respectively Joshua Delboeuf and Sir Walter Hamilton.

> Delboeuf has discussed afresh the questions which belong to the inability to compare the conception with its object. He uses the formula: $A + f(a, x)$; that is, the real result, A, is not known as such, but must be brought about by a,

that is, the object-phenomenon, and x, that is, the nature of our mind. Sir W. Hamilton's explanation is not unlike Delboeuf's. Suppose that the total objects of consciousness in perception = *12*, and that the external reality contributes *6*, the material sense *3*, and the mind *3*. This may enable us to form some rude conjecture of the nature of the object of perception.[137]

If we paraphrase the two formulas, the world as in-itself is in Delboeuf's formula designated 'A,' unknown in-itself but appearing as known when we add the function of 'a' and 'x,' representing respectively the object-phenomenon and the nature of our mind. In Hamilton's formula, the represented world has the designation '12,' and is a function of partly '6' ("external reality"), partly '3' (the "material sense"), and partly '3' ("the mind"). Hamilton must here assume that parts of the represented world have been transferred from partly external objectivity, 6, partly from the sense-impressions, 3, and partly from the mind's reconstruction of the image of the object, 3.

Expanding on the formulaic expressions, we notice that the in-itself in the formulas is re-constructed as phenomenon as an outcome of what we insert in the function. If we designate the thing-in-itself as 'X' and the end-product, i.e., the re-created phenomenon, by a hieroglyph, Δ,[138] the function designates how a perceptive-cognitive process transforms X to Δ. The function itself may thus list a number of known or hypothetical agencies responsible for this transformative work. Thus interpreted, an expanded formula may consequently look like follows:

$$X = \int (x, y, z, \ldots) = \Delta$$

We have as such created a 'master-formula,' which in its form allows many different possibilities for the investment of contents. Helmholtz master-formula would approximately look like follows:

$$X = \int (\textit{sense-data, retina, brain}, \ldots) = \textit{sensible sign}$$

In Helmholtz, we receive data as effects of an external world, the retina then distorts the data, as does the visual centers of the brain, producing Helmholtz's hieroglyph, the sensible sign; that is, the arbitrary sign by which we learn to perceive our environment as a reality. Helmholtz is explicit in his emphasis of the 'x,' i.e., 'external cause': "Our sensations are precisely effects produced by external causes in our organs, and the manner in which one such effect expresses itself depends, of course, essentially on the type of apparatus which is affected."[139]

Helmholtz's insistence that 'sensual signs' as effects of external things seemed to more radical neo-Kantians like African Spir to indicate that he had still not abandoned the idea of a thing-in-itself and the dubious concept of cause. Spir therefore counter Helmholtz's view in this critical assessment:

> When we take a precise look at *which* things Helmholtz considers as causes for our representations, then it shows that he as these causes precisely understands things. [...] However, since Helmholtz himself says that what we imagine [*Vorstellen*] is completely incommensurable with real external things, he should as such also admit that we have no right to claim that actual external things are causes for our representations.[140]

Spir repeats the neo-Kantian argument of inconsistency when philosophers overstep Kant's Transcendental Aesthetics and apply categorical forms as if they are things-in-themselves (cf. Part I, "Nietzsche and Empiricist Neo-Kantianism"). Spir objects that even if we admit that the external thing may be a 'possibility' for our sensations, we still have no idea of what is might consist, adopting a positions reminiscent of Nietzsche's in TL. The "enigmatic x" is still an indefinable possibility of an exteriority, but it is so vaguely proposed that is has no epistemic authority, not even as 'cause' as 'sufficient reason' for impressions. We have "no right to claim that actual external things are causes for our representations," says Spir, in a statement that will reverberate in Nietzsche. The 'thing-in-itself' as 'cause' gives way for our more concrete 'sense-impressions' that are thereupon transformed into 'images'; finally, being transformed into 'words' and 'concepts.' The vague possibility of the enigmatic X is in any case lost in the end-product, i.e., Nietzsche's 'metaphors.' They at best only represent human ('anthropomorphic') versions of 'things/truths,' thus 'things/truths as illusions.' Our master-formula above might, in Nietzsche's case, be filled in as follows:

$$X = \int(nerve\text{-}stimuli, images, words, \dots\,) = metaphors$$

2. From Agnosticism to Positivist Nihilism

1. Epistemological Positivism and Affirmative Nihilism

Toward the end of the century, positivists and/or phenomenalists, such as Fr. Lange, R. Avenarius, E. Mach, H. Vaihinger, and Nietzsche, among many others, reject the preoccupation with the 'thing' from a pragmatic position, because the concept is useless and fulfills no purpose for the scientific researcher.

Emphasizing the psychological and cognitive element in our reception of 'world' implies already to Lange and other neo-Kantians that the knowledge we believe we produce about an 'outside world' must be conditional upon our inadequate perceptive apparatus. In Lange's 'naturalistic correction' of Kant, the inaccessible 'in-itself' is therefore a designation of that 'outside world' that we are constitutionally incapable of perceiving, as such making the notion of an 'in-itself' a limitative concept. The obvious question, lurking just around the corner, became quickly a philosophical theme in the following decades, i.e., 'what is the use and value of preoccupying oneself with a notion of something constitutionally inaccessible, given that we only understand appearances?' To Nietzsche at least, this idle preoccupation reminded too much of another precious idea to which we have absolutely no access, but continues to occupy idle minds, God!

In his *Geschichte*, Lange had explained that scientific discoveries were indeed impeded, not advanced, if or when scientists started searching for substances, essences, causes, and the like, in order to 'explain' their subject-matter.

> Physical science will never discover to us the internal constitution of things, which is not phenomenon, yet can serve as the ultimate ground of explanation of phenomena, but it does not require this for its physical explanations. [...] [Such] explanations must only be grounded upon that which, as an object of sense, can belong to experience, and be brought into connection with our real perceptions, according to the laws of experience.[141]

Lange draws the conclusion and asks pertinently, why at all occupy ourselves with the 'thing-in-itself.'

> Who says that we are to occupy ourselves at all with the, to us, inconceivable 'things-in-themselves'? Are not the natural sciences in every case what they are, and do they not accomplish what they accomplish, quite independently of the ideas as to the ultimate grounds of all nature to which we are ourselves conducted by philosophical criticism?[142]

Since the natural sciences accomplish whatever they accomplish independently of whether scientists believe in 'things' or not, it seems to Lange that the abandonment of the 'thing' only makes scientific observation more rigorous, because we then release ourselves from any residual belief in absolute essences, substances, foundations, or 'things,' and liberate ourselves from a futile constraint. Instead of chasing shadows, we accept our confinement to the apparent surface-world and resign ourselves to observing available data. From ignoring the shadow world, we ascent into the positive world of the phenomenon.

Lange understands his epistemology as a "corrected Kantianism" solidly planted in the real world, which, in a qualified sense, continues *Materialism* rather than *Idealism*. He describes it as "a materialism of the phenomenon," what implies that we are not impelled to study 'ideas,' but rather phenomena as material objects. Material *objects 'in-themselves'* are irrelevant for scientific study, *ideas* are equally irrelevant, but *phenomena as material objects* is the true entry point into this newly conceived positive world.[143]

Scientific formula that increase our understanding never aspire to understand substances or the true nature of the issue in question. The law of gravity, for example, is expressed as an equation between something called the *Gravitational Force*, F_g, and a functional relationship between two masses, their distance, and the relationship between their masses and distance. In order for the formula to work, no scientist needs to speculate about the nature of the 'gravitational force,' beyond that which is already expressed by the functional relationship on the right side of the equation,

$$F_g = GMm/d^2$$

There is in the equation nothing to the left side of the symbol for the gravitational force (F_g) that is worthwhile speculating about, no *thing-in-itself* or *enigmatic X*, which we consequently and in good conscience may cross out:

$$\sout{Enigmatic\ 'X'} = F_g = GMm/d^2$$

The substance, force, or energy (because we do not know what) that we would be searching for as 'explanation' of F_g is identical to the 'thing-in-itself,' the indefinable and enigmatic 'X'; consequently, identical to a purely speculative, metaphysical, and theological notion. This 'search' for idle knowledge is dis-allowed in the new naturalist-pragmatic-scientific thinking; the relationship expressed below gives us adequate and satisfactory knowledge.[144]

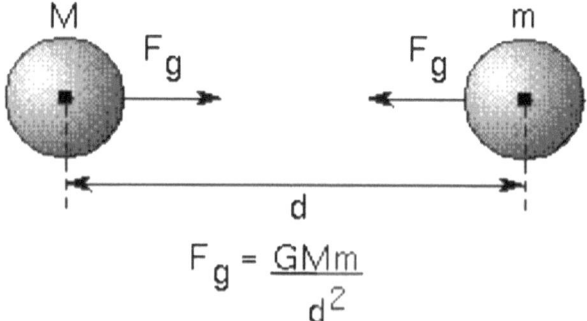

Figure 1   A Functional Relationship Explains the Gravitational Force, not Metaphysical Principles.

Whether one submits to Du Bois-Reymond's *Ignoramus* or *Ignorabimus*, whether one declares the 'I do not know' or 'we shall never know,' in either case, one seems to be asserting a spurious reference to the *unknown itself*, to *pure negativity or absence*. It now seems paradoxical that we, one the one hand, resign ourselves to our ignorance, but, on the other, continue to appeal to the *unknown thing*, construing effectively the *thing* as a *known unknown*. This is an obvious paradox, because if we cannot *know* the *unknown* we cannot know *if* the *unknown* is there in the first place; it is meaningless to assume that there is an unknown realm beyond the limits of knowledge, because it only presumes a world of eternally irresolvable problems that cannot be articulated as discernible problems within *our* world of appearances. The negating position continues to accept the thesis of a 'true' world as meaningful; it continues to tacitly assume a higher intelligence who *might* know all answers to our questions about the 'true' world. Ergo, one continues to assume an extra-worldly intelligence better informed than the ignorant human.[145]

However radical the ignorance-argument was when proposed by Du Bois-Reymond, it is now itself regarded as paradoxical, because it apparently continues the appeal to an unknowable in-itself while simultaneously insisting of our ignorance of this realm. This reiterated appeal is seen as the last refuge for an animated world. Now the new epistemologists suggest we rid ourselves of these last remnants of theological thinking, and instead restrict ourselves to affirming our encounter with a surface of appearances and our descriptions of this surface in our formal-conceptual languages. Science has as such no longer the task to explain or discover the pre-given, but to observe, describe, and reconstruct the given.

The new Pragmatic Positivists, Avenarius, Mach, Vaihinger, and Nietzsche, begin to question Du Bois-Reymond's 'world-riddle,' when they challenge the notion of a hidden world and aspire to replace it with knowledge that is and can be only positive. There can be *no knowledge of absence* and consequently *no appeal to the absent*, but only of that which *presents* itself. It is no longer relevant to try to determine Du Bois-Reymond's "Grenzen des Naturerkennens," because addressing the purely apparent, nothing is incomprehensible to our thinking; it is only within the limits of our experience that we can ask questions that are in principle answerable. Going outside this boundary indicates metaphysical speculation, which has no value. If or when we ask questions that do not have any conceivable answer, they are asked wrongly or illogically. One of the strongest commentators of this new epistemology, Joseph Petzoldt, summarize the project of Avenarius, Mach, and Nietzsche as follows: "The fundamental characteristic of the metaphysical consists in the assumption that there is an Absolute. The metaphysical speculation is consequently futile, a waste of time. These are fundamental assumptions in Avenarius, Mach, and Nietzsche's thinking."[146]

We notice that the 'agnostic position,' perhaps rather in its consequences than its intentions, was tacitly accepting a religious world-order reconfirming the Christian idea that, after all, our human intellect is powerless and impotent. The supposedly daring declaration that we 'only know that we do not know' had the tacit implication that *a deity does know the thing-in-itself.* It creates 'room for God,' as it re-creates a furtive chamber for all the hidden treasures of God's infinite intellect. However, the destruction of this last sanctuary for hidden knowledge leaves us (from a theological perspective) with *nothing*, and the resulting *Nihilism* becomes the new clean slate on which we create conceptual knowledge.

Nietzsche, often seen by the early positivists as the most poetic mind advancing their creed, will see this new-orientation of epistemology as an absolute break with theological thinking and an introduction to his particular *affirmative Nihilism* where the human is finally acknowledging its power to create values in an absolutely superficial surface world. *Affirmative Nihilism* is no longer a cry of despair over living in a meaningless universe; nor is it the late nineteenth century's entry-point into the science-hostile doctrines of the much later emerging postmodernism; nor does it resign itself to the meaninglessness of 'playful' discourse. Being 'affirmative,' it rather celebrates the potential of human reason for stabilizing a multifaceted and chaotic world in simplified formal languages. *Affirmative Nihilism* as *Epistemological Positivism* advances rather than degrades human reason. As such, it seems to the participants in the paradigm to represent a kind of *Epistemological Emancipation.*

It is a characteristic that the leading members of this movement attempt to think beyond the two general positions, *Materialism* and *Idealism*, as a traditional but over-simplifying classification of the current epistemological discussions. They routinely point out problems in both the consistent Materialist and the consistent Idealist position and attempt to think beyond these boxes, for example by replacing the lingering dualism in both of the positions with a monistic understanding of knowledge. The theorists we here refer to, i.e., Fr. Lange, R. Avenarius, E. Mach, H. Vaihinger, and (late) Nietzsche, attempt this strategy, although they in posterior discussions typically have been dragged back into the traditional dualism by self-declared 'materialists,' 'realists,' or 'objectivists,' accusing them of defending the familiar Idealist positions. They themselves denounce that characterization, but since Avenarius's radical empiricism, Mach's phenomenalism, and Nietzsche's interpretation-philosophy may be seen as dismissing the 'in-itself' (as such, objectivity *as such*), in favor of emphasizing the cognitive and psychological reception or 'interpretation' of things, they invariably seen as proponents of *Idealism*, defending a theory no different from Bishop Berkeley's. It is an allegation that was proposed already by W. I. Lenin, writing in opposition to R. Avenarius, E. Mach, J. Petzoldt, and A. Bogdanov; for example according to following assessment: "The 'recent' Machists have not adduced a single argument against the materialists that had not been adduced by Bishop Berkeley."[147] Had Lenin known Nietzsche, he would undoubtedly have seen him as another "Machist."

The so-called 'Machists' themselves devote much energy on refuting Idealism. They are adamant about defending a theory of knowledge that is 'naturalist,' 'empirical,' and 'pragmatic.'[148] They are usually polemically engaged in *criticizing* traditional epistemology as *covertly* idealistic and theologian in its appeal to absolute objectivity, i.e., appealing to the traditional view of objectivity as *pre-given self-identity*. Polemically, they understand themselves as anti-foundational, anti-metaphysical, anti-transcendental, anti-theologian, anti-romantic, but usually always as *pro-scientific*, in their thinking. They are typically inspired by predecessors like Hume, Kant, and Schopenhauer (more so than by the Hegelian tradition), but tend to see the thought of these masters being brought to fruition by nineteenth century's emerging evolutionists, physicists, physiologists, psychologists, epistemologists, and linguists. Nietzsche is living and breathing within this paradigm and attempts to shape a thinking able to articulate its fundamental tenets when applied to various topics, such as (in his TL) the topic of 'knowledge' (in other work, he famously addresses religion, morals, culture, and the arts as well).[149]

2. Sunrise for the Gay Scientists

In 1886, Ernst Mach publishes a first version of his *Die Analyse der Empfindungen* (*The Analysis of Sensations*; 1886).[150] It is highly likely that Nietzsche read the work since he reportedly held an underlined copy of it in his library.[151] To what degree Nietzsche used Mach for inspiration, we can of course never know, but Mach's subject must have played straight into his hands in the mid-1980s, and he must have been captivated by a work starting by proclaiming its anti-metaphysical allegiances in developing a post-Kantian epistemology (cf. the title of chapter one of the work, "Preliminary Anti-Metaphysical Remarks" [*Antimetaphysische Vorbemerkungen*]), thereupon introducing a theory of our conceptual simplifications of a relativistic world, and furthermore defending a theory of mind that involves the introduction of the fragmentary subject. As has been well established by scholars from various schools of commentary, these are key issues occupying the later Nietzsche.[152]

In his work, Mach introduces his famous theory of the 'elements' (for detailed discussion below). Instead of thinking the world as divided in reality and appearances, world and mind, *physis* and *psyche*, he suggests that these two distinct realms can never be anything other than our encounter of them. In this encounter, they are made up of 'elements'—not caused by fixed, fast, and frozen things or substances. These elements stand is certain relationships to each other, which have (*as relationships*) a certain stability and permanence. However, elements change their appearances according to perspectives and circumstances, and cannot reasonably be led back to one abstract unity or singularity. The postulate of thing-ness is therefore an abstraction added to an encountered world (a world of 'becoming,' constantly stabilized and de-stabilized). We experience complexes of functional relationships, some of which exhibit a relatively greater permanence than others, and the relatively more permanent complexes, we name 'things.'

'What is a table?' Mach asks himself on page one, and answers essentially, 'that depends!' It is by the human onlooker presented from different perspectives, in different lights; to our tactile system, it is a surface that varies in temperature; over time, it changes as it wears down, needs repair, new varnishing, etc. Still, on our casual understanding, its complex of elements has a certain permanence in the relationship they stand to each other, and we experience the table as the same table. In that pragmatic sense is it a 'thing.'

Hence, to Mach as well as to Nietzsche, the 'thing-world' becomes a necessary abbreviation of the encountered element-world. There is no denying that it is extremely useful to have definite names for complexes of elements that recur as the same or near the same, and this pragmatic usefulness of the habitual understanding of *world* is always emphasized by Mach.[153]

The phenomenalism or positivism envisioned by them is primarily affirmative of that which is given as presenting itself. Metaphorically speaking, according to metaphors produced by the authors themselves, these new nihilists walk about in the sun, enjoying their sense-impressions—as if personifications of Nietzsche's so-called "gay scientists."

Let me give two examples of this 'sunny world' summoned forth by respectively Mach and Nietzsche.

In *Analysis of Sensations*, Mach adds a longer footnote where he offers a brief auto-biographical narrative recording how he came upon the idea of a phenomenal sensation-world. After prolonged Kant-studies in his teenage years, one bright summer day, it dawned upon him that the world is only a "mass of sensations."

> I have always felt it as a stroke of especially good fortune, that early in life, at about the age of fifteen, I found in the library of my father a copy of Kant's *Prolegomena to any Future Metaphysics*. The book made at the time a powerful and ineffaceable impression upon me, the like of which I never afterwards experienced in any of my philosophical readings. Some two or three years later the superfluity of the role played by 'the thing in itself' abruptly dawned upon me. On a bright summer day in the open air, the world with my ego suddenly appeared to me as one coherent mass of sensations. [...] This moment was decisive for my whole view.[154]

On the account of the narrative, we have decisively moved out of Plato's cave. This is not a world of shadows painted on walls, but a world of summer and sunshine worthy of Claude Monet. It is also not a world of 'truth' that we painstakingly have to learn as philosopher-kings when we ascent from the cave. It is rather the world of the child, who still sees the world immediately.

We encounter the same affirmative 'yes' to the merely appearing, the same suspicion of the cave and shadow world, when we compare to the passage by Nietzsche from *Götzendämmerung* that we have discussed, and which we will here revisit for its 'sunshine' metaphors. Nietzsche too glorifies the superficiality of the world, when he cites his stages of the rise of reason on the sky of knowledge. From Nietzsche's stage 4 to stage 6, we are moving from darkness into light. Stage 4 indicates "Grey morning. First yawn of reason. Cockcrow of positivism." Thereupon follows stage 5 as "Bright day; breakfast; return of bon sense and cheerfulness; Plato blushes in shame; pandemonium of all free spirits." Finally, we arrive to absolute insight in stage 6 which is also absolute light: "Noon; moment of shortest shadow; end of longest error; high point of humanity; INCIPIT ZARATHUSTRA)."[155]

In the aphorism, we are obviously progressing from 'grey morning' to 'breakfast' to 'noon,' i.e., from early dawn to morning to noon. We are back to the motive of the sun, which in Nietzsche is rising over humanity and bringing with it reason and cheerfulness and enlightenment. Sunrise has three phases, where the first is referred to as 'positivism' (by which, as generally assumed, he must be referring to A. Comte) as the beginning of reason, and the last is the noon of fulfillment. The last position is the highest point of humanity and the end of "the longest error" in the history of humanity, i.e., the idea of a "true world," a 'thing-in-itself.' At this zenith for humanity, a new human type enters the stage of philosophy, the so-called super-human, the absolute nihilist, or in Nietzsche's imaginative gallery of characters, Zarathustra.

At this final stage, mankind has realized that there is no double world, no hierarchical distinction between a 'true' and an 'apparent' world, and since the opposition as such disappears, the 'apparent world' as the title of one position in the opposition, as such *continuing to breathe life* into the opposition, is gone too. Now, we only confirm what *is*; i.e., *presence* without absence as its logical opposite.

3. A Nietzsche-Machean Theory of Knowledge

1. From Substances to Appearances

The affinity between Nietzsche and Mach's epistemology was understood by several of Mach's supporters such as H. Kleinpeter, J. Petzoldt, P. Frank, M. Schlick, R. Carnap, H. Vaihinger, and R. von Mises in the beginning of the twentieth century. They were especially impressed by Nietzsche's criticism of the Kantian 'thing-in-itself' and his emphasis on a relational sensation-world replacing the old "school-philosophical" belief in a world of substances. They frequently wrote in appreciation of the evolutionary-biological and pragmatic understanding of knowledge they saw in Nietzsche. In his letter to Ernst Mach, Kleinpeter applauds these theoretical positions.

> First of all, Nietzsche's theory of knowledge [*Erkenntnislehre*] is thoroughly biological. Everywhere do we feel the formative influence of Darwin, even in the details. Strongest revealed in Nietzsche is however the opposition to the Absolute; he is perhaps the most radical representative for relativism in the theory of knowledge [*er ist vielleicht der radikalste Vertreter des Relativismus in der Erkenntnistheorie*]. His thoughts are only available in the form of aphorisms; he was less a scientific thinker than a philosopher in the artistic sense, who in the form of lightning fast intuitions were able to conjecture deeper relations. [...] Pragmatism is entirely part of Nietzsche. The truth of the categories, logic, he views in their use for advancing our insight and our actions, in the last analysis to advance the organism. [*Die Wahrheit der Kategorien, der Logik, erblickt er in ihrer Nützlichkeit zur Förderung unserer Einsicht und unseres Handelns, in letzterer Linie zur Förderung der Organizmus*].[156]

In Phillip Frank, we find the same positive appraisal of the agreement between Mach and Nietzsche: "I am strengthened by the striking agreement of his [Mach] views with [...] Friedrich Nietzsche. [...] The more one delves into the posthumous works of Nietzsche, the more clearly one observes the agreement, particularly in the basic ideas related to the theory of knowledge."[157]

The emphasis on this connection between Nietzsche and Critical Positivism, Phenomenalism, and/or Pragmatism virtually disappears in later twentieth-century receptions, as 'Positivism' (this general and vague term for several different traditions) became increasingly unpopular among the intelligentsia of the second half of the twentieth century. One obstacle may have been the typical, but crude, conflation of nineteenth-century *Positivism* with *Logical Positivism* as a later twentieth-century phenomenon. In any case, the positivist connection to Nietzsche were ignored or dismissed by Continental disciplines such as hermeneutics, existentialism, postmodernism, as well as by analytic philosophy.[158] Only relatively recently, Nietzsche's relation to the early critical positivism has resurfaced thanks to a growing number of scholars, often with a background in intellectual history (cf., references in Introduction); in the latter half of twentieth-century commentary, it was virtually absent.[159]

We quoted Mach's brief autobiographical digression from the beginning of *The Analysis of Sensations*, where he after finishing reading Kant's *Prolegomena* as teenager had an epiphany of sorts, not of the coming of Christ, but of the superficiality of the world.[160] On my classification of the in-itself above, Mach was here grasping the superfluity of the thing-in-itself as hidden in the traditional sense. That "bright summer day in the open air" was obviously more attractive than the dusty old 'thing' stored away in hidden dark places beyond the reaches of the sun. The appreciation of 'bright summer days,' or to be more theoretical, the appreciation of *openness* and the *affirmation* of what *is*, is of course in the spirit of Nietzsche too.

In *Populär Wissenschaftliche Vorlesungen*,[161] Mach returns to the issue and dismisses again the traditional belief in *substance* as a "crude notion" of a "mysterious lump," which we in vain seek outside our minds.

> That obscure, mysterious lump which we involuntarily add in thought, we seek for in vain outside the mind. [...] It is always, thus, the crude notion of substance that is slipping unnoticed into science, proving itself constantly insufficient, and ever under the necessity of being reduced to smaller and smaller world-particles.[162]

In his *Erkenntnis und Irrtum* (1905),[163] his criticism of substances is further elaborated as Mach here returns to the idea as a "monstrous" belief in substances that exist apart from their predicates:

> Inasmuch as it is possible to take away singly every constituent part without destroying the capacity of the image to stand for the totality and to be recognized again, it is imagined that it is possible to subtract all the parts and to have something still remaining. Thus naturally arises the philosophical notion, at first impressive, but subsequently recognized as monstrous, of a 'thing-in-itself,' different from its 'appearance,' and unknowable.[164] [...] Thing, body, matter, are

nothing apart from the combinations of the elements,—the colors, sounds, and so forth—nothing apart from their so-called attributes. That protean pseudo-philosophical problem of the single thing with its many attributes arises wholly from a misinterpretation of the fact, that summary comprehension and precise analysis [...] cannot be carried on simultaneously.[165]

Like in Nietzsche, a 'thing-in-itself' is a "monstrosity" because it presupposes the possibility of a *relation-less, context-less, subject-less* entity. Barring this monstrosity, we are consigned to a perspectival world of relations that is, *first*, arranged on the phenomenal surface of the world, and, *second*, arranged according to the needs and interests of a biological species, *Homo Sapiens*, viewing the world according to its own values and with a *will to power* to compel the world to obey its needs and interests.

Mach is objecting to the notion of 'object' as substance, i.e., as unitary, distinct, and self-identical. He objects to the idea that we can peel off the qualities of a 'thing' and be left with its essence in form of its substance—like Descartes in his chimney corner could make all the sense-qualities of his lump of wax disappear and still be left with a lump that had to be the essence of the wax. From Descartes's chimney corner to Mach's bright summer day, it is almost as if the wax returns with its sweet taste of honey and smell of Jasmines. Mach restores all its former qualities as possible 'elements' in their variable relationships constituting the wax as perceived and dismisses that bland lump that Descartes in his shadow-world was left with and saw as the 'real' wax.

In Mach's view, we perceive the 'thing' as distinct and self-identical in our '*summary comprehension*' of the world (in Nietzsche's view, the distinct 'thing' emerges from our *simplified/abbreviated* understanding of the world). In this commonsensical 'summary comprehension,' the 'thing' becomes a stand-in for a totality of elements, such as color, taste, touch, smell, and perspectival seeing, because a thing-representation is easier to store in memory and recall at our convenience than is our collection of multiple sense-data. A thing-representation is only a spontaneous and very rapid *interpretation* of a complex of elements represented as 'thing.' In a Machean analysis, when Descartes melts his wax and forms a sensually different object from what he had in his hand just a moment ago, he still recalls his original piece of wax as memory-image. He now wonders what could be the common denominator between perceptive image and memory-image, and arrives at the conclusion that since nothing ever left his hand, the two versions (melted 'thing' and memory-image of the 'thing') must have a common substance, unseen and unknown in the original thing-representation itself, because predicates and qualities have been subtracted, leaving the leftover of a lump in his hand.

Thus, according to *summary comprehension*, we *see* the object immediately as unity and casually *use* it as a point of reference and orientation. Our perceptive-cognitive sense-apparatus constructs spontaneously a unified and permanent object-world outside ourselves. However, under Mach's "*precise analysis*," we understand that an 'object' is an abstraction of complexes of relations in a sense-world of becoming and change, and is therefore lacking that substantiality we spontaneously impose upon it. We falsely conclude that from the thing-image as facilitator for our memories, there must be a corresponding substance. It is this spontaneous inference from image to substance that is a *'falsification'* and a *'fiction,'* in the language of Nietzsche, Vaihinger, and Mach alike. When philosophers make this jump from image to object, they are introducing metaphysics into a world of change and becoming.

To Mach the nether epistemological unit is therefore not the 'substance' but the 'element' (to Nietzsche, the 'sense-impression'). One has been discussing what Mach exactly means by 'elements,' and we may attempt to approach an answer by taking a step back to some of his most important influences, G. Th. Fechner, E. Herring, and H. von Helmholtz.[166] In particular, understanding the Machean 'element' seems to be clarified in a comparison to Fechner's 'sensation.'[167]

On the one hand, an element must belong to possible experience. It cannot belong to the postulated objective 'thing-itself' world; it also cannot belong to a transcendental world of 'forms,' 'ideas,' 'categories,' or the like; finally, it cannot be entirely unconscious. Any of these realms are not given as possible experience, and not as *appearing*. Furthermore, an element must be related to the sensuous realm and cannot be identical to a *linguistic* or *conceptual* construct. An element must be emerging before language is emerging in both a phylo- and onto-genetic sense.

We recall that Fechner in a number of experiments demonstrated that 'raw' stimuli had to be increased to a certain magnitude of intensity before they were noticed by his test-subjects. One could for example keep increasing the intensity of a light source, which at first was too weak to be perceived by the test-subject, but at a point would reach a threshold above which it was perceived. Fechner concluded "that every stimulus [...] must already have reached a certain finite magnitude before it can be noticed at all—that is, before our consciousness is aroused by a sensation."[168] This implied that there was a threshold below which the subject did not sense and register stimuli, but remained unconscious about them (which would hold true for both Fechner's "extensive" and "intensive" stimuli; i.e., exogenous and endogenous stimuli caused respectively from the outside and the inside of the organism). When stimuli became conscious, it happened as if in a *qualitative* jump from a zero-sensation response to a sensation-response. At an arbitrary point, which Fechner could measure, the mind was affected and it started to become aware.[169] This awareness is the precondition of a Machean *element* as well; a Machean *element* is a stimulus of which the mind has become aware; in a qualitative jump, an anonymous sense-datum starts manifesting itself. As such, we cannot be aware of a chaotic world of becoming and change below the so-called 'threshold' for registration of data, although we may hypothesize the existence of such a chaotic "force-point world" as Lange would describe it.

We find a similar observation in Nietzsche, when he remarks that it must be *sensed qualities* we arrange in functional relationships, and from which we form 'complexes' we call 'objects.' This interpretation is suggested in various passages from his later notebooks, for example in the following passage on perspectivism addressing the distinction between quantities and qualities.

> Qualities are our insurmountable barriers; we cannot help feeling that mere quantitative differences are something fundamentally distinct from quantity [...] Everything for which the word "knowledge" makes any sense refers to the realms of counting, weighing, measuring, i.e., to the realm of quantity; while by contrast, all our feelings of value (i.e., all our sensations) adhere to qualities, that is, to the perspectival "truths" that are ours alone and simply cannot be "known." It is obvious that every being different from us senses different qualities and consequently lives in another world from the one we live in.[170]

> Qualities are our so-called "insurmountable barrier," beyond or below which we cannot reach, although we in our notion of 'knowledge' have invented a term that aspires to refer to an outside world objectified by means of numbers (to count, to weigh, to measure; therefore, quantify). Qualities are our real nether limit of knowledge, insofar as "all our feelings of value (i.e., all our sensations) adhere to qualities, that is, to the perspectival "truths" that are ours alone and "simply cannot be *known*," because we cannot know ourselves as agent of knowledge without activating our agency and thus being caught up in a vicious circle.

> Qualities are our real human idiosyncrasy: wanting our human interpretations and values to be universal and perhaps constitutive values is one of the hereditary insanities of human pride, which still has its safest seat in religion.[171]

Our "perspectival truths" are applied *by us to us* as human species as our "real human idiosyncrasy." When we impose them on the world, we are guilty in one of our "hereditary insanities of human pride." That 'idiosyncrasy,' that 'hereditary insanity,' is perspectivism in the most profound Nietzschean sense. Since we cannot look around the corner of ourselves, this perspectival world will present itself as given for-us. This qualitative world is *our* world invested with feelings and values, prior to the world counted, weighted, or measured, which Nietzsche seems to see as a secondary elaboration communicating objectified knowledge (or rather "knowledge" in his scare quotes).

We may speculate about how it is to perceive the world like a fly, a snake, a shark, or a bat, but we can never know, because "every being different from us feels different qualities and consequently lives in another world from the one we live in." It is *as homo sapiens* we construct the world according to *our* perspective in contrast to the perspective of other species. We notice that Nietzsche in this note from 1886 sees 'perspective' as *species-specific* as he did already in 1872. This idea of perspectivism is identical to the 'Biological Perspectivism' introduced already in TL, and then again in GS (cf. Part I, A.8 and Part II, A.4).

The idea does not seem to undergo any fundamental change in Nietzsche. It uniformly states that as humans, we sense only qualities, which are therefore our "barriers" within which we 'construct' our world. They manifest a 'truth' that is *our own*, i.e., 'perspectival' rather than universal. Experiences are thereupon quantified as after-reconstruction and as secondary elaboration of the given. We generally order, schematize, conceptualize, organize, interpret, and quantify a world that is from the very first seen from our perspective.[172] Nietzsche apparently finds this point self-evident, when he continues the passage above by insisting,

> Need I add, conversely, that quantities 'in themselves' do not occur in experience, that our world of experience is only a qualitative world, that consequently logic and applied logic (such as mathematics) are among the artifices of the ordering, overwhelming, simplifying, abbreviating power called life, and are thus something practical and useful, because life-preserving, but for that very reason not in the least something 'true'?[173]

In conclusion, the "objective world" is not a foundation of things to which we *apply perspectives*, the "perspectival world" is the foundation to which we *apply things*. We certainly walk around things and gaze at them from different angles or perspectives, but more profoundly, our gaze itself is a perspectival construction of something we call 'things.'[174]

2. Elements, Relations, and Construction of Objectivity

In Mach, too, we only sense 'qualities,' never 'quantities' or 'forces.' We experience a sensed world of 'elements,' by Mach heuristically differentiated in three groups as physical, physiological, and psychological, respectively referring to the physical world, to the physiological world of bodily sensations, or to mental capacities like memories. However, the elements presenting these different classes of impressions are always themselves 'neutral' or 'indifferent' to any epistemological value-ranking. The class of physical elements is not regarded as closer to 'truth' than the class of psychological elements; elements referring to the tree as physical object are not privileged over elements that refer to the tree as processed image in the visual cortex, etc.

Mach's three different classes of 'elements' repeats the conventional distinction between elements existing outside ourselves (such as trees), elements belonging to our body (such as visual perception or pain), and finally elements belonging to thinking as imaginary (such as memories or fantasies). However, these different classes of elements are not organized causally, but in functional relationships, which we after-the-fact re-construct as 'thing.' Our perception of the *object* is not the perception of the *object-itself*, but is a *coming-together* of variables depending on other variables, such as perspective, distance, light, and even our particular mood.[175] An 'object' is constructed from strings of physical and physiological elements woven together to form what we call 'object.' According to this 'string-theory,' we cannot precisely determine what is objective and what subjective.[176]

Mach suggests his three proto-typical sets of elements respectively: (1) $A\ B\ C\ldots$ (complexes referring to outside, physical, spatio-temporal, objects); (2) $K\ L\ M\ldots$ (complexes referring to bodily sensations); and (3) $\alpha\ \beta\ \gamma\ldots$ (complexes referring to imagination, memory-images, etc.).

> Let us denote the above-mentioned elements by the letters $A\ B\ C\ldots, K\ L\ M\ldots$ and $\alpha\ \beta\ \gamma\ldots$ Let those complexes of colors, sounds, and so forth, commonly called bodies, be denoted, for the sake of clearness, by $A\ B\ C\ldots$; the complex, known as our own body, which is a part of the former complexes distinguished by certain peculiarities, may be called $K\ L\ M\ldots$; the complex composed of volitions, memory-images, and the rest, we shall represent by $\alpha\ \beta\ \gamma\ldots$ Usually, now, the complex $\alpha\ \beta\ \gamma\ldots K\ L\ M\ldots$, as making up the ego, is opposed to the complex $A\ B\ C\ldots$, as making up the world of physical objects.[177]

On this new notational system, our perception of an object (or of something we spontaneously construct as an object) is the coming-together of a string of elements, say $A\ C\ L\ M\ \beta\ \gamma\ldots$, in such a way that the string ($A\ C\ L\ M\ \beta\ \gamma\ldots$) *is* our representation of the object.

If we elaborate the thinking by means of an example, the sense of pain is also emerging as such a string of interrelated elements. A pain-sensation impresses itself from the 'outside' while being interpreted from the 'inside' as 'pain,' and as *'this* pain' (recognized as idea). In Mach's formulaic language we may explain 'pain' as follows: something, say a needle, (element-group *A B C* . . .) touches the skin (element-group *K L M* . . .) and is felt as pain (element-group *K L M* . . .), but as *this* characterized, recognized, and remembered pain (element-group $\alpha\ \beta\ \gamma$ . . .), which is partly recognized by perceiving that which touches the skin (element-group *A B C* . . .), remembering one's fear of needles (elements group $\alpha\ \beta\ \gamma$ . . .), hereby augmenting the pain-sensation (element-group *K L M* . . .), etc. Where exactly ("under precise analysis") is the *cause* of pain located in these element-groups? The outside helps defining 'pain' as much as the inside. 'Pain' is *A*, *K*, and α-elements; remove one of the sequences, and there is *no pain*! It is not clearly determinable whether 'pain' belongs to the outside, the inside, or that in-between we call *the skin*.

One might object that the example is twisted because 'pain' is from the beginning not an object, and 'objectivity' is after all the crux of our discussion. However, if we extrapolate and apply Mach's string-theory to visual perception, we ask the same question and get the same answer: does an impression of some-thing emerge from the outside, as *object*; from the inside as *recognized/remembered image* in our visual cortex, or from that in-between we call the *retina*? It is again the case that 'perception' is a combination of *A*, *K*, and α-elements; remove one of the sequences, and there is *no perception*!

In our commonsensical construction of the world (i.e., our spontaneous 'naïve realism'), we tend to draw a line between *world* and *ego* as between the set *A B C* . . . (perceived as belonging to the 'outside'; i.e., physical objects, bodies, etc.) and the two sets, *K L M* . . . and $\alpha\ \beta\ \gamma$ . . . (perceived as belonging to the 'inside,' respectively as body and mind). We tend to see the complexes *A B C* as standing as physical objects over and against the Ego, as comprised of the complexes *K L M* and $\alpha\ \beta\ \gamma$. However, as P. Gori correctly points out, as a consequence of Mach's string-theory, we can alternatively set up the distinction between outside and inside, nature and spirit, object and self, physical and psychical, by collapsing the element groups A B C and K L M, see the human body as part of nature, and reserve the last element group, $\alpha\ \beta\ \gamma$, as properly belonging to the inside self. The point is that the spontaneous distinction between outside and inside remains fragile.[178]

Mach's writing disk is an example of an 'object' that vibrates between such elements groups: "My table is now brightly, now dimly lighted. Its temperature varies. It may receive an ink stain. One of its legs may be broken. It may be repaired, polished, and replaced part by part. But, for me, it remains the table at which I daily write."[179] The 'disk' is broken up in elements; some refer to the 'object,' others to our sensation of the 'object,' others again to our 'self' as memory of the object. We reconstruct the desk as *object*, but we 'see' a desk actually 'vibrating' from image to image, from stage to stage, etc., depending of different light, temperature, and other, conditions. We remember that the disk itself has changed appearance from wear and tear; parts have been replaced, etc. Still, we represent to ourselves the vibrating and unstable disk as the same disk and in our excusable and legitimate 'naïve realism.' We understand the disk to be a *body* with attributes like substance, extension, and permanence.

Only applying "precise analysis," there *is* no such *body* except as an *abstraction* (or to Nietzsche, as an *abbreviating interpretation*), and we are instead presented with certain elements standing in relations to each other and to the perceiving subject, where only *relations* remain permanent, while the properties are in constant flux and change. The thinking has obvious family-resemblances with Nietzsche's *Relations-Welt* of constant *becoming*. Whether in Mach or Nietzsche, the view does not idealistically assert that there is no 'disk' by whimsically reducing it to our idea, our hallucination, or our language. It rather argues that the *disk-object* is *interpretable* and therefore not *determinable*. I can walk around the disk, view it from different angles, under different light, feel its texture, or in frustration, imitating honorable Dr. Johnson in conversation with Bishop Berkeley, give it a good kick to prove its existence, but I remain lost in these and multiple other sensations. They may all prove us right that there *is* a disk-object (and the pain in Dr. Johnson's toe will remind him again and again of the existence of a hard object, which as such resists further philosophical discussion in his wishful thinking), but we remain unable to *articulate* this object as that self-identical *body* that can be subtracted from its innumerable aspects.

In Nietzsche and Mach's *Relations-Welt*, the classical distinction between physical and psychical, outside and inside, is now suspended as well as the notion of a thing-in-itself. Finally, they can take epistemology a step further than Du Bois-Reymond, the noble grandfather of the discourse, dared to do. They no longer need to resign themselves to his *ignorabimus* (cf. Part II, B.1: "From Materialism to Agnosticism"), which by default presupposed the 'thing' as a *known unknown*. In Nietzsche and Mach's *Relations-Welt*, the *element* has rather become a *known without unknown*.

At this point, they have 'deconstructed' the dualistic view of the world as consisting of two radically separated domains, the physical and the psychical, the physical being tangible and concrete, the psychical imaginary and ideational.[180] In a *Relations-Welt* of elements the inside/outside, subject/object, mind/matter distinctions collapse because apparent outside objects are interwoven with our perception of them, and are received by us as 'elements,' as Mach explains.[181]

There is no rift between the psychical and the physical, no inside and outside, no "sensation" to which an external "thing," different from sensation, corresponds. There is but one kind of elements, out of which this supposed inside and outside are formed—elements which are themselves inside or outside, according to the aspect in which, for the time being, they are viewed. The world of sense belongs both to the physical and the psychical domain alike.[182]

Mach is not discarding the pragmatic existence of the commonsensical distinction between objects outside and objects inside, but he starts from a chaotic sensation-world, a soup of elements, which he assumes that we conventionally differentiate in inner and outer. In this differentiation, the Ego stabilizes its boundaries against the external world, thanks to, first, repeated experiences of certain sequences, and second, the consolidation of these experiences as memory. Mach suggests an evolutionary and developmental model where the boundaries of the Ego are gradually formed giving an experiential world relative permanence.[183]

3. Filtration, Simplification, and the General Economy of Signs

In Mach and Nietzsche's biological theory of knowledge, the perceptive apparatus becomes a filter rather than a camera, where the filtration screens material and removes superfluities that are unnecessary or irrelevant to the psychical apparatus. In both, we find a biological-evolutionary explanation of this filtration and abbreviation process. The 'subject' does not and cannot see an outside with the neutrality of a camera, but (as also the case in Vaihinger and Avenarius) it must reduce it to what it *needs* and *wants* to see. It removes impressions that are unnecessary and emphasize that which is of immediate interest regarding the strength, growth, or perseverance of its organism. Seeing is no longer an objective gaze directed toward the outside; it finds a secret motivation in the inside as the perseverance of itself as subject or as society.[184]

This aspect of sensation was already discovered by Th. Fechner, who had said about the utility of his 'thresholds' that, "besides the fact that we are saved from disturbances by unwanted and strange perceptions, because any stimulus escapes notice when it fall below a certain point, there is also the fact that a uniform state of perception is assured because stimulus differences cannot be noticed below their threshold."[185] Thus, the filtration of data was to Fechner a positive and necessary operation on part of the psyche. The organism was striving to maintain a state of relaxation, equilibrium, or homeostasis, and would consequently keep the preponderance of impressions below zero, below threshold. Below 'zero,' we may again hypothesize that there is a flurry of activity going on, which the subject does not register and does not know, a chaos of becoming that we ignore and *must* ignore in order to maintain our mental equilibrium.[186]

Whether or not Nietzsche was influenced by Fechner (if not directly, then for example from reading Lange, who in his *Geschichte* refers to him), he conceives in terms similar to Fechner, Helmholtz, and Lange our psyche as a 'filtration,' 'simplification,' or 'abbreviation,' apparatus. In these capacities, we are introducing equilibrium and homeostasis in the psyche. The following well-known passage from GM can now be seen as Nietzsche's only more intuitive expression of Fechner's thinking.

> Forgetfulness is no mere *vis inertiae* as the superficial imagine; it is rather an active and, in the strictest sense, positive capacity for repression. It is responsible for the fact that what we see and experience enters our consciousness as little, while we are digesting it, as does the thousand-fold process related to physical nourishment—so-called 'incorporation.' To close the doors and windows of consciousness for a while; to remain undisturbed by the noise and struggle of our underworld of utility organs working with and against one another; a little quietness, a little tabula rasa of the consciousness, to make room for new things, […] that is the purpose of active forgetfulness, which is like a doorkeeper, a preserver of psychic order, repose, and etiquette. So it becomes immediately obvious that there would be no happiness, no cheerfulness, no hope, no pride, no present, without forgetfulness.[187]

Nietzsche is evidently discussing physiology and biology. Forgetfulness, the ability to create *tabula rasa* in the psyche, maintains the organism in a state of necessary homeostasis. All the activity of our "underworld of utility organs" is below zero, unknown to us as a matter of biological necessity, since we otherwise would drown in impressions. There would for example be no (sense of) *presence* without forgetfulness, as Nietzsche recognizes, because without forgetfulness, the subject would hang on to past experiences without being able to let them go. Memories would drown the psychic system; present experiences would be interlaced with past experiences and the subject would be unable to sort out the tangle. The result would be a "dyspeptic" human that could not "digest" experiences, unable to live in the presence of the present, but only in a chaotic entanglement of present and past. Forgetfulness is therefore a positive quality because it "makes room for new things."

Given that Nietzsche often returns to the question of 'simplification,' it is somewhat odd when Kleinpeter, in his letter to Mach summarizing the similarities between Mach and Nietzsche (cf. above), is at a loss to find in Nietzsche a parallel to Mach's principle of *Denkökonomie*: "I have only in passing been able to find the principle of thought-economy [*Princip der*

Denkökonomie] in Nietzsche."[188] As perceptive a he is, Kleinpeter overlooks this parallel, since Nietzsche's discussions of linguistic and cognitive processes as simplifying, abbreviating, and facilitating *is* his obvious introduction of an *economy*, and specifically (insofar as we here talk about conceptual understanding) a *thought* economy.

We recall that Nietzsche already in TL was discussing the processing of sense-data into proper perceptions as 'metaphors,' since impressions were processed and translated into images, whereupon images were processed and translated into signs adding a second level of 'metaphorization' to our knowledge of 'world.' *The single principle* behind these translation-processes was always to make our 'existence,' our orientation and situation in the world, *simpler*.

In later work, he never abandons this position. In BGE, "our mind is a *simplification-apparatus*,"[189] in the late notebooks, it is an "*Abstraktions- und Simplifikations-apparat*."[190] In order to 'see' and 'know' imply simplification, thus falsification, thus interpretation, as three inter-related aspects of one and the same perceptive-cognitive operation aimed at making the world habitable. We 'interpret' the world and cannot help but 'interpreting' the world whether we see, think, understand, or read (cf. BGE: "As little as a reader today reads all the individual words of a page—he rather takes about five words in twenty haphazardly and 'conjectures' their probable meaning—just as little do we see a tree exactly and entire with regard to its leaves, branches, color, shape; it is so much easier for us to put together an approximation of a tree"[191]). In this sense, we are "accustomed to lying" as Nietzsche asserts in the continuation of the passage. Nietzsche's translations-, simplifications-, or interpretations-principles assert the greatest possible *economy* in both perception and thought. His *Abstraktions- und Simplifikations-apparat* is directly related to Mach and Avenarius's principles of *Denkökonomie* (and we will in the following section see how Vaihinger too subscribes to the same principle).

Notice for comparison to Nietzsche, the following passage from the *Science of Mechanics*, where Mach breaches an issue that is also Nietzsche's. He too points out that our need to simplify comes about thanks to our "limited powers of memory."

> [Given] man's limited powers of memory, any stock of knowledge worthy of the name is unattainable except by the *greatest* mental economy. Science itself, therefore, may be regarded as consisting of the most complete presentation possible of facts with the *least possible expenditure of thought*. [...] The function of science is to replace experience. Thus, on the one hand, science must remain in the province of experience, but, on the other, must hasten beyond it, constantly expecting confirmation, constantly expecting the reverse. Where neither confirmation nor refutation is possible, science is not concerned.[192]

In Nietzsche (*GM II 2*), man's 'limited powers of memory' showed itself when the psyche *erases information* and *creates 'tabula rasa'* in order to preserve itself.[193] Likewise, Mach's general assumption is that humans have "limited powers of memory," but we compensate for this limitation by applying to thinking the greatest possible mental economy with the least possible mental effort in order to bring order into an apparent world of surfaces (Mach is here adopting this idea from Avenarius, cf., Vaihinger's discussion below). As such, we simplify and abbreviate by transforming experiences into concepts, formula, equations, tables, geometrical shapes, etc. Not only is this a simplification of information applied to the benefit of the single individual (in order for the individual to screen and control an unmanageable inflow of data), but its greater effect is that knowledge can be shared by several communities and generations of researchers.

> It is the object of science to replace or save, experiences, by the reproduction and anticipation of facts in thought. [...] Science is communicated by instruction, in order that one man may profit by the experience of another and be spared the trouble of accumulating it for himself; and thus, to spare posterity, the experiences of whole generations are stored up on libraries.[194]

The knowledge resulting from formalized research is stored in libraries, transformed into 'writing,' which can now be revisited whenever necessary. Members of the scientific community share recorded knowledge, saving them from starting over with new research whenever they encounter a new case. When an experience has been formalized into 'law,' we apply one rule that is true for all cases in the present and in the future. The law is seen as derived from experiences and thereupon preserved in the most economic language of a single formula. As such, "Physics is experience, arranged in economical order."[195]

> Physics shares with mathematics the advantages of succinct description and of brief, compendious definition, which precludes confusion, even in ideas where, with no apparent burdening of the brain, hosts of others are contained. Of these ideas the rich contents can be produced at any moment and displayed in their full perceptual light. [...] The communication of knowledge and the necessity, which everyone feels of managing his stock of experience with the least expenditure of thought, compel us to put our knowledge in economical forms. But here we have a clue which strips science of all its mystery, and shows us what its power really is.[196]

As such, our *drive for knowledge* or *will to truth* become essential motivations for our scientific engagements. When Avenarius, Mach, Vaihinger, Nietzsche, et al., are introducing this principle of economy as foundational for scientific thinking, the biological-psychological underground of the sciences is emphasized. We replace a belief in 'thing' with a belief in 'economic expression,' a world of objects is replaced with a world of relations, and eternal knowledge with provisional knowledge.

Nietzsche has several passages to that effect. To Nietzsche, the notions of 'necessity' and 'law' as indicating permanence in his world of becoming, are often under deconstruction, although they are 'necessary' for our survival, advancement, etc.

> Let us remove here the two popular concepts, 'necessity' and 'law': the first imposes a false compulsion, the second a false freedom into the world. "Things" do not behave with regularity, not according to a rule: there is no thing (—this is our fiction); it behaves as little under a compulsion from necessities. Here nothing is obeyed: *when something is what it is*, this strong or this weak, it is not a consequence of obedience, or of a rule, or of a compulsion.[197]

> When I bring a regularly occurring event on formula, I have facilitated, abbreviated, etc., the designation of the entire phenomenon. But I have not recognized [*constatiert*] a "law"; rather I have raised the question, How can it be, that something is here repeating itself: it is an assumption that the formula for the complex corresponds to, for the time being, unknown forces and force-cancelations [*Kraft-auflösungen*]: it is mythology to think that forces are obeying a law.[198]

> Our pleasure in simplicity, transparency, regularity, brightness [...]— I admit that a strong *instinct* of this kind exists. It is so strong that it governs among all the activities of our senses, and reduces, regulates, assimilates, etc., for us the abundance of real perceptions (unconscious ones), *presenting them to our consciousness* only in this trimmed form. This 'logical,' this 'artistic' element is our continual occupation. *What* made this force so sovereign? Obviously the fact that without it, for sheer hubbub of impressions, no living being would live.[199]

Nietzsche talks here about 'simplification,' 'transparency,' and 'regularity' as *instincts*, and indeed, as we read further, as *logical instincts* that have been selected in the human brain as basic instincts for survival (without them "no living being would live"). This must imply that to Nietzsche too, the human species has an ability to *rationally reconstruct* its surrounding world and construct so-called 'laws of nature,' which actually and effectively *anticipate and predict*.

When these laws are in neither Nietzsche nor Mach seen as discoveries of 'things-in-themselves,' we may ask, how is it possible from this positivist-pragmatic vantage-point to explain 'laws of nature' that are actually and unfailingly *predicting* future events?—The answer seems to be that since laws are formalized knowledge of reiterated experiences, we must assume that that which has repeated itself multiple times, will continue to repeat itself as the same also in the future. In the formula, we immediately 'see' the outcome of a sequence of events, instead of having to wait for every single instance of emerge or re-emerge for us in its path toward its conclusion. Consequently, we have gradually evolved a 'logical instinct' in order for us to schematize and formalize repeated experiences, in this adjusting in-itself chaotic nature to necessities required for our survival and advancement.

4. Knowledge as Sign-Economy

As important as this biological explanation-model is in both Nietzsche and Mach, we have not yet sufficiently elucidated the last important step in our reconstruction of their rethinking of epistemology. 'Logical instincts' cannot proclaim laws all by themselves, 'instinctually' as it were. They need a medium, which happens also to be their condition of possibility, namely language. To this rethinking of human knowledge, which elaborates on aspects found in a variety of disciplines or schools emerging in the nineteenth century (Naturalism, Evolutionary Biology, Phenomenalism, Positivism, Pragmatism, etc.), we must add Linguistics as another discipline rising to prominence in the paradigm.

In Mach, language, as the instrument of communication of laws, "is itself an economical contrivance. Experiences are analyzed, or broken up, into simpler and more familiar experiences, and then symbolized at some sacrifice of precision."[200] Different sensational elements are condensed in perception as 'thing,' and then further abstracted by being represented by a sign or symbol. A 'thing' finally ends up as an *abstraction* represented by a 'name' (in Mach, a 'symbolic' expression; in Nietzsche, a 'metaphorical' expression): "The thing is an abstraction, the name a symbol, for a compound of elements from whose changes we abstract. The reason we assign a single word to a whole compound is that we need to suggest all the constituent sensations at once."[201] Nietzsche gives a virtually identical explanation, when he in his notebooks says:

> A concept is an invention to which nothing corresponds *entirely* but many things slightly: a proposition such as 'two things, being equal to a third thing, are themselves equal' assumes (1) things and (2) equalities—neither exists. Yet with this invented and rigid world of concepts and numbers, man gains a means of seizing by signs huge quantities of facts and inscribing them in his memory.[202]

In this thinking, knowledge is not identical to 'facts,' because compounds of individual facts have been reduced to signs, as Nietzsche continues:

> This apparatus of signs is man's superiority, precisely because it is at the furthest possible distance from the individual facts. The reduction of experiences to *signs*, and the ever greater quantity of things which can thus be grasped, is man's *highest strength*. Intellectuality as the capacity to be master of a huge number of facts in signs. *This intellectual world, this sign-world, is pure 'illusion and deception.*'[203]

This is why we do not 'know' but 'schematize': "Not 'to know' but to schematize—to impose upon chaos as much regularity and form as our practical needs require."[204]

5. A Critical Discussion of an Anti-Phenomenalistic Conception of Mach's Epistemology

Erik Banks gives a presentation of Mach's epistemology that is thorough and often profound. Several of his conclusions seem to substantiate my own Nietzsche-inspired reading. In his chapter on the economy of thought, Banks gives for example the following precise explanation of the importance of Mach's *Denkokonomie*:

> Generally speaking, *Denkokonomie* plays the much needed role of a formal principle in Mach's philosophy. Mach generally neglected the need for form, insisting that all that existed for him were elements and their instantaneous functional connections. Hence, the role played by extended objects was a derivative one in his scheme. Objects for Mach were always changing complexes grouped together in a single history for the sake of convenience because it was more economical and less of a strain on memory to do so. There is thus a general skepticism of objects as realities in their own right for Mach, since the temptation, he believed, was to reify them into causally isolated things in themselves or private egos.[205]

Like undersigned, Banks sees Mach's basic idea as 'objects are changing complexes' 'grouped together for the sake of convenience and economy.' Mach, he says, thought that "objects with their boundaries were no more or less than functions, or variations of elements. An 'object' usually stands only for an immediate neighborhood of its effects on other things."[206] Furthermore, he quotes Mach's explicit,

> Complexes of elements (complexes of sensations) make up bodies. If, to the physicist, bodies appear the real, abiding existences, while the "elements" are regarded merely as their evanescent, transitory appearance, the physicist forgets, in the assumption of such a view, that all bodies are merely thought-symbols for complexes of elements (complexes of sensations).[207]

Given the testimony of these and many other passages, we have no reason to question Banks understanding of Mach. Still, Banks has a theoretical position of his own, and when this is applied, he seems to undersigned to slide back into that mind-world dualism, which Mach does his best to escape, and which otherwise is faithfully summarized in Banks's reading.

Banks asks himself, "must every element be both a sensation and a world element, or are there such elements that never end up linked to human consciousness, but make up objects in themselves?"[208] When he answers this question in the positive, he is summoning up the old ghost of traditional metaphysics from its grave. It is a precarious suggestion, because it implies that there may be 'objects in themselves.' Banks's faithful reading has already dismissed what he now suggests, namely the existence of "elements making up the remainder of the physical world beyond immediate observation, but in more or less remote causal interconnection with our sensations," implying that the world inhabits objects composed of qualities causally effecting our sensations.

Is seems to undersigned that Banks makes Mach's neutral monism a variation of *Mechanical Materialism* of the nineteenth century (previously discussed), with the new "world-elements" replacing the old "corpuscular atoms." When Banks says that "the true neutral monist picture emerges [as] a kind of 'cosmic soup' of world elements (including animal sensations and all of the physical qualities of nature) causally linked together in functions,"[209] then we are back to nature in itself, i.e., to "physical qualities of nature" in themselves and to the notion of causality as objectively linking together world-elements. One has to imply a dualism between a mind-independent and mind-dependent world, since the former somehow effects the latter. Bank's 'world-elements' seem to have a role quite similar to the role of the former 'corpuscular atoms' in the discourse of the nineteenth century.

This re-introduction of dualism finds a succinct expression in a model Banks offers to illustrate the difference between world-elements, sensations, and their overlap. As I read his model, helped by his explanation, "the immanent object is thus partly a mind-dependent sensation (s) and partly a mind-independent world element (e),"[210] the s/e notation designates the overlap between mind-dependent sensation (s) and mind-independent elements (e).

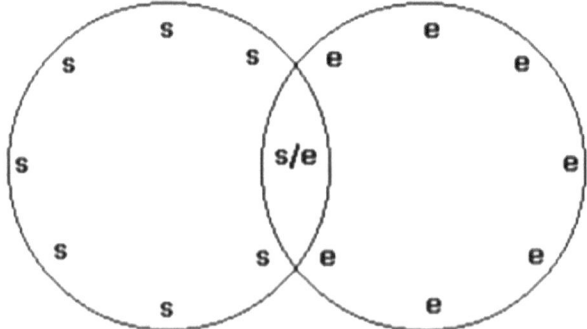

Figure 2 Bank's Dualistic Model on the "Immanent Object" Constructed from Sensations and World-Elements. *Source:* Reprinted by permission from Springer Nature: Springer, *From Sensations to World Elements: Neutral Monism* by Erik C. Banks © 2003.

Independent sensations-element and world-elements have to be taken for granted, while the overlap s/e indicates *the element as appearing to us in perception*. We must presuppose that one part of perception is constituted by the exterior element and another part by the interior sensation, i.e., that one part is given by nature and another part given by our mind. The overlap is now the fusion of the two. In this interpretation, we encounter a world of sensations, situated to the left of the model, and a world of elements, situated to the right of the model, the overlap as the 'immanent object' being that which we actually perceive. However, this distinction between world-elements and sensations, introduces two independent worlds coming together in perception, but supposedly existing as in-themselves before this overlap.

I see several problems in the suggestion, one being that an element-world in-itself has been official philosophical doctrine for centuries as it simply re-introduces the well-known hypothesis of thing-in-themselves as "mind-independent objects." The suggestion of sensations as existing in-themselves as "mind dependent sensations" are difficult to understand as well, as other than dogmatic idealism's *Ideas*. Thus, the conclusion becomes that if we marry *matter* to *idea*, we have *perception*. But where in Mach's work is such a construction defended?

In his elaborations in a more recent work,[211] Bank again argues that 'elements' may be mind-independent; they are explicitly introduced as so-called "Mind-Independent World-Elements," according to the title of the relevant chapter, p. 13.

> A question that arises naturally is what to do about completely mind-independent events and their qualities. If any sensation (s/e) can be interpreted in another context as a physical event, does it follow that all elements are also sensations (e/s) under some interpretation? Some will still defend that reading, but it seems to me to be far too phenomenalistic, as I will show. Should we then admit other elements (pure "e-elements") that are not anyone's sensations, and not even anyone's possible sensations? This question has plagued the literature on Mach, James, and Russell and was a major cause of confusion at the time when they first advanced their positions, but I think it is now possible to give a definitive answer. For Mach and Russell, the sensation-elements (s/e) are only a special class of the mind-independent e-elements, or what I have elsewhere called "world elements. [. . .] it is very wrong to think Mach did not believe in mind independent elements needed to complete our experience of objects."[212,213]

Banks wants to allow the existence of "pure e-elements," i.e., elements not perceived as in any of Mach's three aspects (physical, physiological, or psychological), but living an isolated mind-independent existence as *'things-in-themselves,'* while **s/e**-elements are only a special class of 'world-elements' (**e**-elements).

Explicitly, Mach is "far too phenomenalistic," and Banks reading of Mach turns as such anti-phenomenalist. Unconvinced of this anti-phenomenalism, I will offer an alternative *phenomenalist* reading according to which we are closer to Mach's reasoning, and in which his distinction between *element* and *sensation* differentiates between two aspects of the same, only in various stages of actualization. Element and sensation are equally belonging to an appearing world of sense-impressions, where some elements-groups end up as sensations, while other elements-groups remain potential yet to be actualized as distinct in focused sensation, or perception properly speaking. I see here Nietzsche's distinction between 'nerve-stimuli' and 'images' (or 'sense-impressions' and 'perceptions') coming back into play, and suggest consequently the following model.

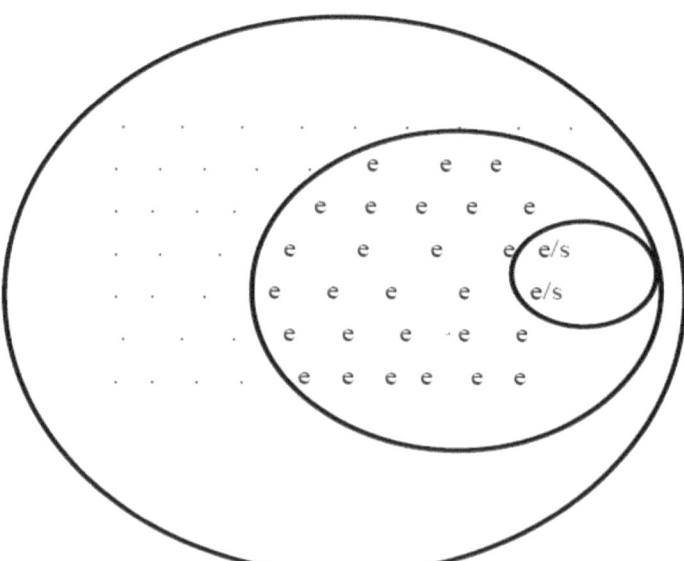

Figure 3 Nietzsche-Machean Model on Chaos World Emerging as Element and Sensation-World.

In this model (recycling Bank's notations 's,' 'e,' and 's/e'), sensations are simply elements attentively seen, while elements are partly sensations and partly unrealized sense-stimuli; i.e., *possible experience*. As our eyes scan the visual field in front of us, it does not scan everything with equal attention; images fall in and out of attention. The two inner ovals of the model, while they both represent the world of appearances, represent this physiological fact. Elements (the *e-field*) are what we can see, and sensations (*the e/s-field*) are what we see. The outer oval represents the incomprehensible thing-in-itself world, represented by points or dots (cf. ...), i.e., that enigmatic x-world that we cannot know and pragmatically speaking do not need to know (in Bank's interpretation, it happens to be the space for 'world-elements'). The 'e' and 'e/s' fields constitute the world of our senses (independent sensations ('s-elements') cannot exist without being associated to elements, therefore only 'e' and 'e/s' are allowed in my model). The world of e-elements is not mind-independent, because it is constituted thanks to our physiological-perceptive capabilities'; i.e., our biologically evolved physiological-perceptive capabilities. This thesis does not radically deny the existence of a 'matter-world,' or, in our notation-system, a point-world [...], but it emphasizes the *encounter* with this 'point-world' as more significant than the empty assertion of a 'world' beyond the *encounter*. Beyond the *encounter*, there is sorry little to see or to talk about. The positivist-pragmatic epistemic position effectively replaces the instinctive urge to *assert existence* with the epistemic interest in *how we know existence*.

If we look at something, focusing now on this and now on that, the impressions in the perceptive field are 'elements' grouped together in relationships making up the various thing-representations. These element-groups move in and out of focus, as my *e-field*, depending on how I direct my gaze. Whenever I redirect my gaze, another world is streaming past me. Only according to this interpretation is it possible to understand Mach's famous dictum "nature is but once there" (quoted by Banks as well), meaning that the world is presented to us in terms of unique unrepeatable states. I fail to see how we otherwise can understand this 'only once,' i.e., how nature can be 'but once,' unless we imply that it glides in and out of existence in our streaming perceptions.

The world is full of 'objects' composed of elements like a "mosaic of tiles," says Mach in another figure, but at any instant, tiles are replaced with other tiles, implying that in this world of "becoming" the objects are constantly changing, appearing, and vanishing.

In order to complete the model of this suggested Nietzsche-Machean theory of knowledge, we would need to add a few extra aspects to the model;

especially the domains of language and conceptualization need representation. The nether limit for knowledge was in Nietzsche's late theory the 'senses,' i.e., the sense-impressions or our *e-field*. They did not lie, Nietzsche declared, but what we *make of them* did (cf. Part II, A.3: "Senses Do Not Falsify"). Only in our processing of sense-impressions did we so-called 'lie'; i.e., in perceptive and linguistic processing of impressions. To Nietzsche, our *e-field* is our original sensation-chaos upon which we create a relatively coherent world thanks to our perceptive and linguistic processing of sense-data. We so-called 'falsify' the reality of sense-data not only by grouping an element world together in familiar perceptive images but helped also by language in this simplification of the *e-field*. To the model above, we would consequently need to add this linguistic processing, as our perceived images are not only sensational in nature, but linguistic as well; consequently, to the *e/s-field* needs to be added an *e/s/l-field* where language and perception cooperate in creating the familiar world of easily identifiable objects. However, in Nietzsche's dramatic language, this is our 'lie' and 'falsification.'[214]

Finally, in a sufficiently complex model, we would need to add a domain for conceptualization. This complex model would approximately correspond to Nietzsche's explanation from TL, where he suggested first the nerve-stimulus (the *e-field*), second, the image (the *e/s-field*), third, the word (an *e/s/l-field*) and finally, the concept (an *e/s/l/c field*).

6. The Exaggerated Fear of Solipsism

An 'anti-phenomenalistic' interpretation of Mach entails the supposed virtue that it avoids 'solipsism.' While Banks introduces this well-rehearsed 'danger' of phenomenal theories of knowledge, in my understanding, this fear is exaggerated, as we are decisively beyond 'solipsism' in the present account of a Nietzsche-Machean theory of knowledge.

Banks believes that this danger comes about if we interpret Mach's elements as "my sensations" (and seems indeed sympathetic to Lenin's rebuttal of the 'Machists' in his criticism of Empirio-Criticsm):

> It often seems that all of Mach's physical elements can be interpreted as *my sensations*, by considering only their psychical variations.[...] Mach's elements were severely limited to one consciousness at a time, and he would be vulnerable to charges of solipsism and idealism despite his own insistence on their objectivity. V. I. Lenin made this point with brio in his *Materialism and Empirio-Criticism*, directed against Russian Machists.[215]

I am unable to see that a Nietzsche-Machean epistemology placing any emphasis on either private ideas or private languages. It does place a strong emphasis on 'sensations,' but in a theory implying that the processing of elements of an appearing world result in 'images' that are approximately identical because we as species share our perceptive apparatus. Thus, the appearing world will appear to everybody as approximately the same, since it is perceived by the same identical perceptive-cognitive apparatus in different individuals. Similarly, it is symbolized as approximately the same thanks to our shared languages. In Nietzsche and peers, there is no room for 'private perceptions' as little as for 'private languages.'

If two individuals look at something within a shared perceptive field, i.e., a shared *e-field*, they will approximately see the same, since they are enveloped by the same appearing world seen by the same perceptive apparatuses, only with the usual variations created by their shifting attention, focus, and visual perspectives, etc. Whether as a single individual or as two, we are enclosed by the same *e-field*, cf., model above, and sense therefore *the same* field because our cleverly evolved sense-apparatus makes us sense the same. Admittedly, but in a rather trivial and obvious sense, we are receiving and processing impressions differently and differently from one moment to the next. Still, we are able to remedy this variation, this inevitable empirical incongruence between two persons who happen to possess two minds instead of one, because we have evolved the habit occasionally to point out particular segments in our perceptive *e-field* to draw it into the perceptive *e/s-field* of the other. Oftentimes we help this pointing exercise by performing a speech-act, "look at the oak," at this point drawing a certain element group into our perceptive-linguistic *e/s/l-field*. We simplify an element-group by means of uttering a word, and the word becomes our signifier for the appointed element-group in our *e-field*. At this point, both of us look at an oak. Our multi-dimensional element world has successfully become one-dimensional, because thanks to our conventional language 'an oak is an oak,' as well as 'a leaf is a leaf,' 'a dog is a dog,' and 'a stone is a stone.'

My model seems, thus, to apply with minor variations, whether it illustrates sensation of one or of two egos. Instead of a single inner oval embedded in the bigger oval of sense-impressions, wrapped up in the same inaccessible enigmatic X-world, we simply add another inner oval, in such a way that two egos instead of one are wrapped up in the same world, seeing this world streaming past them. If they are wrapped up in the same language too, they are able to quickly signify a particular element-group as a 'tree' or an 'oak,' which simplifies their focus and saves time as they orient themselves in the world they see.

Certainly, this successfully achieved agreement is in a Nietzsche-Machean theory of knowledge the end-point of analysis, not the beginning. Indeed, if we go back to 'analysis,' the achieved one-dimensional world becomes again multi-dimensional, because then we must in honesty admit that however strongly we as two individuals focus our attention on the same appearing world, we hardly see the exact self-same, because we can never completely reduce our two minds to one. However, it is difficult here to see this plain fact as a problem, indeed a *logical* problem?

7. Claude Monet's Impressionism as a Model on Positivism

It is interesting to contemplate Claude Monet's paintings as a help to understand the phenomenal epistemology of Nietzsche and Mach, especially his 'series' of motives painted in different seasons or at different times of the day, in different light or from different angles; his haystacks, his water lilies, or his Cathedrals of Rouen are excellent illustrations of Nietzsche-Machean phenomenalism.

His series of no less than twenty-eight paintings of the Cathedral of Rouen, seen at different times of the day and in different light, shows us a cathedral broken up into 'sensation-elements.' It is as such deconstructed into a complex of context-dependent sensations, which antedates our mental construction of the physical-material cathedral. However, it is in this not reduced to a Berkelean or Schopenhaurian idea; let us notice that impressionism or phenomenalism is indeed *anti-idealism*, because the 'idea' is mere form, i.e., the reduction of sense-impressions to their simplest possible, easiest to remember, form, while 'impressions,' 'phenomena,' or 'elements,' as our first perceptive encounters with the appearing world, predate the 'form.'

Painting twenty-eight cathedrals, Monet manages to illustrate the Machean idea that the world is un-repeatable. Monet is not trying to re-present the 'thing-in-itself,' but to *see* the flicker of a world broken up in impressions that change from one moment to the next. It is characteristic of impressionist technique that the *outline* of the object is replaced with brush-stokes or points of color as the painter's best imitation on how we cognitively construct an object. The speed with which a painting is conceived is another characteristic; the impressionist is always up against time destroying the moment, and must do his or her best to capture the moment in as few brush-strokes as possible. The best of the impressionists have internalized an economics of brush-strokes.

If Monet had painted only one cathedral, he would already have made his point; by painting a series of twenty-eight, he demonstrates it even better, namely how the 'permanent enduring object' is broken up in an infinite series of flickers of impressions. He insists on repeating the same object, the Cathedral, but he shows that repetition of the same is never repetition of the self-same, but rather an eternal repetition of variations of the same. His series of twenty-eight painting of the 'same' in a state of becoming 'deconstructs' the notion of the *thing-itself=truth*, and illustrates the Machean idea that 'we see nature but once.' We do not hold that Monet's cathedrals are true seen from one angle but false from another, true in one season but false in another, true at one time of the day but false at another. We do not assign truth-values to his cathedrals, his water lilies, or his haystacks.

The dogmatic realist may look at Monet's cathedrals and assure him or herself that behind the many versions we would find the same objective cathedral. Monet could be seen as a perspectivist in the harmless sense, insofar as he sees *the same* from different angles at different hours of the day. His many cathedrals may thus serve as illustration of the repeatability of the same true object-world. The realist presupposing that behind the many canvases we have the implicit cathedral as it could be captured by a good camera, objectively standing *there* frozen in time caught at one universal time on one universal day in one universal season under one universal weather condition. The 'implicit' cathedral, i.e., as thing-in-itself, has no time of day, no season, and no weather; it is the same whether at dawn, at noon, or at dusk; it is the same whether the day is sunny, grey, rainy, or snowy.

The Nietzsche-Machean positivist might reply that the 'implicit' cathedral is in actuality the 'idea' of the cathedral, formed after it has appeared to us in all kinds of weather. The 'implicit cathedral' is in fact *ideal form*, which, ironically, the *realist* keeps insisting upon as the true *material object*. It is this *ideal form* proposed to be *material object* that is under questioning in Nietzsche, Mach and Monet alike.

4. The Fictional Concept in Vaihinger and Nietzsche

1. "Fictionalism" as Radical Neo-Kantianism

Vaihinger was one of the important neo-Kantian philosophers at the turn of the nineteenth century. He was the founding father of the still prominent journal *Kant-Studien* and the author of a two volume monograph on Kant's *Critique of Pure Reason*, (*Kommentar zu Kants Kritik des reinen Vernunft*, 1881 and 1892), but he is best known for his *Die Philosophie 'Als Ob'* (1911; *The Philosophy 'As If'*; 1925).[216] Like Nietzsche, he was profoundly influenced by Schopenhauer and Fr. Lange, and was as such imbedded in contemporary debates on neo-Kantianism, naturalism, positivism, and pragmatism.

In juxtaposition to Nietzsche, it is Vaihinger' major opus, *Die Philosophie des 'Als Ob,'* which is interesting for our purposes. Its publications-date, 1911, seems to indicate that there is a gap of a generation or two between Nietzsche and Vaihinger. However, this is misleading, because, as Vaihinger explains in his preface, its first and most important part was written already in 1876/1877 as his doctoral dissertation. Thereupon he started preparing the manuscript for publication, a revision-work he would keep delaying and interrupting for various reasons (illness, other engagements, and doubts regarding the relevance of his work), before he finally, after no less than thirty-five years, was able to publish the book in 1911. This piece of historical information is interesting because it makes Nietzsche and Vaihinger intellectual contemporaries. They have apparently been working out their thinking simultaneously (however independently), with Vaihinger writing the first version of his *Die Philosophie des 'Als Ob'* about the same time as Nietzsche is writing his *Menschliches, Allzumenschlisches* (1876–1879).

In the preface to his work, Vaihinger reports that it was the discovery of Nietzsche's writings in 1898 that gave him the impetus to revisit and rework his neglected dissertation.

> Now I saw, that the time for my book had arisen. [...] When I read Nietzsche in the end of the nineties, [...] I realized to my happy surprise the deep familiarity between our life and world understanding, which partially derived from the same sources, Schopenhauer and F. A. Lange.[217]

Vaihinger and Nietzsche are inspired by the same primary sources (Schopenhauer and Lange), imbedded in the same contemporary Kantian and neo-Kantian discussions, and committed to the new "Biological Theory of Knowledge" (Vaihinger's label), which is gaining ground thanks to Darwin and inspiring other contemporaries, e.g., R. Avenarius and E. Mach.[218] Vaihinger mentions Pragmatism too as an influence, especially in the version of C. S. Peirce, while he distances himself from a so-called "uncritical pragmatism," characterized as an "epistemological Utilitarianism of the worst kind," falsely proclaiming that "what is of use for us, what helps us to endure life, is true."[219] Supposedly, Vaihinger is here referring to J. Bentham and J. Stuart Mill's Utilitarianism, which also receives harsh reviews by Nietzsche around in his work.

Vaihinger characterizes his *Als Ob* philosophy alternately as "Idealistic" or "Critical" Positivism. It is first *positivism*, because it "with complete determination and candor alone moves in the direction of the basis of the given, the empirical sense-content."[220] It is secondly *idealism*, because it "recognizes and adopts any idea emerging from intellectual and ethical needs, as useful and valuable fictions of humankind, without which human thinking, feeling, and action would wither away."[221] In the latter regard, he furthermore characterizes his thinking as a "phenomenology of the ideational and reproductive consciousness."[222] Qua these self-descriptions, he relates his thinking to at least three major 'schools' developing and coming into prominence during the first of half of the twentieth century, namely Positivism, Pragmatism, and Phenomenology.[223]

In Vaihinger's review of Nietzsche, he sees him as sharing the same intellectual background and suggesting solutions to current epistemological problems identical to his own. In other words, his own *Fictionalism* and Nietzsche's *Interpretation-philosophy* start out from the same critical premises and end with the same radical conclusions.[224]

As we have noted, there was at the turn of the nineteenth century nothing particularly controversial about placing Nietzsche in the Naturalist, Positivist, and Pragmatic camps. Only after the Second World War, this affiliation virtually disappears in Nietzsche-commentary, as it becomes commonplace to see him first as an 'existentialist' and later as the patron saint of postmodernism (both among prominent proponents of the postmodernist movements and by prominent detractors). Habermas, for example, complains in his *The Philosophical Discourse of Modernity*[225] about Nietzsche's over-emphasis on the so-called 'poetic dimension' in the context of his own tables for 'communicative actions'[226] and regards Nietzsche as an *anti-enlightenment* thinker. To temper this authoritative and dominant assessment of Nietzsche, it is worthwhile here to mention that one of the prominent Machean positivists, Philipp Frank, regarded Nietzsche as *continuing the enlightenment project*.

> Nietzsche is the other great enlightenment philosopher of the end of the nineteenth century. The harmony of his epistemological views with those of Mach, who had gone through an entirely different course of instruction and possessed an entirely different temperament and entirely different ethical ideals, seems to me to be evidence for the fact that such view must have penetrated to the enlightened minds of that time.[227]

When Nietzsche frequently has been cited for promoting a theory of knowledge where 'truth' is an 'illusion,' 'metaphor,' or 'falsification,' then he is seen as asserting something that postmodernists also would assert, but as has been discussed, it goes largely unnoticed that the assertions are uttered in intellectual contexts different from those of the postmodernists. To express a truth-critical theory of knowledge coming from a Kantian background, is different than expressing it coming from a Saussurian (or pseudo-Saussurian) background as Derrida and followers do.

The same provision we can apply to Vaihinger. Vaihinger's metaphysical fictionalism does not entail a claim about the world, but about the knowledge we form, qua concepts, about the world. In his *Als Ob* philosophy, we present these concepts *as if* true, while they are 'fictional' in the precise sense of 'abstract,' 'simplifying,' and 'constructed.'[228] 'Fictionalism' is in agreement with Nietzsche's philosophy of interpretation when he argues that we are 'interpreting' and 'falsifying' our world when we create concepts like 'thing-in-itself,' 'substance,' 'cause,' 'force,' and 'atom' in order to facilitate our understanding. In both writers, first and foremost the *conceptual* and *theoretical* world is 'fictional.' Various important axioms are constructed as so-called fictions in scientific disciplines such as physics, chemistry, biology, psychology, and economics. However, it is usually emphasized in them both that these conceptual fictions are *useful* and even *necessary* in order to produce theoretical results and/or cultural advancement.[229]

As we have seen in the discussion of Mach, in Vaihinger and Nietzsche, a 'material' or 'objective' world is inaccessible, as they have learnt from Kant that it is 'in-itself.' This implies that the concepts we form about it have no reference to an *identifiable objective something*. The concept is as such a 'fiction,' while the material world would be, if anything, radically non-fictional, but precisely therefore also inaccessible. Briefly, the naked matter-world would be radically language-independent, non-human, and amoral. It would be a world '*as is*,' in contrast to our constructed theory-world, which is '*as if*.' The 'as is' world, however, would not give us hard evidence of pre-existing 'natural laws,' ultimate causes, or other objectivities, but would rather manifests itself as random, chaotic, and ever-changing in multiple different directions.[230] This distinction between an inexpressible 'as is' world and a conceptually expressed 'as if' world is well explained by Vaihinger, when he writes,

> It is impossible for us to express the sequences, which we observe without the intervention of discursive thought. But to regard this as an expression of reality is an antiquated attitude. We must therefore accept as actually real only certain sequences of sensation from which there arise [...] structures that are treated as fictions. [...] It is however not possible without the aid of discursive thought to make ourselves intelligible to others. Without this discursive aid [...] there would be nothing left for us to do but to remain silent and stare vacantly into space.[231]

We are in the neo-Kantian paradigm not able to access the 'thing-in-itself,' but we are able to perceive sequences of sensations and to form 'discursive thought,' which can thereupon be communicated to other participants in a scientific community. Nietzsche's interpreted world is conceptually identical to Vaihinger's fictional '*as if*' world. It is the world where the 'thing-in-itself' has disappeared and been replaced with 'interpretations' starting already with our species-specific perception of the world, which is thereupon being further 'interpreted' in speech and finally in theoretical concepts (cf. Part I, A.4) in order for us to explain, understand, and give meaning to the silent and vacant space enveloping us as a species.

As one of the leading Kantian thinkers in his day, it is unsurprising that Vaihinger is applying Kant's critique of the 'thing-in-itself' in his thinking. To illustrate his 'as if' philosophy he uses pertinently Kant's own master-concept, 'thing-in-itself,' which Vaihinger now sees as a *necessary fiction* allowing the distinction of the world into subject and object, and thus producing the *idea* of 'objectivity.'

> The fiction of the thing-in-itself would thus be the most brilliant of all conceptual instruments. Kant introduces the concept of the thing in itself as an x to which a y, the ego, as our organization, corresponds. By this means, the whole world of reality can be dealt with. Subsequently the 'ego' and the thing-in-itself are dropped and only sensations remain as real. From our point of view, the sequence of sensations constitutes ultimate reality, and two poles are mentally added, subject and object.[232]

Although the 'thing-in-itself' is a non-existing fiction, it is a good concept; as idea it is a good idea. It remains a construct, a *fiction*, but a *useful fiction* as long as it is only asserted as idea. It becomes an error, when it degenerates into a *hypothesis*. When the fiction becomes hypothesis, we start to believe that it can possibly be verified or falsified depending on further observation and collection of evidence. By contrast, the *fictional* concept is like an artificial symbol in mathematical equations that eventually 'drops out' when it has fulfilled its purpose.[233] The thing-in-itself as fiction asserts an opposition between thing and appearance, between object and subject, and when eventually the notion drops out as it must, so does the classical dualism between 'thing' and 'appearance' and we are left with *sensational reality*, the so-called world of appearances as the only 'real.'

> The division of the world in things-in-themselves = objects and things-in-themselves = subjects is the primary fiction upon which all other depend. From the standpoint of critical positivism, there is no absolute, no thing-in-itself, no subject, and no object. All that remains is sensations, which exist, and are given, and out of which the whole subjective is constructed with its division into physical and psychical complexes. Critical Positivism asserts that [...] only the observed sequence and co-existence of phenomena exist, and upon these alone it takes its stand.[234]

When Kant in the second edition to the *Critique of Pure Reason* rehabilitates the 'thing-in-itself,' Vaihinger, in agreement with most neo-Kantians as well as Nietzsche, is convinced that Kant has misunderstood himself as he has started treating the thing-itself as a *hypothesis*.[235]

Vaihinger sees Nietzsche as promoting a critique similar to his own: "Nietzsche also recognizes the distinction between thing-in-itself and appearances as an artificial one and consequently as a conceptual invention: 'the true essence of things is an invention of the conceiving being, without which it would not be able to represent things to itself.'"[236] The view is shared by Fr. Lange, this master-thinker of both Nietzsche and Vaihinger, when Lange describes the 'thing' as simply a "thought thing" or a "limit concept" [*ein blosses Gedankending . . . ein blosser Grenzbegriff*], or when Lange elaborates, "When one asks why there are things, then the answer is: thanks to the appearances. The more the 'thing in itself' vanishes as simple idea, the more the world of appearances gains in reality. The natural disposition of our reason leads us necessarily beyond the world, which we perceive by our senses."[237]

In Lange, Nietzsche, and Vaihinger we arrive to a position in which the apparent sensation-world becomes the *nether limit for knowledge*, while the linguistic and conceptual super-structure is a 'fiction' or 'interpretation.' The language of Vaihinger and Nietzsche is near identical when they describe this all-important world of *sensations*. In Vaihinger we read, "the sequence of sensations constitutes ultimate reality," while Nietzsche has it, "the sensations are the ultimate reality" [*die Sensationen sind die letzte Realität*]."[238] Like Nietzsche in his late writings, Vaihinger too emphasizes the positivist creed that only sense-reality is objectively real: "The only thing that is real and will remain real is the observable unchangeability of phenomena, their relations, etc. Everything else is a mere illusion with which the psyche plays about."[239]

Although concepts are fictions, they are still grounded in sensational reality, having been devised with the purpose of resolving a problem. Without these conditions, they devolve into "empty husks" says Nietzsche, "husks without content," says Vaihinger: "As soon as a fiction is regarded apart from the ground on which it has developed and apart from the purpose it fulfils, then it is a husk without content."[240] This thinking can only remind us of Nietzsche's 'dead metaphors' (cf. Part I, A.6); i.e., metaphors claiming an existence of their own, alienating themselves from the human who originally used them as creative abbreviations of states of affairs too complex in themselves to be expressed. In Vaihinger's vocabulary, 'fictions' degrade into 'hypotheses' when they gain independence. At this point they are "illusions." Concepts, Vaihinger says (again in language reminiscent of Nietzsche's), "possess validity only in relation to reality; without it they are dead. Regarded apart from their purpose they are valueless."[241]

2. The Biological Theory of Knowledge in Vaihinger, Avenarius, and Nietzsche

In addition to the obvious inspiration from Kant, continued in neo-Kantianism and Critical Positivism, Nietzsche and Vaihinger adhere almost uniformly to the newly emerged 'biological theory of knowledge' deriving from the evolutionary thinking of Darwin and other naturalists. Like Lange, Vaihinger subscribes to Darwinism and he believes that Nietzsche too belongs to that tradition, despite of his "misunderstandings" of Darwin (as well as, according to Vaihinger, Nietzsche belongs to the Kantian tradition despite his "misunderstandings" of Kant):

> The Kantian or, if you will, neo-Kantian origin of Nietzsche's doctrine has hitherto been completely ignored, because Nietzsche [...] has repeatedly and ferociously attacked Kant whom he quite misunderstood. As well as he attacked Darwin, to who he was just as much indebted.[242]

In *Nietzsche als Philosoph* (1902),[243] Vaihinger sees Nietzsche's teaching as a "positively applied Schopenhaurianism," reversed and revaluated "under the influence of Darwin";[244] Nietzsche turns away from Schopenhauer's a-historicism, and adopts the evolutionary point of view of Darwin:

> In this context, the historical evolutionary point of view of Darwinism becomes object for his profound interest and understanding. Particularly, he turns his interest toward the development of the moral ideas and the problem of cultural progress. [...] In this, we have located the inner core of the specific Nietzschean view of life: it is simply the Schopenhaurian teaching of Will but seen positively under the influence of Darwinism and the teaching of the struggle for existence.[245]

This adopted naturalist and evolutionary thinking is seen as the most logical theoretical foundation of Fictionalism. Lange, Vaihinger, and Nietzsche take for granted that physical processes have evolved in order to respond to stimuli most expediently. Thought-processes too are such expedient physiological processes participating in the struggle for existence, and the phenomenon of thought has as such a primary biological function. This makes thought a biological rather than a rational phenomenon. In Vaihinger's description, which would apply to Nietzsche too,

> The organic function of thought goes on mostly *unconsciously*. [...] The actual fundamental processes happen in the darkness of the unconscious. [...] They are completely instinctive and unconscious, even if they later emerge in the luminous circle of consciousness.[246]

The narrative is approximately the following, during our evolutionary history, we adopted, out of survival concerns, an intellectual ability to process that which is given, i.e., sensational reality where we encounter regularity in coexistence and succession of events and instances. However, as thinking starts to evolve as a trait in homo sapiens, it begins to take on a life of its own and it develops into an activity exercised for its own purpose. It emancipates itself from its original practical purposes and becomes an end in itself, as it develops into theoretical thinking preoccupied with problems that are impossible to answer. After this decline, thought becomes a mere fiction forming an 'as if' world that now becomes as important as, if not more important than, the 'real' sensational world.[247]

It is one of the many consequences of this naturalism concluding to fictionalism that the organism is not a mere receptacle into which matter is poured; consciousness is not a 'passive mirror' reflecting reality. In Vaihinger's words.

> Consciousness is not like a passive mirror that reflects rays according to purely physical laws; consciousness receives no external stimulus without forming it according to its own matter. The psyche is *an organic formative force [Gestalungskraft]*, which independently and purposefully changes received material. [...] The mind not merely appropriates, it is also assimilates and constructs. During growth, *its creates the ability of its organs* [...] and *adapts them to external circumstances*. [...] Logical thought is an active appropriation of the outer world and is therefore an organic function of the psyche.[248]

In the naturalist evolutionary conception, thinking becomes a biological adaptation as it facilitates the human species in its struggle for survival; knowledge is required for acquisition of food and for the protection from the elements, and thinking helps to solve these basic problems. This view had been introduced most originally by Richard Avenarius, who Vaihinger is explicitly citing on several occasions in his work, and who seems to have been known by Nietzsche as well.

Today, Avenarius is virtually forgotten. The fact that he has never been translated into English together with the inaccessibility of his German has probably held him back in obscurity.[249] Ironically, he is best known because Lenin found it necessary to write a treatise denouncing his so-called 'Empirio-Criticism,' which he perceived as a threat to the official doctrine of Dialectical Materialism.[250]

Vaihinger is dedicating a section to a discussion of Avenarius's so-called economy-principle as proposed in Avenarius's, *Philosophie als Denken der Welt gemäss dem Princip des kleinsten Kraftmasses* (1876).[251] Here it becomes clear how evolutionary biology is merged with epistemology, as according to Vaihinger's account of Avenarius.

> The psyche must be regarded as a machine. [...] A machine is an appliance of practical mechanics by means of which a given movement is accomplished

with the least expenditure of force. This requirement is to a great extent fulfilled by the human psyche, when is seen as a psychical machine; in this sense it is purposeful and efficient [*zweckmässig*]. [...] The work demanded of the human psyche is movement is the broadest sense of the word; first the purely external movements and reflex movements, and thereupon voluntary movements for the sake of preserving the organism. The total psychical machine must therefore be regarded as an energy-saving machine, as an arrangement enabling the organism to perform its movements as efficiently as possible, i.e., as quickly, elegantly, and with the least expenditure of force [*geringstem Kraftaufwand*] as possible. [...] We must consider that as the human being continually improves upon its machine, it will perform its required work still quicker, better, more efficiently, and with still improved conservation of force [*Kraftersparnis*]. [...] The psyche is a continually self-improving machine, which fulfills the purpose to perform as safe and as quick and with the least expenditure of force the life-preservative movements of the organism; i.e., movements in the broadest sense of the word, as the ultimate end-goal for all action. Our sensations [*Empfindungen*] are the roots for all our mental life, and culminates in movement; what lies in-between are merely transit-points [*Durchgangspunkt*]. The gradual perfection of the thought-machine is for example clearly expressed in the law of the condensation of ideas. [...] Condensation is in the psychical machine of no less importance than in the machine of physical Mechanics. The entire concept-formation can be reduced to a condensation-process through which the working capacity is considerably increased. [...] To regard concepts as ends in themselves is an error. [...] The resolution of the entire world of representations in such thought-devices is the proper task for a theory of knowledge; the methodology of these devices forms logic. All logical methods, including here the fictive, are only aiding and assisting this machine. [...] The essential task of methodology is to learn to manipulate this thought-machine and thought-device [*Denkmaschine und Denksmittel*].[252]

Vaihinger's presentation of the psyche as a 'machine' working according to the principle of the least expenditure of force (or energy), refers to Avenarius's idea that our psyche functions according to "the principle of the smallest masses of force." The principle is an economy-principle stating that we as biological organisms always prefer to solve problems with the 'least effort.' Thus, as species, not only do we have a drive to solve problems, but to solve them as efficiently as possible. We are so to speak *constitutionally lazy* (at least when we function at our optimum) insofar as our minds conserve as much energy as possible when applied to problems. We notice that Avenarius and Vaihinger are inheriting discussions from the scientific context of the late nineteenth century, namely the energy-conservation law as it had been proposed by scientists like H. von Helmholtz, L. Boltzmann, and E. Mach. Now, this energy-conservation law from cutting-edge physics is applied to the functioning of the human organism.

Our thinking, too, and by extension philosophy, is performed according to this principle of 'least effort' or 'highest efficiency.' From a biological psycho-physical perspective, our conceptual constructions of systems are performed because *systematization* in itself is conservation of force (*Krafter-sparniss*). Avenarius explains it this way: When we systematize, we organize various 'masses of representations' into a complex that are subjected to one overriding central representation (a so-called *Centralvorstellung*). This ordering enhances our ability to better apperceive, survey, and orient ourselves in the mass of representations that always encounter and overwhelm us. Now, the more *familiar* the *Centralvorstellung*, the easier is it to organize new content under its label; as such, it stabilizes the system by connecting everything to everything else. According to Avenarius, the biological mind chooses to represent material in the most familiar and customary fashion; it always prefers that which is easiest, that which it has already learnt and internalized. As well as the mind is striving to adjust itself to the *familiar*, it attempts to avoid the *unfamiliar*. As well as thinking the familiar fills the mind with pleasure, the thinking of the unfamiliar fills it with displeasure since the unfamiliar presents to the mind representations not already internalized by its system. The unfamiliar forces us into thinking something new instead of the old, which creates discomfort and even 'fear.' Therefore, old and familiar apperceptions (so-called *Gewohnheitsapperceptionen*) are preferred.[253] Avenarius lists their advantages as follows, they are: (1) immediately understood, implying that we do not need to waste energy on consulting alternative representations; (2) they do not need to be activated in all details; and (3) they are not necessarily represented with full consciousness; they have been over-learned to the point that they are largely reflexes.[254]

In speech and theoretical thinking, too, we economize masses of apperception, striving to delimit them to the fewest possible. Avenarius surmises that language historically develops from tribal societies having a vocabulary of few and relatively vague words, into societies employing still more distinct words. Originally, words would be vague and include several different representations. However, as language develops, words become more precise and better able to express more exact groups of representations; speakers would communicate 'ideas' still more precisely, and the more distinct the language, the better speakers are saving themselves from having to seek a meaning in a multitude of representations, i.e., the more words in a language, the more refined and precisely do speakers delimit their masses of apperception. Language is therefore itself evidence of a force-economical principle; it is in Avenarius, as also in Nietzsche, a 'simplification-' or an 'abbreviation-apparatus.'[255]

In his discussions of language, Mach too offers an analysis similar to Avenarius and Nietzsche's as he sees language as an economical device making an appearing world simpler and thus cognizable. Like in Avenarius and Nietzsche, language simplifies and familiarizes an otherwise too multifarious and complex reality.

> Language, the instrument of communication, is itself an economical contrivance. Experiences are analyzed, or broken up, into simpler and more familiar experiences, and then symbolized at some sacrifice of precision.[256]

> The most wonderful economy of communication is found in language. [...] Language, with its helpmate, conceptual thought, by fixing the essential and rejecting the unessential, constructs its rigid pictures of the fluid world on the plan of a mosaic, at a sacrifice of exactness and fidelity but with a saving of tools and labor.[257]

> No inalterable thing exists. The thing is an abstraction, the name a symbol, for a compound of elements from whose changes we abstract. The reason we assign a single word to a whole compound is that we need to suggest all the constituent sensations at once.[258]

In Avenarius, Mach, Vaihinger, and Nietzsche, the mind is an "energy saving machine"; it operates according to a force-economical principle by condensing ideas, as it, thanks to this condensation-process, heightens its performance. This biological-economical conception has the implication that there is no simple correspondence between 'idea' and 'object,' that "thought processes are not copies of reality itself, they are not in agreement with 'things,' logical processes are not the same as objective events."[259] Thought processes are from this biological-economic principle instead "instruments for finding our way about more easily in this world."[260] The thinking has an obvious pragmatic dimension, because ideas are not pursued for their own sake, but for the utility they may have to the human species as an organism.

On several occasions, Nietzsche adopts the view when he explicitly discusses the construction of our world as a process that simplifies and abbreviates, when he describes the mind as a 'simplification-' and 'abbreviation-apparatus.'[261] He believes, like Avenarius, that the mind does its best to repeat the familiar and avoid the unfamiliar. In his published work as well as in unpublished notes, he too sees the mind as transforming the new into the old, the unfamiliar into the familiar, the unknown into the known, and the inhuman into the human; suggested in language similar to Avenarius.'

> The strength of the spirit to appropriate what is foreign manifests itself in a strong tendency to assimilate the new to the old, to simplify the manifold, to overlook or put aside what is utterly contradictory—just as it arbitrarily highlights certain features and lines in what is foreign, in every piece of the 'external world.'[262]

> One wonders, one is anxious, one wants something familiar, which one can hold on to. . . As soon as something new is referred back to something old, we are calmed down. The so-called causality-instinct is only the fear of the unusual and an attempt to uncover therein something familiar. A search not for causes but rather for the familiar.[263]

> What is "knowledge" ["*erkennen*"]? To lead something strange back to something well-known and familiar. First principle: that which we have *gotten used to*, counts no longer as enigma, as problem.[264]

Regarding the question of causality that we addressed, Nietzsche suggested that humans actively construct causal sequences, not because a Kantian category is dictating a certain necessity in our perception, but because we "fear the unusual." Nietzsche's explanation turned biological and psychological; as humans we have an *active desire* to find causes, because we out of "fear" search for the "familiar." His thinking suggests that if I cannot see the *cause* of something experienced, the experience becomes unsettling (i.e., 'unfamiliar' and 'new'). If someone displays an unusual behavior or utters an incomprehensible remark, I seek to remedy my confusion by restoring the lost meaning by supplying a plausible cause for the behavior or the remark. If an unfortunate accident befalls me, I start to look for a cause that could *explain* why this random event is happening to *me*, etc. If we in these and other cases are able to construct a *cause* (some well-known principle), Nietzsche claims that "something new is referred back to something old" and we are "calmed down."

The bottom-line is that the world *in itself* is a chaotic and inaccessible ground, unto which we as humans apply our *interpretations* in order to familiarize the strange. Eventually, given the *relentless interpretive pressure we apply to this vacant space of nothing*, the world will eventually 'open' itself as 'meaning.' At that point, it is being constituted as Human ground, obeying our desire to see ourselves again in everything surrounding us. It is as such, we are 'humanizing the world' (cf. Part II, B.3: "Chronological Reversal of Cause and Effect").

As mentioned, this is not a uniquely Nietzschean thought; the idea was often asserted in nineteenth-century science discussions, for example in the discussions of Du Bois-Reymond and Lange discussed, when they maintained that before the theoretical construction, the non-representable necessarily had to be *personalized* and *pictured* in concepts familiar to the contemporary scientist.[265] The ground as such, the world beyond our sensations, the thing-in-itself, is nothing, and claims about the beyond the purely sensational are fictional. Therefore, Vaihinger concludes that, "the only fiction-less doctrine in the world is that of Critical Positivism. Any *more detailed or elaborate* claim about existence as such is fictional."[266]

5. Nietzsche's Positivism According to Habermas

Jürgen Habermas, in *Erkenntnis und Interesse* (1968) and in a *Nachwort* to an anthology of Nietzsche's epistemological writings (1968),[267] is one of the relatively few commentators of Nietzsche who in the 1860s understood that his theory of knowledge was situated in the positivist tradition.

Habermas may be best known for his criticism of Nietzsche in his *Der Philosophische Diskurs der Moderne* (1985),[268] where he sees Nietzsche as initiator of the increasingly influential postmodern and deconstructionist paradigm, and reacts to that influence. This association between Nietzsche and postmodernism, I have consistently discarded as misreading, adopted in much late twentieth century Nietzsche commentary without historical critical reflection (cf. Introduction 2.1: "Incompatibilities between the Naturalist and Deconstructive Project").

Although Habermas eventually falls into the same trap in his 1985 work, in earlier work, he is more accommodating in his analysis of Nietzsche, who he even regards as continuing the fundamentally progressive project of Enlightenment. In this early work, we find a highly relevant discussion of Nietzsche's epistemology that places it in agreement with the early neo-Kantian, Naturalist, and Positivist receptions.

> Nietzsche shares the positivist conception of science. Only that information which meets the criteria of empirical = scientific results counts as knowledge in rigorous sense. [...] Like Comte before him, Nietzsche conceives the critical consequences of scientific technical progress as overcoming metaphysics. [...] The process of enlightenment made possible by the sciences is critical, but the critical dissolution of dogmas produces not liberation but indifference. It is not emancipatory but nihilistic.[269]

Habermas is explicit that Nietzsche belongs in the Positivist tradition, with Comte as the influential predecessor, as he like Comte pursues the ideal of overcoming metaphysics by replacing old dogmas with empirical-scientific knowledge. In this, Nietzsche is indeed seen as an enlightenment thinker, with the caveat that Nietzsche's enlightenment thinking is not emancipatory but "nihilistic." To his credit, so Habermas, Nietzsche puts an emphasis on empirical-scientific knowledge in order to defeat the dogmas of superstition, religion, and metaphysics, but he does in this critique not produce liberation but "indifference."

This is the crux of early Habermas's critique of Nietzsche. In the context of the present work, we notice that Habermas is sufficiently clear-minded to see the connection between Nietzsche and Positivism, but fails in understanding how the *logic of positivist thinking* necessarily must lead to Nietzsche's conclusion, i.e., 'Nihilism.'

However, before elaborating on this critique of Habermas, let us address another issue, which Habermas understands better that the typical commentator writing in the 1960s and 1970s. With great clarity, he understands the importance of Nietzsche's evolutionary thinking and the theme of human self-preservation as a foundation for epistemology, promoted by Nietzsche in order to replace the appeal to transcendental categories in Kant and Schopenhauer with biological necessities.

> Nietzsche's 'theory of knowledge' [...] consists in the attempt to comprehend the categorical framework of the natural sciences (space, time, event), the concept of laws (causality), the operational axis of experience (measurement), and the rules of logic and calculation as the *relative a priori* of a world of objective illusion that has been produced for the purposes of mastering nature and of preserving existence: "the entire cognitive apparatus is an apparatus for abstraction and simplification—not directed at knowledge but at the control of things: 'end' and 'means' are as far from the essence as are 'concepts.'" [...] Nietzsche conceives science as the activity through which we turn 'nature' into concepts for the purpose of mastering nature. The compulsion to logical correctness and empirical accuracy exemplifies the constraint of the interest in possible technical control over objectified natural processes, and thereby the compulsion to preserving existence.[270]

The self-preservation motive in Nietzsche, Habermas describes as a "relative a priori," which strictly speaking is a contradiction in terms, but in his context seems to indicate that the universal and transcendental a priori-concepts have been replaced with the principle of self-preservation. As such, a Nietzschean world reduced to "objective illusion" has been replaced with evolutionary processes, implying that what we do and think is first and foremost a question of survival. In this sense, we are "a priori" under the "compulsion to preserve existence"; we are subjected to natural but random selective processes. Now, knowledge serves self-preservation interests as it brings nature under control; the intellect "has the function both of bringing under control an environment that threatens existence and of securing the reproduction of life. Biological self-preservation is thus the deepest motive for our production of knowledge."[271] The "relative a priori" of our self-preservation, not the 'absolute a priori' of 'universal truth,' is our 'deepest motive' in the production of knowledge.

In reference to TL, Habermas again joins the discussion we have pursued here and draws many of the same conclusions. He refers to Nietzsche's triadic model of the production of knowledge between nerve-stimuli, images, and words (cf. Part I, A.4), realizing the arbitrariness of the 'transferences' and the lack of correspondence between the different levels, when he writes.

> The elementary level of symbolic meaning consists of images that are produced poetically on the occasion of external stimuli. Between 'image' and 'nerve stimulus' there exists no reversible definite relation of correspondence: it depends much more on the meaning-inventing subjectivity as it transfers the external cause into metaphorical significance—in this way we play a 'groping game on the backs of things.'[272]

In the formation of symbolic meaning thanks to Nietzsche's "metaphors," Habermas realizes that these symbols need to be immediately forgotten as our own contribution so as to uphold the "objectivizing illusion." The actor does not comprehend his own production, and creates the objectivizing illusion in order to create an interpretation that is foundational and an illusion that can guarantee the security of knowledge.[273]

> Only the conventional solidification of conventional metaphors confers on the fanciful production an illusion of correspondence and thus 'truth.' Indeed, this poetic assimilation of the environment, the 'metamorphosis of the world in men,' takes place always in the framework of primary grammatical forms. If we acted only at the level of metaphors, we would remain captured in a world of dreams. Only the apparatus of concepts and abstractions grounds an intersubjective world of waking life. This construction of concepts is pre-formed in language.[274]

As Habermas says, we exist under the meta-logical force of our natural history, our contingent evolution into a species that not only perceives in a certain manner but also has a particular capacity to symbolize. In Nietzsche, Kantian categories are subsumed under the meta-logical principle of natural selection, as stated in later *Nachlaß* material (quoted here from Habermas): "We would not have the intellect we have if we did not *need* to have it" (Nietzsche, WM 498).[275] [...] "In the formation of reason, logic, and the categories, it was *need* that was authoritative" (Nietzsche, WM 515).[276] Thus, Kantian synthetic a priori judgments are not true in the sense that a concept corresponds to reality itself, they are 'true' in the sense that they have proven themselves useful in the service of preserving life. If truth is a fiction, and if the thing-in-itself as truth is a fiction, the correspondence theory of truth also becomes impossible to uphold. It all comes down to the preservation of man and, as Nietzsche says, "the preservation of man is not a proof of truth" (Nietzsche, WM 497).[277] Also noted by Habermas, Nietzsche always presupposes the classical metaphysical-ontological concept of truth, when he criticizes the 'transcendental a priori' or the 'thing-in-itself.' Against this exacting ideal of truth, truth-claims have to fail, and they seem to dwindle into the insignificant and random.

If it seems as if Nietzsche has replaced the true with the false, as if we live in an utterly arbitrary universe where nonsense is as good as carefully measured judgment, Habermas as well as undersigned resist this interpretation, because truth is never replaced with the random, but with the exigency of our evolutionary and linguistic competences. As species, we share our perceptive reception of the world and our capacity to arrange this world in language. These capacities are not uniquely individual, nor do they change from tribe to tribe, from class to class, from nation to nation, or from historical age to historical age. Communicative competences we share with the prehistoric human and visual perception we share with numerous animals and with almost all the mammals because we like them live in a spatial-temporal world illuminated by a bright star called the sun. These shared species-specific generally-evolved capacities warrant that we receive Nietzsche's 'nerve-stimuli' as approximately the same (with approximately similarly evolved organs), enabling us to see the same world.

In his work, Habermas even sees Nietzsche as participating in the Enlightenment tradition, insofar as his criticism of limiting modes of theoretical and social life, pursues the autonomy of reason. However, in Habermas's assessment, Nietzsche is taking his thinking too far toward the nihilism that emerges as a consequence of absolute positivism. Nietzsche in other words ignores or overlooks the normative component of human knowledge that Habermas keeps insisting on, which requires social responsibility and political commitment in the man of knowledge. It is in posing this political imperative, I see Habermas committing a mistake.

That Nietzsche may be seen as a late participant in the 'enlightenment' tradition seems correct also to undersigned. However, the now emancipated autonomous reason must *adopt* Nietzsche's 'nihilism' as its most logical and unbiased conclusion, not *repressing* this conclusion by regressing to Habermas's insistence on moral, social, or political responsibility in the formation of knowledge.

My fundamental argument is simple: the critical dissolution of dogmas should not lead us to the erection of new dogmas. 'Liberation' and 'emancipation' in Habermas imply that humans take social-political-ideological control over the sciences, in order to produce a scientific knowledge 'serving mankind.' That may sound correct, but it is a trap to subdue scientists under the arbitrary will of the politicians and the ideologues. It is also a step back from that empirical-scientific ideal that Habermas otherwise defends and sees Nietzsche defending. We cannot on the one hand devise a scientific methodology that bases its production of knowledge on empirical observation and scientific conceptualization, and then, on the other hand, demand that scientists need to follow political ideals.

Undersigned, however appreciative of Habermas's early readings of Nietzsche, sees contrary to Habermas, 'nihilism' as a great emancipative motive that if watered down by political-normative ideals starts an almost immediate and uncontrollable degeneration into ideology that eventually dulls critical consciousness. The emancipative ideal imposed as a moral imperative quickly coagulates and sediments itself as dogma. Only absolute nihilism prevents this coagulation, this almost immediate sedimentation of a new 'good' and 'evil.'

Instead of Habermas's 'critical theory,' we need today, rather, a 'hyper-critical theory,' and only "Nihilism" provides a good theoretical foundation for this hyper-criticism. If Nietzsche's 'super-human' is the figure par excellence embracing Nihilism, he or she personify this anti-priest and anti-ideologue, embracing absolute Nihilism as a hyper-critical 'politics' that never loses its vigilance against the self-righteous reiterations of new self-other, good-evil formations.[278]

C: FINAL ASSESSMENT

1. What Is 'True' and What Is 'False' in Nietzsche's Discussion of Knowledge?

'*Was is also Wahrheit?*' is Nietzsche's guiding question in TL. Paraphrasing Nietzsche, we may ask the same question, but with specific reference to his work: '*Was is also Wahrheit*' in Nietzsche?

After our reconstructive reading, we understand that the human *drive for Truth* (in the metaphysical and theological sense) and its *drive for lying* is the same thing—a surprising and paradoxical equation, to be sure. However, to Nietzsche, the human being seeking final and absolute answers *essentially* lies when it tells itself that its answers are Truths. The 'drive for truth' is a 'drive for deception,' as we often read in Nietzsche (e.g., BGE 1). Setting up a truth table for Nietzsche's discussion, we can say without much hesitation that the classical concept (i.e., the 'metaphysical,' 'theological,' 'absolute,' 'universal,' 'unconditional,' etc.) of Truth *is false*. By contrast, Nietzsche's many replacements of Truth are true, including perceptive and linguistic concepts. Our sense-perceptions as such are 'true' when they record appearances; our speech-acts are 'true' when they convey a conventional correspondence between utterances and references; our conceptual formula are 'true' when they as economical tools facilitate our biological and social advancement and survival.[279] I have argued that Nietzsche, in the second part of TL (TL2), introduces a type-different concept of 'truth' belonging in the Romantic paradigm, according to which 'truth' as intuitive insight grasped by the myth-creating artist *is true*.[280] In Nietzsche's later work, he seems to have corrected himself and rejected this idea as *false*.

Nietzsche, far from being a 'truth-denier,' is as such a defender of truth, because in this criticism of the false concept of Truth, he always carefully suggests alternative *positive* concepts of the true. He criticizes 'Truth' understood as a metaphysical and theological concept, exactly because it is unscientific, dogmatic, and religious. It presupposes a designed world waiting to be discovered, and a designed world takes a designer (an outrageous proposition to Nietzsche). In conformity with his age, Nietzsche defends *pragmatic scientific* concepts of truth, as these alternative concepts of 'truth' always are context-dependent, albeit 'context-dependent' in a sometimes exceptionally broad sense. The 'context' on which they depend may be as general as our shared visual perception and our shared linguistic conventions. In the context of our physiology, we have evolved an ability to perceive, orient ourselves in, and react to one single for-us world (not to several different parallel worlds), and in the context of our languages, we have become able to identify and communicate to each other interesting segments of this for-us world. Within these general contexts, we may refer correctly or incorrectly to things and states of affairs, and we may be sincere or insincere in our linguistic interactions. Within these contexts, we form knowledge of certain states of affairs. Still, the knowledge we form is *not* absolute and unconditional.

If the validity of our truth-claims is defined within such a broad context, what is it Nietzsche tells us that we *cannot know*? First, he tells us that we cannot know the world *as such*, as something *in-itself*; this consequence comes about thanks to the principle of 'biological perspectivism' (cf. Part I, A.8). Consequently, we cannot discover objective correspondences between ourselves and the world *as such*; i.e., the single for-us world and another in-itself world. The latter construction is pure hypothesis; the in-itself world might for that sake be a multiplicity of parallel worlds, rather than that hard reassuring objectivity the dogmatic realist always seems to appeal to. Second, Nietzsche denies that our concepts can fully exhaust the world for its essential contents (laws, causes, substances, etc.). Concepts, as our constructions or 'schematizations,' merely simplify by selecting and deselecting identified segments of the perceived world; they fragmentize the world in order to put it together again as a simpler and more abstract version of itself. This simpler version Nietzsche describes as 'falsifying' or 'fictional,' but only because he for a second refers to the false comparison-background of a metaphysical 'real' world, i.e., the false assumption that we might have access to a fully 'True' version of the world. Third, he points out that relativizing the notion of truth entails relativizing the notion of the 'good' as well. This has not been my issue in the present work, but whether we examine historical societies and their ideologies or scrutinize our innermost intentions, it is granted that we cannot determine *the* 'Good.' Nietzsche's 'naturalist deconstruction' of Truth must imply a deconstruction of the Good, too, because according to the naturalist paradigm, inherited selfish survival motives immediately overrides putative unselfish intentions. Our ability to *understand* our intentions and ourselves is in question also because the ego-centered narcissistic self cannot carry out a pure objectifying illumination of itself. In any case, our selves are in our way in achieving truly objective knowledge, because *we* perceive, *we* conceptualize, and *we* judge. We cannot dispense with the 'we' and get a glimpse of what is *there* without *us*.

We thus see the following tendency in Nietzsche, whenever he encounters the claim that there is one *Truth* about any of our worlds (e.g., the exterior world of perception, the communicative world of languages, the scientific world of concepts, the interior world of self-reflection, or the ethical world of moral judgments), he sees such a theory of knowledge as *False*. However, when it is the claim that we, as situated in any of these worlds, produce provisional 'truths' about them, he will see the theory of knowledge as *true* (although knowledge produced within the framework of a correct theory of knowledge is never guaranteed to be *True*, but at best only *provisionally true*).

Appendix
"On Truth and Lies in a Non-Moral Sense"

A new translation of Nietzsche's,
"Ueber Wahrheit und Lüge im außermoralischen Sinne"
(Sämtliche Werke, *KSA* 1, pp. 875–90)

Part I
§ 1
– 875 –

In irgend einem abgelegenen Winkel des in zahllosen Sonnensystemen flimmernd ausgegossenen Weltalls gab es einmal ein Gestirn, auf dem kluge Tiere das Erkennen erfanden. Es war die hochmütigste und verlogenste Minute der "Weltgeschichte": aber doch nur eine Minute. Nach wenigen Atemzügen der Natur erstarrte das Gestirn, und die klugen Tiere mußten sterben.—So könnte jemand eine Fabel erfinden und würde doch nicht genügend illustriert haben, wie kläglich, wie schattenhaft und flüchtig, wie zwecklos und beliebig sich der menschliche Intellekt innerhalb der Natur ausnimmt. Es gab Ewigkeiten, in denen er nicht war; wenn es wieder mit ihm vorbei ist, wird sich nichts begeben haben. Denn es gibt für jenen Intellekt keine weitere Mission, die über das Menschenleben hinausführte. Sondern menschlich ist er, und nur sein Besitzer und Erzeuger nimmt ihn so pathetisch, als ob die Angeln der Welt sich in ihm drehten. Könnten wir uns aber mit der Mücke verständigen, so würden wir vernehmen, daß auch sie mit diesem Pathos durch die Luft schwimmt und in sich das fliegende Zentrum dieser Welt fühlt.

Part I
§ 1

In some remote corner of a universe in which numerous flickering solar systems are scattered there was once upon a time a star upon which clever creatures invented knowing. That was the most arrogant and dishonest minute of "world history," but it was after all only a minute. After nature had drawn a few breaths, the star froze and the clever creatures had to die.—One might invent such a story, and would still not have adequately described how miserable, how shadowy and transient, how aimless and arbitrary the human intellect looks within nature. There were eternities during which it did not exist; and when eventually it is over, nothing will have happened. For this intellect has no additional mission which takes it beyond human life. Rather, the intellect is human, and only its possessor and creator takes it seriously, as if the axis of the world was turning within it. Could we understand the mosquito, we might learn that it too glides through the air with such a self-importance, feeling itself as the flying center of this universe.

—Continued

Es ist nichts so verwerflich und gering in der Natur, was nicht, durch einen kleinen Anhauch jener Kraft des Erkennens, sofort wie ein Schlauch aufgeschwellt würde; und wie jeder Lastträger seinen Bewunderer haben will, so meint gar der Stolzeste Mensch, der Philosoph, von	There is nothing in nature so repugnant and low that it would not immediately swell up like a balloon at the slightest puff of the power of knowing. And just as every doorkeeper wants to have an admirer, so even the proudest of men, the philosopher,

– 876 –

allen Seiten die Augen des Weltalls teleskopisch auf sein Handeln und Denken gerichtet zu sehen.	supposes that everywhere around him he sees the eyes of the universe telescopically directed at his action and thought.
§ 2	§ 2
Es ist merkwürdig, daß dies der Intellekt zustande bringt, er, der doch gerade nur als Hilfsmittel den unglücklichsten, delikatesten, vergänglichsten Wesen beigegeben ist, um sie eine Minute im Dasein festzuhalten, aus dem sie sonst, ohne jene Beigabe, so schnell wie Lessings Sohn zu flüchten allen Grund hätten. Jener mit dem Erkennen und Empfinden verbundene Hochmut, verblendende Nebel über die Augen und Sinne der Menschen legend, täuscht sie also über den Wert des Daseins, dadurch daß er über das Erkennen selbst die schmeichelhafteste Wertschätzung in sich trägt. Seine allgemeinste Wirkung ist Täuschung—aber auch die einzelnsten Wirkungen tragen etwas von gleichem Charakter an sich.	It is peculiar that this was brought about by the intellect, which was only included as a helpful accessory to these most unfortunate, delicate, and transitory beings in order to keep them a minute in existence. Without this addition they would have had every reason to escape this existence as quickly as Lessing's son. Every pride connected with knowing and sensing lies like a blinding fog over the eyes and senses of humans, deceiving them about the value of existence insofar as it in itself carries this most flattering evaluation of knowledge. For this pride contains within itself the most flattering estimation of the value of knowing. Its most general effect is deception—but even the most particular effects carry within themselves something of similar nature.
§ 3	§ 3
Der Intellekt, als ein Mittel zur Erhaltung des Individuums, entfaltet seine Hauptkräfte in der Verstellung; denn diese ist das Mittel, durch das die schwächeren, weniger robusten Individuen sich erhalten, als welchen einen Kampf um die Existenz mit Hörnern oder scharfem Raubtier-Gebiß zu führen versagt ist. Im Menschen kommt diese Verstellungskunst auf ihren Gipfel: hier ist die Täuschung, das Schmeicheln, Lügen und Trügen, das Hinter-dem-Rücken-Reden, das Repräsentieren, das im erbogten Glanze Leben, das Maskiertsein, die verhüllende Konvention, das Bühnenspiel vor anderen und vor sich selbst, kurz das fortwährende Herumflattern um die eine Flamme Eitelkeit so sehr die Regel und das Gesetz, daß fast nichts unbegreiflicher ist, als wie unter den Menschen ein ehrlicher und reiner Trieb zur Wahrheit aufkommen konnte.	As a means for preserving the individual, the intellect develops its greatest powers in its capacity for pretense, as this is the means by which the weaker, less robust individuals preserve themselves, since they are denied the horns or sharp teeth of the predators in the struggle of existence. This art of pretense reaches its peak in man: here the illusion, the flattering, the lie and the deceit, the backbiting, the false appearances, the life in borrowed splendor, the masquerading, the hiding behind convention, the play-acting of others and of oneself, in brief, where the constant fluttering around the flame of vanity and conceit becomes so much the rule and the law that it is nearly incomprehensible how among men an honest and pure drive for truth could even have arisen.

—Continued

Sie sind tief eingetaucht in Illusionen und Traumbilder, ihr Auge gleitet nur auf der Oberfläche der Dinge herum und sieht "Formen," ihre Empfindung führt nirgends in die Wahrheit, sondern begnügt sich, Reize zu empfangen und gleichsam ein tastendes Spiel auf dem Rücken der Dinge zu spielen. Dazu läßt sich der Mensch nachts, ein Leben hindurch, im Traume belügen, ohne daß sein moralisches Gefühl dies je

– 877 –

zu verhindern suchte: während es Menschen geben soll, die durch starken Willen das Schnarchen beseitigt haben. Was weiß der Mensch eigentlich von sich selbst! Ja, vermöchte er auch nur sich einmal vollständig, hingelegt wie in einen erleuchteten Glaskasten, zu perzipieren? Verschweigt die Natur ihm nicht das Allermeiste, selbst über seinen Körper, um ihn, abseits von den Windungen der Gedärme, dem raschen Fluß der Blutströme, den verwickelten Fasererzitterungen, in ein stolzes, gauklerisches Bewußtsein zu bannen und einzuschließen! Sie warf den Schlüssel weg: und wehe der verhängnisvollen Neubegier, die durch eine Spalte einmal aus dem Bewußtseinszimmer heraus und hinabzusehen vermöchte, und die jetzt ahnte, daß auf dem Erbarmungslosen, dem Gierigen, dem Unersättlichen, dem Mörderischen der Mensch ruht, in der Gleichgültigkeit seines Nichtwissens, und gleichsam auf dem Rücken eines Tigers in Träumen hängend. Woher, in aller Welt, bei dieser Konstellation der Trieb zur Wahrheit!

§ 4

Soweit das Individuum sich, gegenüber andern Individuen, erhalten will, benutzt es in einem natürlichen Zustand der Dinge den Intellekt zumeist nur zur Verstellung: weil aber der Mensch zugleich aus Not und Langeweile gesellschaftlich und herden weise existieren will, braucht er einen Friedensschluß und trachtet danach, daß wenigstens das allergrößte bellum omnium contra omnes aus seiner Welt verschwinde.

They are deeply immersed in illusions and dream images; their eyes merely glide over the surface of things and see "forms"; nowhere do their senses lead them to truth, but make them instead content with receiving stimuli and to play a fumbling game on the back of things. In addition to this, man lets himself be deceived every night in dreams, throughout life, without trying to prevent this with his moral sentiments; while there are humans who through strong willpower have stopped themselves from snoring. What does man actually know about himself? Is he just once able to perceive himself completely, as if displayed in an illuminated glass case? Does not nature withhold almost all things from him, even his body—the windings of the intestines, the rapid flow of the bloodstream, the intricate quivering of the fibers—in order to banish and confine him to a proud deceptive consciousness? She threw away the key, and woe to the fatal curiosity that should attempt to peer out through a crack in the chamber of consciousness, guessing that man is suspending in the pitiless, the greedy, the insatiable, and the murderous; in the indifference of his ignorance, as if hanging on the back of a tiger in dreams. If this is the condition, how on earth did the drive for truth derive?

§ 4

Insofar as the individual wants to preserve itself over and against other individuals, it needs in the natural order of things the intellect mostly for pretense; while when men from necessity and boredom also want to live socially and as group, they need a peace treaty and attempt to banish at least the worst *bellum omnium contra omnes* from their world. This peace treaty brings with it something which seems to be the first step in acquiring the enigmatic truth-drive.

—Continued

Dieser Friedensschluß bringt etwas mit sich, was wie der erste Schritt zur Erlangung jenes rätselhaften Wahrheitstriebes aussieht. Jetzt wird nämlich das fixiert, was von nun an "Wahrheit" sein soll, das heißt, es wird eine gleichmäßig gültige und verbindliche Bezeichnung der Dinge erfunden, und die Gesetzgebung der Sprache gibt auch die ersten Gesetze der Wahrheit: denn es entsteht hier zum ersten Male der Kontrast von Wahrheit und Lüge. Der Lügner gebrauchte die gültigen Bezeichnungen, die Worte, um das Unwirkliche als wirklich erscheinen zu machen; er sagt zum Beispiel: "ich bin reich," während für seinen Zustand gerade "arm" die richtige Bezeichnung wäre. Er mißbraucht die festen Konventionen durch beliebige Vertau-	From now on that which shall count as "truth" is being established; that is, one invents a uniform and binding designation for things, and this legislation of language gives also the first laws of truth. From here emerges for the first time the contrast between truth and lie. The liar uses valid designations, the words, for making the unreal appear as if it is real. He says for example, "I am rich," while "poor" would have been the correct designation for his condition. He abuses the established conventions by means of arbitrary substitutions

— 878 —

schungen oder gar Umkehrungen der Namen. Wenn er dies in eigennütziger und übrigens Schaden bringender Weise tut, so wird ihm die Gesellschaft nicht mehr trauen und ihn dadurch von sich ausschließen. Die Menschen fliehen dabei das Betrogen werden nicht so sehr als das Beschädigtwerden durch Betrug: sie hassen, auch auf dieser Stufe, im Grunde nicht die Täuschung, sondern die schlimmen, feindseligen Folgen gewisser Gattungen von Täuschungen. In einem ähnlichen beschränkten Sinne will der Mensch auch nur die Wahrheit: er begehrt die angenehmen, Leben erhaltenden Folgen der Wahrheit, gegen die reine folgenlose Erkenntnis ist er gleichgültig, gegen die vielleicht schädlichen und zerstörenden Wahrheiten sogar feindlich gestimmt. Und überdies: wie steht es mit jenen Konventionen der Sprache? Sind sie vielleicht Erzeugnisse der Erkenntnis, des Wahrheitssinnes, decken sich die Bezeichnungen und die Dinge? Ist die Sprache der adäquate Ausdruck aller Realitäten?	or even reversals of names. If he does this in a manner that is selfish and causes harm, society will no longer trust him and will thereby exclude him. Humans do not so much shun being deceived as being harmed by the deceit. Even at this stage, they actually do not hate the deception as much as the bad and harmful consequences from certain kinds of deceit. In a similar limited sense, man wants only truth: he desires the pleasant and life-preserving consequences of truth, while he is indifferent toward pure knowledge without consequences; he is even hostile toward perhaps harmful and destructive truths. And besides, how is it with these linguistic conventions themselves? Are they perhaps products of knowledge, of the senses of truth; do the designations and the things correspond? Is language the adequate expression of all realities?
§ 5	§ 5
Nur durch Vergeßlichkeit kann der Mensch je dazu kommen zu wähnen, er besitze eine "Wahrheit" in dem eben bezeichneten Grade. Wenn er sich nicht mit der Wahrheit in der Form der Tautologie, das heißt mit leeren Hülsen begnügen will, so wird er ewig Illusionen für Wahrheiten einhandeln.	It is only by means of forgetfulness that man arrives to the illusion that he possesses "truth" to the extent just indicated. When he is no longer satisfied with truth in the form of tautologies, that is, is no longer content with empty husks, then he will always exchange truths for illusions.

—Continued

Was ist ein Wort? Die Abbildung eines Nervenreizes in Lauten. Von dem Nervenreiz aber weiterzuschließen auf eine Ursache außer uns, ist bereits das Resultat einer falschen und unberechtigten Anwendung des Satzes vom Grunde. Wie dürften wir, wenn die Wahrheit bei der Genesis der Sprache, der Gesichtspunkt der Gewißheit bei den Bezeichnungen allein entscheidend gewesen wäre, wie dürften wir doch sagen: der Stein ist hart: als ob uns "hart" noch sonst bekannt wäre, und nicht nur als eine ganz subjektive Reizung! Wir teilen die Dinge nach Geschlechtern ein, wir bezeichnen den Baum als männlich, die Pflanze als weiblich: welche willkürlichen Übertragungen! Wie weit hinaus geflogen über den Kanon der Gewißheit! Wir reden von einer "Schlange": die Bezeichnung trifft nichts als das Sich winden, könnte also auch dem Wurme zukom-

– 879 –

men. Welche willkürlichen Abgrenzungen, welche einseitigen Bevorzugungen bald der bald jener Eigenschaft eines Dinges! Die verschiedenen Sprachen, nebeneinander gestellt, zeigen, daß es bei den Worten nie auf die Wahrheit, nie auf einen adäquaten Ausdruck ankommt: denn sonst gäbe es nicht so viele Sprachen. Das "Ding an sich" (das würde eben die reine folgenlose Wahrheit sein) ist auch dem Sprachbildner ganz unfaßlich und ganz und gar nicht erstrebenswert. Er bezeichnet nur die Relationen der Dinge zu den Menschen und nimmt zu deren Ausdrucke die kühnsten Metaphern zu Hilfe. Ein Nervenreiz, zuerst übertragen in ein Bild! Erste Metapher. Das Bild wieder nachgeformt in einem Laut! Zweite Metapher. Und jedesmal vollständiges Überspringen der Sphäre, mitten hinein in eine ganz andre und neue. Man kann sich einen Menschen denken, der ganz taub ist und nie eine Empfindung des Tones und der Musik gehabt hat: wie dieser etwa die chladnischen Klangfiguren im Sande anstaunt, ihre Ursachen im Erzittern der Saite findet und nun darauf schwören wird, jetzt müsse er wissen, was die Menschen den "Ton" nennen, so geht es uns allen mit der Sprache.

What is a word? The copy of a nerve-stimulus in sounds. But to infer from the nerve-stimulus to a cause outside us is already the result of a false and unjustified application of the principle of sufficient reason. If in the genesis of language truth alone had been the deciding criterion for certainty in designations, how could we then say: the stone is hard; as if 'hard' was already known to us, and not merely a purely subjective stimulus!

We divide things into gender as we designate the tree as masculine and the plant as feminine; but what arbitrary assignments! How far does this not exceed the canon of certainty! We talk about a "snake," but this designation touches only upon the coiling and twisting and could apply equally to the worm.

What arbitrary demarcations, what one-sided preferences for soon this soon another property of a thing! Juxtaposing different languages shows that regarding words, it is never truth, never the adequate expression that matters, because otherwise we would not need so many languages. The "thing-in-itself" (i.e., pure truth without consequences) is also for the creator of language quite incomprehensible and is not worthwhile striving for at all. He designates only the relations of the things to humans and helps himself expressing them by the most audacious metaphors. A nerve-stimulus is first transferred into an image! First metaphor. The image is again transformed into a sound! Second metaphor. Each time there is a complete leap from one sphere right into the middle of a completely new and different one. One can imagine a person who is completely deaf and never has had the sensation of tones and music. He would in astonishment look at Chladni's sound-figures in the sand, might discover their cause in the vibrations of the string, and hereby swear that he knows what humans call 'tone.' The same applies to us all with respect to language.

—Continued

Wir glauben etwas von den Dingen selbst zu wissen, wenn wir von Bäumen, Farben, Schnee und Blumen reden, und besitzen doch nichts als Metaphern der Dinge, die den ursprünglichen Wesenheiten ganz und gar nicht entsprechen. Wie der Ton als Sandfigur, so nimmt sich das rätselhafte X des Dings an sich einmal als Nervenreiz, dann als Bild, endlich als Laut aus. Logisch geht es also jedenfalls nicht bei der Entstehung der Sprache zu, und das ganze Material, worin und womit später der Mensch der Wahrheit, der Forscher, der Philosoph arbeitet und baut, stammt, wenn nicht aus Wolkenkuckucksheim, so doch jedenfalls nicht aus dem Wesen der Dinge.

§ 6

Denken wir besonders noch an die Bildung der Begriffe. Jedes Wort wird sofort dadurch Begriff, daß es eben nicht für das einmalige ganz und gar individualisierte Urerlebnis, dem es sein Entstehen verdankt, etwa als Erinnerung dienen soll, sondern zugleich für zahllose, mehr oder weniger ähnliche, daß heißt streng ge-

– 880 –

nommen niemals gleiche, also auf lauter ungleiche Fälle passen muß. Jeder Begriff entsteht durch Gleichsetzen des Nichtgleichen. So gewiß nie ein Blatt einem andern ganz gleich ist, so gewiß ist der Begriff Blatt durch beliebiges Fallenlassen dieser individuellen Verschiedenheiten, durch ein Vergessen des Unterscheidenen gebildet und erweckt nun die Vorstellung, als ob es in der Natur außer den Blättern etwas gäbe, das "Blatt" wäre, etwa eine Urform, nach der alle Blätter gewebt, gezeichnet, abgezirkelt, gefärbt, gekräuselt, bemalt wären, aber von ungeschickten Händen, so daß kein Exemplar korrekt und zuverlässig als treues Abbild der Urform ausgefallen wäre. Wir nennen einen Menschen "ehrlich." Warum hat er heute so ehrlich gehandelt? fragen wir. Unsere Antwort pflegt zu lauten: seiner Ehrlichkeit wegen. Die Ehrlichkeit! Das heißt wieder: das Blatt ist die Ursache der Blätter.

We believe that we know something about the things themselves when we talk about trees, colors, snow, and flowers, although we adhere to nothing but metaphors of things, with no correspondence at all to their original essences. Like the tone as sand-figure, so is it with the enigmatic X of the things in themselves appearing first as nerve-stimulus, then as image, and finally as sound. In any case, language does not originate logically, and the entire material in and with which the man of truth, the researcher or the philosopher, works and constructs, derives—if not entirely from some imaginary never-never land—at least not from the essences of things.

§ 6

Let us specifically consider the formation of concepts. Every word immediately becomes a concept when it no longer serves as a reminder of the unique and completely individualized original experience to which it owes its origin, but also fits the numerous more or less similar—which strictly speaking means

never similar—non-identical cases. Every concept emerges by equalizing the unequal. As certain as it is that one leaf is never completely identical to another leaf, as certain is it that the concept leaf is formed thanks to arbitrarily discarding these individual differences. In forgetting these differences, the idea is now formed that there is something in nature which besides the leaves gives us *the* "leaf," something like an arché-form according to which all leaves have been woven, outlined, measured, colored, curved, and painted, but by incompetent hands so that no copy ever turned out as a correct and faithful true imitation of the original form. We call a person "honest." Why did he act so honestly today, we ask? Our answer usually is, because of his honesty. Honesty! That is to say that the leaf is the cause to the leaves. We know nothing whatsoever of an essential quality called "honesty," but only of numerous individualized, and therefore unequal actions, which we because we ignore the unequal equalizes and now designate as an honest act.

—*Continued*

Wir wissen ja gar nichts von einer wesenhaften Qualität, die "die Ehrlichkeit" hieße, wohl aber von zahlreichen individualisierten, somit ungleichen Handlungen, die wir durch Weglassen des Ungleichen gleichsetzen und jetzt als ehrliche Handlungen bezeichnen; zuletzt formulieren wir aus ihnen eine qualitas occulta mit dem Namen: "die Ehrlichkeit." Das Übersehen des Individuellen und Wirklichen gibt uns den Begriff, wie es uns auch die Form gibt, wohingegen die Natur keine Formen und Begriffe, also auch keine Gattungen kennt, sondern nur ein für uns unzugängliches und undefinierbares X. Denn auch unser Gegensatz von Individuum und Gattung ist anthropomorphisch und entstammt nicht dem Wesen der Dinge, wenn wir auch nicht zu sagen wagen, daß er ihm nicht entspricht: das wäre nämlich eine dogmatische Behauptung und als solche ebenso unerweislich wie ihr Gegenteil.

§ 7

Was ist also Wahrheit? Ein bewegliches Heer von Metaphern, Metonymien, Anthropomorphismen, kurz eine Summe von menschlichen Relationen, die, poetisch und rhetorisch gesteigert, übertragen, geschmückt wurden, und die nach langem Gebrauch einem Volke fest, kanonisch und verbindlich dünken: die Wahr-

– 881 –

heiten sind Illusionen, von denen man vergessen hat, daß sie welche sind, Metaphern, die abgenutzt und sinnlich kraftlos geworden sind, Münzen, die ihr Bild verloren haben und nun als Metall, nicht mehr als Münzen, in Betracht kommen.

§ 8

Wir wissen immer noch nicht, woher der Trieb zur Wahrheit stammt: denn bis jetzt haben wir nur von der Verpflichtung gehört, die die Gesellschaft, um zu existieren, stellt: wahrhaft zu sein, das heißt die usuellen Metaphern zu brauchen, also moralisch ausgedrückt: von der Verpflichtung, nach einer festen Konvention zu lügen, herdenweise in einem für alle verbindlichen Stile zu lügen.

Finally, we articulate out of this a *qualitas occulta* with the name, "honesty."

By overlooking the individual and the real we get the concept which also gives us the form, while within nature there are no forms and concepts, therefore also no species, only a for us inaccessible and indefinable X. As such, also our opposition between the individual and the species is anthropomorphic and derives not from the essence of things, although we would not dare to claim that it does not correspond to them; that would namely be a dogmatic assertion, and as such, just as indemonstrable as its opposite.

§ 7

What is then truth? A mobile army of metaphors, metonymies, and anthropomorphisms; in short, a sum of human relations, which, poetically and rhetorically intensified, have been transferred, embellished, and after long usage of a people seem fixed, canonical, and compulsory.

Truths are illusions, which one has forgotten that that is what they are, metaphors, which have become outworn and sensuously powerless, coins, which have lost their stamp and now only are regarded as metal, no longer as coins.

§ 8

We still do not know from where the drive for truth derives, because we have so far only heard about is as an obligation, which society imposes for the sake of existence. To be truthful implies that one uses the common metaphors, or expressed morally, one follows the obligation to lie according to the established conventions and lies in herd-fashion in a manner applying to everybody.

—Continued

Nun vergißt freilich der Mensch, daß es so mit ihm steht; er lügt also in der bezeichneten Weise unbewußt und nach hundertjährigen Gewöhnungen—und kommt eben durch diese Unbewußtheit, eben durch dies Vergessen zum Gefühl der Wahrheit. An dem Gefühl verpflichtet zu sein, ein Ding als "rot," ein anderes als "kalt," ein drittes als "stumm" zu bezeichnen, erwacht eine moralische auf Wahrheit sich beziehende Regung: aus dem Gegensatz des Lügners, dem niemand traut, den alle ausschließen, demonstriert sich der Mensch das Ehrwürdige, Zutrauliche und Nützliche der Wahrheit. Er stellt jetzt sein Handeln als "vernünftiges" Wesen unter die Herrschaft der Abstraktionen; er leidet es nicht mehr, durch die plötzlichen Eindrücke, durch die Anschauungen fortgerissen zu werden, er verallgemeinert alle diese Eindrücke erst zu entfärbteren, kühleren Begriffen, um an sie das Fahrzeug seines Lebens und Handelns anzuknüpfen. Alles, was den Menschen gegen das Tier abhebt, hängt von dieser Fähigkeit ab, die anschaulichen Metaphern zu einem Schema zu verflüchtigen, also ein Bild in einen Begriff aufzulösen. Im Bereich jener Schemata nämlich ist etwas möglich, was niemals unter den anschaulichen ersten Eindrücken gelingen möchte: eine pyramidale Ordnung nach Kasten und Graden aufzubauen, eine neue Welt von Gesetzen, Privilegien, Unterordnungen, Grenzbestimmungen zu schaffen, die nun der andern anschaulichen Welt der ersten Eindrücke gegenübertritt, als das Festere, Allgemeinere,	Obviously, man forgets that this is the case, and he therefore lies in the indicated sense unconsciously and according to century old habits; precisely thanks to this unconsciousness and forgetfulness, he arrives to a sense of truth. From being obligated to the feeling that one designates a thing as 'red,' another as 'cold,' a third as 'silent,' a moral impulse emerges regarding truth. In contrast to the liar, who nobody trusts and everybody excludes, the person demonstrates to himself the venerable, trustful, and useful aspects of truth. He now subjects his behavior as a "rational" being to the rule of abstractions; he no longer tolerates that his standpoints are disrupted by sudden impressions; he generalizes all these impressions first into colorless and cool concepts in order to then entrust them with the guidance of his life and action. Everything that raises man above the animal depends upon this ability to transfer visual metaphors into a schema, that is, to transform an image into a concept. Because in the realm of these schemata something is possible, which never could have been accomplished in the visual first impressions, namely the construction of a pyramidal order of classes and gradations, the creation of a new world of laws, privileges, subordinations, boundaries, which now stands over and against the other visual world of first impressions as something more solid and universal,

– 882 –

Bekanntere, Menschlichere und daher als das Regulierende und Imperativische. Während jede Anschauungsmetapher individuell und ohne ihresgleichen ist und deshalb allem Rubrizieren immer zu entfliehen weiß, zeigt der große Bau der Begriffe die starre Regelmäßigkeit eines römischen Kolumbariums und atmet in der Logik jene Strenge und Kühle aus, die der Mathematik zu eigen ist. Wer von dieser Kühle angehaucht wird, wird es kaum glauben, daß auch der Begriff, knöchern und achteckig wie ein Würfel und versetzbar wie jener, doch nur als das Residuum einer	more familiar and human, and with this also more regulative and authoritative. Whereas each pictorial metaphor is individual and without equal and therefore always able to elude all classification, the great conceptual construction shows the rigid regularity of a Roman columbarium, breathing the logical strictness and coolness that characterizes mathematics.

—*Continued*

Metapher übrig bleibt, und daß die Illusion der künstlerischen Übertragung eines Nervenreizes in Bilder, wenn nicht die Mutter, so doch die Großmutter eines jeden Begriffs ist. Innerhalb dieses Würfelspiels der Begriffe heißt aber "Wahrheit'," jeden Würfel so zu gebrauchen, wie er bezeichnet ist, genau seine Augen zu zählen, richtige Rubriken zu bilden und nie gegen die Kastenordnung und gegen die Reihenfolge der Rangklassen zu verstoßen. Wie die Römer und Etrusker sich den Himmel durch starre mathematische Linien zerschnitten und in einen solchermaßen abgegrenzten Raum, als in ein templum, einen Gott bannten, so hat jedes Volk über sich einen solchen mathematisch zerteilten Begriffshimmel und versteht nun unter der Forderung der Wahrheit, daß jeder Begriffsgott nur in seiner Sphäre gesucht werde. Man darf hier den Menschen wohl bewundern als ein gewaltiges Baugenie, dem auf beweglichen Fundamenten und gleichsam auf fließendem Wasser das Auftürmen eines unendlich komplizierten Begriffsdomes gelingt: - freilich, um auf solchen Fundamenten Halt zu finden, muß es ein Bau wie aus Spinnefäden sein, so zart, um von der Welle mit fort getragen, so fest, um nicht von jedem Winde auseinander geblasen zu werden. Als Baugenie erhebt sich solchermaßen der Mensch weit über die Biene: diese baut aus Wachs, das sie aus der Natur zusammenholt, er aus dem weit zarteren Stoffe der Begriffe, die er erst aus sich fabrizieren muß. Er ist hier sehr zu bewundern—aber nur nicht wegen seines Triebes zur Wahrheit, zum reinen Erkennen der Dinge.

– 883 –

Wenn jemand ein Ding hinter einem Busche versteckt, es ebendort wieder sucht und auch findet, so ist an diesem Suchen und Finden nicht viel zu rühmen: so aber steht es mit dem Suchen und Finden der "Wahrheit" innerhalb des Vernunft-Bezirkes.

Everybody who has inhaled this coolness can hardly believe that also the concept—bony and square like a dice, and replaceable with everything—after all is only the remnant of a metaphor, and that the illusion of the artistic transference of a nerve-stimulus into an image, is, if not the mother, then at least the grandmother of every concept. In this conceptual game of dice, "truth" means to use every dice according to its markings, to accurately count its spots, to form correct categories, and never violate the order of classes and the sequence of rankings.

Just as the Romans and Etruscans divided heaven in rigid mathematical lines, and then exiled God to such a space segmented like a template, so every people has above themselves such a mathematically divided concept-heaven and understand now by the demand of truth that every concept-god may be sought only within his own sphere. One is certainly allowed to admire the human being as a formidable genius of construction, succeeding in rising the tower of an endlessly complicated dome of concepts on a moving foundation, as if on running water. Obviously, in order to find support for such a foundation, his construction must be like a spider's web, delicate enough to be carried along by the ripples of the waves, strong enough not to be blown apart by the wind. As a genius of construction the human raises itself far above the bees: they built from wax, which they gather in nature, but humans build from the far more delicate material of concepts, which they must first fabricate out of themselves. In this, they are very admirable—but not due to their drives for truth or for a pure knowledge of things.

When somebody hides something behind a bush, then looks for it in the same place and finds it there again, there is not much to admire in such seeking and finding; however, this is the situation regarding the seeking and finding of "truth" within the realms of reason.

—Continued

Wenn ich die Definition des Säugetiers mache und dann erkläre, nach Besichtigung eines Kamels: "siehe, ein Säugetier," so wird damit eine Wahrheit zwar ans Licht gebracht, aber sie ist von begrenztem Werte, ich meine, sie ist durch und durch anthropomorphisch und enthält keinen einzigen Punkt, der "wahr an sich," wirklich und allgemeingültig, abgesehn von dem Menschen, wäre. Der Forscher nach solchen Wahrheiten sucht im Grunde nur die Metamorphose der Welt in den Menschen, er ringt nach einem Verstehen der Welt als eines menschenartigen Dinges und erkämpft sich bestenfalls das Gefühl einer Assimilation. Ähnlich wie der Astrolog die Sterne im Dienste der Menschen und im Zusammenhange mit ihrem Glück und Leide betrachtete, so betrachtet ein solcher Forscher die ganze Welt als geknüpft an den Menschen, als den unendlich gebrochenen Widerklang eines Urklanges, des Menschen, als das vervielfältigte Abbild des einen Urbildes, des Menschen. Sein Verfahren ist, den Menschen als Maß an alle Dinge zu halten: wobei er aber von dem Irrtum ausgeht, zu glauben, er habe diese Dinge unmittelbar, als reine Objekte vor sich. Er vergißt also die originalen Anschauungsmetaphern als Metaphern und nimmt sie als die Dinge selbst.	If I create the definition of the mammal and then, after observing a camel, declare: "look, a mammal," then a truth is brought to light, but it is of limited value. I mean, it is anthropomorphic through and through and does not contain a single speck that apart from man would be really and universally "true in itself." The researcher of such truths seeks essentially only the metamorphosis of the world into man, he struggles to understand the world as a human-like thing and at best, he acquires laboriously a sense of assimilation. Similar to the astrologer who sees the stars in service of the human in relation to luck and suffering, so the researcher regards the entire world as tied up with the human being, as an infinitely broken reverberation of an arché-sound, the human, as a manifold replica of an arché-image, the human. His method is to hold man to be the measure of all things. In this assumption, however, he proceed from the error to believe that he has these things immediately as pure objects in front of him. He forgets therefore the original pictorial metaphors as metaphors and takes them to be things in themselves.
§ 9	§ 9
Nur durch das Vergessen jener primitiven Metapherwelt, nur durch das Hart und Starrwerden einer ursprünglichen in hitziger Flüssigkeit aus dem Urvermögen menschlicher Phantasie hervorströmenden Bildermasse, nur durch den un besiegbaren Glauben, diese Sonne, dieses Fenster, dieser Tisch sei eine Wahrheit an sich, kurz nur dadurch, daß der Mensch sich als Subjekt, und zwar als künstlerischschaffendes Subjekt, vergißt, lebt er mit einiger Ruhe, Sicherheit und Konsequenz: wenn er einen Augenblick nur aus den Gefängnis wänden dieses Glaubens heraus könnte, so wäre es sofort mit seinem "Selbstbewußtsein" – 884 – vorbei. Schon dies kostet ihm Mühe, sich ein zugestehen, wie das Insekt oder der Vogel eine ganz andere Welt perzipieren als der Mensch, und daß die Frage, welche von beiden Weltperzeptionen richtiger ist, eine ganz sinnlose ist, da hierzu bereits mit dem Maßstabe der richtigen Perzeption,	Only by forgetting this primitive metaphor-world, only by making hard and rigid the mass of images that originally streamed like a stormy flood through the primary constitution of human imagination, only thanks to the unshakable belief that this sun, this window, this table possess truth in itself, in short, only because the human beings forgot themselves as subjects, and indeed as artistic-creative subjects, do they live somewhat tranquilly, securely, and consistently. But if they could escape the prison-walls of this faith for only an instant, then it would quickly be over with their "self-consciousness." It is already difficult for man to acknowledge that the insect and the bird perceive an entirely different world than humans, and that the question which of the two world-perceptions is the correct one is quite meaningless, as it hereby already assumes the correct perception as measuring

—Continued

das heißt mit einem nichtvorhandenen Maßstabe gemessen werden müßte. Überhaupt aber scheint mir "die richtige Perzeption"—das würde heißen: der adäquate Ausdruck eines Objekts im Subjekt—ein widerspruchsvolles Unding: denn zwischen zwei absolut verschiednen Sphären, wie zwischen Subjekt und Objekt, gibt es keine Kausalität, keine Richtigkeit, keinen Ausdruck, sondern höchstens ein ästhetisches Verhalten, ich meine eine andeutende Übertragung, eine nachstammelnde Übersetzung in eine ganz fremde Sprache: wozu es aber jedenfalls einer frei dichtenden und frei erfindenden Mittelsphäre und Mittelkraft bedarf. Das Wort "Erscheinung" enthält viele Verführungen, weshalb ich es möglichst vermeide: denn es ist nicht wahr, daß das Wesen der Dinge in der empirischen Welt erscheint. Ein Maler, dem die Hände fehlen und der durch Gesang das ihm vorschwebende Bild ausdrücken wollte, wird immer noch mehr bei dieser Vertauschung der Sphären verraten, als die empirische Welt vom Wesen der Dinge verrät. Selbst das Verhältnis eines Nervenreizes zu dem hervorgebrachten Bilde ist an sich kein notwendiges: wenn aber dasselbe Bild millionenmal hervorgebracht und durch viele Menschengeschlechter hindurch vererbt ist, ja zuletzt bei der gesamten Menschheit jedesmal infolge desselben Anlasses erscheint, so bekommt es endlich für den Menschen dieselbe Bedeutung, als ob es das einzig notwendige Bild sei und als ob jenes Verhältnis des ursprünglichen Nervenreizes zu dem hergebrachten Bilde ein strenges Kausalitätsverhältnis sei; wie ein Traum, ewig wiederholt, durchaus als Wirklichkeit empfunden und beurteilt werden würde. Aber das Hart- und Starr-Werden einer Metapher verbürgt durchaus nichts für die Notwendigkeit und ausschließliche Berechtigung dieser Metapher.

– 885 –

§ 10

Es hat gewiß jeder Mensch, der in solchen Betrachtungen heimisch ist, gegen jeden derartigen Idealismus ein tiefes Mißtrauen empfunden, so oft er sich einmal recht deutlich von der ewigen Konsequenz, Allgegenwärtigkeit und Unfehlbarkeit der

rod, that is, assumes a non-existing standard. In any case, it seems to me that "the correct perception"—i.e., the adequate expression of an object in the subject—is a self-contradictory absurdity. Because between two absolutely different spheres, as between subject and object, there is no causality, no correctness, no expression, but at best only an aesthetical relation; I mean a suggestive transference, a stammering translation into a completely foreign language—for which one at any rate needs a freely poeticizing and freely inventive mediating sphere and mediating force. The word 'appearance' contains many seductions, why I try to avoid it as much as possible: because it is not true that the essence of things 'appears' in the empirical world. If a painter in the absence of hands had to express an image in front of his eyes in song, he would with this confusion of spheres always reveal more, than the empirical world reveals about by the essences of things. Even the relation between a nerve-stimulus and the resulting image is in itself not necessary. However, when the same image has been generated a million times, and hereby have been inhere tied through numerous human generations, and finally by the entire humanity appears every time according to the same events, then it finally achieves for humans the same meaning, as if it is the only necessary image and as if every relation between the original nerve-stimuli and the appearing image is a strong causal relationship. It is like a dream, which is eternally repeated is finally regarded as reality and judged as such. However, a metaphor's becoming hard and rigid does not reveal the necessity and the decisive verification of this metaphor.

§ 10

Every person, familiar with such considerations, must certainly have felt a deep mistrust against any such idealism whenever he clearly had convinced himself of the eternal consistency, omnipresence, and infallibility of the laws of nature.

—Continued

Naturgesetze überzeugte; er hat den Schluß gemacht: hier ist alles, soweit wir dringen, nach der Höhe der teleskopischen und nach der Tiefe der mikroskopischen Welt, so sicher, ausgebaut, endlos, gesetzmäßig und ohne Lücken; die Wissenschaft wird ewig in diesen Schachten mit Erfolg zu graben haben, und alles Gefundene wird zusammenstimmen und sich nicht widersprechen. Wie wenig gleicht dies einem Phantasie erzeugnis: denn wenn es dies wäre, müßte es doch irgendwo den Schein und die Unrealität erraten lassen. Dagegen ist einmal zu sagen: hätten wir noch, jeder für sich, eine verschiedenartige Sinnesempfindung, könnten wir selbst nur bald als Vogel, bald als Wurm, bald als Pflanze perzipieren, oder sähe der eine von uns denselben Reiz als rot, der andere als blau, hörte ein dritter ihn sogar als Ton, so würde niemand von einer solchen Gesetzmäßigkeit der Natur reden, sondern sie nur als ein höchst subjektives Gebilde begreifen. So dann: was ist für uns überhaupt ein Naturgesetz? Es ist uns nicht an sich bekannt, sondern nur in seinen Wirkungen, das heißt in seinen Relationen zu andern Naturgesetzen, die uns wieder nur als Summen von Relationen bekannt sind. Also verweisen alle diese Relationen immer nur wieder aufeinander und sind uns ihrem Wesen nach unverständlich durch und durch; nur das, was wir hinzubringen, die Zeit, der Raum, also Sukzessions verhältnisse und Zahlen, sind uns wirklich daran bekannt. Alles Wunderbare aber, das wir gerade an den Naturgesetzen anstaunen, das unsere Erklärung fordert und uns zum Mißtrauen gegen den Idealismus verführen könnte, liegt gerade und ganz allein nur in der mathematischen Strenge und Un verbrüchlich keit der Zeit- und Raum-Vorstellungen. Diese aber produzieren wir in uns und aus uns mit jener Notwendigkeit, mit der die Spinne spinnt; wenn wir gezwungen sind, alle Dinge nur unter diesen Formen zu begreifen, so ist es dann	He has concluded that however far we penetrate into the heights of the telescopic and into the depths of the microscopic world, everything is certain, well-constructed, infinite, lawful, and complete; that science will successfully be excavating these chambers forever, to discover that everything is consistent and non-contradictory. How far this is from resembling a phantasm creation; because if this were what it was, it would have to suppose illusion and unreality to be anywhere. Against this, we must first of all say that if each of us had different sense-perceptions, if we could perceive now as a bird, now as a worm, now as a plant, or if one of us saw the same stimulus as red, another as blue, and a third ever heard it as a tone, then nobody would talk about such a lawfulness of nature, but instead comprehend it as an extremely subjective construction. So, what at all is law of nature for us? It is not known by us in-itself, but only in its effects, that is, in its relations to other laws of nature, which again are known to us only as the sum-total of relations. In other words, all these relations refer always only to each other and are completely incomprehensible to us in their essence. Only that what we bring to the relations—time and space, that is, successive sequences and numbers—is really known to us in them. However, all the marvelous that we correctly admire about the laws of nature, that which requires our explanation and may seduce us into mistrusting idealism, is strictly and exclusively contained only within the mathematical rigor and indestructibility of our representations of time and space. These, however, we produce in and from ourselves with the same necessity with which the spider spins. If we are forced to comprehend all things only under these forms,
– 886 –	
nicht mehr wunderbar, daß wir an allen Dingen eigentlich nur eben diese Formen begreifen: denn sie alle müssen die Gesetze der Zahl an sich tragen, und die Zahl gerade ist das Erstaunlichste in den Dingen. Alle Gesetzmäßigkeit, die uns im Sternen lauf	then it is no longer astonishing that we essentially only comprehend all things according to these forms. All of them must carry within them the law of number, and the number is indeed the most amazing about things.

—*Continued*

und im chemischen Prozeß so imponiert, fällt im Grunde mit jenen Eigenschaften zusammen, die wir selbst an die Dinge heranbringen, so daß wir damit uns selber imponieren. Dabei ergibt sich allerdings, daß jene künstlerische Metapherbildung, mit der in uns jede Empfindung beginnt, bereits jene Formen voraussetzt, also in ihnen vollzogen wird; nur aus dem festen Verharren dieser Urformen erklärt sich die Möglichkeit, wie nachher wieder aus den Metaphern selbst ein Bau der Begriffe konstituiert werden konnte. Dieser ist nämlich eine Nachahmung der Zeit-, Raum- und Zahlenverhältnisse auf dem Boden der Metaphern.

Part II

§ 11

An dem Bau der Begriffe arbeitet ursprünglich, wie wir sahen, die Sprache, in späteren Zeiten die Wissenschaft. Wie die Biene zugleich an den Zellen baut und die Zellen mit Honig füllt, so arbeitet die Wissenschaft unaufhaltsam an jenem großen Kolumbarium der Begriffe, der Begräbnisstätte der Anschauungen, baut immer neue und höhere Stockwerke, stützt, reinigt, erneut die alten Zellen und ist vor allem bemüht, jenes ins Ungeheure aufgetürmte Fachwerk zu füllen und die ganze empirische Welt, das heißt die anthropomorphische Welt, hineinzuordnen. Wenn schon der handelnde Mensch sein Leben an die Vernunft und ihre Begriffe bindet, um nicht fortgeschwemmt zu werden und sich nicht selbst zu verlieren, so baut der Forscher seine Hütte dicht an den Turmbau der Wissenschaft, um an ihm mithelfen zu können und selbst Schutz unter dem vorhandenen Bollwerk zu finden. Und Schutz braucht er: denn es gibt furchtbare Mächte, die fortwährend auf ihn eindringen und die der wissenschaftlichen "Wahrheit" ganz anders geartete "Wahrheiten" mit den verschiedenartigsten Schildzeichen entgegenhalten.

– 887 –

§ 12

Jener Trieb zur Metapherbildung, jener Fundamentaltrieb des Menschen, den man keinen Augenblick wegrechnen kann, weil man damit den Menschen selbst wegrechnen würde, ist dadurch, daß aus

All lawfulness, which so impresses us in the movements of the stars and in the chemical processes, is fundamentally identical to the properties that we ourselves bring to things; so, we are in this impressed about ourselves. From this, it must of course follow that every artistic metaphorical construction, with which every sensation in us begins, already presupposes those forms and thus is executed according to them. Only thanks to the unmovable persistence of these arché-forms can we explain how it is possible build an edifice of concepts out of metaphors. It is namely an imitation of time-, space-, and number-relations on the foundation of metaphors.

Part II

§ 11

As we have seen, it is originally language that works on the construction of concepts, in later ages the work is taken over by the sciences. Just as the bees simultaneously build the cells and fill them with honey, so the sciences work constantly on this great columbarium of concepts, this graveyard for sense-impressions, when it continues to build still new and higher stories and reinforcements, cleaning and renovating the old cells, as it attempts to fill out this enormous towering framework and arrange within it the entire empirical world, i.e., the anthropomorphic world. If the man of action binds his life to reason and its concepts in order not to be carried away and lose himself, the researcher builds his hut close to the tower of science so it can assist him and give him protection beneath its already existing bulwark. And support he needs, because there are terrible powers that constantly imposes themselves upon him and confront scientific 'Truth' with quite different kinds of 'truths' displaying the most varied inscriptions on their shields.

§ 12

That drive to form metaphors, that fundamental human drive, which one cannot ignore for even an instant because one would then discard the human being itself, is in fact neither defeated nor tamed

—*Continued*

seinen verflüchtigten Erzeugnissen, den Begriffen, eine reguläre und starre neue Welt als eine Zwingburg für ihn gebaut wird, in Wahrheit nicht bezwungen und kaum gebändigt. Er sucht sich ein neues Bereich seines Wirkens und ein anderes Flußbette und findet es im Mythus und überhaupt in der Kunst. Fortwährend verwirrt er die Rubriken und Zellen der Begriffe, dadurch daß er neue Übertragungen, Metaphern, Metonymien hinstellt, fortwährend zeigt er die Begierde, die vorhandene Welt des wachen Menschen so bunt unregelmäßig, folgenlos unzusammenhängend, reizvoll und ewig neu zu gestalten, wie es die Welt des Traumes ist. An sich ist ja der wache Mensch nur durch das starre und regelmäßige Begriffsgespinst darüber im klaren, daß er wache, und kommt eben deshalb mitunter in den Glauben, er träume, wenn jenes Begriffsgespinst einmal durch die Kunst zerrissen wird. Pascal hat recht, wenn er behauptet, daß wir, wenn uns jede Nacht derselbe Traum käme, davon ebenso beschäftigt würden als von den Dingen, die wir jeden Tag sehen: "wenn ein Handwerker gewiß wäre, jede Nacht zu träumen, volle zwölf Stunden hindurch, daß er König sei, so glaube ich, sagt Pascal, daß er ebenso glücklich wäre als ein König, welcher alle Nächte während zwölf Stunden träumte, er sei Handwerker." Der wache Tag eines mythisch erregten Volkes, etwa der älteren Griechen, ist durch das fortwährend wirkende Wunder, wie es der Mythus annimmt, in der Tat dem Traume ähnlicher als dem Tag des wissenschaftlich ernüchterten Denkers. Wenn jeder Baum einmal als Nymphe reden oder unter der Hülle eines Stieres ein Gott Jungfrauen wegschleppen kann, wenn die Göttin Athene selbst plötzlich gesehn wird, wie sie mit einem schönen Gespann, in der Begleitung des Pisistratus, durch die Märkte Athens fährt—und das glaubte der ehrliche Athener—so ist in jedem Augenblicke, wie im Traume, alles möglich, und die ganze Natur umschwärmt	when it, from its transient creations, the concepts, builds a regular and rigid new world as its fortress. It seeks a new realm for its activity, a new riverbed, and finds it in mythology, and generally in art. This drive is constantly confusing the classifications and cubicles of the concept by which new transferences, metaphors, and metonymies are suggested; it constantly manifests the desire to refashion the present world of the waking human being, which is so colorful, irregular, causally incoherent, alluring, and forever new, as if it were a dream-world. In and for themselves the waking human beings are only sure that they are awake thanks to of the rigid and regular net of concepts, and are therefore sometimes impelled to believe that they dream, if once this net of concepts happens to be torn apart by art. Pascal is right when he claims that if we every night had the same dream, we would be as occupied with it as we are with the things that we see every day: "if a worker could be sure that he for a full twelve hours every night was dreaming that he was a King, then I believe," says Pascal, "that he would be as happy as a King who for twelve hours every night dreamt that he was a worker." For a mythological inspired people like the ancient Greeks, the waking day will thanks to the constant miracle that is assumed in myths better resemble dream-work than the day of the sober scientific thinker. If every tree could speak as a nymph or a god could carry away a virgin in the guise of a bull; if the goddess Athena suddenly was seen riding her beautiful chariot, in company with Pisistratus, through the market places of Athens—and that was what the honest Athenian believed—then in every moment everything is possible, like in dreams, and the entire nature is embracing
– 888 –	
den Menschen, als ob sie nur die Maskerade der Götter wäre, die sich nur einen Scherz daraus machten, in allen Gestalten den Menschen zu täuschen.	humans as if they were merely the masquerade of the gods, having fun deceiving humans in every possible shape.

—*Continued*

§ 13

Der Mensch selbst aber hat einen unbesiegbaren Hang, sich täuschen zu lassen, und ist wie bezaubert vor Glück, wenn der Rhapsode ihm epische Märchen wie wahr erzählt oder der Schauspieler im Schauspiel den König noch königlicher agiert, als ihn die Wirklichkeit zeigt. Der Intellekt, jener Meister der Verstellung, ist so lange frei und seinem sonstigen Sklavendienste enthoben, als er täuschen kann, ohne zu schaden, und feiert dann seine Saturnalien. Nie ist er üppiger, reicher, stolzer, gewandter und verwegener: mit schöpferischem Behagen wirft er die Metaphern durcheinander und verrückt die Grenzsteine der Abstraktionen, so daß er zum Beispiel den Strom als den beweglichen Weg bezeichnet, der den Menschen trägt, dorthin, wohin er sonst geht. Jetzt hat er das Zeichen der Dienstbarkeit von sich geworfen: sonst mit trübsinniger Geschäftigkeit bemüht, einem armen Individuum, dem es nach Dasein gelüstet, den Weg und die Werkzeuge zu zeigen, und wie ein Diener für seinen Herrn auf Raub und Beute ausziehend, ist er jetzt zum Herrn geworden und darf den Ausdruck der Bedürftigkeit aus seinen Mienen wegwischen. Was er jetzt auch tut, alles trägt im Vergleich mit seinem früheren Tun die Verstellung, wie das frühere die Verzerrung an sich. Er kopiert das Menschenleben, nimmt es aber für eine gute Sache und scheint mit ihm sich recht zufrieden zu geben.

Jenes ungeheure Gebälk und Bretterwerk der Begriffe, an das sich klammernd der bedürftige Mensch sich durch das Leben rettet, ist dem freigewordnen Intellekt nur ein Gerüst und ein Spielzeug für seine verwegensten Kunststücke: und wenn er es zerschlägt, durcheinanderwirft, ironisch wieder zusammensetzt, das Fremdeste paarend und das Nächste trennend, so offenbart er, daß er jene Notbehelfe der Bedürftigkeit nicht braucht und daß er jetzt nicht von Begriffen, sondern von Intuitionen geleitet wird. Von diesen Intuitionen aus führt kein regelmäßiger Weg in das Land der gespenstischen

§ 13

However, humans have an indestructible penchant for letting themselves be deceived and are like spellbound by happiness when the rhapsodist tells them epic fairy tales as if they were true, or when the actor on the stage plays the king more royally than he actually is. The intellect, this master of pretense, is free and relieved from its other slave-duties as long as it can deceive without harming, and celebrates then its Saturnalia. Never is it more sensual, more opulent, more proud, more adroit and bold. With creative pleasure, it throws metaphors into chaos and displaces the boundary stones of abstraction, so that for example the 'stream' designates a moving path carrying man to where he otherwise would have to walk. As such, the intellect throws off itself the suggestions of servility. Sometimes it attempts to show, with depressing eagerness, the poor individual lusting for existence, the way and the tools; and like a servant stripping its master of booty and prey, it becomes itself master and can wipe off its face the expression of indigence. Everything it does now implies an act of pretention in comparison with its earlier actions, which implied distortion. It copies human life, but takes this life to be something good and seems quite satisfied with it.

Every enormous timber and woodwork of the concept, onto which the needy human clings throughout life, is for the emancipated intellect merely a platform and plaything for its audacious magic tricks. And when it smashes it, throws it into a chaotic mess, ironically to put it together again, pairing the most foreign and dividing the most familiar things, then it reveals that it does not need this deficient substitute, and that it will not be guided by concepts, but by intuitions. No straight pathway leads from these intuitions to the land of the ghostly

—Continued

– 889 –

Schemata, der Abstraktionen: für sie ist das Wort nicht gemacht, der Mensch verstummt, wenn er sie sieht, oder redet in lauter verbotenen Metaphern und unerhörten Begriffsfügungen, um wenigstens durch das Zertrümmern und Verhöhnen der alten Begriffsschranken dem Eindrucke der mächtigen gegenwärtigen Intuition schöpferisch zu entsprechen.

§ 14

Es gibt Zeitalter, in denen der vernünftige Mensch und der intuitive Mensch nebeneinander stehn, der eine in Angst vor der Intuition, der andere mit Hohn über die Abstraktion; der letztere ebenso unvernünftig, als der erstere unkünstlerisch ist. Beide begehren über das Leben zu herrschen: dieser, indem er durch Vorsorge, Klugheit, Regelmäßigkeit den hauptsächlichsten Nöten zu begegnen weiß, jener, indem er als ein "überfroher Held" jene Nöte nicht sieht und nur das zum Schein und zur Schönheit verstellte Leben als real nimmt. Wo einmal der intuitive Mensch, etwa wie im älteren Griechenland, seine Waffen gewaltiger und siegreicher führt als sein Widerspiel, kann sich günstigenfalls eine Kultur gestalten und die Herrschaft der Kunst über das Leben sich gründen: jene Verstellung, jenes Verleugnen der Bedürftigkeit, jener Glanz der metaphorischen Anschauungen und überhaupt jene Unmittelbarkeit der Täuschung begleitet alle Äußerungen eines solchen Lebens. Weder das Haus, noch der Schritt, noch die Kleidung, noch der tönerne Krug verraten, daß die Notdurft sie erfand: es scheint so, als ob in ihnen allen ein erhabenes Glück und eine olympische Wolkenlosigkeit und gleichsam ein Spielen mit dem Ernste ausgesprochen werden sollte. Während der von Begriffen und Abstraktionen geleitete Mensch durch diese das Unglück nur abwehrt, ohne selbst aus den Abstraktionen sich Glück zu erzwingen, während er nach möglichster Freiheit von Schmerzen trachtet, erntet der intuitive Mensch, inmitten einer Kultur stehend, bereits von seinen Intuitionen, außer der Abwehr des Übels, eine fortwährend einströmende Erhellung, Aufheiterung, Erlösung. Freilich leidet er heftiger, wenn er leidet: ja er leidet auch öfter, weil er aus der

schemata, the abstractions; no word is created for them; man falls silent when he sees them. Or else, man speaks purely in forbidden metaphors and unheard-of conceptual combinations, for at least, in the shattering and mockery of the old conceptual boundaries, to match creatively the impression of the powerful present intuition.

§ 14

There are ages, in which the rational and the intuitive human being exist side by side, one in fear of intuition, the other with disdain for abstraction—the latter being just as irrational as the former is being inartistic. Both have a desire to rule over life; one, because he through precaution, wisdom, and regularity knows how to meet basic needs; the other, because he as an "over joyful hero" ignores these needs and only counts as real the life represented as appearance and beauty. Where once upon a time the intuitive human being, like for example in ancient Greece, wields his weapons more powerfully and victoriously than his opponent, a culture may in favorable circumstances emerge establishing the rule of art over life: i.e., the pretense, the denial of necessity, the brilliance of the metaphorical perspective, and generally, the immediacy of the illusions that accompanies all expressions of this life. Neither the house, nor the gait, nor the garment, nor the clay jug, reveal that they were created out of need. It seems as if they all want to express a sublime happiness and a cloudless Olympian sky, as if they play with seriousness.

Whereas the human guided by concepts and abstractions only prevents misfortune, without being able to squeeze happiness out of the abstractions while striving toward the highest possible freedom from pain, the intuitive human is rewarded with illumination, cheerfulness, and redemption continuously streaming toward him. Obviously, he suffers more intensely when he suffers; yes, he suffers far more frequently, since he does not

—*Continued*

– 890 –

Erfahrung nicht zu lernen versteht und immer wieder in dieselbe Grube fällt, in die er einmal gefallen. Im Leide ist er dann ebenso unvernünftig wie im Glück, er schreit laut und hat keinen Trost. Wie anders steht unter dem gleichen Mißgeschick der stoische, an der Erfahrung belehrte, durch Begriffe sich beherrschende Mensch da! Er, der sonst nur Aufrichtigkeit, Wahrheit, Freiheit von Täuschungen und Schutz vor berückenden Überfällen sucht, legt jetzt, im Unglück, das Meisterstück der Verstellung ab, wie jener im Glück; er trägt kein zuckendes und bewegliches Menschengesicht, sondern gleichsam eine Maske mit würdigem Gleichmaße der Züge, er schreit nicht und verändert nicht einmal seine Stimme, wenn eine rechte Wetterwolke sich über ihn ausgießt, so hüllt er sich in seinen Mantel und geht langsamen Schrittes unter ihr davon.	know how to learn from experience and always stumbles into the same hole twice. In his suffering, he is as irrational as in his happiness; he cries out loudly and is beyond consolation. How different it is with the stoic man, who, when effected by the same misfortunes, learns from experience how to control himself thanks to concepts. He, who otherwise seeks sincerity, truth, freedom from illusions, and protection from enchanting intrusions, executes now in his misfortune a masterful deception, just as the other type of man did in his happiness. His human face is not elastic and flexible, but is rather like a mask of dignified monotonous features. He never shouts and does not even change his tone of voice when a real thundercloud pours down on him; he only wraps himself up in his overcoat and walks with measured steps into the rain.

Translation, Peter Bornedal

Notes

INTRODUCTION

1. Nietzsche, "Über Wahrheit und Lüge im aussermoralischen Sinne" (1873) in, *Sämtliche Werke Kritische Studienausgabe*, edited by G. Colli and M. Montinari (Berlin/New York: Walter de Gruyter, 1967–1977). Translation is added below in a bilingual German/English version: "On Truth and Lies in a Non-Moral Sense."

2. In a previous work, I distinguished between an "Ur-ground," unknown in-itself, but necessarily (in Nietzsche' vocabulary) 'falsified' by a human 'optics' (i.e., our human sensory apparatus as evolved over millions of years), and as such 'falsified' providing us with a "Human Ground" as the for-us appearing world; also this ground must be seen as falsified, but on a higher, linguistic and conceptual, level. Cf. Peter Bordenal's "A Silent World: Nietzsche's Radical Realism; World, Sensation, Language," *Nietzsche-Studien* 34 (2005): pp. 1–47; Cf. also Peter Bordernal, *The Surface and the Abyss* (Berlin/New York: de Gruyter, 2010).

3. It does not seem to undersigned that the creative capacity of the philosophical, theoretical, or scientific writer is significantly determined according to how he or she responds to the classical metaphysical tradition. For example, even if we traditionally agree that Plato is an advocate of 'Truth,' it would be meaningless to conclude that he is a more 'serious' less 'playful' writer than is Nietzsche, who we tend to agree is a 'skeptic.' Their attitudes to absolutistic truth-metaphysics are not conditional upon their theoretical 'playfulness.' 'Truth' or 'Belief in Truth' is hardly like a suppressive super-ego, which when deconstructed liberates our creative potentials. One might even say that people who 'believe in Truth' have a highly vivid imagination.

4. We will later determine 'naturalistic deconstruction' in contradistinction to the 'formalistic deconstruction' suggested by J. Derrida and P. de Man in the late twentieth century (cf. below).

5. Compare, for example, to the "foreword" to Nietzsche's *Beyond Good and Evil* (: "The fight against the Cristian-ecclesiastical pressure of millennia—for Christianity is Platonism for 'the people'—has created in Europe a magnificent tension of the spirit the like of which had never yet existed on earth: with so tense a bow we can now shoot for the most distant goals. To be sure, European man experiences this tension as need and distress. […] We *good Europeans* and free, very free spirits—we still feel it, the whole need of the spirit and the whole tension of its bow. And perhaps also the arrow, the task, and, who knows, the goal." Nietzsche, *Beyond Good and Evil* (1885; Translation by W. Kaufmann, New York: Vintage, 1966), pp. 3–4.

6. Jacques Derrida, 1967: *De la Grammatologie* (Les Editions des Minuit, 1967). Translated by G. Spivak as *Of Grammatology* (Baltimore: Johns Hopkins University Press, 1974), p. 158.

7. Freidrich Albert Lange, *History of Materialism and Critique of Its Present Importance*, vol. 2, p. 302.

8. Derrida, *Of Grammatology*.

9. Derrida, *Of Grammatology*, p. 19.

10. I speculate that such statements are intentionally vapid in order to force us to listen for another more profound meaning in or behind them, which we tend to assume Derrida possesses even if we do not seem to find it ourselves. The promised profundity in the trivial and banal are meant, I think, to suggests meta-logical intuitions in the author, whom we are now seduced into acknowledging as absolute master.

11. Derrida, *Of Grammatology*, p. 70.

12. See Derrida's "Freud and the Scene of Writing" in *Writing and Difference*. Translated by A. Bass (Chicago: The University of Chicago Press, 1978).

13. Jacques Derrida, *Spurs: Nietzsche's Styles/Éperons: Les Sytles de Nietzsche*. Translated by B. Harlow (Chicago: The University of Chicago Press, 1979); See also Derrida's later interview-article (interview by Richard Beardsworth), "Nietzsche and the Machine," *Journal of Nietzsche Studies* 7 (1994): pp. 7–66.

14. Derrida, *Spurs*, p. 123.

15. Derrida, *Spurs*, p. 131.

16. I cannot completely rule out that it has been mentioned somewhere in the considerable literature on Nietzsche, but I do not recall discussions of the fragment, nor any obsession with the 'intimate reaches of Nietzsche's thoughts' among Nietzsche-commentators from the Schools I am best acquainted with.

17. The same strategy is applied in Derrida's reading of Austin, and subsequently questioned by Derrida's most intelligent critic, John Searle, in an exemplary debate between Derrida and Searle. Cf. J. L. Austin, *How to Do Things with Words* (Cambridge, MA: Harvard University Press, 1975). Austin is subjected to Derrida's reading in *Margins of Philosophy*. Translated by A. Bass (Chicago: The University of Chicago Press, 1982). Searle writes a critical response in 1977: "Reiterating the Differences. A Reply to Derrida," in H. Sussman and S. Webster, eds., *Glyph 1*, no. 2 (1977), and Derrida responds in essays eventually published as *Limited Inc*. Translated by S. Weber and J. Mehlman (Evanston: Northwestern University Press, 1988). Finally, Searle has a discussion of problems in deconstruction in John Searle's "A World Turned Upside Down," in G. Madison, ed. *Working Through Derrida* (Evanston: Northwestern University Press, 1993).

18. Derrida, *Spurs*, p. 131.

19. Derrida, *Spurs*, p. 133; Nehamas has a similar exposition of Derrida's *Éperons* in his "Introduction" to an edition of Nietzsche's early notebooks; see A. Nehamas, *Nietzsche: Writings from the Early Notebooks* (Cambridge: Cambridge University Press, 2009), p. xi.

20. So according to the translation of D. Breazeale to which de Man refers: cf. Breazeale, Daniel (ed.): *Philosophy and Truth* (Amherst/New York: Humanity Books, 1999), p. 84. See my alternative translation in the appendix to this volume (pp. 175–91).

21. Paul de Man, *Allegories of Reading* (New Haven/London: Yale University Press, 1979), p. 109.

22. G. Abel is right in emphasizing that to Nietzsche we utilize any available sign-system in order to familiarize the strange, also pictorial sign-systems: "There is no reason to adopt the thesis that we have to limit our concept of mental representation, as well as generally the question of the relationships between consciousness, mind, and world to linguistic systems and forms in a narrow sense. [...] Linguistic and propositional representation-symbols were never the only means for mental, imaginary representations and presentations. A comprehensive theory about human consciousness, mind, thinking, and action requires the inclusion also of non-linguistic, as well as of non-propositional sign and interpretation systems." Günter Abel, "Bewußtsein—Sprache—Natur. Nietzsches Philosophie des Geistes," *Nietzsche-Studien* 30: 1 (2001): (pp. 1–43) p. 39.

23. Cf. Clark, M. and Dudrick, D., 2012, *The Soul of Nietzsche's Beyond Good and Evil*. (New York: Cambridge University Press). The esoteric reading-strategy is on Clark and Dudrick's own account supposed to penetrate into a "hidden Nietzsche"; since "Nietzsche is trying to show us something that he does not say, [...] one must attempt to figure out what Nietzsche leaves unsaid and attempt to decipher not only the strategy embodied in the writing but also the strategy behind the writing." Clark, M. and Dudrick, D., 2013, ibid., pp. 48–49. Following a critical reception of this work, the authors defend their views in the follow-up article, Clark and Dudrick, 2014: "Defending Nietzsche's Soul" (*The Journal of Nietzsche Studies*, Volume 45, 3), where we are told that Nietzsche is being "deliberately misleading": "It may seem, then, that an esoteric reading is simply a rigorous interpretation, and that is largely what we take our esoteric reading of *BGE* to be. But there *is* another aspect to it: mistrusting the author, recognizing that he is sometimes *deliberately* misleading. [...] To make sense of a philosophical text when the author is sometimes being deliberately misleading, one has to do a lot of philosophy." Clark, M. and Dudrick, D.: "Defending Nietzsche's Soul," pp. 332 and 333. The reading-strategy has been met with incredulity by several Nietzsche scholars, too many to cite at this place. For a few objections, see for example H. Heit: "One function of Clark and Dudrick's distinction between "esoteric" and "exoteric" therefore seems to be to explain away whatever opposes their interpretation." Heit, Helmut, 2014: "Advancing the Agon: Nietzsche's Pre-texts and the Self-Reflexive Will to Truth" (in *Journal of Nietzsche Studies*, v. 45). p. 35. Or R. Schacht: "They proceed to the further idea that Nietzsche sometimes means something very different from—or even the exact opposite of—what he seemingly is saying; and that he was expecting "good readers" to see what his game is [...] and "figure out" what he actually means instead." Schacht, Richard, 2014: "Clack and Dudrick's New Nietzsche," (in *Journal of the History of Philosophy*, v. 52), p. 341.

24. Feuerbach, Ludwig, 1846: *Das Wesen des Christenthums* (Leipzig).

25. Nietzsche's 'Darwinism' is already acknowledged by himself in his preparations for TL in *Notebook 19*, where he says: "The terrible consistency of Darwinism, which, incidentally, I regard as true." Notebook 19, summer 1872—beginning 1873, 19[132] in Guess and Nehamas (eds.), 2009: *Nietzsche: Nietzsche: Writings from the Early Notebooks* (Trans. L. Lob, Cambridge: Cambridge University Press). It was

taken for granted in his early reception-history; e.g., mentioned by Hans Vaihinger in both his *Die Philosophie des 'Als Ob'* (Berlin, 1911) and his *Nietzsche als Philosoph* (Porta Westfalica, reprint 2002) (cf. discussion of Vaihinger below). Ernst Mach's follower, Hans Kleinpeter, describes positively Nietzsche's Darwinism in *Der Phenomenalismus: Eine Naturwissenshcaftliche Weltanschauung*. (Leipzig, 1913), and in a series of "Letters to Ernst Mach, 1912." (cf. Nietzsche Studien 40 (Berlin/New York, 2012; ed. P. Gori). In contemporary receptions, we find several discussions of Nietzsche's relation to Darwinism, notably Stegmaier, Werner, 1987: "Darwin, Darwinismus, Nietzsche. Zum Problem der Evolution," (in Nietzsche Studien 16. Berlin/New York), and Richardson, John, 2004: *Nietzsche's New Darwinism* (Oxford).

26. It is an approach I first found in Robin Small in *Nietzsche in Context* (Aldershot, 2001) years ago, where Small demonstrated that Nietzsche's epistemological positions 'in context' became almost completely obvious and lucid—cleansed, as it were, from all the so-called 'puzzlements' and 'inconsistencies.'

27. See Kofman, Sara, 1972: *Nietzsche et la métaphore*. Editions Galilée, Paris. (*Nietzsche and Metaphor*, translated by D. Large; Stanford, 1993). De Man, Paul, 1974: "Nietzsche's Theory of Rhetoric," in Symposium: A Quarterly Journal in Modern Literatures, 28:1, pp. 33–51. Yale UP; and De Man, *Allegories of Reading*. Cf. discussion below.

28. In later writings, Nietzsche is explicitly critical of these his early views inspired by Romanticism, Schopenhauer, and Wagner, and he denounces them as they found expression in his early work in a new foreword to second publication of his *Geburt der Tragödie*. We may see this later self-criticism as a manifestation of his mature realization of his commitment to the naturalist and pragmatic paradigm in which he was imbedded from the beginning, but had apparent difficulties reconciling with his early fascination with Schopenhauer and Wagner's arts-metaphysics. We will return to this discussion in Part I, B.5: "Nietzsche's Later Self-Criticisms."

29. In the following reading of TL, I will often be quoting from *Notebook 19*, with its many illuminating alternative formulations of Nietzsche's early epistemological thinking.

30. A. Nehamas discusses this discrepancy between Nietzsche's *Birth of Tragedy* and later writing, cf. Nehamas, Alexander, 2009: "Introduction" from *Nietzsche: Writings from the Early Notebooks* (Cambridge, Cambridge University Press), p. xi. (see further discussion, Part I, A.10.5: "Nietzsche's Later Self-Criticisms").

31. Cf. Clark, M., 1990, *Nietzsche on Truth and Philosophy*, Cambridge University Press. Clark defended the correspondence theory of truth in her first book (*Nietzsche on Truth and Philosophy* (1991), as she argued that only in *Wahrheit und Lüge* Nietzsche was "falsifying truth," while he in later work revised and reversed himself and adopted a virtually pro-analytic position by starting "verifying truth." Nietzsche's early work was "juvenilia," which he after mature reflection revises, ending up as "a defender of truth." It is a position Clark has been defending since her first work, and we see it reiterated in her later (with D. Dudrick), *The Soul of Nietzsche's Beyond Good and Evil* (2013).

32. Büchner, Ludwig, 1855/1872: *Kraft und Stoff*. Steiger Verlag (184l; *Force and Matter or Principles of the Natural Order of the Universe*, Leibniz). Drossbach,

Maximilian, 1884: *Über die Scheinbaren und die Wirklichen Ursachen des Geshehens in der Welt.* C. E. M. Pfeffer, Halle, and Drossbach, Maximilian, 1865: *Über die Objecte der Sinnlichen Wahrnehmung.* C. E. M. Pfeffer, Halle.

33. Cf. Du Bois-Reymond, Emil, 1872: "Über die Grenzen des Naturerkennens," in *Wissenschaftliche Vorträge*, ed. J. Howard Gore, Boston, Ginn and Company 1896. (English trans, "The Limits of our Knowledge of Nature." Popular Science Monthly, v. 5, 1874). Du Bois-Reymond, Emil, 1874: "Die Sieben Welträthsel," in *Wissenschaftliche Vorträge*; ed. J. Howard Gore, Boston Ginn and Company. (1896; English trans, "The Seven World-Riddles," Popular Science Monthly, v. 5, 1874). Helmholtz, Hermann von, 1995: *Science and Culture: Popular and Philosophical Lectures.* Edited by D. Cahan. Chicago (The University of Chicago Press). Lange, Friedrich Albert, 1873: *Geschichte des Materialismus und Kritik seiner Bedeutung in der Gegenwart*, bd. 1 and 2. Iserlohn (Verlag con J. Daedeker).

34. I will in the present work keep referring to these four writers, especially the following works are crucial. Lange, Friedrich Albert, 1873: *Geschichte des Materialismus und Kritik seiner Bedeutung in der Gegenwart* bd. 1 and 2. Iserlohn, Verlag con J. Daedeker); Avenarius, Richard, 1876: *Philosophie als Denken der Welt gemäss dem Princip die kleinsten Krafmasses.* Leipzig, Fues's Verlag; Mach, Ernst, 1886/1922: *Die Analyse der Empfindungen und das Verhältnis des Physischen zum Psychischen*, Jena, Gustav Fischer. (1914, *The Analysis of Sensations and the Relation of the Physical to the Psychical.* Translation T. J. McCormack. New York (Dover Publications), 1959. Mach, Ernst, 1905: *Erkenntnis und Irrtum.* Leipzig (Verlag von Johann Ambrosius Barth) (1976; *Knowledge and Error: Sketches on the Psychology of Enquiry*; translation T. J. McCormack Dordrecht: Reidel Publishing Company). Mach, Ernst, 1898: *Popular Scientific Lectures.* Translation T. J. McCormack. Chicago/London (Open Court). Mach, Ernst: *Science of Mechanics: A Critical and Historical Account of its Development.* Translation T. J. McCormack. Chicago/London (Open Court) 1919; and Vaihinger, Hans, 1911: *Die Philosophie des 'Als Ob'* (Berlin).

35. Vaihinger realizes to his "happy surprise the deep familiarity" between Nietzsche's and his own world understanding, which he sees as having "derived from the same sources, Schopenhauer and F. A. Lange." Vaihinger. 1911: *Die Philosophie des 'Als Ob'*, p. xiv. Kleinpeter is describing this familiarity in his work on Phenomenalism, Kleinpeter, Hans, 1913: *Der Phenomenalismus: Eine Naturwissenshcaftliche Weltanschauung* (Leipzig, J. A. Barth), as well as in correspondence to Mach.

36. Permitting here a rephrasing of Nietzsche, who largely examined the *cultural consequences* of this new thinking, we may give this particular 'Nihilist Enlightenment Thinking' the title *Exit God, Enter the Super-Human*. As I will argue below, if we see 'nihilistic' 'enlightenment thinking' in juxtaposition to Habermas's famous promotion of the continuation of the enlightenment project, Habermas's Critical Theory and my reconstructed Critical Positivism have two different social-political-ethical aspirations, where I happen to see 'Critical Positivism' as the most radical and emancipative (cf. Part II, B.5: "Nietzsche's Positivism According to Habermas").

37. There are several fine translations on the market of this popular essay. My favorite was always Breazeale, Daniel (ed.), 1999: "On the Truth and Lie in an

Extra-Moral Sense," in *Philosophy and Truth: Selections from Nietzsche's Notebooks of the Early 1870's* (Amherst, Humanities Books). Opportunely, Breazeale also translated and added several entries from Nietzsche's notebooks from around the time he composed TL. See also Ronald Speirs' translation in Geuss, R. and Speirs R. (eds.), 1999: *Nietzsche: The Birth of Tragedy and other Writings* (Cambridge, Cambridge University Press). For a newer translation, one may consult Ladislaus Lob's in Geuss. and Nehamas (eds.), 2009: *Nietzsche: Writings from the early Notebooks*, op. cit. This volume is the most comprehensive in its introduction to Nietzsche's notes for his early work, and offers in addition an excellent "Introduction" by A. Nehamas, discussing Nietzsche's early work up to *Human, all too Human*.

PART I: NIETZSCHE'S EARLY THEORY OF TRUTH AND KNOWLEDGE

1. R. Small too is discussing intellectual paradigm or 'context' as well in Small, Robin, 2001: *Nietzsche in Context* op. cit.

2. Cf. Brobjer, Thomas, 2008: *Nietzsche's Philosophical Context* (Urbana, University of Illinois Press), and Scheibenberger, Sarah, 2016: *Kommentar zu Nietzsche's, Ueber Wahrheit und Lüge im außermoralischen Sinne* (New York, Berlin, de Gruyter). Several other commentators have been engaged in establishing this theoretical context, see for example, Small, Robin (op. cit.), Emden, Christoph, 1990: *Language, Consciousness, and the Body* (Cambridge) and Emden, Christoph, 2014: *Nietzsche's Naturalism* (Cambridge); Stack, Georg, 1983: *Lange and Nietzsche* (Berlin/New York); Crawford, Claudia, 1988: *The Beginnings of Nietzsche's Theory of Language* (Berlin/New York); Moore, Gregory, 2002: *Nietzsche: Biology and Metaphor* (Cambridge). Recent articles by Pietro Gori about Nietzsche's intellectual affinities to psycho-physiology, pragmatism, and positivism are highly relevant to the current approach, prominently Gori, P., 2009: "The Usefulness of Substances. Knowledge, Science and Metaphysics in Nietzsche and Mach." in *Nietzsche Studien* bd. 38 (Berlin/New York); see also list of literature.

3. This has been incontrovertibly established by Meijers and Stengelin in their juxtaposition of Gerber's *Die Sprache als Kunst* and Nietzsche's TL, showing that entire passages in TL paraphrase, even plagiarize, Gerber. See Meijers, A. und Stengelin, M.: "Kondordanz zu . . . Gustav Gerbers Die Sprache als Kunst . . . und Nietzsches Über Wahrheit und Lüge," Nietzsche Studien 17. Berlin, New York (Walter de Gruyter), 1888. See also, Meijers, Anthonie: "Gustav Gerber und Friedrich Nietzsche. Zum historischen Hintergrund der sprachphilosophichen Auffassungen des frühen Nietzsche," in Nietzsche Studien 17. Berlin, New York (Walter de Gruyter), 1888. See also Scheibenberger's discussion in Scheibenberger, Sarah, 2016: Kommentar zu Nietzsche's, Ueber Wahrheit und Lüge, ibid., pp. 7–12. Brobjer too reports: "In September 1872, Nietzsche borrowed Gustav Gerber's Die Sprache als Kunst (Language As Art) (Bromberg, 1871). [...] And much of the content of Gerber's book found its way into Nietzsche's text "Ueber Wahrheit und Lüge." T. Brobjer, op.

cit., p. 42. This paraphrase or plagiarism has necessarily been a point of controversy because it seems to deflate the importance of TL. A note on my personal take on this discussion may therefore be in place. We need understand the circumstances for the composition of Nietzsche's early essay. What we today read as Nietzsche's *Wahrheit und Lüge* was a preparatory draft for a larger intended work (sometimes referred to as his Philosophenbuch). The essay was never published by himself and was apparently never submitted for publication (cf. Scheibenberger, op. cit., pp. 7–12). We feel we are reading a completed monograph, but are in fact reading merely a collection of notes that has been undergoing various revisions by different editors. If so, as the author of an early draft for a larger work, Nietzsche has like virtually any other writer included a mixture of his own and other people's thoughts in whatever state of completion. In notes and first drafts, one does not falsely represent other writer's work as one's own, because the draft is not intended to circulate beyond one's narrow office space into the public sphere. This at least applies 'extenuating circumstances' to the charge of 'plagiarism.'

4. In the appendix to this volume (pp. 175–91), I provide an original translation of the essay facing Nietzsche's German original (cf. "Ueber Wahrheit und Lüge im aussermoralischen Sinne" / "On Truth and Lies in a non-moral Sense"). See alternative translations by Breazeale, D. (ed.), 1999: *Philosophy and Truth* op. cit., Speirs in Geuss, R. and Speirs R. (eds.), 1999: *Nietzsche: The Birth of Tragedy and other Writings* (op. cit.), and L. Lob's in Geuss and Nehamas (eds.), 2009: *Nietzsche: Writings from the early Notebooks* (op. cit.).

5. WL, 875–76; see appendix pp. 175–77. This passage beginning WL we also find in Nietzsche's earlier essay, "Über das Pathos der Wahrheit." (cf. KSA 1, p. 759).

6. Schopenhauer is already influenced by the biological paradigm in his references to Lamarck in his early essay, *Über die vierfache Wurzel des Satzes des zureichenden Grunde* (1813) as well as in *Die Welt als Wille und Vorstellung*. Lange discusses Darwin in a separate chapter in his *Geschichte des Materialismus* (1866).

7. Schopenhauer: *Die Welt als Wille und Vorstellung* II. SW 2, p. 11. cf. above, we know that Nietzsche reread Schopenhauer in 1872 while writing *WL*.

8. Helmholtz, Hermann von: *Science and Culture: Popular and Philosophical Lectures*. Edited by D. Cahan. Chicago (The University of Chicago Press), 1995, p. 366.

9. In 1780, French astronomer C. Messier had published a list including 32 galaxies. In the early 19th century thousands of galaxies had been identified by British astronomers W. Herschel, C. Herschel, and J. Herschel. The nebular hypothesis proposed by Kant and Laplace also suggested an enormous universe.

10. Lamarck publishes his *Philosophie Zoologique* in 1809, Darwin his *On the Origin of Species* in 1856, and Heackel his *Generelle Morphologie der Organismen* in 1866; Darwin is explicitly applying the theory of evolution to the human being in his *The Descent of Man, and Selection in Relation to Sex* from 1871. Although the young Nietzsche probably did not read Darwin directly, it is certain that he read Fr. A. Lange's *Geschichte des Materialismus* (1866) several times, in which work Lange dedicates a long chapter to Darwin and evolutionary theory.

11. We notice that several influential figures of the century, e.g., Schopenhauer, Hartman, Nietzsche, and later Freud, all end up concluding that we as humans are more 'instinct' than 'reason,' more 'will' than 'purpose.' Paradigmatically, they share this fundamental premise, albeit they will espouse very different conceptions of 'will.' The premise finds its way into the popular mind as well, perhaps most famously in R. L. Stevenson's *Dr. Jekyll and Mr. Hyde.*

12. Johannes Müller dealt with the mechanism of the senses in his magnum opus, *Handbuch der Physiologie des Menschen*, published between 1833 and 1840, which became the leading textbook in physiology for most of the nineteenth century. Gustav Theodor Fechner had published his groundbreaking *Elemente der Psychophysik* in 1860, which became influential for several generations of physiologists and psychologists, such as, Hermann von Helmholtz, Wilhelm Wundt, Ernst Mach, Sigmund Freud, and William James. German physician and physiologist, Emil du Bois-Reymond, became best known for two brief philosophical essays, drawing up conclusions for the new naturalistic paradigm, *Die Grenzen des Naturerkennens*, 1872, and *Die Sieben Welträthsel*, 1880. Finally, H. von Helmholtz, spanning several disciplines like physics, physiology, and philosophy, consolidated the thinking in his monumental *Handbuch der physiologischen Optik*, 1867. Nietzsche may not have read these scientific writers directly, but he read Fr. Überweg's *Grundriss der Geschichte der Philosophie* (1862–1866) and Lange's *Geschichte des Materialismus*, who both have elaborate discussions of these developments and their philosophical implications; the discussion is present also in Schopenhauer (cf. above).

13. Cf. Helmholtz and Lange, op. cit.

14. WL 876; see appendix pp. 176–77.

15. This critique of anthropocentrism of Nietzsche's is possibly inherited from Ludwig Feuerbach, who, in *On the Essence of Christianity*, points out that if lower species like plants or insects had a God, he would merely be a reflection of themselves as species. "Every being is in and by itself infinite—has its God, its highest conceivable being, in itself." (ibid., p. 7). "If the plants had eyes, taste, and judgment, each plant would declare its own flower the most beautiful." (ibid., p. 8). The suggestion has philological support, insofar as Nietzsche had read Feuerbach in the 1860s, according to the records of T. Brobjer (ibid.).

16. Cf. Nietzsche's *Human, All Too Human* (1878/1879).

17. On a 'paradigmatic' approach, we notice that Freud's celebrated discoveries of the 'unconscious' is an effect of 'naturalism' too; it is a conclusion correctly drawn by a bold mind from understanding various systemic relationships already existent within the paradigm in which he is imbedded (Schopenhauer, Darwin, Fechner, and Helmholtz were part of Freud's education). On a 'paradigmatic' approach, such 'bold minds' have the ability to understand the logic of a paradigm with sufficient clarity to be able to draw from it conclusions that have not been drawn before, but are defensible within the logic of the paradigm, and therefore appear to be worthwhile pursuing in further research. Rather than making 'discoveries,' they are strong in analysis and synthesis of what is presented to them as regulated experience and conceptual language.

18. WL 876–77; see appendix pp. 176–78.

19. Derrida makes a similar observation in his posthumous *Histoire du mensonge. Prolegomene* (2012, Paris), as he sees that to Nietzsche the lie is not an error. Derrida does not, however, give us Nietzsche's advanced biological-naturalist explanation of these states of affairs, as here introduced. From his earliest to his latest work, it is enough for Derrida to point out that the difference between 'true' and 'false' is not a difference after all, but a "Différance with an 'a.' This generally is the 'master-gesture,' the 'master-argument,' of all Deconstruction. Somebody suggests a 'difference,' with this a conceptual opposition, and the deconstructionist response is invariably, 'but no, there is no difference!' (by implication, no conceptual opposition). (For critical discussions of de Man and Derrida, see "Introduction," 2; and Part II, A.3).

20. WL 876; see appendix pp. 176–77.

21. Cf. Du Bois-Reymond, Emil: "Über die Grenzen des Naturerkennens" (1872; "The Limits of our Knowledge of Nature"); cf. Part II, B.1: "From Materialism to Agnosticism."

22. The 'categorical imperative' is Kant's rational determination of the morally good. In the performance of the moral act, we apply to ourselves an imperative that in one of Kant's versions reads, "Act only according to that maxim whereby you can at the same time will that it should become a universal law. [...] Act as if the maxim of your action were to become through your will a universal law of nature." Kant: *Grounding of a Metaphysics of Morals*, 1785 (Hackett, ibid., p. 30)

23. Cf. Hobbes: "To this war of every man, against every man, this also is consequent, that nothing can be unjust. The notions of right and wrong, justice and injustice have there no place. Where there is no common power, there is no law; where no law, no injustice. Force and fraud are in war the two cardinal virtues." Hobbes, *Leviathan* (1651), p. 6. In Hobbes as in Nietzsche, war is a more natural condition to human beings than social order. Social order is possible only when human beings abandon their own interests that delegate their inclinations to a sovereign for their safety and well-being. The transfer of power is a mutual promise and entered collectively for the general benefit of all. Each individual says to the next individual, "I transfer my right of governing myself to X (the sovereign) if you do too." This constitutes Hobbes's 'social contract' and indicates the beginning of the formation of the state.

24. Cf. Hobbes: "[The contract] is void, but if there be a common power set over them both, with right and force sufficient to compel performance. For he that performeth first has no assurance the other will perform after, because the bonds of words are too weak to bridle men's ambition, avarice, anger, and other passions, without the fear of some coercive power; which in the condition of mere nature, where all men are equal, and judges of the justness of their own fears, cannot possibly be supposed." Hobbes, *Leviathan* (1651), p. 9.

25. For further discussion, see also Bornedal, P., 2014: "On the Institution of the Moral Subject: On the Commander and the Commanded in Nietzsche's Discussion of Law." In *Kriterion, Nietzsche and the Kantian Tradition*. Ed. R. Lopes, Brazil.

26. WL 876; see appendix pp. 176–77.

27. About a quarter of a century later, F. de Saussure would clarify this idea in another vocabulary arguing that in our use of language correspondences between sound and concept, *signifier* and *signified*, were *arbitrary* and *conventional*. Saussure ignored the epistemological discussion of the 'thing-in-itself,' not because he did not believe in 'things,' but because the epistemological world-mind problem was beyond the scope of a linguistics that aimed to become 'scientific,' and whose first requisite was to describe only linguistic phenomena, not extra-linguistic essences.

28. WL 877–78; see appendix pp. 177–79.

29. Paul de Man offers an alternative reading of this passage that seems obscure, esoteric, and idiosyncratic: "The deconstruction of the self as a metaphor does not end in the rigorous separation of the two categories (self and figure) from each other but ends instead in an exchange of properties that allows for their mutual persistence at the expense of literal truth. This process is exactly the same as what Nietzsche describes as the exemplary 'lie' of language: 'The liar uses the valid designations, words, to make the unreal appear real. He misuses the established linguistic conventions by *arbitrary substitutions or even reversals* of the names.' By calling the subject a text, the text calls itself, to some extent, a subject. The lie is raised to a new figural power, but it is nonetheless a lie. By asserting in the mode of truth that the self is a lie, we have not escaped from deception. We have merely reversed the usual scheme which derives truth from the convergence of self and other by showing that the fiction of such a convergence is used to allow for the illusion of selfhood to originate." De Man, Paul: "Nietzsche's Theory of Rhetoric," in *Symposium: A Quarterly Journal in Modern Literatures* 28: 1, 33–51. Yale, 1974, p. 40. I fail to see how Nietzsche in the previous discussion is 'deconstructing the self'; is the 'lying subject' supposed to indicate this 'deconstruction'?—On the contrary, a lying individual abusing established linguistic conventions must be highly conscious and reflective about his or her utterances. Moreover, where does Nietzsche 'call the subject a text, and the text a subject,' and what has this to do with the phenomenon of lying? When we lie, we (as Nietzsche puts it) 'reverse names' of states of affairs, which we as such misrepresents. We succeed in lying because we believe that the conventional correspondence between sign and thing is functional and operative. The liar is in his act of lying therefore displaying a strong belief in this functionality, rather than throwing his subjectivity into textual disarray and indetermination.

30. Nietzsche: *Nachlaß* 1872/1873, KSA 7, 19[97]. Cf. Guess and Nehamas, 2009: *Nietzsche: Writings from the Early Notebooks*, op. cit. Notebook 19, summer 1872—beginning 1873.

31. Nietzsche: *Nachlaß* 1872/1873, KSA 7, 19[230]. Cf. Guess and Nehamas, 2009: *Nietzsche: Writings from the Early Notebooks*, op. cit. Notebook 19, summer 1872—beginning 1873.

32. For further discussion, see also Bornedal, Peter, 1996: *The Interpretations of Art*. (Lanham/New York).

33. Vanessa Lemm arrives to a similar conclusion, when she says, "a common shortcoming of those interpretations that simply see Nietzsche as a 'denier' of truth is their failure to distinguish his practical discourse on truth from his theoretical treatment of truth. Nietzsche's practical treatment of truth belongs to the genre of social criticism,

or what has come to be called a 'critical theory' of society. Here 'truth' refers to a basic, normative presupposition of all social beings living together and all communicative action among human beings. 'Truth' in this practical sense, therefore, needs to be distinguished from both metaphysical and singular truth." Lemm, Vanessa, 2009: *Nietzsche's Animal Philosophy: Culture, Politics, and the Animality of the Human Being* (New York: Fordham UP), p. 113; See also Brigati, Roberto, 2015: "Veracity and Pragmatism in Nietzsche's On Truth and Lies," in *Parrhesia* 23, pp. 78–102.

34. The phrase comes from Clark, Maudemarie: *Nietzsche on Truth and Philosophy* (Cambridge: Cambridge University Press), 1991.

35. *Nachlaß* 1872/1873, KSA 7, 19[229]. Cf. Guess and Nehamas, 2009: *Nietzsche: Writings from the Early Notebooks*, op. cit. Notebook 19, summer 1872—beginning 1873.

36. WL 883; see appendix pp. 183–84.

37. WL 880; see appendix pp. 180–81.

38. Given that we conventionally define the camel as belonging to the mammals, the tautology of the statement becomes clear when we expand the statement and includes its implicit premise: '*if* we define a camel as belonging to the mammals, *then* it follows that a camel is a mammal.' "Empty husks" are Nietzsche's designation of such empty tautological statements; to be compared to Kant's perhaps better-known example of an analytic proposition, 'a bachelor is an unmarried man' or expanded, '*if* we define a bachelor as an unmarried man, *then* if follows that a bachelor is an unmarried man.'

39. WL 878; see appendix pp. 178–79.

40. *Nachlaß* 1872/1873, KSA 7, 19[229]. Cf. Guess and Nehamas, 2009: *Nietzsche: Writings from the Early Notebooks*, op. cit. Notebook 19, summer 1872—beginning 1873.

41. In German, '*der Baum*' is masculine, while '*die Pflanze*' is feminine.

42. Nietzsche understands here the German, 'die schlange' (snake), used as noun, as a derivative of the verb 'schlingen' (twisting, winding, wrapping).

43. WL 878–79; see appendix pp. 178–80.

44. The idea is well-known from a number of philosophers, and we see it entertained already in J. Locke's *Essays Concerning Human Understanding* (1690). In the example of the stone's hardness, Nietzsche is likely to have been inspired by his contemporary, Gustav Gerber, who has a near-identical formulation in *Die Sprache als Kunst*: "We say: the stone is hard, as if the hardness was something different from our judgment." Claudia Crawford notices Gerber's influence on Nietzsche in Crawford, C., 1988: *The Beginnings of Nietzsche's Theory of Language*, op. cit., p. 203, and Meijers, A., 1988: "Gustav Gerber und Friedrich Nietzsche," op. cit.

45. Cf. Saussure, Ferdinand de, 1916: *Cours de linguistique générale* (Translation: *Course in General Linguistics*, 1966).

46. To the commonsense realist, this view (which to undersigned seems self-evident) often implies the idealist view that the world as externality is reduced to ideas. Reacting to this supposed idealism in Nietzsche, B. Williams (among many others) objects that entities in the world, such as 'dogs' and 'snakes,' are obviously known as existing as such: "Some deniers [of truth] have indeed been attached to

confused formulations in the philosophy of language, in part derived from a mangling of Saussure, to the general effect that language consists of "arbitrary signs" which "get their meaning" from their relations to other signs, and since this is so, it cannot relate to a non-linguistic world. This is a tissue of mistakes. If *dog* is an "arbitrary" sign for a dog, it is at any rate a sign for a dog, and that must mean that it can refer to a dog: and a dog is a dog, not a word." Williams, 2003: *Truth and Truthfulness* (Princeton), p. 6. I do not see the often rehearsed criticism applies. Williams and other defenders of realism object to straw men, fantasy opponents, making extravagant idealist claims; these fantasy opponents are supposed to believe that we live in a world of ideas, and not in that concrete world that is here and everywhere. The resistances of floors, tables, and other nearby objects 'prove' the obvious existence of a 'hard' external world. But *that* the world is, does not explain *what* the world is. *That-ness* is not the same as *what-ness*. 'A dog is a dog!' Williams says, countering the linguistic notion of the "arbitrary sign," but why in this example is the word 'dog' not arbitrary, if it emphatically is not a dog? My thesis is that commonsense realists are actually 'ultra-strong conventionalists,' convinced that conventions are universal and permanent, making it silly to call the origin of these conventions into question. Hence, if we 'call' a dog a dog, it is not because of the disturbing 'arbitrary sign,' but because convention has dictated the sign for dog, and because we as ultra-strong conventionalists cannot tolerate distinctions between *language and object*, between *conventional and universal*, or between *knowledge and existence*. Williams says: "It is trivially true that "snake" is a human concept, a cultural product. But it is a much murkier proposition that its use somehow *falsifies* reality—that "in itself" the world does not contain snakes, or indeed anything else you might mention." Williams, 2003, *Truth and Truthfulness*, p. 17. The false inference of the last sentence (attributed to fantasy opponents) that 'falsification' implies 'annihilation' of reality, that conclusion does not follow from the 'arbitrary sign,' whether in Nietzsche or Saussure. When the sign 'falsifies,' is falsifies a world, and the falsification entails the existence of a world. Without the sign, this world is in Nietzsche and Saussure regarded as undifferentiated, not yet actively denominated, but still *being there* in its undifferentiated state. It is not far-fetched to entertain the idea that our hominid ancestors lived in a world where so-called 'snakes' were not yet singled out in contrast to other crawling or wriggling animals, and the example does not imply that 'the world did not contain snakes.' Even if Nietzsche believes that concepts make the "un-identical identical," individual instances *exist*, perceived by eyes having evolved into perceiving them. However, Nietzsche and his peers do not make simple judgments of existence from which nothing else follows than the *assertion of existence*. They rather question *what* and *how* we *know*. At least, "my" Nietzsche is not questioning the *existence* of snakes or dogs, but how concepts introduce necessary segmentation of our infinitely variegated perceptions of reality that eventually settle as *strong linguistic conventions*—but never into *ultra-strong conventions identical to things-in-themselves*.

47. Hartman, E. von: *Die Philosophie des Unbewussten*, 3 vols. (*The Philosophy of the Unconscious*; 1870), Lange, Fr. A, 1866.: *Geschichte des Materialismus* (ibid.). The most thorough discussion of Nietzsche's inspiration from Lange, we find

in Stack, G., 1883: *Lange and Nietzsche* (Berlin-New York: Walter de Gruyter). For further discussions, see T. Brobjer (2008), C. Emden (2005), Emden (2014) and R. Small (2001).

48. As we will discuss below, Nietzsche is here referring Schopenhauer's discussion in *On the Fourfold Root*, op. cit.

49. WL 879; see appendix pp. 179–80.

50. Nietzsche's tri-partition of our perceptive-cognitive apparatus is far from original; it recapitulates a way of thinking the psyche common among psychologists and philosophers of knowledge in the nineteenth century. In the Continental tradition, we find the thinking in A. Schopenhauer, G. A. Fechner, L. Ueberweg, H. von Helmholtz, F. A. Lange, A. Spir, E. Mach, W. Wundt, and the young Freud. In the nineteenth Anglo-Saxon tradition, we find it in G. Hamilton, Stuart Mill, and later in W. James.

51. A. Meijers alternatively presents a model that leaves out Nietzsche's 'nerve-stimulus,' but includes the thing-in-itself in its stead, which I see as an error. However, like undersigned, Meijers differentiates between 'Wort' and 'Begriff': "Ding an sich → Bild (oder Anschauungsmetapher) → Laut (oder Wort) → Begriff." Meijers, A., 1988, "Gustav Gerber und Friedrich Nietzsche" in *Nietzsche Studien* 17 (Berlin and New York: Walter de Gruyter), p. 386. Claudia Crawford notices Gerber's influence, and summarizes Gerber's reconstruction of the genesis of language as follows: "First, the thing in itself presumably prompts a nerve stimulus (*Nervenreiz*), which produces in the human being a sensation (*Empfindung*). The sensation, quite spontaneously produces a sound (*Laut*). This sound is a purely natural reaction to stimulus, whether a cry, a scream, or any other sound, it is primarily an action, which reduces the tension created by the perception of the stimulus. Already in this first phase of its development, the language sound produce by the sensation does not directly represent the original prepetition. The movement between sensation and sound is arbitrary and here the art instinct becomes active." C. Crawford: *The Beginnings of Nietzsche's Theory of Language*, op. cit., p. 203.

52. Schopenhauer, Arthur, 1847: *Über die vierfache Wurzel des Satzes des zureichenden Grunde*, in *SW*3 (Translation, 1889: *On the Fourfold Root of the Principle of Sufficient Reason*, London: George Bell and Sons.)

53. Schopenhauer: *Über die vierfache Wurzel*, SzG, *SW3*, p. 69.

54. Schopenhauer: *Über die vierfache Wurzel*, SzG, *SW3*, pp. 69–70.

55. Schopenhauer: *Über die vierfache Wurzel*, SzG, *SW3*, p. 60.

56. It is a creed that is variously described as 'primitive materialism' in Fr. Lange or 'naïve materialism' in Fr. Engels, who are equally hostile to this simple linear model (cf. discussion Part II, A.1).

57. See Drossbach, 1865: *Über die Objecte der Sinnlichen Wahrnehmung*, op. cit. and Drossbach, 1884: *Über die Scheinbaren und die Wirklichen Ursachen des Geschehens in der Welt*, op. cit.

58. The idea of simple cause-effect relationships in inner mental life is under deconstruction already in TL, and will be continued in Nietzsche's later work.

59. WL 883; see appendix pp. 183–84.

60. Locke, John, 1690: *Essay Concerning Human Understanding*, op. cit.

61. In the later *Nachlaß* material (e.g., KSA 12, 1886/1887, 6[14]), Nietzsche will see stimuli as quantities and images as qualities, assuming that 'quality' comes about from an abbreviation-/simplification-process making quantities perceptible. Quantities imply a sensation-overflow that has to be made manageable before the human species is able to perceive properly speaking. This distinction between 'qualities' and 'quantities' is actually present already in the early *Nachlaß* material, cf. *Notebook 19*.

62. Contemporary psychology still accepts various parts of this nineteenth-century perceptive-cognitive model. One assumes that there is a process whereby sensory stimuli are translated into structured experience, the latter often seen as the joint product of the sensory stimulation and of the psychological process itself. However, psychologists tend not to ask the question preoccupying the epistemologists of the nineteenth century, namely whether a real world exists independently of human experience and, if so, how the truth of experiences may be determined. Professional psychologists tend to bypass such questioning in favor of problems that can be methodologically resolved.

63. Ernst Chladni had published his experiment in *Entdeckungen über die Theorie des Klanges*, Leipzig 1787.

64. WL 879; see appendix pp. 179–80.

65. Nietzsche is likely to have seen it is Lange, who cites the example in his *Geschichte*: "That *our* things are different from things *in themselves* may be made plain to us, therefore, even by the simple opposition between a tone and the vibrations of the string that occasions it." Lange: *The History of Materialism*, book 2, section 1, p. 188.

66. The dictionary-correct translation of Nietzsche's "Wolkenkuckucksheim" is "cloud-cuckoo-land." The phrase refers to Aristophanes's comedy "The Birds" where birds build cities in the clouds. Generally, the expression connotes an impossible non-existing dream or fantasy-land, thus—among several possible alternative translations—an 'imaginary never-never land,' as I have opted for.

67. WL 884; see appendix pp. 184–85.

68. Schopenhauer: *Die Welt als Wille und Vorstellung* I, SW1, p. 79.

69. Schopenhauer: *Die Welt als Wille und Vorstellung* I, SW1, p. 113.

70. Nietzsche: *Nachlaß* 1872/1873, KSA 7, 23[13].

71. Nietzsche: *Nachlaß* 1872/1873, KSA 7, 19[66]. Cf. Guess and Nehamas, 2009: *Nietzsche: Writings from the Early Notebooks*, op. cit. Notebook 19, summer 1872—beginning 1873.

72. Cf. Freud's preoccupation with this kind of 'proto-thinking' in his *Traumdeutung* (1900) a few decades later.

73. Schopenhauer: *Die Welt als Wille und Vorstellung* I, SW1, p. 78. The distinction between perceptive and linguistic representations, images and words, is relatively simple and had been around long before Schopenhauer and Nietzsche. We see this distinction between intuitive perceptions and concepts already in Kant, for example when in his *Logic*, he observes: "All knowledge, that is, all representations consciously related to an object, are either intuitive perceptions or concepts [*entweder Anschauungen oder Begriffe*].—The intuitive perception is an individual [*einzelne*]

representation, the concept a general [*allgemeine*] or reflective representation. (Kant: *Logik*, WA VI, p. 521).

74. Schopenhauer: *Die Welt als Wille und Vorstellung* I, SW1, p. 78. Notice here the similarity to Nietzsche's language in TL.

75. Schopenhauer: *Die Welt als Wille und Vorstellung* I, SW1, p. 81. Notice again the similarity to Nietzsche's language.

76. Schopenhauer: *Die Welt als Wille und Vorstellung* I, SW1, p. 155.

77. Schopenhauer: *Die Welt als Wille und Vorstellung* 2, SW2, p. 87.

78. Schopenhauer: *Die Welt als Wille und Vorstellung* I, SW1, p. 156.

79. Nietzsche: *Nachlaß* 1872/1873, KSA7, 19[66]. Cf. Guess and Nehamas, 2009: *Nietzsche: Writings from the Early Notebooks*, op. cit. Notebook 19, summer 1872—beginning 1873.

80. Schopenhauer: *Die Welt als Wille und Vorstellung* 2, SW2, p. 86.

81. Cf. Schopenhauer: *Die Welt als Wille und Vorstellung* I, SW1, p. 81.

82. Schopenhauer *Die Welt als Wille und Vorstellung* 2, SW2, p. 87.

83. See also Crawford, who spends a chapter outlining some of the convergences between Nietzsche and Schopenhauer in Crawford, Claudia: *The Beginnings of Nietzsche's Theory of Language*, op. cit., p. 184.

84. WL 880; see appendix pp. 180–81.

85. We notice that Nietzsche's first model, *nerve-stimulus* → *image* → *sound/word*, addresses different theoretical disciplines such as physiology, psychology, cognitive science, and linguistics, and applies essentially to our perceptive-cognitive apparatus, while his second and expanded model, *nerve-stimulus* → *image* → *sound/word* → *concept*, adds the inevitable epistemological dimension to the discussion. Epistemic language is conceptual, i.e., the language of knowledge, as cultivated in science, theory, and philosophy.

86. WL 880; see appendix pp. 180–81.

87. However, in order to avoid confusion at this point, Nietzsche's 'words' never refer to *things in-themselves*, never to unmediated objectivity or 'reality'; in this sense, his neo-Kantian criticism of the thing-in-itself is never in dispute. They exclusively refer to Nietzsche's images or my 'thing-representations.'

88. WL 880; see appendix pp. 180–81.

89. WL 880; see appendix pp. 180–81.

90. WL 880; appendix pp. 180–81. In a note apparently written as a draft to *TL*, Nietzsche describes the problem with concepts as the introduction of "false perceptions": "The concept originates from equalizing the non-equal. [...] The equal is taken for granted because one presupposes identity; therefore because of *false perceptions* [italics added]. One sees a human walking, and names it 'walking.' Then a monkey, a dog: and one says again, 'walking.'" Nietzsche: *Nachlaß* 1872/1873, KSA7, 23[11]. Nietzsche's '*walking*' is another generalization, added to his two other examples, leaf and honesty. It indicates that a unique human motor-activity is being applied to all animals, as if their various motor movements are reduced to human motor movements.

91. As indicated, in the second part of his essay, Nietzsche returns with a vengeance to his second theory, arguing with great eloquence how the concept alienates us from the supposedly *intuitive and immediate* language of words for sense-reality

(thing-representations). There, he suggests a distinction between authentic and inauthentic language, where, as typical in the romantic paradigm, the authentic is represented in the languages of fantasy, dreams, imagery, myth, and poetry, while by contrast concept-formation destroys this linguistic immediacy. It is this emphasis on the proper and authentic applied to the word (with its connotations to poetry, myth, and literature), I see as a regress to a 'romantic-aesthetic' or 'romantic-sentimental' paradigm (cf. Part I, B.10: "Regressions to Romantic Arts-Metaphysics").

92. Nietzsche: WM 506 = KSA 11, 25[168].

93. Especially as mediated by Paul de Man. We find the authoritative discussions in: (1) Paul De Man,"Nietzsche's Theory of Rhetoric," *Symposium: A Quarterly Journal in Modern Literatures* 28: 1 (1974): 33–51; (2) De Man, *Allegories of Reading*; (3) De Man, Paul: The Rhetoric of Romanticism. (New York: Columbia University Press), 1984. Also Kofman, Sara, 1972: *Nietzsche et la métaphore*. Editions Galilée, Paris. (*Nietzsche and Metaphor*, translated by D. Large; Stanford, 1993).

94. WL 881; see appendix pp. 181–82.

95. Cf. C. Emden: "Language, Nietzsche seems to suggest, is a figurative discourse in itself [...], but the metaphoricity of language result from a more fundamental metaphorical process located beyond or perhaps before language. At stake here are the relationships among the materiality of nervous processes, the formation of introspective mental images, and the ensuing representations of these images in verbalization. Nietzsche's use of the term *metaphor* here might be confusing, for metaphor can exist only within language." Emden, C.: *Nietzsche on Language*, op. cit., p. 106. See also Crawford discussion in Crawford, Claudia, 1988: *The Beginnings of Nietzsche's Theory of Language* op. cit.

96. Cf. Aristotle, *Poetics*, XXI, 1457a. See also Perelman and Olbrechts-Tyteca, 1959: *The New Rhetoric: A Treatise on Argumentation* (Notre-Dame: University of Notre dame Press).

97. Cf. Schlimgen: "Nietzsche's concept of image should here not be thought as a copy in relation to reality; it already replaces something (and has as such sign-character) which has no ontic status, of which it could not be a copy." Schlimgen: *Nietzsches Theorie des Bewußtseins* (Berlin/New York: Walter de Gruyter, 1998), p. 73; See also Emden: "The transition from perception to language accordingly proceeds in a 'metaphorical' manner [...] and does not start with any kind of external reality or some pseudo-Kantian thing-in-itself." Emden: Nietzsche on Rhetoric and Neurophysiology, op. cit., p. 101; See also A. Meijers: "Gustav Gerber und Friedrich Nietzsche" in Nietzsche Studien, op. cit., p. 385.

98. Scientists write in metaphors all the time and are typically aware that they do. They know that the 'gravitational force' or the 'big bang' are metaphorical expressions of something we do not fully understand. Less scientific minds, however, may be compelled into literalizing these metaphors in the belief that they here encounter the reassuring expressions of objective scientific knowledge.

99. See especially GM, Part II.

100. Four works by M. Foucault stands to undersigned out as such re-discoveries of coagulated meaning in various fields: Foucault, Michel, 1961: *Folie et déraison: histoire de la folie à l'âge classique* (1965; *Madness and Civilization: A History of*

Insanity in the Age of Reason); Foucault, Michel, 1963: *Naissance de la clinique: une archéologie du regard médical* (*The Birth of the Clinic: An Archaeology of Medical Perception*, 1973); Foucault, Michel, 1966: *Les Mots et les choses* (*The Order of Things*, 1970); Foucault, Michel, 1975: *Surveiller et punir: naissance de la prison* (*Discipline and Punish: The Birth of the Prison*, 1977).

101. Cf. Brobjer, Thomas H., 2008: *Nietzsche's Philosophical Context*, op. cit.
102. Feuerbach, Ludwig: *The Essence of Christianity*. Translated by G. Eliot. Amherst, New York (Prometheus Books), 1989, p. 4. This repeats Hegel's analysis from *The Phenomenology of Mind*, notably as developed in his chapter on 'master and slave.'
103. Feuerbach: *The Essence of Christianity*, p. 5.
104. Feuerbach: *The Essence of Christianity*, p. 11.
105. Feuerbach: *The Essence of Christianity*, p. 8.
106. Feuerbach: *The Essence of Christianity*, p. 25.
107. Feuerbach: *The Essence of Christianity*, p. 12.
108. Feuerbach: *The Essence of Christianity*, p. 25.
109. Feuerbach: *The Essence of Christianity*, pp. 29–30.
110. Feuerbach: *The Essence of Christianity*, p. 26.
111. Feuerbach comes across as a reluctant atheist, equaly able to understand the anthropomorphism in the religious ideal and embrace its fundamental necessity. Nietzsche is of course less schizophrenic.
112. WL 881 pp. 181–82.
113. WL 881 pp. 181–82. *A propos* the vague and indecisive distinction between 'word' and 'concept' in Schopenhauer and Nietzsche, we notice that when Nietzsche is here talking about the transformation of image into a linguistic form, he is using the term 'concept' (*Begriff*) for that form, where it would have been accurate to describe this *second* transfer (after the *first* transfer of stimuli into images) as a process transforming an 'image' into a 'word.' Thereupon, we encounter the *third* transformation of 'word' into the proper 'concept,' as acknowledged elsewhere.
114. UBII, KSA1, p. 248. For a closer reading of Nietzsche's UBII, See also Jensen, Anthony K., 2013: *Nietzsche's Philosophy of History* (New York: Cambridge University Press).
115. E. von Hartman, one of the possible sources of inspiration of the early Nietzsche, had suggested a similar thesis: "All conscious human thought is only possible by the help of language, since we see that human thought without language [...] in the most favorable case, very little exceeds that of the cleverest domestic animals." Hartman, Eduard von: *Philosophy of the Unconscious*, bd. 2 (Reprint. London: Routledge, 2000), p. 298.
116. Schopenhauer: *Die Welt als Wille und Vorstellung* I, SW1, p. 74.
117. WL 881–82; see appendix pp. 181–83.
118. More about the 'spider' metaphor in Part I, A.9.
119. We find in Sara Kofman the following commentary to the relevant passage of Nietzsche's: "The scientific edifice, full of splendor, is compared to that of a miserable insect, with such small cells, in order to ridicule science's claim to cut the world down to its size, a presumption which takes metaphors for essences. Science can never

explain the world; it can only describe it in terms of metaphorical schemata, which are human, all too human. It is a pure 'system of signs' (a semiology), a mythology (a world of fictions). It is of the same nature as ordinary language, which is simply extends. It originates in the same metaphorical activity and is constructed on the basis of concepts which it just multiplies and renovates, using the same materials." Kofman, Sara, 1993: *Nietzsche and Metaphor*, op. cit., p. 62. When Nietzsche compares scientific concept-formations with the constructions of bees and spiders, it is explicitly in order to emphasize the far more delicate nature of (and the extreme complexity of) human construction in comparisons to that of bees and spiders. I fail to see the scientists depicted as 'as miserable' as bees, but rather admirable in the comparison; scientific constructions are not as such ridiculous, they rather become ridiculous if or when they are alienated from the intellectual scientific process and taken to represent essences in and of themselves. Kofman writes that science is "a mythology, a world of fictions," which reads like the critical positivist view of later Nietzsche, Vaihinger, and Mach (cf. discussion Part II, A.4), but she thinks that 'fiction' is poetry, while properly understood, a *positivist 'fiction'* refers to scientific concept-language, while rigorously denouncing its references to metaphysical 'essences.' In the Naturalist-Positivist paradigm, scientific concept-language *is* deconstruction of metaphysics.

120. WL 881 pp. 181–82.

121. See also discussion of Nietzsche's 'anthropocentrism' in Stack, George, 2005: *Nietzsche's Anthropic Circle: Man, Science, and Myth* (New York: University of Rochester Press).

122. WL 882; see appendix pp. 182–83.

123. WL 882; see appendix pp. 182–83.

124. WL 882; see appendix pp. 182–83.

125. WL 883; see appendix pp. 183–84.

126. As we find this naturalized 'corrected Kantianism' defended and discussed by especially Fr. A. Lange in *Geschichte des Materialismus*, op. cit.

127. WL 885; see appendix pp. 185–86.

128. *Nachlaß* 1872/1873, KSA7, 19[157]. Cf. Guess and Nehamas, 2009: *Nietzsche: Writings from the Early Notebooks*, op. cit. Notebook 19, summer 1872—beginning 1873.

129. *Nachlaß* 1872/1873, KSA7, 19[158]. Cf. Guess and Nehamas, 2009: *Nietzsche: Writings from the Early Notebooks*, op. cit. Notebook 19, summer 1872—beginning 1873.

130. Cf. Jameson, Frederick, 1975: *The Prison House of Language* (Princeton, NJ: Princeton University Press).

131. Nietzsche: FW, KSA5, 374.

132. See also W. Stegmaier's detailed discussion of book five of FW in Stegmaier, Werner, 2012: *Nietzsches Befreiung der Philosophie: Kontextuelle Interpretation des V. Buchs der 'Fröhlichen Wissenschaft* (Berlin/New York: W. de Gruyter).

133. Nietzsche's statements about 'truth,' 'perspectivism,' or 'interpretation' have for several decades been an issue of vivid debate, as they to commentators of particularly the analytic persuasion appeared to be inconsistent or self-contradictory.

If Nietzsche declares 'truth' to be 'false,' he is repeating the classical Liar Paradox, i.e., he is asserting a statement, which in its content is stating that there is no truth, and therefore self-referentially is stating that it is itself false, because if the statement pronounces that there is no truth, then this statement applies in equal measure to itself, and is therefore self-undermining. One may recall one of the first renditions of the Liar Paradox in Ancient Greek thinking attributed to Eubulides of Miletus, who should have said: "A man says that he is lying. Is what he says true or false?" See e.g. Dowden on the paradox: Dowden, Bradley: "Liar Paradox" in: Stanford Encyclopedia of Philosophy; see also Russell, Bertrand. *Logic and Knowledge: Essays 1901–1950*, ed. by Robert C. Marsh, George Allen and Unwin, Ltd. (1956). When Nietzsche is proposing his 'perspectival' theory of knowledge, he is allegedly producing only another variation of the liar paradox. If he says that everything is perspectival (for example in GM: "There is *only* a perspective seeing [*ein perspektivisches Sehen*], *only* a perspective "knowing" [*ein perspektivisches 'Erkennen'*]" (GM III, 12), this statement is spoken either from Nietzsche's own perspective or it is extra-perspectival; in any case, it is self-undermining. Maudemarie Clark, for example, finds Nietzsche's perspectivism inconsistent or self-refuting, at least in what she calls its 'radical interpretation': "In addition to the general problem regarding truth, the problem of self-reference plagues the radical interpretation of perspectivism." Clark, Maudemarie, 1991: *Nietzsche on Truth and Philosophy*. Cambridge, Cambridge University Press, p. 151. If he apparently says that 'everything is interpretation,' as for example in the sentence, "I would say: no, facts is exactly what there is not, only interpretations. We cannot establish any fact 'in itself'." (NF 1886/1887, KSA 12, 7[60]), he has produced yet another variation of the Liar Paradox, as the logical-analytic readings will take for granted that 'interpretation' has the connotation 'false,' while 'facts' have the connotation 'true,' what catches Nietzsche in a non-sense, because he purportedly has made the radical claim that *truth* is *false*. (Other commentators have more accommodating or rescuing readings of Nietzsche's so-called paradoxès: e.g. Nehamas, Alexander, 1985: *Nietzsche: Life as Literature* (Cambridge, MA.); see e.g. Nehamas, ibid., pp. 66–68; and Hales, S. D. and Welshon, R., 2000: *Nietzsche's Perspectivism* (Urbana and Chicago). As I understand Nietzsche in his intellectual context, Nietzsche's idea of a 'biological perspectivism' suspends the discussions of formal logical puzzles, since it concludes from the fact of the evolution of our cognitive apparatus that we perceive the world differently than other species, and therefore from *another perspective*. On that background, rehearsing various formal logical puzzlements cannot be the concern of neither Nietzsche nor any other theorist of science. Their claim of a 'perspectival world' is not an extra-perspectival truth-claim, but a statement confirming a biological fact. They are not confused in their application of logic, but prove their rigor by applying consistent reasoning *to the topic* they have under discussion. During the nineteenth, twentieth, and twenty-first centuries, the evolutionary hypothesis assumed the status of a fact, and Nietzsche's *sound logical reasoning* becomes a tool to advance this new naturalist understanding. His reasoning is generally always organic and internalized, never pretentious and demonstrative. For example, when he reasons that if he and peers can conclude (i) to 'biological perspectivism' as a general and indisputable condition, then (ii), the appearing world is interpreted according to different perspectives, and then (iii), we can no longer assert that there is one 'true world,' and then (iv), we can rightfully conclude, in reference to this issue, that 'there are no *facts*, but only *interpretations*.' These and other inferences he does not formalize into tables of simple syllogisms, but that does not take away the consistency of the thinking, given our acceptance of the biological-naturalist premise.

134. Kant: *Prolegomena* § 46, WAV, p. 205.

135. Nietzsche: *Nachlaß* 1872–1873, KSA 7, 19[236]. Cf. Guess and Nehamas, 2009: *Nietzsche: Writings from the Early Notebooks*, op. cit. Notebook 19, summer 1872—beginning 1873.

136. Nietzsche: *Nachlaß* 1872/1873, KSA 7, 19[242]. Cf. Guess and Nehamas, 2009: *Nietzsche: Writings from the Early Notebooks*, op. cit. Notebook 19, summer 1872—beginning 1873.

137. As we will see below, the thinking anticipates E. Mach, who will develop this theory of 'elements' in his work on perception and knowledge (cf. Mach, E.: *The Analysis of Sensations and the Relations of the Physical to the Psychical*. Translation T. J. McCormack. New York (Dover Publications), 1959, and Mach: *Popular Scientific Lectures*. Translation T. J. McCormack (Chicago/London: Open Court, 1898). A few Nietzsche commentators, such as N. Hussain and P. Gori, have defended this theoretical affinity between Nietzsche and Mach, which seems evident also to undersigned; See, e.g., Hussain, N.: "Nietzsche's Positivism," in *European Journal of Philosophy* 12: 3, 2004, pp. 326–68; and "Reading Nietzsche through Ernst Mach," in Moore, G., and Brobjer T. (eds.): *Nietzsche and Science*. London (Ashgate), 2004; Gori, P.: "The Usefulness of Substances. Knowledge, Science and Metaphysics in Nietzsche and Mach," in *Nietzsche-Studien* 38, 2009.

138. This is a thinking that again reminisces Feuerbach, who also insisted that a 'real God' was never an abstract nature or thing-in-itself, but a God of predicates, i.e., a God personified by the qualities that a tribe, a people, or a civilization bestowed upon him (cf. Part I, A.2: "God as 'Dead Metaphor': Nietzsche and Feuerbach on Anthropocentrism").

139. Nietzsche: *Nachlaß* 1872/1873, KSA 7, 19[236]. Cf. Guess and Nehamas, 2009: *Nietzsche: Writings from the Early Notebooks*, op. cit. Notebook 19, summer 1872—beginning 1873.

140. WL, 883; see appendix pp. 183–84.

141. WL 883; see appendix pp. 183–84.

142. WL 885; see appendix pp. 185–86.

143. WL 885; see appendix pp. 185–86. We notice that we are here back to the issue of biological Perspectivism, but in this context used as an irrefutable argument against truth-metaphysics.

144. It is perhaps surprising that Nietzsche is presenting a version of 'Machist' epistemology already in his early TL, but even if the young Nietzsche may not have read Mach at this point, he is well acquainted with several ideas in the neo-Kantian paradigm *anticipating* Mach, not least by Fr. Lange, who, with his influential discussions of the new sciences in his *Geschichte*, stands out as an indispensable *common*

source of inspiration for several of the prominent writers of the late nineteenth century.

145. WL 885; see appendix pp. 185–86.
146. WL 884–85; see appendix pp. 184–86.
147. Nietzsche, 1881: *Morgenröte (Daybreak,* translation Hollingdale), p. 117.
148. Schopenhauer, *Die Welt als Wille und Vorstellung* I, p. 422.
149. Schopenhauer, *Die Welt als Wille und Vorstellung* I, p. 439. The issue is discussed already in *On the Principle of Sufficient Reason*, paragraph 21.
150. Liebmann, Otto, 1865: *Kant und die Epigonen* (Berlin), pp. 21–22.
151. Schopenhauer, *Die Welt als Wille und Vorstellung* I.
152. Liebmann, Otto, 1865: *Kant und die Epigonen*, op. cit.
153. Fischer, Kuno, 1883: *Kritik der kantischen Philosophie*, op. cit. (1888, *Critique of Kant*, trans. W. S. Hough, London). As Fischer's English translator explains in the preface to his translation, Fischer's small opus is a summary of work on Kant from his monumental *Geschichte der moderne Philosophie*, München, published during the 1860s.
154. Lange, Fr. A., 1873: *Geschichte des Materialismus*, op. cit.
155. Schopenhauer: *Die Welt als Wille und Vorstellung* I, pp. 502–3.
156. Fischer: *Critique of Kant*, op. cit.
157. Fischer: *Critique of Kant*, op. cit., p. 98
158. Liebmann: *Kant und die Epigonen*, op. cit., pp. 25–26.
159. Fischer: *Critique of Kant*, op. cit., pp. 26–27.
160. Scheiberberger sees this discrepancy as well in Nietzsche's uses of the concept of concept. Cf. Scheibenberger, "Die Ambivalenz der Sprache ist im Besonderen abzulesen an der (metaphorischen) Unterscheidung zwischen Wort und Begriff. Zunächst stellt N. die Metapher als notwendigen Vorläufer des Begriffs unter den Begriff, zweitens aber stellt er sie als lebendigen Antipoden dem starren Begriff entgegen. Die Metapher der ersten Art ist aber wiederum nur in einer Metapher (wie jener des Nervenreizmodells) denkbar, da sie, der Sprache entzogen, in individuellem Erleben gründet. Wenn aber ein solches Erleben bewusst gemacht, wenn es erinnert wird, dann unterliegt es schon den sprachschemata, die Schemata auch des Bewusstseins sind." Scheibenberger, Sarah, 2016: *Kommentar zu Nietzsche's Ueber Wahrheit und Lüge im außermoralischen Sinne*, p. 17.
161. WL 886; see appendix pp. 186–87.
162. WL 882; see appendix pp. 182–83.
163. Cf. discussions of Fr. Schiller and Fr. Schlegel below.
164. This aspect is contributing to the conclusion Sara Kofman is drawing from her reading of TL. Cf. Kofman, Sara, 1993: *Nietzsche and Metaphor*, op. cit.
165. WL 887; see appendix pp. 187–88.
166. Nietzsche starts out his essay describing a "Trieb zur Wahrheit" (TL 876), and introduces towards the end the new "Trieb zur Metapherbildung" (TL 887). The two drives are at least partially overlapping, since 'Truth' in the first part of the essay is seen as an 'army of metaphors.' It is again a confusion, on Nietzsche's part, when he in the latter part of his essay mobilizes the 'metaphor-drive' *against* scientific

conceptualizations, seemingly forgetting that he generally classified these as a kind of metaphors. However, in TL1, an epistemological 'metaphor' is (like Vaihinger's 'fiction') not poetic. In TL2 Nietzsche seemingly goes back on this first general determination of 'metaphors,' and postulates that 'metaphors' are poetic and artistic in their most authentic form. He seems to be paraphrasing G. Gerber's "Kunsttrieb" from his *Die Sprache als Kunst*, op. cit., p. 132.

167. WL 887; see appendix pp. 187–88. Quoted from Pascal, Blaise, 1658: *Pensées* (English trans., "Thoughts," 1962).

168. WL 887; see appendix pp. 187–88.

169. WL 888; see appendix pp. 188–89.

170. WL 888; see appendix pp. 188–89.

171. Cf. Kofman, Sara, 1993: *Nietzsche and Metaphor*, op. cit., and De Man, Paul, 1974: "Nietzsche's Theory of Rhetoric," op. cit., and De Man, *Allegories of Reading*.

172. Still, although family-resemblances are obvious, there is no complete overlap between the deconstructionist paradigm and Nietzsche's Romantic. Nietzsche introduces a consideration that is at odds with at least the more rigorous forms of deconstruction, because his linguistically emancipated human destroys conceptual constructions *in order to capture the self-presence of the intuition*. Hence, the linguistically emancipated human is not in Nietzsche engaged in textual playfulness for its own sake, but for the sake of restoring a fully self-present phono-centric universe. His poetic-poeticizing human questions conceptual constructions *in order to* "match creatively the impression of the powerful present intuition." It is again the thinking of Schopenhauer, Nietzsche is here paraphrasing when he proposes a self-present world of intuitions; i.e., as "images in the eye," as thing-*representations* in closest possible proximity to the *living word*.

173. Sara Kofman, too, notices and comments on this distinction: "Thus, already in the *Philosophenbuch* Nietzsche distinguishes and opposes two types of man: 1) Rational man, who is insensitive to art and masters life through foresight, prudence, regularity; led by the abstractions which protect him from unhappiness without procuring him any happiness, he basically aspires to be freed from suffering. [...] 2) Irrational man, the joyous hero, freed from neediness since he considers only a life disguised as appearance and beauty to be real. This human type, thanks to art, is happy, lives more than the other in the acceptance of joy and suffering, through love of life. He also suffers more because he lacks 'memory' and does not learn any lessons from experience. The prototype of this kind is the pre-Socratic Greek." Kofman, *Nietzsche and Metaphor*, op. cit., pp. 79–80. Kofman provides a precise reading of Nietzsche's opposition. My difference with the deconstructive approach is essentially that deconstruction do not and cannot see Nietzsche's affirmation of Naturalism and prefers by default to read him for his Romanticism (therefore the de-emphasis of the sciences and the stronger emphasis of 'irrational man' in Kofman). In the subsequent section below, we will see how strongly Romanticism, in the representation of Schiller and Schlegel, emphasizes 'playfulness' as part of authentic creation. One and a half century later, this emphasis is reiterated in Deconstruction, where 'playful creativity' again is brought to the fore apparently to challenge the monolithic sciences. In this sense, one could argue that *Deconstruction is a Romanticism*, or at least, have

family-resemblances with the latter and its appropriation of Nietzsche consequently inherits this tonality too. By contrast, I argue that the later Nietzsche is a Naturalist, a Pragmatist, and a Positivist.

174. WL 889; see appendix p. 190.

175. WL 889–90; see appendix pp. 190–91.

176. For a detailed description of the 'priest' and as a first tentative attempt to reconstruct a Nietzschean 'critique of ideology,' one may consult P. Bornedal, 2010: *The Surface and the Abyss*, chap. 5, op. cit.

177. I see this interpretation being more straightforward, and less committed to Deconstructive idiom, than Scheibenberger's de Manian reading suggesting that Nietzsche produces an analogy between the figure of the intellectual and language as metaphorical, as if this wrapped up figure is itself a metaphor of language as rhetoric. "Das Wechselspiel von Ver- und Enthüllung in WL, das N. am Problem der Sprache, insbesondere am Begriff der Metapher exemplifiziert, wird am Ende des Textes sinnfällig im Bild des ummantelten Philosophen. Wenn sich der Gelehrte in seinen Mantel hüllt, dann hüllt sich auch der Text in seine (metaphorische) Textualität ein und verweist auf den Eingang von *WL*: auf das Fabulieren." Scheibenberger, Sarah, 2016: *Kommentar zu Nietzsche*, ibid., p. 17.

178. "Der Begriff von klassischer und romantischer Poesie, der jetzt über die ganze Welt geht und so viel Streit und Spaltungen verursacht, ist *ursprünglich* von mir und Schiller ausgegangen." Goethe quoted from Behler, Ernst: *Einleitung*, in Schlegel, Friedrich, 1979: *Kritische Friedrich Schlegel Ausgabe*, bd. I (Paderborn: Ferdinand Schöningh Verlag), p. CLXXI.

179. Friedrich Schiller: *On Naive and Sentimental Poetry*, in: Nisbet, ed.: German Aesthetic and Literary Criticism (Cambridge: Cambridge University Press, 1985), p. 181. and *Über Naive und Sentimentale Dichtung*, in: Theoretische Schriften, Werke, bd. VIII (Frankfurt a/M: Deutscher Klassiker Verlag, 1992), p. 708.

180. Schiller: *On Naive and Sentimental Poetry*, op. cit., p. 181; *Über Naive und Sentimentale Dichtung*, op. cit., p. 708.

181. Schiller: *On Naive and Sentimental Poetry*, op. cit., p. 193; *Über Naive und Sentimentale Dichtung*, op. cit., p. 732.

182. Schiller: On Naive and Sentimental Poetry, op. cit., p. 186; *Über Naive und Sentimentale Dichtung*, op. cit., p. 719.

183. Schiller: On Naive and Sentimental Poetry, op. cit., p. 193; *Über Naive und Sentimentale Dichtung*, op. cit., p. 732.

184. Schiller: On Naive and Sentimental Poetry, op. cit., p. 190; *Über Naive und Sentimentale Dichtung*, op. cit., p. 727.

185. Fr. Schlegel: "Über das Studium der Griechischen Poesie," in *Kritische Friedrich Schlegel Ausgabe*, bd. I, op. cit.

186. Fr. Schlegel: Quoted from Ernst Behler: *Friedrich Schlegel in Selbstzeugnissen und Bilddokumenten* (Hamburg: Rowohlt Verlag, 1966), p. 39 [my translation].

187. F. Schlegel: "Über Griechen und Römer," *Kritische Friedrich Schlegel Ausgabe*, bd. I, p. 217 [my translation].

188. F. Schlegel: "Über Griechen und Römer," *Kritische Friedrich Schlegel Ausgabe*, bd. I, p. 228 [my translation].

189. F. Schlegel: "Über Griechen und Römer," *Kritische Friedrich Schlegel Ausgabe*, bd. I, p. 241 [my translation].
190. Fr. Schlegel: "Die Griechen und Römer," *Kritische Friedrich Schlegel Ausgabe*, bd. I, p. 211 [my translation].
191. F. Schlegel: "Über Griechen und Römer," *Kritische Friedrich Schlegel Ausgabe*, bd. I, p. 242 [my translation].
192. F. Schlegel: "Über Griechen und Römer," *Kritische Friedrich Schlegel Ausgabe*, bd. I, p. 253 [my translation].
193. F. Schlegel: "Dialogue on Poetry," op. cit., p. 96; F. Schlegel: "Gespräch über die Poesie," *Kritische Friedrich Schlegel Ausgabe*, bd. I, p. 312.
194. F. Schlegel: "Über der Grieschishe Poesie," *Kritische Friedrich Schlegel Ausgabe*, bd. I, p. 288 [my translation].
195. The same theme is also spelled out in the *Arthenäum* fragments: "The romantic type of poetry is still becoming; indeed *its peculiar essence is that it is always becoming and that it can never be completed*. It cannot be exhausted by any theory, and only a divinatory criticism might dare to characterize its ideal." F. Schlegel: *Selected Aphorisms from the Athenaem*, in: Willson, ed.: *German Romantic Criticism*, op. cit., p. 127.
196. They are available in the *Nachlaß* material published in the *Kritischen Studien Ausgabe* (KSA), vol. 7, which usually I am referring to; and in the now completed comprehensive digital version of Nietzsche's *Sämtliche Werke*; see Nietzsche, Fr.: *Digitale Kritische Gesamtausgade: Nachgelassene Fragmente: Fragmente 1869–1874*. The early notes have recently been translated into English in Geuss, R. and Nehamas, A. (eds.), 2009: *Nietzsche: Writings from the early Notebooks* op. cit.
197. Nietzsche: KSA1 153. Compare to Prange, *Nietzsche, Wagner, Europe*: "The child [...] symbolizes the liberation or transcendence from the moral and dialectical interpretation of the world, the moment in which humanity is finally able to let life be, and let it be *in* the world instead of being locked up in a subject-object relationship to it. Hence, the child symbolizes the moment in which humankind has stopped judging, and plays, subsisting in one endless realm of imagination and fantasy. The child, thus, represents the moment of transcendence of common, daily life and of immanence or unity insofar as it is *in* the world, in a way that transcends the common involvement with reality (therefore it is stronger than being 'part' of the world or 'to partake in being'). The imagery of the child symbolizes Schiller's famous adage in his education letters that 'man only plays when he is in the fullest sense of the word a human being, and he is *only fully a human being when he plays*' ('der Mensch spielt nur, wo er in voller Bedeutung des Worts Mensch ist, und *er ist nur da ganz Mensch, wo er spielt*'). It is *beauty* as 'living form' with which man plays: 'with beauty man shall *only play*, and it is *with beauty only* that he shall play' ('der Mensch sollmit der Schönheit *nur spielen*, und er soll *nur mit der Schönheit* spielen')." Prange, Martine, 2013: *Nietzsche, Wagner, Europe* (Berlin, de Gruyter), pp. 141–42.
198. It is not an issue that seems to have received much attention, and insofar as Nietzsche's *aesthetics* is not the topic of the present work it is also not an issue I will explore in depth, but some of the social-political sacrifices Nietzsche deems necessary in order to create an aesthetic culture are, in my view, indefensible: "To supply

the soil for a greater development of art, the vast majority, in the service of a minority, must be enslaved to the demands of life beyond their individual need. The privileged class must be freed from the struggle for existence at the expense of the majority, in order to create a new world of need. Accordingly, we must be prepared to declare that slavery, as the cruel fundamental condition of any culture, is an integral part of the essence of a culture […]. The misery of the struggling mass must be made even greater to enable a number of Olympian men to produce the world of art." Guess and Nehamas (eds.): *Writings from Nietzsche's Early Notebooks*. Notebook 10, beginning of 1871 10[1], p. 70.

199. Nehamas, A., 2009: "Introduction" in Guess and Nehamas: *Nietzsche: Writings from the early Notebooks*, op. cit., pp. xxi–ii.

200. Nehamas, A, 2009: "Introduction" from Nietzsche: *Writings from the Early Notebooks*, op. cit., pp. xxxvi–vii.

201. Nietzsche: "Attempt at a self-criticism" in *The Birth of Tragedy* (Trans. S. Whiteside, Penguin, 1993), pp. 41–42

202. Notebook 34, April–June, 1885, p 1; in Bittner, Rüdiger, 2003: *Nietzsche: Writing from the Late Notebooks* (Cambridge: Cambridge University Press).

203. Nietzsche, 1878/1879: *Menschliches, Allzumenschliches*, KSA 2. *Human, All too Human* (Trans. by R. J. Hollingdale. Cambridge: Cambridge University Press).

204. Nietzsche: *Human, All Too Human*, 1986 (Trans. by R. J. Hollingdale. Cambridge: Cambridge University Press), pp. 26–47.

205. The human seeing itself as the measurer of all things is back in *Human, all too Human*; cf. Nietzsche: "*Man as the Measurer*. Perhaps all human morality had its origin in the tremendous excitement that seized primitive man when he discovered measure and measuring, scales and weighing (for the word Mensch [man] means "the measurer"—he wished to name himself after his greatest discovery!). With these ideas they mounted into regions that are quite beyond all measuring and weighing, but did not appear to be so in the beginning." *Human, all too Human*, II: The Wanderer and His Shadow, 22.

206. Nietzsche, ibid., 14–15.
207. Nietzsche, ibid., 24.
208. Nietzsche, ibid., 15.
209. Nietzsche, ibid., 24–25.

PART II: NIETZSCHE'S POSITIVIST-PRAGMATIC PARADIGM

1. Cf., *Die fröhliche Wissenschaft* (1882), augmented by book 5 (1887) (translation W. Kaufman, *The Gay Science* [GS]), *Jenseits von Gut und Böse* (1886) (translation R. J. Hollingdale, *Beyond Good and Evil* [BGE]), *Zur Genealogie der Moral* (1887) (translation W. Kaufman, *On the Genealogy of Morals* [GM]), and Nietzsche's *Nachlaß material* associated to these works.

2. We may see this *in-itself indifferent world* as Nietzsche's *externally real*, as his chaotic reality, which is elaborated into a human interpretation thanks to agencies

like perception, cognition, and language. We may as such take the world's *that-ness* for granted but not its *what-ness*. *That* the world is given in its chaotic existence manifesting itself for example as impenetrability and obstruction, as hardness and resistance, to all living beings alike, that we must accept. However, the explanations of *what* that obstructive world *is* and *how* it *becomes* perception, we cannot take for granted. Thus, the acceptance of *that-ness* gives us sorry little insight in *what-ness*; it cannot derive an epistemological argument, but is rather a mere repetition in words of an experience we share with all animals. Hence, we cannot conclude from the world's *that-ness* that we know its *what-ness*. *That-ness* has no language, while *what-ness* cannot be expressed without language. This seems to be a point proposed also by some contemporary constructivists; i.e., it is an empty postulate to claim that *that-ness* gives us knowledge of *what-ness* (e.g., Tom Rockmore; cf., following note).

3. Nietzsche seems to undersigned anticipating a position that has been defended by for example Rockmore, Thomas, 2004: *On Foundationalism: A Strategy for Metaphysical Realism* (Lanham, MD: Rowman & Littlefield) and Rockmore, Thomas, 2005: *Constructivism as Epistemology* (Lanham, Rowman and Littlefield); cf. discussions below. See also Remhof, Justin, 2018: *Nietzsche's Constructivism: A Metaphysics of Material Objects* (London: Routledge).

4. Nietzsche: *Nachlaß* 1885/1886, KSA 12, 2[83]. Cf. G. Beam's assessment of the relations between Hume and Nietzsche: "Hume and Nietzsche are more akin to one another than anyone has ever acknowledged. Both are pioneers of a mode of philosophizing that is naturalistic, anti-metaphysical, and focused on human nature," in Beam, "Hume and Nietzsche: Naturalists, Ethicists, Anti-Christians" (1996, p. 318); See also, D. C. Hoy in "Nietzsche, Hume, and the Genealogical Method," in Schacht, ed., 1994: *Nietzsche, Genealogy, Morality*, op. cit.

5. Nietzsche: *Der Wille zur Macht* 551, p. 374.

6. Nietzsche, ibid., 551, p. 375.

7. Nietzsche, ibid., 552, p. 375.

8. Nietzsche, ibid., 633, p. 426.

9. Cf. Hume, David: *An Enquiry Concerning Human Understanding*, op. cit., Section 11, p. 20.

10. Kant, with his emphasis on causal law and a mind predisposed to think this law as a *synthetic a priori*, is by both Nietzsche and Mach understood as a regressive step back from Hume's insights. There are several discussions of Nietzsche arguing his commitment to the *synthetic a priori*, even to see him as an heir of Kant on this issue; See e.g., Clark and Dudrick, *The Soul of Nietzsche* (ibid.) or T. Doyle, 2009: *Nietzsche on Epistemology and Metaphysics*.

11. Nietzsche: FW 112, KSA 3, p. 473.

12. It seems likely that Nietzsche has read Avenarius's *Philosophie als Denken der Welt gemäss dem Princip de kleinsten Krafmasses* (Leipzig: Fues's Verlag, 1876), which discusses these matter in the same vocabulary.

13. Nietzsche: *Nachlaß* 1885/1886, KSA 12, 2[83].

14. Nietzsche: *Nachlaß* 1885, KSA 12, 2 [83]. Stack gives a similar assessment of Nietzsche's notion of causality: "Nietzsche repeatedly questions the ontological significance and reference of the concept of causality. He argues that we do not

experience any 'cause,' that 'Hume was right' to argue that the idea of causality is rooted in habit. However, this is not a habit of the mind of an individual, but of mankind. Our belief in causality is derived from our fallacious assumption. That there is a metaphysical 'subject' that is capable of efficacious action. We derive the notion of cause-effect from the belief that 'we are causes.' [...] Relying once again on a familiar analogy, Nietzsche argues that the idea of causality has its origin in a false account of a 'subject' effecting an action. Therefore, it is itself a fictional notion." See Stack, G. J.: *Nietzsche's Anthropic Circle: Man, Science, and Myth* (New York: University of Rochester Press, 2005), pp. 107–8.

15. Nietzsche: *Nachlaß* 1885, KSA 12, 2 [83].
16. Nietzsche: *Nachlaß* 1885/1886, KSA 12, 2[139].
17. Nietzsche: *Nachlaß* 1886/1887, KSA 12, 7[1], p. 249.
18. Nietzsche: WP 515, p. 351. One finds a similar position well described in work by T. Rockmore, who sees the position emerging from Kant when he is announcing the 'Copernican revolution' of knowledge, while Kant conceiving the categories still belongs in the foundationalist tradition. "Kant's commitment to foundationalism is visible in different ways in the critical philosophy, including his proposed deduction of a univocal categorical framework which, in his opinion, is the condition of the possibility of experience and knowledge off objects. This type of knowledge depends, according to the critical philosophy, on invariant knowledge of the human mind. He is committed, on the contrary, to anti-foundationalism through his claim, central to his Copernican turn, that we must in some sense 'construct' what we know as a necessary condition of knowing it. This claim commits Kant to a constructivist approach to knowledge as well as to the view that we cannot claim to know what is as it is. [...] Kant's Copernican turn undermines any claim to know the mind-independent external world as it is." Rockmore, Thomas, 2004: *On Foundationalism: A Strategy for Metaphysical Realism* (Lanham: Rowman and Littlefield), p. 7. Rockmore's foundational Kant seems to be approximately equivalent to Nietzsche's "anti-Kant," i.e., the Kant arguing for the synthetic a priori and the Kant reviving the 'thing-in-itself,' the belief in 'causes,' etc., in the second edition of his CPR, while Rockmore's constructivist Kant, Kant of the Copernican turn, is roughly equivalent to Nietzsche's insistence of the anthropocentric component of our production of knowledge. Nietzsche's claims that knowledge is an 'error' or a 'falsification'—which has troubled some of the realists among his commentators, and which they consequently attempt to rectify—is in my reading nothing more than the overly dramatic labels for the claim that knowledge in non-representational and has no objective foundation, i.e., if we provisionally assume that the metaphysical notion of an objective foundation is 'True,' knowledge must to Nietzsche be seen as 'falsification' of the assumed 'True.' In later notes, he has the good sense to realize that the metaphysical assumption of a 'true thing' is in itself nonsense, and realizes consequently that there is a misnomer to talk about knowledge as 'falsification.' As discussed below, this does not imply that Nietzsche falls back into 'naïve realism,' but that the dichotomy between a 'True' and a 'false' world is suspended, since the world is only ONE as phenomenal.
19. Nietzsche: *Nachlaß* 1885/1886, KSA 12, 4[8].
20. Nietzsche: GM I.13, KSA 5, p. 279.

21. See also JGB 20, KSA 12, 2[84]; NF 1885/1886, KSA 12, 2 [70]; NF 1885/1886, KSA 12, 2[78]; and NF 1885/1886, KSA 12, 2[84].
22. Nietzsche: GM I 13, KSA 5, p. 279.
23. For interpretations of Nietzsche's GM I, 13, see, e.g., Hatab, Lawrence: *Nietzsche On the Genealogy of Morality* (Cambridge: Cambridge University Press, 2008); Janaway, Christopher: *Beyond Selflessness: Reading Nietzsche's Genealogy* (Oxford: Oxford University Press, 2007); Leiter, Brian: *Nietzsche on Morality* (London: Routledge, 2002); Ridley, Aaron: *Nietzsche's Conscience: Six Character Studies from the Genealogy.* (New York: Cornell University Press, 1998), pp. 27–28; Acampora, Christa Davis: *Contesting Nietzsche* (Chicago: University of Chicago Press, 2013), pp. 140–45; and Pippin, Robert: *Nietzsche, Psychology, and First Philosophy.* (Chicago: The University of Chicago Press, 2006), p. 75; Stegmaier, Werner: *Nietzches "Genealogie der Moral"* (Darmstadt: Wissenschaftliche Buchgesellschaft, 1994); Wolfgang Müller-Lauter: "On Judging in a World of Becoming" in B. Babich (ed.): *Nietzsche, Theories of Knowledge, and Critical Theory*, op. cit., p. 168. And Hamacher, Werner: "The Promise of Interpretation" in Rickels, Laurence A.: *Looking After Nietzsche: Interdisciplinary Encounters with Merleau-Ponty* (New York: SUNY Press, 1990), p. 35.
24. Sometimes commentators have surmised that Nietzsche is criticizing the ignorance about the different speeds of light and sound waves, resulting in the false conjectures that the flash is *causing* thunder. It is true that such a conjecture would constitute another example of a false cause-effect relation; since light-waves travel faster than sound waves, we do indeed perceive light before we hear sound, but not because the flash *causes* thunder. But apart from the fact that Nietzsche does not talk about 'thunder,' this interpretation is not sufficiently abstract to apply to the other examples he thinks he is illustrating; i.e., 'I think' and 'forces move.'
25. *Nachlaß* 1872/1873, KSA 7, 19[209]. Cf. Guess and Nehamas, 2009: *Nietzsche: Writings from the Early Notebooks*, op. cit. Notebook 19, summer 1872—beginning 1873.
26. Bois-Reymond quoted from Lange: *A History of Materialism*, book 2, section 2, op. cit., p. 378.
27. Lange, Fr. A.: *A History of Materialism*, op. cit., book 2, section 2; See also Stack, George J., 1983: *Lange and Nietzsche*, op. cit.
28. Lange: *A History of Materialism*, op. cit., book 2, section 2, p. 379.
29. Hartmann, Eduard von, 1870: *Philosophie des Unbewußtsen*, bd. 1 (Berlin: Carl Dunckers Verlag), p. 240.
30. Some scholars question Nietzsche's acquaintance with Mach's work and discount their theoretical affinities. It is a question, I believe, we can regard as today settled thanks to T. Brobjer's research into Nietzsche's sources: "According to Max Oehler, Nietzsche read texts by Ernst Mach in a public reading room in Zürich in 1884. It is also possible that Nietzsche would have read contributions by Mach or reviews and discussions of him in philosophical journals. Later, probably in 1886 or 1887, Nietzsche bought and read one of Mach's most important works, *Beiträge zur Analyse der Empfindungen.* […] We know that he read it, for two pages contain annotations." Brobjer, Th.: *Nietzsche's Philosophical Context: An Intellectual Biography.*

(Chicago: The University of Illinois Press, 2008), p. 94. Why the resistance in both the Analytic and Postmodern camp to the idea of the rather obvious affinities between Nietzsche and Mach?—Perhaps because a Nietzsche with affinities to empiricist, positivist, or phenomenalist science discussions (via Hume, Fechner, Helmholtz, Lange, Spir, Avenarius, and Mach) contradicts *both* the passionate dismissals of the sciences in the postmodernist camp *and* the interpretation of science as 'finding' and 'discovering' Truth in the analytic camp. At least, we are here introduced to an extremely rare instance of agreement between the Postmodernist and the Anglo-Saxon philosophers.

31. Mach: *The Analysis of Sensations.* op. cit., pp. 96–97.

32. Nietzsche: *Nachlaß* 1888, KSA 13, 14[82].

33. Mill, John Stuart: "Utilitarianism" in *On Liberty and Other Essays*, edited by J. Gray. (Oxford: Oxford University Press, 1991), p. 137.

34. Nietzsche: GD, 'The Four Great Errors 5,' KSA 6, p. 93.

35. Nietzsche: *Nachlaß* 1886/1887; KSA 12, 5[10].

36. Nietzsche: *Nachlaß* 1888, KSA 13, 14[98].

37. Nietzsche: *Nachlaß* 1885, KSA 11, 34[82].

38. Nietzsche: JGB 11, KSA 5, pp. 24–25.

39. Molière: *Le Malade imaginaire* 1674 (trans. as *The Imaginary Invalid* by B. H. Clark, 1925).

40. Kant, 1996: *Critique of Pure Reason.* (Translated by W. S. Pluhar; Indianapolis: Hackett Publishing Company), B 3.

41. Kant, 1996: *Critique of Pure Reason*, op. cit.

42. Important discussions of Kant's discussions of the paralogism can be found in various work. I am especially impressed by Fischer, Kuno, 1866: *A Commentary on Kant's Critick of the Pure Reason.* (London: Longmans, Green, and Co.). Kemp Smith, Norman, 1918: *A Commentary to Kant's Critique of Pure Reason.* (London: Macmillan); Kaulbach, Friedrich, 1982: *Immanuel Kant.* (Berlin-New York: Walter de Gruyter); Kitcher, Patricia: "Kant's Paralogisms" (In *The Philosophical Review* 91: 4 [October 1982], pp. 515–47.) Guyer, Paul, 2006: *Kant.* (London-New York: Routledge). And Proops, Ian, 2010: "Kant's First Paralogism" (In *Philosophical Review* 119: 4).

43. Nietzsche: GD, 'The Four Great Errors 3,' KSA 6, p. 91.

44. Nietzsche: TL, KSA 1, p. 883.

45. Let us notice in passing that the distinction is taken for granted in today's neuro- and cognitive sciences, where it is established knowledge that the image of the 'outer world' received on the retina is different from the image emerging after data have been processed by the visual cortex of the brain. Cf. discussions in Dennett, Daniel, 1991: *Consciousness Explained* (Boston and New York, Little, Brown, and Company). See also Dennett, Daniel, 1995: *Darwin's Dangerous Idea: Evolution and the Meaning of Life* (New York: Touchstone).

46. Nietzsche: *Nachlaß* 1885; KSA 11, 26[44].

47. Cf. discussion in Part I, A.8, as well as more detailed discussions in Part II, B.3.

48. The view implies that there is no privileged perceptive apparatus; we have seen previously that Nietzsche sometimes talks about human 'pride' or 'vanity' in cases where we forget or ignore the perspectivism of our animal seeing.

49. Nietzsche: TI, "The Four Great Errors," 4, KSA 6.

50. Nietzsche: *Nachlaß* 1885; KSA 11, 26[35].

51. Brobjer notices that Nietzsche in this example may be paraphrasing a paragraph in E. Mach's *Analysis of Sensations*, where he refers to the anachronisms in sleeping and waking life; cf., Brobjer, op. cit., pp. 174–75.

52. See also Stack, George J.: *Nietzsche's Anthropic Circle: Man, Science, and Myth* (New York: University of Rochester Press, 2005). In this work on Nietzsche, Stack remarks on the similarity between Nietzsche and eighteenth-century physicist Lichtenberg, quoting a passage from Lichtenberg with obvious similarity to Nietzsche's thinking: "Wenn wir glauben wir sahen Gegenstande, so sehen wir bloß uns. Wir können von Nichts in der Welt Etwas eigentlich erkennen, als uns selbst und die Veranderungen, die in uns vorgehen." Compare also to Nietzsche: "*der Mensch findet zuletzt in den Dingen nichts wieder als was er selbst in sie hineingesteckt hat.*" Quoted here from Stack: *Lange and Nietzsche*, op. cit., pp. 103–4.

53. I made a first attempt to render this model in Bornedal, 2010, *The Surface and the Abyss*, op. cit., but since it suffered from various imprecisions, have improved it in the present version.

54. My references to de Man below are from the following three main sources: de Man, Paul: *The Rhetoric of Romanticism* (New York: Columbia University Press, 1984); de Man, *Allegories of Reading*; and de Man, Paul, 1974: "Nietzsche's Theory of Rhetoric," in *Symposium: A Quarterly Journal in Modern Literatures*, 28: 1, pp. 33–51. Yale University Press.

55. The passage is found in the *Nachlaß* material from spring 1888, cf. Nietzsche, *Nachlaß* 1888, KSA 13, 15[90], and in WM 479. Following de Man, the fragment has been discussed by Culler in Culler, Jonathan: *On Deconstruction: Theory and Criticism after Structuralism* (Ithaca, NY: Cornell University Press, 1982), p. 86. It re-appeared in Klein's commentary to Nietzsche's early essay in Klein, Wayne: *Nietzsche and the Promise of Philosophy* (New York: State University of New York Press, 1997). Erwin Schlimgen too discusses the fragment in Schlimgen, Erwin: *Nietzsches Theorie des Bewußtseins*. (Berlin and New York: Walter de Gruyter, 1999), pp. 134–35.

56. C. Norris discusses this passage in his book on Paul de Man, dismissing it as one of Nietzsche's "immoderate or downright nonsensical claims." Norris, Christopher, 1988: *Paul de Man* (London: Routledge), p. 42. Norris seems generally to be under the impression that Derrida is the more 'serious,' while Nietzsche is the postmodernist philosopher. Although I share many views with Norris, I am obviously turning around this evaluation on Derrida and Nietzsche's 'seriousness.'

57. De Man, *Allegories of Reading*, pp. 107.

58. De Man, "Nietzsche's Theory of Rhetoric," p. 37; Cf. De Man, *Allegories of Reading*, p. 108.

59. Cf. Lange, *Geschichte des Materialismus*.

60. Cf. Fechner, *Elements of Psychophysics*.
61. Cf. Mach, *Die Analyse der Empfindungen*.
62. Nietzsche, *Nachlaß*, 1885/1986, KSA 12, 2[85].
63. Nietzsche: *Nachlaß*, 1885/1886, KSA 12, 2[149].
64. Nietzsche: *Nachlaß*, 1885/1886, KSA 12, 2[154].
65. Nietzsche: *Nachlaß*, 1886/1887, KSA 12, 9[40].
66. Nietzsche: *Nachlaß*, 1886/1887, KSA 12, 10[202].
67. Nietzsche: *Nachlaß*, 1888, KSA 13, 14[122].
68. Other objections to Clark, we may find in L. Anderson: "Overcoming Charity: The Case of Clark's *Nietzsche on Truth and Philosophy*." (*Nietzsche-Studien* 25 [1996]); in N. Hussain (2004): "Nietzsche's Positivism." N. Hussein counters Clark's analytic readings of Nietzsche by developing Nietzsche's positions in conjunction with Mach's. This strategy—adopted also by undersigned (cf. Part II, B)—helps Hussain to save Nietzsche as a potential pro-scientific writer: "The interpretation of Nietzsche as a Machian positivist or 'sensualist' allows us to interpret him as simultaneously rejecting the thing-in-itself, accepting a falsification thesis and defending empiricism. […] Such a view will allow Nietzsche both to be science-friendly and to accept a falsification thesis." Hussain, 2004, op. cit., pp. 327 and 357. We find Clark's critical response to Hussain's position in Clark and Dudrick, 2004: "Nietzsche's Post-Positivism" in *The European Journal of Philosophy* (Blackwell).
69. WL 883; see appendix pp. 183–84.
70. For a careful philological reading of *Götzendämmerung*, see also Urs Sommer, Andreas, 2012: *Kommentar zu Nietzsches Der Fall Wagner and Götzendämmerung* (Berlin: De Gruyter).
71. GD, "Wie die 'wahre Welt' endlich zur Fabel wurde," KSA 6, p. 81.
72. GD, "Wie die 'wahre Welt' endlich zur Fabel wurde," KSA 6, p. 81.
73. Tsarina Doyle too suggests that position 4 and 5 "may in fact be construed as two aspects of just one position." Doyle, Tsarina, 2009: *Nietzsche on Epistemology and Metaphysics* (Edinburgh: Edinburgh UP), p. 72.
74. That epistemological Nietzsche should have a 'Schopenhaurian,' a 'Positivistic,' in order to arrive to a genuinely 'Nietzschean' period as purportedly equivalent to the three positions '4', '5', and '6' from GD, seems first to have been forwarded by Hans Vaihinger in his brief work, *Nietzsche als Philosoph* (Berlin: Reuther und Reichard, 1902) and then by Friedrich Rittelmeyer in his *Friedrich Nietzsche und das Erkenntnisproblem* (Leibniz, 1908). With all respect of Vaihinger and Rittelmeyer, I see the classification as misleading. First, I see greater continuity in Nietzsche's thinking and cannot detect, therefore, a specific 'Nietzschean' period. Second, I cannot see why Nietzsche's HH indicates a particular 'positivist' period, which I rather locate in his latest writing (albeit noticing that Vaihinger refers to Comte's positivism, while I refers to Mach's). Third, Nietzsche's latest writings are not *him arriving to himself* as 'Nietzschean,' but are developments and clarifications of the dominant naturalist-positivist-pragmatic paradigm. So, Vaihinger/Rittelmeyer's classification, in my opinion, makes no sense any longer. If one (in all brevity) should try to suggest a three-prong classification of Nietzsche's work, I would suggest the following: The

very young Nietzsche is Wagnerian (cf. Part I, B.10). The early to middle Nietzsche from the 1870s into the 1880s is chiefly neo-Kantian. The late Nietzsche from the eighties, is largely overlapping so-called early to middle Nietzsche, but is chiefly Positivist-Pragmatic. These boxes have porous walls, and various trains of thought move in and out of the different compartments.

75. Several scholars have rightly reacted to the typical postmodernist 'fictional' interpretation of position '6' from GD, so D. Conway: "Does this double abolition [of true and apparent world] perhaps betoken the dawn of a post-metaphysical era, which Nietzsche inaugurates by deconstructing the most stubborn binarism of Western philosophy. Many scholars have reached precisely this conclusion, happily conscripting Nietzsche as the progenitor of postmodern philosophy. If the true and apparent worlds are both abolished [...] then the world *must* be a fiction, a construct, a narrative artifact created by that exceedingly clever animal, *homo faber*." Conway, D., 1999: "Beyond Truth and Appearance," in B. Babich: *Nietzsche, Epistemology, and Philosophy of Science*. Dordrecht (Kluwer Academic Publishers), p. 110. After we have learnt that Vaihinger's *positivist fictionalism* is not identical to *postmodern fictionalism*, I believe that we no longer need to take seriously the claim that *the world* is a fiction applied to Nietzsche or peers, because we now know that it applies only to *the concepts we form of 'world.'*

76. Nietzsche: *Nachlaß*, 1886/1887, KSA 12, 6[23].
77. Nietzsche: *Nachlaß*, 1886/1887, KSA, 12, 6[23].
78. Nietzsche: *Nachlaß*, 1887, KSA 12, 9[91].
79. Ernst Mach is stating the same idea, when in *Science of Mechanics* he says "*Sensations are not signs of things*. [...] *The world is not composed of 'things' as its elements*, but of colors, tones, pressures, spaces, times, in short what we ordinarily call individual sensations." Mach, Ernst: *Science of Mechanics: A Critical and Historical Account of its Development*. (Trans. T. J. McCormack. Chicago-London: Open Court, 1919), p. 483.
80. Nietzsche: GD II, "Die Vernunft in der Philosophie," II, 2.
81. Nietzsche: FW 354, KSA 3, p. 593.
82. Today, we can precisely locate the seat of this so-called 'falsification' as the part of the brain called the 'visual cortex,' although no contemporary neuroscientist would insinuate that the processing of data in the visual cortex is responsible for 'lying.' That senses should be 'falsifying,' 'lying,' or 'fictionalizing' would to most scientists be over-dramatic, misleading, and unscientific language. For multiple reasons, our human mind, as a product of evolution, is not 'lying.' If anything, it is telling us the truth of what we *need* to know.
83. Cf. Hussain, commenting on the same passage: "The senses do not lie. It is our language, and reasoning, that can lead to confusion [...] Nietzsche will talk about falsification brought on by language." Hussain, N., 2004: "Nietzsche's Positivism," op. cit., p. 348.
84. We recall that Schopenhauer anticipated Nietzsche when already in the *Fourfold* he talked about the "intellectual character of perception." He already then distinguished between 'raw sense data' and 'perceptive reason.' In the relevant passage, Schopenhauer criticizes philosopher who have argued that "perception of the

outer world is a thing of the senses" without mentioning the "intellectual character of perception, [...] the fact, that it is mainly the work of the Understanding, which [...] primarily creates and produces the objective, outer world out of the raw material of a few sensations." Schopenhauer: *Fourfold*, op. cit., p. 58.

85. See discussion of Mach and Vaihinger below. See also Hussain, op. cit., p. 349.
86. Nietzsche: *Nachlaß* 1887, KSA 12, 9[91].
87. Nietzsche: *Nachlaß* 1888, KSA 13, 14[79].
88. Nietzsche: *Nachlaß*, 1888, KSA 13, 14[184].
89. Nietzsche: *Nachlaß*, 1887/1888, KSA 13, 11[50].
90. Nietzsche: *Nachlaß*, 1887, KSA 12, 9[106] = WM 569.
91. Nietzsche: GD, Die Vernunft in der Philosophie, II 2.
92. In M. Haar's, Nietzsche and Metaphysics, we find similar observations, as he suggested that when Nietzsche gives up his old binary, a new is created on a second-order level however strongly Nietzsche refutes the old binary between appearance and reality. Although Nietzsche has succeeded in deconstructing one binary, he immediately slips back into another. Cf. Haar, Michel, 1996: Nietzsche and Metaphysics. (New York: State University of New York Press), p. 49.
93. Nietzsche: GD, Die Vernunft in der Philosophie, II. 2.
94. As a consequence of the persistent criticism of the 'in-itself' and the simultaneous promotion of the purely phenomenal world Nietzsche and peers realize that we construct knowledge only thanks to our languages and metalanguages (concept-formations). Knowledge is explained as constructed on top of original chaotic sense-impressions, coming about thanks to our cognitive 'drive' to simplify and is therefore not in any way representational. This economical aspect of knowledge-production is discussed extensively in Avenarius, Mach, Vaihinger, and Nietzsche. Thus, Nietzsche has his false start in Wagner and Schopenhauer's aesthetics, but when he later reads Fr. Lange, H. Helmholtz, neo-Kantians like K. Fischer, O. Liebmann, and A. Spir, and probably R. Avenarius and E. Mach, he tries to assimilate their naturalism, biologism, and positivist-pragmatic thinking into his epistemology as well as into his ethics. Again, Nietzsche's view seems strongly affiliated to what in today's discussions we sometimes see addressed as 'Constructivist Epistemology'; cf., Rockmore: "According to the constructivist approach to knowledge that Kant focuses, we do not uncover, discover, find, or reveal the object of knowledge, which we construct or make. In Kant's wake, and to avoid not already constituted but rather as constructed by the subject of subjects as a condition of knowledge. The result is a view of the object of knowledge as no longer independent of, but rather dependent on, the knower. [...] First, since we cannot show we know a mind-independent external object, metaphysical realism fails; and, second, the minimal condition of knowledge is that the subject in some way 'constructs' what it knows." Rockmore, Thomas, 2005: *On Constructivist Epistemology* (Lanham, MD: Rowman & Littlefield), pp. 4–5.
95. Nietzsche: FW 374, KSA 3.
96. Nietzsche: *Nachlaß* 1888, KSA 13, 14[93].
97. Here a Machean 'element' and a 'Nietzschean 'point' existing in a relationship world cannot be seen as analogous to Roger Boscovich's force-point world, which is applied to elementary particles. Mach's elements and Nietzsche's points

exist on the sensational data-level of experiences, not on a nuclear quantum level. Whether Nietzsche in other regards has been inspired, and to which extent, by Boscovich is a different discussion, taken up by a number of commentators such as Whitlock, Greg: "Roger Boscovich, Benedict de Spinoza, and Friederich Nietzsche: The Untold Story." In *Nietzsche-Studien* bd. 25 (Berlin-New York: Walter de Gruyter, 1996); Small, Robin, 2001: *Nietzsche in Context*, op. cit.; Stack, George J., 1983: *Nietzsche and Lange*, op. cit.; and Abel, Günter, 1998: *Nietzsche: Die Dynamik des Willen zur Macht und die Ewige Wiederkehr*, op. cit.

98. In Einstein's theory of relativity, movement and velocity is relative because there is no absolute rest that the velocity of moving bodies can be measured against. This relativity is regarded as objective, as our best and most precise understanding of bodies in the universe. It does not resign itself to subjectivism.

99. Nietzsche: *Nachlaß* 1888, KSA 13, 14[93].

100. Nietzsche: *Nachlaß* 1886, KSA 12, 6[23].

101. Nietzsche: FW 354, KSA 3, p. 593. A note from the notebooks repeats the same issue: "Insofar as the word 'Knowledge' [*Erkenntniß*] has any meaning, is the world knowledgeable: but it is in some way interpretable, it has no meaning behind this, only innumerable meanings, "Perspektivism." Our needs are interpreting the world: our drives and their for and against." Nietzsche: *Nachlaß* 1886, KSA 12, 7[60].

102. Mach, Ernst, 1914. *The Analysis of Sensations and the Relation of the Physical to the Psychical* (Trans. C. M. Williams from German edition 1897. Chicago/London: Open Court), p. 331.

103. Nietzsche: FW 112, KSA 3.

104. Nietzsche: FW 293, KSA 3.

105. Nietzsche: FW 335, KSA 3; See also Nietzsche's eulogies of the sciences and the scientists in, *Menschliche Allzumenschliche* II, 206.

106. Nietzsche: *Nachlaß* 1886/1887; KSA 12, 5[10].

107. In Schopenhauer, it is for example seen as placeholder for two foundational constituents of the universe, matter and force, cf. his early essay, Schopenhauer, A., 1847: *Über die vierfache Wurzel des Satzes des zureichenden Grunde*. (1974: *On the Fourfold Root of the Principle of Sufficient Reason*; tr. Paine) op. cit.

108. George J. Stack too relates these arguments of Lange's to Nietzsche: "[Lange] claims that the very conception of "things" existing in themselves in a spaceless, timeless realm in which there can be no sense to causal action is a paradoxical, if not an absurd, conception. In all probability, Nietzsche's critical comments about the idea of *Dinge-an-sich* were inspired by Lange's queries and doubts. [...] What Lange held was that we cannot speak of the realm of things in themselves as the 'cause' of our *a priori* categories for the simple reason that the concept of cause cannot be used 'transcendentally.'" Stack, G.: *Lange and Nietzsche*, op. cit., pp. 217–18.

109. R. H. Grimm's authoritative work, *Nietzsche's Theory of Knowledge* (Berlin and New York: de Gruyter) from 1977 has been influential in the discussions of Nietzsche's concepts of truth, knowledge, and the distinction between reality and knowledge. Grimm's essential thesis is, however, very different from the one suggested by undersigned, as he seems to regress to the materialist discussion of

truth determined as 'power-quanta' or 'forces.' Accordingly, Nietzsche is replacing one metaphysical concept of truth with another metaphysical concept of truth, i.e., replacing one concept of the thing-in-itself as unchanging *substance* with another concept of the thing-in-itself as ever-changing *forces*. In commentary, it is not uncommon to see Nietzsche's anti-metaphysics as consisting in this replacement of *substances* with *forces*. In the analysis of undersigned, this proposed 'over-coming' of metaphysics in the replacement of the 'enigmatic x' as *substance* with an equally 'enigmatic y' called *force* is merely creating a different duality between appearances and 'thing.' In the present work, I have rejected the thesis, first, because I see Nietzsche supporting a pragmatic concept of truth, and, second, because I see him replacing *any metaphysical concept of Truth as 'thing-in-itself'* with rationalizations, formalizations, and conceptualizations of a purely apparent world. As such, we are in Nietzsche entirely beyond the concept of the 'thing-in-itself' whether interpreted as substance or as force. Creating room for a new 'Thing' in the name of power-quanta or forces only repeats metaphysics' most essential gesture. In Nietzsche and peers, it is rather the 'concept' that will replace of 'Truth.' If, as Grimm suggests, 'reality' or 'being' for Nietzsche "consists of nothing less than a vast number of power-quanta, which differ among themselves only quantitatively," (Grimm, op. cit., p. 18), if "reality is a chaos of power-quanta" (Grimm, ibid., p. 30), and if we are somehow receiving these power-quanta, then Nietzsche's view is no different from that of the mechanical materialists and we are back to an understanding of forces as some ultimate but hidden 'reality,' cf., Saint-Simon Laplace, Ludwig Büchner, and Maximilian Drossbach.

110. Comte, Auguste: *Cours de philosophie positive* 1–6 (1830–1842). Translated and abridged as *Introduction to Positive Philosophy*, by F. Ferré (Hackett, 1988).

111. Mill, John Stuart, 1865: *Auguste Comte and Positivism* (Createspace Independent Publishers, 2013).

112. Mill, John Stuart, 1865: *Examination of Sir William Hamilton's Philosophy* (xxx).

113. Comte, Auguste, 1988: *Introduction to Positive Philosophy*, op. cit. p. 2.

114. To distinguish between this early Positivism and the later Logical Positivism emerging in the first half of the twentieth century, Richard von Misses makes a useful distinction between a 'material' and 'logical' positivism (one might alternatively suggest that the distinction runs between an 'onto-logical' versus a 'logical' positivism, and argue that the positivism we apply to Nietzsche and his peers is 'ontological,' since it is thoroughly engaged in rephrasing the fundamental ontic/ontological question). See Mises, Richard von, 1956: *Positivism: A Study in Human Understanding* (New York: George Braziller).

115. See Du Bois-Reymond, Emil, 1872: "Über die Grenzen des Naturerkennens," in *Wissenschaftliche Vorträge*. Ed. J. Howard Gore (Boston: Ginn and Company, 1896). English translation, "The Limits of our Knowledge of Nature," in *Popular Science Monthly* 5, 1874; See also Du Bois-Reymond, Emil, 1880: "Die Sieben Welträthsel," in *Wissenschaftliche Vorträge*. Ed. J. Howard Gore (Boston: Ginn and Company, 1896). English translation, "The Seven World-Riddles." *Popular Science Monthly* 5, 1874.

116. Laplace, Pierre-Simon: *Essai philosophique sur les Probabilitè*, Paris, 1814. Translation, *Philosophical essay on Probabilities*, p. 2. D'Alembert too had suggested that perhaps "the universe is one single fact and one great truth." D'Alembert in *Encyclopé du Discours préliminaire*, Paris, 1751, vol. 1, p. ix.

117. Du Bois-Reymond, 1874: "The Limits of our Knowledge of Nature," op. cit., p. 2.

118. See Drossbach, 1865: *Über die Objecte der Sinnlichen Wahrnehmung*, op. cit., and Drossbach, 1884: *Über die Scheinbaren und die Wirklichen Ursachen des Geschehens in der Welt*, op. cit. Drossbach did not enjoy much recognition among his 19th century peers. Lange has no mention of him in his *Geschichte* (1865) and Überweg mentions him only in two insignificant footnotes in his otherwise encyclopedic, Ueberweg, Friedrich: *Grundriss der Geschichte der Philosophie: Das Neunzehnte Jahrhundert*. Berlin, 1902. However, he has enjoyed some recognition in newer Nietzsche commentary, for example by Mattia Riccardi in "Nietzsche's Sensualism," European Journal of Philosophy (Oxford: Blackwell, 2011). Riccardi seems to argue that Drossbach's talk about 'forces' is equivalent to Nietzsche's and seems to endorse that we, as prescribed in Drossbach, can establish a relationship between the inaccessible outer world and the interior world of consciousness thanks to these 'moving forces.'

119. Nietzsche's mockery of the so-called "*Klümpchen-atom*," also lead back to Roger Boscovich and Fr. Albert Lange, arguing against the notion of a smallest unit in form of an indivisible atom—the so-called 'clump-atom' in Nietzsche's jargon. Studies of the relations between Boscovich, Lange, and Nietzsche, we find in a number of commentators; for example, Whitlock, Greg, 1996: "Roger Boscovich, Benedict de Spinoza, and Friederich Nietzsche: The Untold Story" in *Nietzsche-Studien* bd. 25 (Berlin and New York: de Gruyter). See also Stack, George J., 1983: *Nietzsche and Lange* (Berlin-New York: de Gruyter). Also Abel, Günter, 1998: *Nietzsche: Die Dynamik des Willen zur Macht und die Ewige Wiederkehr* (Berlin-New York: de Gruyter). Also Small, Robin, 1986: "Boscovich Contra Nietzsche" in *Philosophy and Phenomenological Research* 46: 3.

120. Du Bois-Reymond: *Über die Grenzen des Naturerkennens*, op. cit., p. 22.

121. Du Bois-Reymond: ibid., p. 21.

122. Du Bois-Reymond: ibid., p. 27.

123. Du Bois-Reymond: ibid., pp. 27–28.

124. Du Bois-Reymond: ibid., p. 32.

125. Seven years later, in his second important essay, Du Bois reintroduced his ignorabimus-argument concerning knowledge escaping us, as the "World Riddle." The two phrases would ring over the rest of the century and well into the twentieth. It gave for example title to German evolutionary biologist Ernst Haeckel's monograph, *Der Welträtsel* (1899), where he ambitiously attempted to resolve the enigma. Haeckel, Ernst, 1899: *Der Welträtsel. The Riddle of the Universe* (Trans. J. McCabe, London: Watts and Co, 1929).

126. Lange, *Geschichte* II, op. cit. p., 156.

127. Helmholtz: "The Facts in Perception" in *Science and Culture*, op. cit., p. 347.

128. Helmholtz, 1867: *Physiologische Optik*, (Leibzig: Leopold Voss).
129. Helmholtz: *Physiologische Optik*, op. cit., vol. 3, p. 18.
130. Helmholtz: *Physiologische Optik*, op. cit., ibid.
131. Helmholtz: "The Recent Progress of the Theory of Vision," in *Science and Culture*, op. cit., p. 179.
132. Helmholtz: "The Recent Progress of the Theory of Vision," in *Science and Culture*, op. cit., p. 179.
133. Ueberweg, Friedrich, 1857: *System der Logik* (Berlin); 1871: *System of Logic and History of Logical Doctrines* (Translation T. M. Lindsay, London).
134. Ueberweg, 1871: *System of Logic*, op. cit., p. 103
135. Ueberweg, 1871: ibid., p. 79.
136. Ueberweg, 1871: ibid., pp. 80 and 102.
137. Ueberweg, 1871: ibid., p. 80
138. In his work *Materialism and Empiro-Criticism*, Lenin designates mockingly these 'signs' with no apparent relation to material reality, "hieroglyphs." It is as precise a designation as anything I have read, so why not take Lenin's formulation seriously and use for our own purposes.
139. Helmholtz: "The Facts in Perception" in *Science and Culture*, op. cit., p. 347.
140. Spir, African, 1873: *Denken und Wirklichkeit. Versuch einer Erneuerung der Kritischen Philosophie* (Leipzig), p. 134.
141. Lange, *History of Materialism*, book 2, p. 163.
142. Lange: *History of Materialism*, book 2, p. 200.
143. Cf. George J. Stack: "With this conception of a *materiale Idealismus* Lange, before the phenomenologists, and independent of them, was seeking a mediation between materialism and idealism, a "third way." And even though it is difficult to piece together Nietzsche's fragmentary statements on this complex issue, I believe that he absorbs and reflects the materio-idealism or ideo-materialism that Lange sketches." Stack, George J.: *Lange and Nietzsche* (Berlin-New York: Walter de Gruyter, 1983), p. 97.
144. Lange gives another example of the irrelevance of investigating the 'thing-in-itself.' He remarks that researchers into electricity and magnetism, such as Ørsted and Faraday, would have achieved nothing had they started out with the assumption that they needed a speculative explanation of the nature of magnetism. The *power* of magnetism is and remains an unknown, a thing-in-itself, but exactly because they suspend this speculative research-strategy into the unknown, they facilitate their discoveries of the relations between magnetism and electricity. To ruminate over the nature of forces 'inside' the magnet would have been a sterile enterprise.
145. See also P. Frank: *The Law of Causality and its Limits* (Vienna: Springer Verlag, 1932), pp. 260ff.
146. Petzoldt, Joseph, 1900: *Einführung in die Philosophie der Reinen Erfahrung, Erster Teil, Die Bestemmtheit der Seele (*Leibniz, Teubner), p. 352. Notice, that Petzoldt takes for granted that Nietzsche belongs in this exclusive club of new epistemologists.
147. W. I. Lenin, 1906/1909: *Materialism and Empirio-Criticism: Critical Comments on a Reactionary Philosophy* (Collected Works, vol. 14. Moscow, Progress Publishers, 1909, p. 38. Lenin's primary polemical target seems to be Aleksandr Bog-

danov, who had written positively about Mach and Avenarius, but moreover was the leading theoretician of the so-called Proletarskaya Kultora (the "Proletkult"), an organization meant to provide the foundations for a truly proletarian art—art produced by proletarians for proletarians. Lenin later withdrew his support of Bogdanov's project, and his work must be seen in that political context. Although Lenin is extremely well-read in the contemporary 'Machists' he criticizes, I see a major problem in Lenin's polemics. In his defense of 'Dialectical Materialism,' which he sees as the true Marxist position, it becomes near impossible to defend 'Historical Materialism,' which to my mind Machists would do a much better job defending. We notice that Lenin's dogmatic Marxist criticism of Mach and Avenarius reverberates in contemporary debate when dogmatic realists espouse very similar criticisms of phenomenalist and positivist positions.

148. They advocate a position that since has been advanced under a profusion of different labels, e.g., Positivism, Phenomenalism, Phenomenology, Empirio-Criticism, Ideo-Materialism, Impressionism, Fictionalism, Pragmatism, or Constructivism. Here, it of course does not help our understanding much to call the paradigm they defend one thing or the other, but generally, we notice that they all appeal to a theory of knowledge that either directly or indirectly involves empiricism, pragmatism, perspectivism, relativism, and nihilism.

149. We notice that late nineteenth century epistemologists lay the groundwork for the early twentieth century discussions, branching out in major schools like Pragmatism, Positivism, and Phenomenology. These schools are in contemporary discussions often regarded as distinct, but have at least 'common ancestry' in these neo-Kantian discussions. Authoritative research in the relationships between R. Avenarius, E. Mach, and E. Husserl, we may find in Sommer, Manfred, 1985: *Husserl und der Frühe Positivismus* (Frankfurt: Vittorio Klostermann).

150. Mach, Ernst, 1886/1922: *Die Analyse der Empfindungen und das Verhältnis des Physischen zum Psychischen*, Jena, Gustav Fischer (1914; *The Analysis of Sensations and the Relation of the Physical to the Psychical*, trans. C. M. Williams, Chicago: Open Court).

151. Cf. Brobjer, 2008: *Nietzsche's Philosophical Context,* op. cit., p. 94. Follower of Mach, Hans Kleinpeter, claimed that Nietzsche's sister Elisabeth Förster-Nietzsche in conversation reported that Nietzsche was well-acquainted with Mach. Cf. Kleinpeter, Hans, 2012: "Letter to Ernst Mach," 22.12.1911; in *Nietzsche Studien* bd. 40, ed. P. Gori (Berlin/New York: de Gruyter).

152. Cf. Hussain, op. cit., Riccardi, op. cit., Gori, op. cit., C. Emden, op. cit. A recently published work by J. Remhof has a thorough discussion on the 'Analytic-Positivist divide'; cf. Remhof, Justin, 2018: *Nietzsche's Constructivism: A Metaphysics of Material Objects* (London: Routledge)). Among scholars from the 'Anglo Saxon' traditions having denied a link between Nietzsche and Mach, Clark seems the most prominent; see e.g. Clark, M. and D. Dudrick, 2004, in "Nietzsche's Post-Positivism," op. cit.

153. This usefulness of an abbreviated 'thing' world returns in other pragmatic philosophers such as W. James. I will not in this work attempt to discuss how James's pragmatism is related to the Mach-Nietzschean project, however evident that seems

to appear in several of James's key writings: *Pragmatism: A New Name for some Old Ways of Thinking* (New York, 1906), and *The Meaning of Truth* (New York: Longmans and Green, 1909). I hope to return to this important discussion in another work.

154. Mach: *The Analysis of Sensations*, op. cit., p. 30n.

155. Nietzsche: *GD*, "Wie die 'wahre Welt' endlich zur Fabel wurde," *KSA* 6, p. 81.

156. Kleinpeter, Hans: "Letter to Ernst Mach," op. cit., p. 295. Also Kleinpeter's admirably clear discussion of phenomenalism, *Der Phenomenalismus: Eine Naturwissenshcaftliche Weltanschauung* (Leipzig, 1913), contains several positive references to Nietzsche—who indeed happens to be his most quoted source after Mach and Kant.

157. See Frank, Phillip, 1941: *Between Physics and Philosophy* (Cambridge: Harvard University Press), p. 51. Frank has several references to Nietzsche also in his, Frank, Phillip, 1932: *The Law of Causality and its Limits* (Vienna: Springer Verlag). In Petzoldt, Joseph, 1900: *Einführung in die Philosophie der Reinen Erfahrung, Erster Teil, Die Besternmtheit der Seele* (Leibniz) and in R. von Mises, 1956: *Positivism: A Study in Human Understanding* (New York: George Braziller), we find again a number of positive references to Nietzsche. Mach's biographer John Blackmore states about the relationship: "The basic facts are that both men were epistemological phenomenalists, advocated the subordination of science and truth to satisfying human 'biological needs,' and had similar ontological views of 'matter,' 'ego,' and 'God.'" Blackmore, John, 1972: *Ernst Mach: His Work, Life, and Influence*. (Berkeley: University of California Press), p. 123. As mentioned, Brobjer has found evidence that Nietzsche is likely influenced by Mach, cf. Brobjer, *Nietzsche's Philosophical Context*, op. cit., p. 94.

158. See also P. Pojman's assessment: "Positivism is really a collection of traditions, connected often by misunderstandings as much as by actual intellectual agreement. Furthermore, the word today has come to mean something so far removed from its nineteenth century origins as to be practically harmful in understanding the how it was used in the nineteenth century." Pojman, P.: "Ernst Mach," in *The Stanford Encyclopedia of Philosophy*. Winter 2011, p. 1. The reason why a Nietzsche-Machean relationship has been meet with resistance in both the Continental and Analytic camps of Nietzsche research may well be that a Nietzsche with affinities to empiricist, positivist, or phenomenalist science discussions (via Hume, Fechner, Helmholtz, Lange, Spir, Avenarius, and Mach) seems to reject *both* the dismissals of the sciences in the postmodernist camp *and* the correspondence theory of truth promoted in the analytic camp.

159. J. Habermas and A. Danto stand out as exceptions to the neglect of the positivist connection in Nietzsche-commentary. So Danto: "I want only to emphasize that Nietzsche, who is so naturally taken as a predecessor of the irrationalistic tendency in contemporary philosophy, in his own writings exhibits attitudes toward the main problems of philosophy which are almost wholly in the spirit of Logical Positivism." Danto: *Nietzsche as Philosopher*, op. cit., p. 65. Here, I would only replace Danto's reference to "Logical Positivism" with the early Positivism of the late nineteenth century, whether we call it "Machist," "Critical," or "Ontological." Habermas is being discussed in more detail below (cf. Part II, B.5: "Nietzsche's Positivism according to Habermas").

160. Mach, Ernst, 1886: *Beiträge zur Analyse der Empfindungen*; op. cit. Translation 1959, *Contributions to an Analysis of Sensations and the Relations of the Physical to the Psychical* (New York, Dover Publications), p. 30.

161. Mach, Ernst, 1903: *Populär-Wissenschaftliche Vorlesungen* (Leipzig). Translation 1894: *Popular Scientific Lectures*, (London).

162. Mach, 1894: *Popular Scientific Lectures*, p. 203.

163. Mach, 1905: *Erkenntnis und Irrtum: Skizzen zur Psychologie des Forschung* (Leipzig). Translation 1926: *Knowledge and Error: Sketches on a Psychology of Inquiry*, (Dordrecht and Boston).

164. Mach, 1926: *Knowledge and Error*, op. cit. pp. 6–7.

165. Mach, 1926: *Knowledge and Error*, op. cit. pp. 6–7.

166. As suggested before by R. von Mises, op. cit., and Pojman, op. cit. Erik Banks seems to defend a somewhat different interpretation in a discussion of Mach, cf. Banks, Erik, 2003: *Ernst Mach's World Elements. A Study in Natural Philosophy* (Springer-Science). See further discussion below.

167. Cf. Fechner, Gustav Theodor, 1860: *Elemente der Psychophysik* (Leipzig). Translated by H. Adler; edited by D. Howes and E. Boring, as *Elements of Psychophysics* (New York/Chicago: Holt, Rinehart and Winston), 1966.

168. Fechner, 1966: *Elements of Psychophysics*, op. cit. p. 199.

169. For a more elaborate discussion of Fechner see Bornedal, *The Surface and the Abyss*, 2010, op. cit. Also Gori, Pietro, 2015: "Psychology without a Soul, Philosophy without an I. Nietzsche and 19th century Psychophysics" in *Nietzsche and the Problem of Subjectivity*. Ed. J. Constancio et al (de Gruyter).

170. Nietzsche: NF, KSA 12, 1886/1887, 6[14] = WM 565.

171. Nietzsche: NF, KSA 12, 1886/1887, 6[14] = WM 565.

172. *En passant*, this view of knowledge seems to undersigned to support M. Foucault's view, although it is here derived from sources and discussions different from Foucault's.

173. Nietzsche: NF, 1886/1887, KSA 12, 6[14]. This continuation of the passage is by the original editors not included in WM.

174. In several Nietzsche-commentators, we often encounter the discussion of a simple and self-evident 'perspectivism' in the references to the obvious possibility for humans to see objects differently insofar as we can walk around them and look at them from different angles. The introduction of this particular understanding of Nietzsche's 'perspectivism' usually ends by *contradicting* Nietzsche's proper perspectivism, as one infers that from the fact that we can see an 'object' from different angles, it must follow that there is *an object* to be seen in the first place. Since this inference is irrefutable, Nietzsche's 'enigmatic x' is no longer enigmatic, because if we see 'x' from angle 1, angle 2, and angle 3, we are only confirming the existence of the extremely un-enigmatic object x. Thanks to this analysis, it is possible to restore Nietzsche as an objectivist and a realist. In an alternative analysis of the example of us walking around an object looking at it from different angles, in this confirming the objectivity of the object-world, let us first notice that our eyes scan the world from infinitely many angles and perspectives in just brief intervals of time. From *any* angle, the eye scans a world of becoming, i.e., an element-world, not an object-world. Thus,

from *any* angle, we receive an ocean of information that needs subjective processing and ordering. It is *the physiological principle* of this ordering—which comes about as an outcome of the biological evolution of our sense organs—that is at the core of Nietzsche's 'perspectivism,' not the fact that many angles point toward the same center—as if we are walking around on the circumference of a circle, where our gaze is directed toward the center; as if the object-world is logically proved by this implicit (pre-reflective) model of a circle with its circumference and center—because irrefutably, if there is a circumference, then there is a center.

175. P. Gori offers a similar explanation: "The component parts of reality acquire qualities only in relation with other body complexes; their being physical or psychical objects depends on the perspective from which we look at them, and any element can play different roles in both these areas of investigation. *Therefore, all the qualities of the entities one studies depend on the functional relation of the elements*, and the constituent parts of any complex doesn't have properties in itself." Gori: *On the Usefulness of Substances*, op. cit. p. 122.

176. For sure, a Machean 'element' is not the same as an elementary particle in physics, since it related to psycho-physiology, but for pedagogical reasons, it may help if we see the idea as modeled over *elementary nuclear particles*, which in their combinations form different chemical elements, but only qua the multiple arrangements of their interrelated protons, neutrons, and electrons. Notice that the relationships between the three basic subatomic particles in an atom is *functional*, not *causal*. We cannot see a proton as a *cause* of an electron, or vice versa, but they exist in a functional relationship according to certain laws.

177. Mach, *On the Analysis of Sensations*, ibid., p. 9; See also Gori, op. cit., and Banks, op. cit.

178. Cf. Gori: "What is really important in his defining the complexes of elements is that it is not possible to clearly differentiate between ego and body (or soul and matter), since Mach admits that one can see $\alpha \beta \gamma \ldots$ and K L M $\ldots$ as making us the ego (and consider this complex as opposed to A B C $\ldots$, that makes up the world of physical objects), but also that , sometimes, $\alpha \beta \gamma \ldots$ alone is viewed as ego, and K L M $\ldots$ together with A B C $\ldots$ as the world of physical object." Gori, P.: *The Usefulness of Substances*, ibid., p. 120. See also Banks: "Now, with the aid of remembrances, and by trial and error, we learn to divide our experiences into three classes. The first class, labeled A, B, C ... refers to our sensations of physical objects with color and shape and sensed as if external to our bodily surfaces. The second, labeled K, L, M ... refers to sensations we have of our own bodies (such as local signs). Finally, in the third class labeled $\alpha \beta \gamma, \ldots$ are the phenomena of afterimages, memory representations, imagination, and the like." Banks, 2003: *Ernst Mach's World Elements*, op. cit., p. 105.

179. Mach: *On the Analysis of Sensations*, op. cit., p. 2.

180. A caveat, I am consistently claiming that phenomenalism, positivism, or neutral monism are 'naturalistic deconstructions' of classical dualism, and rejections of the self-present or self-identical thing, but with emphasis on the qualifier "naturalistic." Although the *critique of metaphysics* is a strong motive in Mach and Nietzsche's thinking, it is not a critique that belongs in the postmodern tradition, but rather in an

ultra-modern tradition where the biological and cognitive sciences are forming the core in a new naturalist and pragmatic philosophy.

181. We often see this aspect of the thinking introduced under the label 'Neutral Monism.' E.g., Banks, 2003, *Ernst Mach's World Elements*, ibid.

182. Mach: *The Analysis of Sensations and the Relation of the Physical to the Psychical* (Translation C. M. Williams from German edition 1897. Chicago/London: Open Court, 1914), p. 310.

183. Banks offers the following narrative account of Mach's evolutionary and developmental explanation. "Mach's analysis is in one way the biography of human experience as it rises from a primordial soup of elements and slowly delimits itself from the environment into its own boundaries of an ego, with a strong command of its body, good association between its different sensory modalities, and a relative permanence provided by memory and time sensation. [...] Awareness is mostly dependent upon experiencing the same events again and remembering them to be the same." Banks, 2003: *Ernst Mach's World Elements*, op. cit., p. 105.

184. Gori compares this selectivist aspect of Nietzsche-Machean epistemology to more recent attempts in 'evolutionary epistemology': "If one compares Nietzsche's theory of knowledge with Mach's 'principle of economy of thought,' one can find a deep similarity in their conceiving the cognitive process as based upon the Darwinian selectivist model. That's why I think that both Nietzsche and Mach can be included in the list of those scholars who upheld a natural selection epistemology or, as Donald Campbell wrote in his essay devoted to the philosophy of Karl Popper, an *evolutionary epistemology*." Gori, 2009: "On the Usefulness of Substances," op. cit., p. 125n. It is the first time I have seen Nietzsche related to Karl Popper; it is an interesting comparison that deserves further discussion.

185. Fechner, 1966, *Elements of Psychophysics*, op. cit., p. 208.

186. Freud, too, adopted the idea, especially in his neuro-psychological essay, *Project to a Scientific Psychology* (1898), and again in his much later essay about the so-called 'death-drive,' introduced in *Beyond the Pleasure Principle*; cf.: Freud, Sigmund, 1920: *Jenseits des Lustprincips* (Leipzig, Internationaler Psychoanalytischer Verlag). Freud's participation in the intellectual paradigm of the era is evident. Not only is Freud directly inspired by Fechner, but generally speaking Freud too belonged in that group of 'naturalist' 'evolutionary' Central European philosophers we are here discussing, applying for example Darwinism to the psychology of human sexuality. It is unsurprising that we find several agreements between the projects of Nietzsche, Mach, Avenarius, Vaihinger, and Freud; they are all naturalist philosophers, attempting to take thinking beyond metaphysics, religion, and dogma, faithful to observation and reason, even those of them who chose to think about the 'irrational,' such as Nietzsche and Freud. I allow myself to take for granted that to try to understand the logic of the irrational is a task adopted only by the excessively rational character-type. To try to understand what chaotic forces are playing their games behind the fig-leaf of a theologized and divinized '*reason*' is to undersigned enlightenment-thinking at its best, albeit darker in its prospects than usually advertised.

187. Nietzsche: GM II 1, KSA 5, p. 291. Therefore, Nietzsche assigns the highest importance to the principle of simplification (cf. "O sancta simplicitas" [JGB 55], paraphrasing the Catholic interpellation "O sancta Christi").
188. Kleinpeter, Hans: Letter to Mach, op. cit., p. 296.
189. Nietzsche, JGB 192, KSA 5.
190. Nietzsche: NF, KSA 11, 26[61]; See also W. Stegmaier: *"Thinking as a use of signs is, according to Nietzsche, an "art of schematizing and abbreviating" ("Schematisir- und Abkürzungskunst"), even in science and logic.* Nietzsche looked upon Thinking in a consequently pragmatic way." Stegmaier, W., 2006: "Nietzsche's Doctrines, Nietzsche's Signs." *The Journal of Nietzsche Studies*, 31, p. 24.
191. Nietzsche, JGB 192, KSA 5.
192. Mach, 1919: *Science of Mechanics*, op. cit., p. 490.
193. In the particular context of the second part of GM, Nietzsche argues that forgetfulness is making it difficult for the governor to institute Law, since the feebleminded human does not retain material well; consequently, people's ability to remember a few social rules has to be impressed by graphic displays of violence and torture inflicted upon those who have 'forgotten,' 'ignored,' 'violated,' or 'broken' law, and on the scaffold, Law returns with a vengeance, as the perpetrator literally is being broken as a punishment for his forgetfulness. This violence is as "mnemonic technique" encouraging the spectators to remember in the future.
194. Mach, 1919: *Science of Mechanics*, op. cit., p. 481.
195. Mach, 1903: *Popular Scientific Lectures*, op. cit., p. 197.
196. Mach, 1903: *Popular Scientific Lectures*, op. cit., p. 197.
197. Nietzsche: *Nachlaß* 1888; KSA 13, 14[79].
198. Nietzsche: *Nachlaß* 1886/1887; KSA 12, 7[14]).
199. Nietzsche: *Nachlaß* 1885, KSA 11, 34[49].
200. Mach, 1919: *Science of Mechanics*, op. cit., p. 482.
201. Mach, 1919: *Science of Mechanics*, op. cit., p. 482.
202. Nietzsche: *Nachlaß* 1885, KSA 11, 34[131].
203. Nietzsche: *Nachlaß* 1985, KSA 11, 34[131].
204. Nietzsche: WM 515, p. 351 = KSA 13, 14[152].
205. Banks, 2003: *Ernst Mach's World Elements*, op. cit., p. 123.
206. Banks, 2003: ibid., p. 107.
207. Mach: *The Analysis of Sensations*, op. cit., p. 25.
208. Banks, 2003: *Ernst Mach's World Elements*, op. cit., p. 108.
209. Banks, 2003: ibid., p. 108.
210. Banks, 2003: ibid., p. 107.
211. Banks, Eric, 2014: *The Realistic Empiricism of Mach, James, and Russell: Neutral Monism Reconceived* (Cambridge: Cambridge UP).
212. Banks, 2014: ibid., p. 13.
213. Banks, 2014: ibid., p. 14.
214. We recall that Schopenhauer anticipated Nietzsche when already in the *Fourfold* he talked about the "intellectual character of perception." He already then

distinguished between 'raw sense data' and 'perceptive reason.' In the relevant passage, Schopenhauer criticizes philosopher who have argued that "perception of the outer world is a thing of the senses" without mentioning the "intellectual character of perception, [...] the fact, that it is mainly the work of the Understanding, which [...] primarily creates and produces the objective, outer world out of the raw material of a few sensations." Schopenhauer: *Fourfold*, op. cit., p. 58.

215. Banks, 2003: *Ernst Mach's World Elements*, op. cit. p. 4. We rarely see Lenin introduced in the defense of commonsense realism, but Banks reference to his political-ideological defense of Dialectical Materialism against the "Idealism" of Empirio-Criticism, which Lenin saw dangerously introduced by Avenarius, Mach, Petzoldt, and Bogdanov, is quite pertinent. I am apparently not alone in noticing this overlap between Lenin's defense of Materialism and the Analytic defense of Realism, when mobilized against Positivism, Phenomenalism, and/or Pragmatism. In contemporary defense-strategies, we frequently encounter variations of Lenin's materialist arguments as well as his refutations of biological, cognitive, and/or linguistic modifications of the supposed monolithic existence of a truly objective matter-world.

216. See Vaihinger, Hans, 1911: *Die Philosophie des 'Als Ob'* (Berlin). 1935: *The Philosophy of 'As if'* (Trans. C. K. Ogden, London: Routledge and Kegan Paul).

217. Vaihinger, *Die Philosophie des 'Als Ob'*, p. xiv.

218. Explicitly in *Die Philosophie des 'Als Ob'*, Vaihinger refers to Mach's *Beiträge zur Analyse der Empfindungen* (1886; Contributions to the Analysis of the Sensations) and Avenarius' *Philosophie als Denken der Welt gemäss dem Princip des kleinsten Kraftmasses* (1876) and his *Kritik der reinen Erfahrung*, 2 vols. (1888–1900).

219. Vaihinger, 1911: *Die Philosophie des 'Als Ob'* op. cit., p. xv.

220. Vaihinger, 1911: *Die Philosophie des 'Als Ob'* op. cit., p. xx.

221. Vaihinger, 1911: *Die Philosophie des 'Als Ob'* op. cit., p. xx. I will in the following describe the Positivism of Vaihinger, Nietzsche, Avenarius, Mach, and several other of their followers as "Critical Positivism" in order to distinguish it from the later developing "Logical Positivism."

222. Vaihinger, 1911: *Die Philosophie des 'Als Ob'* op. cit., p. xx.

223. Vaihinger refers to multiple other labels for his thinking besides "Positivism," "Pragmatism," "Phenomenology," and generally "Fictionalism,' such as "Biological Theory of Knowledge," "Idealistic" or "Critical Positivism," "Neo-Kantianism." They are schools that in contemporary debate frequently are perceived as distinct, but to Vaihinger's mind share in the same fundamental neo-Kantian paradigm.

224. Vaihinger is far from the only member of the positivist tradition who understands Nietzsche's epistemology as positivism. This understanding he shares with several members of this broadly defined positivism emerging on the theoretical stage at end of the 19th century and beginning of the twentieth. Hans Kleinpeter, Moritz Schlick, Joseph Petzoldt, Phillip Frank, and Rudolph Carnap sport explicitly positive assessments of Nietzsche's epistemology. Later in the twentieth century, Eugen Fink too describes Nietzsche's epistemology as a "fictional theory of knowledge." Fink, Eugen, 1960: *Nietzsches Philosophie*. Stuttgart (Verlag W. Kohlhammer), 1960; p.

165; as well as Jürgen Habermas (in *Erkenntnis und Interesse* (Frankfurt, Suhrkamp), 1968. Translation, J. J. Shapiro: *Knowledge and Human Interests* (Beacon Press, 1971) sees this affinity to the positivist-pragmatist tradition. In recent commentary the assessment has been reiterated by R. Small, C. Emden, N. Hussain, and P. Gori (among others). Of particular relevance for the relations between Nietzsche and Vaihinger, see Gentili, Carlo: "Kant, Nietzsche, und die 'Philosophie des Als Ob'" in *Wirklich. Wirklichkeit. Wirklichkeiten. Nietzsche uuber 'wahre' und 'scheinbare' Welten* (ed. R. Rescheke). Nietzscheforschung bd. 20.

225. Habermas, Jürgen, 1996: *The Philosophical Discourse of Modernity*. Translated by F. G. Lawrence (Cambridge, MA: MIT Press, 1996).

226. See Habermas, 1996: *The Philosophical Discourse of Modernity*, op. cit. See also Norris, Christopher, 1990: *What's Wrong with Postmodernism: Critical Theory and the Ends of Philosophy* (Baltimore: Johns Hopkins University Press).

227. Frank, Phillip, 1941: *Between Physics and Philosophy* (Cambridge: Harvard University Press), p. 51; See also Frank: *The Law of Causality and its Limits* (Vienna: Springer Verlag, 1932), p. 260ff.

228. As Vaihinger explains, 'fiction' derives from the Latin *Fictio*, which designates partly an *activity*, partly a *product*. It designates in the first place the activity of *Fingere*; that is, of constructing, forming, giving shape to, elaborating, presenting, conceiving, thinking, imagining, assuming, planning, devising, inventing. It refers in the second place to the product of these activities, i.e., the fictional assumption, the fabrication, the creation, the imagined case. Cf. Vaihinger, 1911, op. cit., p. 81.

229. E.g. Nietzsche: "Without granting as true the fictions of logic, without measuring reality against the purely invented world of the unconditional and self-identical, without a continual falsification of the world by means of numbers, mankind could not live." (JGB 4).

230. In an attempt to imagine such a 'world,' I proposed in an earlier work a so-called "Ur-ground" for insects, fish, reptiles, mammals, and primates alike (approximately equivalent to Nietzsche's 'world of becoming'), as a necessary minimum for organisms to *react to* and *evolve within* (cf. Bornedal, 2005: "A Silent World: Nietzsche's Radical Realism; World, Sensation, Language." In *Nietzsche-Studien* 34, p. 1–47). Such an 'Ur-ground' was not supposed to be nothing and was opposed to Berkeley's 'idea.' It was not formed and shaped by any organism, but was rather like an abundance of material, relationships, and movements as a potentiality of indefinitely many possible aspects. If one imagines that at some point in distant prehistory the first primitive eyes begin to discern light from darkness, this primordial Ur-ground started to reveal itself *as something* to certain organisms, but still only in a single of its multiple aspects, its indefinite number of potentialities. As such, I suggested that any organism exposes this "Ur-ground" to a primary falsification simply given their species-specific perception. As Homo Sapiens, we would necessarily share this condition with other living organisms, although we perceive the world differently according to our different evolved 'optics' (Nietzsche's term). In contrast to the 'Ur-ground,' I added therefore a second layer of falsification, namely of a specific "Human ground" as that, which shows itself for-us as the apparent world (the world

that we perceive). To Nietzsche, we falsify also this ground by forming it in language and eventually transforming it into concepts (with this bringing order into the world, i.e., transforming a perceived world into a world of knowledge) in cognitive-linguistic processes surpassing those of most animal. It is well known that to Schopenhauer and Nietzsche, animals do not possess the cognitive capabilities of humans; they for example gaze into a world of ever-new moments unable to hold on to the moments that stream past them, while humans in contrast (more as a curse than a blessing) remember the moment and seems unable to let it go—as such missing the pleasant world of unconcerned self-presence, envying the simplicity of the animal (cf. Nietzsche in "On the Use and Abuse of History"). This seems to have been a theme occupying V. Lemm as well in her recent work: Lemm, Vanessa, 2009: *Nietzsche's Animal Philosophy: Culture, Politics, and the Animality of the Human Being* (New York: Fordham UP), where she has an interesting critical discussion of my thesis and offers the following correction: "Where I diverge from Bornedal is that I also account for why senses ''don't deceive'' more than he does: the senses don't deceive because, as first metaphors, they represent contact with the world as radical multiplicity. This is the way contact is made with becoming, and this contact is truthful and honest (the contact does not, in itself, express that the world is anything other than chaos). Additionally, first metaphors do not deceive because they are the primordial ''artistic'' and ''aesthetic'' relationship with the world (rather than representational and epistemic). Intuitive metaphors are truthful because they are artistic, not, as Bornedal asserts, because they are ''non-conscious and pure perception,'' or ''self-presence of the present'' or an expression of ''animal stupidity'' (ibid., p. 17). In fact, Bornedal's reading emphasizes the radical difference between the world as chaotic Urgrund and the human world as constituted by falsification and anthropomorphism, while simultaneously deemphasizing the continuity between human and animal life. Bornedal thereby accepts the humanist premises of much of the discourse on Nietzschean perspectivism in the literature (Nehamas, Nietzsche: *Life as Literature*, pp. 64–65), despite having consistently rejected them for always starting too late and being unfaithful to the Urgrund. On the other hand, Bornedal does not see that, for Nietzsche, the return to contact with the Urgrund is made possible by the denial of the discontinuity between animal and human life." V. Lemm, ibid., p. 202. As I see it, the crux of this objection is to argue for a return to *the correspondence theory of truth*, but now as correspondence between 'sense-impressions' and chaotic reality in-itself as my previously suggested 'Ur-ground.' Following Kant, the neo-Kantians, and Nietzsche, I obvious argue that neither humans nor any other organism have access to such an in-itself world as Ur-ground (briefly put, take away all sensation, and we have an approximation of the in-itself, but what organism perceive without sensations?) Thus, I follow the neo-Kantian-Nietzschean-Positivist argument that perceptions always will be in the way of understanding the in-itself. Still, I think that the concept of an *Ur-ground* has a rational purpose, because we must take for granted that we and other organisms have evolved in a concrete and material 'world' (in a natural environment, not (e.g.) in a brain, from ideas, from divine designs, or the like), and this fact makes the hypothesis legitimate and necessary. When after millions of years of evolution, the first organism opened its eyes, and saw the color red as indicator of a ripe fruit, it was because there were edible fruits around, and still, this was a very selective perception of redness, not shared with many other creatures. Since this perceptive selectivity applies to all perception (even to perception of *space* and *time*, if we take Kant seriously), we have no access to a *sensation-less in-itself* that we may label 'Ur-ground,' or 'thing-in-itself,' or 'enigmatic x,' or something else. In Nietzsche's thinking, we receive data in the form of stimuli about this 'ground,' but these stimuli are not his 'first metaphors.' Only when his nerve-stimuli are transferred into images in perception properly speaking are we having Nietzsche's 'first metaphors'—i.e., the world according to *our* perceptive representation (I called it previously the 'Human ground'). As sufficiently argued, this perceptive representation must necessarily entail a 'falsification' of stimuli, and when in Nietzsche's model, images are transferred into words, a second 'falsification' emerges. Only in this biological-linguistic sense do we exist in a world of so-called 'metaphors.' Lemm seems to be regressing back to the early, romantic Nietzsche (the Nietzsche of deconstruction, who I critically discussed in Part I, B), according to who artists have special assess into the 'truth,' able to transform an alien and estranged world into mythology and magic. She believes that non-deceiving sense-impressions are able to 'touch reality' as veridical accounts of the in-itself world, and defends in this a variation of *the correspondence theory of truth*. In this particular version, not only artists, but apparently animals as well, have special access to truth, and the crux of her objection is that in deemphasizing "the continuity between human and animal life," and by posing a "radical difference between the world as chaotic Ur-ground and the human world as constituted by falsification and anthropomorphism," I overlook "that the return to contact with the Urgrund is made possible by the denial of the discontinuity between animal and human life," i.e., if we accept 'continuity' between animal and human life, the return to the Ur-ground becomes possible. But in what alternative scientific world do such statements make sense? Is Lemm claiming that animals have access to the in-itself, and furthermore, that we as humans are able to become like animals (granted we accept 'continuity')? If so, these claims are of course incompatible to my own view on which I find it self-evident that animals are caught up on their perceptions of an apparent world no less than humans, therefore 'falsifying' no less than humans. I find it equally self-evident that animals and humans have different experiences of the world given differently evolved perceptive apparatuses; thus, there must necessarily *be discontinuity* in the experience of world among different species, which will tend to be more pronounced the more distant our ancestral roots are. (On the other hand, this does not rule out that there are continuities as well, for example, as often emphasized in Nietzsche's neo-Kantian paradigm, our shared experience of space and time, possibly including the understanding of causality). Finally, I don't understand Lemm's theoretical desideratum, why is it in the first place taken for granted that this return to a dead unfriendly sensation-less in-itself world is desirable? To my mind, the nightmare of all nightmares.

231. Vaihinger, 1925: *The Philosophy of 'As if'*, op. cit., p. 68.
232. Vaihinger, 1925, ibid., p. 76.

233. If the fiction does not 'drop out' after having fulfilled its purpose, it degenerates into *hypothesis*; it becomes essentially a *dogma*, which is a perversion of pragmatic thinking according to both Vaihinger and Nietzsche, who attempted to express the same thought in WL by proposing a distinction between "metaphors" and "dead metaphors." "Metaphors" are Vaihinger's fictions, "dead metaphors" are Vaihinger's hypotheses or dogmas. Vaihinger cautions, "we cannot change the fiction into a dogma, the 'as if' into a 'that'. When this is done, we get all the false philosophical problems as if concepts are realities." Vaihinger, 1925: *The Philosophy of 'As if'*, op. cit., p. 31. See also Vaihinger: "[Hypotheses] are assumptions, which are probable, assumptions the truth of which can be proved by further experience. They are therefore verifiable. Fictions are never verifiable, for they are hypotheses which are known to be false, but which are employed because of their utility." Vaihinger, *Die Philosophie des 'Als Ob'*, p. xlii.
234. Vaihinger, 1925: *The Philosophy of 'As if'*, op. cit., p. 77.
235. Cf., Vaihinger, 1925, ibid., p. 76.
236. Vaihinger, 1925, ibid., p. 351 (quoting Nietzsche).
237. Lange, Fr. A.: *Geschichte der Materialismus*, v. II, p. 57; See also Lange, pp. 28, 49, 50, 63, 126, and 137.
238. Nietzsche, NF, 1887/88, 11[332]. Cf. above, Nietzsche talks about 'sensation-chaos' (in GD, his so-called 'position 6') as indicating the origin of knowledge. We find a similar reading in Gori: "Nietzsche started thinking that the crucial point should be the interpretation of sense data. [. . .] Everything concerning the existence of substantial entities [. . .] is closely related to our brain processing sense data, in its schematizing and simplifying them." Gori, P.: "The Usefulness of Substances," ibid. pp. 114–115. See also Small, R., *Nietzsche in Context*, ibid., p. 158.
239. Vaihinger, 1925: *The Philosophy of 'As if'*, op. cit., p. 124.
240. Vaihinger, 1925, ibid., p. 123.
241. Vaihinger, 1925, ibid., p. 123.
242. Vaihinger, 1925, ibid., p. 342.
243. Vaihinger, Hans, 1902: *Nietzsche als Philosoph* (xxx).
244. Vaihinger, 1925: *The Philosophy of 'As if'*, op. cit., p. 21.
245. Vaihinger, 1902: *Nietzsche als Philosoph*, op. cit., pp. 24–25.
246. Vaihinger, 1911: *Der Philosophie des 'Als Ob'*, op. cit., p., 7. Vaihinger introduction to our physiological processes as unconscious reminiscences Nietzsche's descriptions of our constitutionally necessary 'forgetfulness' in GM II 1, KSA 5, p. 291.
247. Cf. Vaihinger, 1911: *Der Philosophie des 'Als Ob'*, op. cit.
248. Vaihinger, 1911: *Der Philosophie des 'Als Ob'*, op. cit., pp. 2–3.
249. There are only a few book length introductions to Avenarius in the twentieth century. I have been consulting the following: (1) Carstanjen, Friedrich, 1894: *Richard Avenarius' Biomechanische Grundlegung der Neuen Allgemeinen Erkenntnistheorie: Eine Einführung in die "Kritik Der Reinen Erfahrung."* (München, Theodor Ackerman), (2) Petzoldt, Joseph, 1900: *Einführung in die Philosophie der Reinen Erfahrung*, bd. 1 and 2 (Leibniz, Teubner), (3) Ewald, Oskar, 1905: *Richard Avenarius als Begründer des Empiriokritizismus* (Berlin, Ernst Hofmann), (4) One

might include also Lenin's ideological-political dismissal of Avenarius, cf. Lenin, W. I., 1906: *Materialism and Empirio-Criticism: Critical Comments on a Reactionary Philosophy* (Collected Works, vol. 14 (Moscow, Progress Publishers). Finally, of a newer date, (5) Sommer, Manfred, 1985: *Husserl und der Frühe Positivismus* (Frankfurt: Vittorio Klostermann).

250. Lenin, 1906: *Materialism and Empirio-Criticism*, op. cit.

251. Avenarius, R., 1876: *Philosophie als Denken der Welt gemäss dem Princip de kleinsten Krafmasses* (Leipzig, Fues's Verlag).

252. Vaihinger, 1911: *Der Philosophie des 'Als Ob'*, op. cit., pp. 177–81.

253. It is again fruitful to compare to Nietzsche who repeatedly emphasizes the fear of the unfamiliar as well; cf. above.

254. As an aside, this force-economical view also helps us to understand the attraction ideological systems have had for peoples of all ages, today no less that during the history of civilization. Ideologies recruit the simplest possible dogmas and biases, and direct themselves against the new and unfamiliar in their representation of an issue. This must represent a psycho-physiological 'pleasure' nearly impossible to resist for the ideological mind (i.e., the constitutionally lazy mind). Ideological systems typically divide the universe in 'familiar' and 'unfamiliar,' 'self' and 'other,' 'peace' and 'danger,' 'love' and 'fear,' 'inside' and 'outside,' etc. It is a pertinent subject, deserving of much more extensive discussion than I can give it here.

255. It is an aspect of Nietzsche often emphasized in German commentary.

256. Mach: *Science of Mechanics*, op. cit., p. 481.

257. Mach: *Popular Lectures*, op. cit., p. 192.

258. Mach: *Science of Mechanics*, op. cit., p. 482.

259. Vaihinger, 1925: *The Philosophy of 'As if'*, op. cit., p. 8.

260. Vaihinger, 1925: *The Philosophy of 'As if'*, op. cit., p. 8.

261. It is an aspect of Nietzsche often emphasized in German commentary; see for example, Abel, Günter, 2001: "Bewußtsein—Sprache—Natur. Nietzsches Philosophie des Geistes," in Nietzsche-Studien, Band 30. (Berlin/New York: Walter de Gruyter); Schlimgen, Erwin, 1998: Nietzsches Theorie des Bewußtseins. Berlin/New York (Walter de Gruyter); Stegmaier, Werner: "Weltabkürzungskunst. Orientierung durch Zeichen," in Josef Simon (ed.): *Zeichen und Interpretation*.

262. Nietzsche, JGB 230, KSA 5.

263. Nietzsche, *Nachlaß* 1888, KSA 13, 14[98].

264. Nietzsche, *Nachlaß* 1886/1887; KSA 12, 5[10].

265. Lange quoting De Bois-Reymond: "Force [...] is nothing but a more recondite product of the irresistible tendency to *personification* which is impressed upon us; *a rhetorical artifice, as it were, of our brain*, which snatches at a figurative term, because it is destitute of any conception clear enough to be literally expressed. [...] What do we gain by saying it is reciprocal attraction whereby two particles of matter approach each other? Not the shadow of an insight in the nature of the fact. But, strangely enough, our inherent quest of causes is in a manner satisfied by the involuntary image tracing itself before our inner eye, of a hand which gently draws the inert matter to it." (De Bois-Reymond quoted from Lange: *A History of Materialism*, book 2, section 2, p. 378; italics added.) Nietzsche talks about similar issues when he makes

the following observations: "The means of expression of language [*Ausdrucksmittel der Sprache*] is useless: it belongs to our inescapable need for preservation: constantly positing a cruder world of the enduring, the 'thing', etc. Relatively, we may speak of atoms and monads." (Nietzsche: *Nachlaß* 1888, KSA 13, 11[73]) [...] "The presuppositions of Mechanism, the stuff, the atom, pressure, impact, and weight are not "facts as such" [*"Thatsachen an sich"*], but rather interpretations helped by psychological fictions." (Nietzsche: *Nachlaß* 1888, KSA 13, 14[82]). Claudia Crawford too refers to the passage of Du Bois-Reymond, and comments: "Here we find that there are at bottom neither forces nor matter. Both are rather abstractions from things." Crawford: *Nietzsche's beginnings of Language*, op. cit., p. 87.

266. Vaihinger, 1911: *Die Philosophie des 'Als Ob'* op. cit., pp. 75–76. Permitting a digression to a literary example, we may see a fascinating representation of positivist nihilism half a century later in Samuel Beckett's work. Beckett has to my knowledge never been read from this point of view, but in the most familiar of his works, *Waiting for Godot*, it cannot escape us that we are introduced to a disenchanted barren world that resists being fictionalized. This world, in all its purposeless materiality, thwarts all the desperate attempts by the protagonists to create a narrative that might give them a foundation and a belief, not to say a 'truth,' by which to live. The great 'fiction,' invented by Vladimir and Estragon, is now 'Godot,' constructed as their hopeless hope of a semi-divine arrival in a desolate world. However, the play leaves us in no doubt that 'Godot' never arrives, that Godot is a *fiction*. In the two acts of the play, he never arrives *twice*, to be precise; and if there had been a third act, he would still not arrive. *Nihil* rules and *Fictio* is the impotent servant to *Nihil*, nothing but the babble-mouth of the play itself that cannot stop talking, personified by the indefatigable Gogo and Didi.

267. Habermas, Jürgen, 1968: *Erkenntnis und Interesse* (Frankfurt: Suhrkamp). Translation, J. J. Shapiro: *Knowledge and Human Interests* (Beacon Press, 1971). Habermas, Jürgen, 1968: Nachwort" in *Nietzsche: Erkenntnis theoretische Schriften* (Suhrkamp, Frankfurt). Translation found in Babich and Cohen: *Nietzsche, Theories of Knowledge, and Critical Theory: Nietzsche and the Sciences*, vol. 1 (Springer, 1999). In this anthology, we find several insightful articles on the relationship between Nietzsche and Habermas. Individual articles consulted by undersigned are Cohen, Robert: "Preface"; Crowell, Steven: "Nietzsche Among the Neo-Kantians"; Fischer, Kurt Rudolf: "Nietzsche and the Vienna Circle"; Schmid, Holger: "The Nietzschean Meta-Critique of Knowledge"; Swindal, James: "Nietzsche, Critical Theory, and a Theory of Knowledge"; Spiekermann, Klaus: "Nietzsche and Critical Theory"; Rockmore, Tom: "Habermas, Nietzsche, and Cognitive Perspective." I benefit as well from McCarthy's general introduction to Habermas: McCarthy, Thomas, 1985: *The Critical Theory of Jürgen Habermas* (MIT Press).

268. Habermas, Jürgen, 1985: *Der Philosophische Diskurs der Moderne* (Frankfurt: Suhrkamp). Translation, F. Lawrence: *The Philosophical Discourse of Modernity* (MIT Press, 1987).

269. Habermas, 1971: *Knowledge and Human Interest*, op. cit., pp. 291–92.

270. Habermas, 1971, ibid., pp. 295–96.

271. Habermas, 1999, Afterword, op. cit., p. 216.
272. Habermas, 1999, ibid., p. 216.
273. Cf. Habermas, 1999, ibid., p. 216.
274. Habermas, 1999, ibid., p. 216.
275. Nietzsche, WM 498 = KSA11, 26[137].
276. Nietzsche, WM 515 = KSA 13, 14[152].
277. Nietzsche, WM 497 = KSA 11, 26[12].
278. Cf. Bornedal, Peter, 2010: *The Surface and the Abyss* chap. 5, op. cit.
279. The replacements of Truth in the absolute sense, is often introduced in Nietzsche as a '*Für-Wahr-halten*,' Nietzsche here reiterating a Kantian phrase introduced in the *Logic* [Kant, *Logik*, WA VI, p. 494]. There may be no "adequate expressions of an object in a subject" (cf. WL 884; see appendix pp. 184–85), no "correct perception," no correspondence between sense-perception and object, but we still *hold-for-true* that which we see streaming past us as reality.
280. He is here drawn to the romantic fascination with the intuitive and impulsive 'naïve' artist, rather than the 'sentimental' and 'intellectual'; to the simple in the form of images and their immediate representations in words, rather than the formal conceptualizations these simple representations receives by researchers and scientists. He asserts a hard distinction between the conceptualizing sciences and the mythologizing arts, between the reason of the scientists and the intuition of the artists, between the rational and the impulsive man, echoing his distinction between the Apollonian-Dionysian versus the Socratic from *Die Geburt der Tragödie* [cf. Part I, B].

Abbreviations

KrV	Kant: *Kritik der reinen Vernunft*, WA 3 and 4
SzG	Schopenhauer: *Über die vierfache Wurzel des Satzes vom zureichenden Grunde*, SW 3
W1	Schopenhauer: *Die Welt als Wille und Vorstellung* Bd. 1. SW 1
W2	Schopenhauer: *Die Welt als Wille und Vorstellung* Bd. 2. SW 2
SW	Schopenhauer, 1960: *Sämtliche Werke* Bd. 1–5. Edited by W. von Löhneysen. (Frankfurt a/M, Suhrkamp Verlag)
WA	Kant, 1968: *Werkausgabe* Bd. 1–12. Edited by W. Weischedel. (Frankfurt a/M, Suhrkamp Verlag)
BGE	Nietzsche: *Beyond Good and Evil*
BT	Nietzsche: *The Birth of Tragedy*
D	Nietzsche: *Daybreak*
EH	Nietzsche: *Ecce Homo*
EH	Nietzsche: *Ecce Homo*, KSA 6
FW	Nietzsche: *Die fröhliche Wissenschaft*, KSA 3
GD	Nietzsche: *Götzendämmerung*, KSA 6
GM	Nietzsche: *On the Genealogy of Morals*
GM	Nietzsche: *Zur Genealogie der Moral*, KSA 5
GS	Nietzsche: *The Gay Science*
GT	Nietzsche: *Die Geburt der Tragödie*, KSA 1
HH	Nietzsche: *Human, All Too Human*
JGB	Nietzsche: *Jenseits von Gut und Böse*, KSA 5
KSA	Nietzsche, 1967–1977: *Sämtliche Werke Kritische Studienausgabe*. Edited by G. Colli and M. Montinari. (Berlin and New York, de Gruyter)
M	Nietzsche: *Morgenröte*, KSA 3
MA	Nietzsche: *Menschliches, Allzumenschliches*, KSA 2
N	Nietzsche: *Nachgelassende Fragmente*, KSA 7–14
TI	Nietzsche: *The Twilight of the Idols*
TL	Nietzsche: *On Truth and Lies in an Extra-Moral Sense*

UB	Nietzsche: *Unzeitgemässige Betrachtungen*, KSA 1
UM	Nietzsche: *Untimely Meditations*
WL	Nietzsche: *Über Wahrheit und Lüge im aussermoralischen Sinne*, KSA 1
WM	Nietzsche: *Der Wille zur Macht*. Stuttgart (Kröner Verlag), 1996
WP	Nietzsche: *The Will to Power*
Z	Nietzsche: *Also Sprach Zarathustra*, KSA 5

Bibliography

GERMAN EDITIONS

Sämtliche Werke; *Digitale Kritische Gesamtausgade.*
Sämtliche Werke Kritische Studienausgabe, 1967–1977. Edited by G. Colli and M. Montinari. (Berlin and New York, de Gruyter).
Sämtliche Briefe Kritische Studienausgabe, 1986. Edited by G. Colli and M. Montinari. (Berlin and New York, de Gruyter).
Also Sprach Zarathustra, KSA 5.
Der Wille zur Macht (Stuttgart, Kröner Verlag), 1996.
Die fröhliche Wissenschaft, KSA 3.
Die Geburt der Tragödie, KSA 1.
Ecce Homo, KSA 6.
Götzendämmerung, KSA 6.
Jenseits von Gut und Böse, KSA 5.
Menschliches, Allzumenschliches, KSA 2.
Morgenröte, KSA 3.
Nachgelassende Fragmente, KSA 7–14.
Über Wahrheit und Lüge in aussermoralischen Sinne, KSA 1.
Unzeitgemässige Betrachtungen, KSA 1.
Von Nutzen und Nachteil der Historie für das Leben (UB II), KSA 1.
Zur Genealogie der Moral, KSA 5.

ENGLISH EDITIONS

Beyond Good and Evil, 1973. Translated by R. J. Hollingdale (London: Penguin Books).
Beyond Good and Evil, 2002. Translated by J. Norman (Cambridge: Cambridge University Press).
Daybreak, 2002. Translated by R. J. Hollingdale. (Cambridge: Cambridge University Press).
Ecce Homo, 1969. Translated by W. Kaufmann. (New York: Vintage Books).
Human, All Too Human, 1986. Translated by R. J. Hollingdale. (Cambridge: Cambridge *University Press*).

Nietzsche: Writings from the Early Notebooks, 2009. Edited by R. Guess and A. Nehamas; Translated by L. Lob (Cambridge: Cambridge University Press).
Nietzsche: Writings from the Late Notebooks, 2003. Edited by Bittner, Rüdiger (Cambridge: Cambridge University Press).
On the Genealogy of Morals, 1969. Translated by W. Kaufmann (New York: Vintage Books).
On the Genealogy of Morals, 1996. Translated by D. Smith. (Oxford: Oxford University Press).
On the Truth and Lie in an Extra-Moral Sense, 1999. Translated by D. Breazeale; in Breazeale (ed.): *Philosophy and Truth. Selections from Nietzsche's Notebooks of the Early 1820's* (Amherst: Humanities Books).
On Truth and Lying in a Non-Moral Sense, 1999. Translated by R. Speirs, in Clark (ed.): *The Birth of Tragedy and other Writings*. (Cambridge: Cambridge University Press).
The Birth of Tragedy, 1967. Translated by W. Kaufmann. (New York: Vintage Books).
The Birth of Tragedy, 2000. Translated by D. Lange. (Oxford: Oxford University Press).
The Gay Science, 1974. Translated by W. Kaufmann. (New York: Vintage Books, Random House).
The Gay Science, 2001. Edited by B. Williams. Translated by J. Nauckhoff. (Cambridge: Cambridge University Press).
The Twilight of the Idols, 1968. Translated by R. J. Hollingdale (London: Penguin Books).
The Twilight of the Idols, 1998. Translated by Duncan Large (Oxford: Oxford World Classics).
The Will to Power, 1968. Edited by W. Kaufmann. Translated by Kaufmann and R. J. Hollingdale (New York: Vintage Books).
Thus Spoke Zarathustra, 1961. Translated by R. J. Hollingdale (London: Penguin Books).
Untimely Meditations, 1983. Translated by R. J. Hollingdale (Cambridge: Cambridge University Press).

SECONDARY LITERATURE

Abel, Günter, 1995: *Interpretationswelten: Gegenwartsphilosophie jenseits von Essentialismus und Relativismus* (Frankfurt: Suhrkamp), 1995.
Abel, Günter, 1998: *Nietzsche: Die Dynamik des Willen zur Macht und die Ewige Wiederkehr* (Berlin and New York: de Gruyter).
Abel, Günter, 2001: "Bewußtsein—Sprache—Natur. Nietzsches Philosophie des Geistes," in Nietzsche-Studien 30 (Berlin and New York: de Gruyter).
Abel, Günter, 2003: "Wahrheit und Interpretation", www.nietzschesource.org/gabel.
Abel, Günter, 2004: *Zeichen der Wirklichkeit* (Frankfurt: Suhrkamp Verlag).

Abel, Günter, 2011: "Die Aktualität der Wissenschaftphilosophie Nietzsches," in Heit et al: *Nietzsches Wissenschaftsphilosophie*, op. cit.
Acampora, C. D., 2013: *Contesting Nietzsche* (Chicago: University of Chicago Press).
Addis, L., 2013: *Nietzsche's Ontology* (München: Walter de Gruyter).
Allison, David B. (ed.), 1977: *The New Nietzsche* (New York, Delta Book).
Anderson, Lanier, 1996, "Overcoming Charity: The Case of Maudemarie Clark's Nietzsche on Truth and Philosophy", in *Nietzsche-Studien* 25 (Berlin and New York: de Gruyter).
Anderson, Lanier, 1998: "Truth and Objectivity in Perspectivism" in *Synthese* 115 (Dordrecht, Kluwer Academic Publishers).
Aristotle, 1941: *Metaphysics*, in *The Basic Works of Aristotle*, edited by R. McKeon (New York, Random House).
Austin, J. L., 1975: *How to do things with words* (Cambridge, MA: Harvard University Press).
Avenarius, Richard, 1876: *Philosophie als Denken der Welt gemäss dem Princip die kleinsten Krafmasses* (Leipzig: Fues's Verlag).
Babich, B. and Cohen, R. (eds.): *Nietzsche, Theories of Knowledge, and Critical Theory: Nietzsche and the Sciences*, vol. 1 (Springer, 1999).
Babich, Babette (ed.), 1999: *Nietzsche, Epistemology, and Philosophy of Science* (Dordrecht: Kluwer Academic Publishers).
Babich, Babette, 1994: *Nietzsche's Philosophy of Science* (New York: State University of New York Press).
Babich, Babette, 2010: "Towards a Critical Philosophy of Science" in *International Journal of the Philosophy of Science* 24: 4.
Banks, Eric, 2014: *The Realistic Empiricism of Mach, James, and Russell: Neutral monism reconceived* (Cambridge: Cambridge University Press).
Banks, Erik, 2003: *Ernst Mach's World Elements: A Study in Natural Philosophy* (Dordrecht: Springer Science).
Beam, Graig, 1996: "Hume and Nietzsche: Naturalists, Ethicists, Anti-Christians," in *Hume Studies*, 22: 2.
Becher, Erich, 1905: "The Philosophical Views of Ernst Mach" in *The Philosophical Review* 14: 5 (Durham, NC: Duke University Press).
Behler, Ernst, 1966: *Friedrich Schlegel in Selbstzeugnissen und Bilddokumenten* (Hamburg, Rowohlt Verlag).
Berkeley, George, 1999: *Principles of Human Knowledge*. (Oxford: Oxford University Press).
Bittner, Rüdiger (ed.), 2003: *Nietzsche: Writing from the Late Notebooks* (Cambridge: Cambridge University Press).
Blackmore, John, 1972: *Ernst Mach: His Work. Life, and Influence* (Berkeley: University of California Press).
Bornedal, Peter, 1996: *The Interpretations of Art*. Lanham/New York: Rowman & Littlefiled/UPA, 1996.
Bornedal, Peter, 2005: "A Silent World: Nietzsche's Radical Realism; World, Sensation, Language." In *Nietzsche-Studien* 34.

Bornedal, Peter, 2010: *The Surface and the Abyss: Nietzsche as Philosopher of Mind and Knowledge* (Berlin and New York: de Gruyter).
Bornedal, Peter, 2014: "On the Institution of the Moral Subject: On the Commander and the Commanded in Nietzsche's Discussion of Law." In *Kriterion, Nietzsche and the Kantian Tradition* (Brazil: Minas Gerais).
Bornedal, Peter, 2015: "Perspectivism and Phenomenalism: Rethinking Epistemology in Nietzsche and Mach." Manuscript: www.academia.edu/bornedal/papers.
Breazeale, Daniel (ed.), 1999: *Philosophy and Truth: Selections from Nietzsche's Notebooks of the Early 1870's* (Amherst: Humanity Books).
Breazeale, Daniel, 1999: "Introduction," in Breazeale, *Philosophy and Truth*.
Brigati, Roberto, 2015: "Veracity and Pragmatism in Nietzsche's On Truth and Lies" in *Parrhesia* 23.
Brobjer, Thomas, 2008: *Nietzsche's Philosophical Context. An Intellectual Biography* (Chicago: University of Illinois Press).
Brobjer, Thomas, 2011: "Nietzsche's Last View of Science" in Heit et al: *Nietzsches Wissenschaftsphilosophie*, op. cit.
Brobjer, Thomas: "Nietzsche's Reading and Knowledge of Natural Science: An Overview" in Moore/Brobjer: *Nietzsche and Science*, op. cit.
Büchner, Ludwig, 1841/72: *Kraft und Stoff* (New York: Steiger Verlag).
Büchner, Ludwig, 1884: *Force and Matter or Principles of the Natural Order of the Universe* (Leipzig: Theodor Thomas).
Capaldi, Nicholas, 1992: "The Dogmatic Slumber of Hume Scholarship" in *Hume Studies* 18: 2.
Carstanjen, Friedrich, 1894: *Richard Avenarius' Biomechanische Grundlegung der Neuen Allgemeinen Erkenntnistheorie: Eine Einführung in die "Kritik Der Reinen Erfahrung."* (München: Theodor Ackerman).
Cassirer, Ernst, 1922: *Das Erkenntnisproblem in der Philosophie und Wissenschaft der neueren zeit*, bd. 2. (Berlin: Verlag Bruno Cassirer).
Clark, M. and D. Dudrick, 2004, "Nietzsche's Post-Positivism," in *European Journal of Philosophy* 12: 3.
Clark, M. and D. Dudrick, 2012, *The Soul of Nietzsche's Beyond Good and Evil* (New York: Cambridge University Press).
Clark, M. and Dudrick D., 2014: "Defending Nietzsche's Soul" in *The Journal of Nietzsche Studies* 45: 3 (Penn State University Press).
Clark, Maudemarie, 1990: *Nietzsche on Truth and Philosophy* (Cambridge: Cambridge University Press).
Clark, Maudemarie, 1994: "Nietzsche's Immoralism and the Concept of Morality" in Schacht: *Nietzsche, Genealogy, Morality* op. cit.
Classen, J., 1908: *Vorlesungen über moderne Naturphilosophen* (Hamburg: Verlag von Boysen).
Cohen, Robert, 1999: "Preface" in Babich/Cohen: *Nietzsche, Theories of Knowledge, and Critical Theory*, op. cit.
Comte, Auguste, 1830–1842: *Cours de Philosophie Positive* v. 1–6 (Paris)
Comte, Auguste, 1988: *Introduction to Positive Philosophy*, translator F. Ferré (Hackett)

Conway, Daniel W. (ed.), 1998: *Nietzsche: Critical Assessments*, vols. 1–4 (London and New York: Routledge).
Conway, Daniel W., 1999: "Beyond Truth and Appearance," in Babich/Cohen: *Nietzsche, Epistemology, and Philosophy of Science*, op. cit.
Copleston, Frederick, 1963: *A History of Philosophy*, vol. 7: *Modern Philosophy* (London, New York: Doubleday).
Couzens Hoy, Daniel: "Nietzsche, Hume, and the Genealogical Method," in Schacht: *Nietzsche, Genealogy, Morality* (op. cit.).
Cox, Christoph, 1999: *Nietzsche: Naturalism and Interpretation* (Berkeley: University of California Press).
Crawford, Claudia, 1988: *The Beginnings of Nietzsche's Theory of Language* (Berlin and New York: de Gruyter).
Crowell, Steven, 1999: "Nietzsche Among the Neo-Kantians" in Babich/Cohen: *Nietzsche, Theories of Knowledge, and Critical Theory*, op. cit.
Culler, Jonathan, 1982: *On Deconstruction: Theory and Criticism after Structuralism* (Ithaca: Cornell University Press).
Danto, Arthur, 1980: *Nietzsche as Philosopher* (New York: Columbia University Press).
Darwin, C., 2003. *The Origin of Species* (New York: Signet Classics).
Dawkins, Richard, 1996: *The Blind Watchmaker: Why the Evidence of Evolution Reveals a Universe without Design* (New York: W. W. Norton).
De Man, Paul, 1974: "Nietzsche's Theory of Rhetoric," in *Symposium: A Quarterly Journal in Modern Literatures*, 28:1 (New Haven, CT: Yale University Press).
De Man, Paul, 1979: *Allegories of Reading* (New Haven and London: Yale University Press).
De Man, Paul, 1984: *The Rhetoric of Romanticism* (New York: Columbia University Press).
Deleuze, Gilles, 1983: *Nietzsche and Philosophy*. Translated by H. Tomlinson (New York: Columbia University Press).
Dennett, Daniel, 1991: *Consciousness Explained* (Boston and New York: Little, Brown, and Company).
Dennett, Daniel, 1995: *Darwin's Dangerous Idea: Evolution and the Meaning of Life* (New York: Touchstone).
Dennett, Daniel, 2006: *Breaking the Spell: Religion as a natural Phenomenon* (New York: Penguin Books).
Derrida, Jacques, 1972: *Marges de la Philosophie* (Paris: Les Éditions de Minuit).
Derrida, Jacques, 1974: *Of Grammatology*. Translated by G. Spivak (Baltimore, MD: Johns Hopkins University Press).
Derrida, Jacques, 1978: "Freud and the Scene of Writing" in *Writing and Difference*. Translated by A. Bass (Chicago: The University of Chicago Press).
Derrida, Jacques, 1978: *Writing and Difference*. Translated by A. Bass (Chicago: The University of Chicago Press).
Derrida, Jacques, 1979: *Spurs: Nietzsche's Styles/Éperons: Les Styles de Nietzsche*. Translated by B. Harlow (Chicago: The University of Chicago Press).

Derrida, Jacques, 1982: *Margins of Philosophy* (trans. Alan Bass. Chicago: The University of Chicago Press).
Derrida, Jacques, 1988: *Limited Inc.* (Trans., S. Weber and J. Mehlman. Evanston: Northwestern University Press).
Derrida, Jacques, 1988: *The Ear of the Other*. Translated by P. Kamuf. (Lincoln, The University of Nebraska Press).
Derrida, Jacques, 1994: "Nietzsche and the Machine" in *The Journal of Nietzsche Studies* 7 (Penn State University Press).
Descartes, Rene, 1984: *Meditations on First Philosophy*, in *The Philosophical Writings of Descartes*, vol. 2. Translated by J. Cottingham et al. (Cambridge: Cambridge University Press).
Doyle, Tsarina, 2009: *Nietzsche on Epistemology and Metaphysics* (Edinburgh: Edinburgh University Press).
Doyle, Tsarina, 2012: "The Kantian Background to Nietzsche's Views on Causality." *The Journal of Nietzsche Studies* 43:1 (Penn State University Press).
Drossbach, Maximilian, 1865: *Über die Objecte der Sinnlichen Wahrnehmung*. C.E.M/ Pfeffer, Halle.
Drossbach, Maximillian, 1884: *Über die Scheinbaren und die Wirklichen Ursachen des Geschehens in der Welt* (Halle, Pfeffer).
Du Bois-Reymond, Emil, 1872/1974: "Über die Grenzen des Naturerkennens" in: Wollgast, S. (ed.): Vorträge über Philosophie und Gesellschaft (Hamburg).
Du Bois-Reymond, Emil, 1874: "The Limits of our Knowledge of Nature," in *Popular Science Monthly*, vol. 5.
Du Bois-Reymond, Emil, 1874: "The Seven World-Riddles." *Popular Science Monthly*, vol. 5.
Du Bois-Reymond, Emil, 1896: "Die Sieben Welträthsel," in *Wissenschaftliche Vorträge*. Ed. J. Howard Gore (Boston: Ginn and Company).
Du Bois-Reymond, Emil, 1896: "Über die Grenzen des Naturerkennens," in *Wissenschaftliche Vorträge*. Ed. J. Howard Gore (Boston: Ginn and Company).
Emden, Christian J., 2005: *Nietzsche on Language, Consciousness, and the Body* (Urbana and Chicago: Illinois University Press).
Emden, Christian J., 2014: *Nietzsche's Naturalism: Philosophy and the Life Sciences in the Nineteenth Century* (Cambridge: Cambridge University Press).
Emden, Christian: "Metaphor, Perception and Consciousness: Nietzsche on Rhetoric and Neurophysiology," in Moore/Brobjer: *Nietzsche and Science*, op. cit.
Ewald, Oskar, 1905: *Richard Avenarius als Begründer des Empiriokritizismus* (Berlin: Ernst Hofmann).
Fechner, Gustav Theodor, 1860: *Elemente der Psychophysik* (Leibzig: Verlag Breitkopf and Härtel).
Fechner, Gustav Theodor, 1966: *Elements of Psychophysics* (New York and Chicago: Holt, Reinhart and Winston).
Feuerbach, Ludwig, 1846: *Das Wesen des Christenthums* (Leipzig).
Feuerbach, Ludwig, 1989: *The Essence of Christianity*. (Translated by G. Eliot, Amherst and New York: Prometheus Books).

Figal, Günter, 2001: *Nietzsche: Eine philosophische Einführung* (Stuttgart: Reclam).
Fink, Eugen, 1960: *Nietzsches Philosophie* (Stuttgart and Berlin, Verlag Kohlhammer).
Fink, Eugen, 2003: *Nietzsche's Philosophy.* Translated by G. Richter (London and New York: Continuum).
Fischer, Kuno, 1865: *System der Logik und Metaphysik: Oder Wissenschaftlehre.* Heidelberg, F. Bassermann.
Fischer, Kuno, 1866: *A Commentary on Kant's Critick of the Pure Reason.* (London: Longmans, Green, and Co.).
Fischer, Kuno, 1883: *Kritik der Kantischen Philosophie* (München: Verlag Fr. Bassermann).
Fischer, Kuno, 1888: *A Critique of Kant.* Translation by W. S. Hough (London: Swan Sonnenschein and Lowrey).
Fischer, Kurt Rudolf: "Nietzsche and the Vienna Circle" in Babich/Cohen, 1999, *Nietzsche, Theories of Knowledge, and Critical Theory,* op. cit.
Foucault, Michel, 1961: *Folie et déraison: histoire de la folie à l'âge classique* (1965; *Madness and Civilization: A History of Insanity in the Age of Reason*).
Foucault, Michel, 1963: *Naissance de la clinique: une archéologie du regard médical* (*The Birth of the Clinic: An Archaeology of Medical Perception,* 1973).
Foucault, Michel, 1966: *Les Mots et les choses* (*The Order of Things,* 1970).
Foucault, Michel, 1975: *Surveiller et punir: naissance de la prison* (*Discipline and Punish: The Birth of the Prison,* 1977).
Foucault, Michel, 1989: *Archaeology of Knowledge* (London: Routledge).
Foucault, Michel, 2002: *The Order of Things* (London: Routledge).
Foucault, Michel, 2006: *History of Madness* (London: Routledge).
Frank, Philipp, 1932: *Das Kausalgesetz und Seine Grenzen* (Vienna: Julius Springer).
Frank, Philipp, 1932: *The Law of Causality and its Limits* (Vienna: Springer Verlag).
Frank, Philipp, 1941: *Between Physics and Philosophy* (Cambridge: Harvard University Press).
Frank, Philipp, 1950: *Modern Science and Its Philosophy* (Cambridge: Harvard University Press).
Freud, Sigmund, 1920: *Jenseits des Lustprincips* (Leipzig: Internationaler Psychoanalytischer Verlag).
Freud, Sigmund, 1966: *Project for a Scientific Psychology* in *The Standard Edition of the Complete Psychological Works of Sigmund Freud,* vol. 1; ed. J. Strachey. London.
Gemes, Ken, 1992: "Nietzsche's Critique of Truth" in *Philosophy and Phenomenological Research* 52: 1.
Gemes, Ken, 1992: Nietzsche's Critique of Truth in Philosophy and Phenomenoligical Research 52: 1.
Gemes, Ken, 2001: "Postmodernism's Use and Abuse of Nietzsche" in *Philosophy and Phenomenological Research* 62: 2.
Gentili, Carlo: "Kant, Nietzsche, und die Philosophie des Als Ob," in *Wirklich. Wirklichkeit. Wirklichkeiten. Nietzsche uuber 'wahre' und 'scheinbare' Welten* (ed. R. Rescheke, Nietzscheforschung bd. 20).

Gerber, Gustav, 1885: *Die Sprache als Kunst*, bd. I and II (Berlin, R. Gaertners Verlagsbuchhandlung).
Gerhardt, Volker, 1996: *Vom Willen zur Macht: Anthropologie und Metaphysic der Macht am exemplarischen Fall Friedrich Nietzsches* (Berlin and New York, de Gruyter).
Geuss, R. and Nehamas, A. (eds.), 2009: *Nietzsche: Writings from the early Notebooks* (Cambridge, Cambridge University Press).
Gori, Pietro, 2009: "The Usefulness of Substances. Knowledge, Science and Metaphysics in Nietzsche and Mach" (In Nietzsche-Studien 38).
Gori, Pietro, 2011: "Nietzsche as Phenomenalist?" in Heit et al: *Nietzsches Wissenschafts philosophie*, op. cit.
Gori, Pietro, 2015: "Psychology without a Soul, Philosophy without an I. Nietzsche and 19th century Psychophysics" in *Nietzsche and the problem of Subjectivity* (ed. Constancio et al, de Gruyter).
Gori, Pietro: "Nietzsche on Truth. A Pragmatic View?" in *Wirklich. Wirklichkeit. Wirklichkeiten. Nietzsche über 'wahre' und 'scheinbare' Welten* (ed. R. Rescheke) Nietzscheforschung bd. 20.
Granier, Jean, 1966: *Le problème de la Vérité dans la philosophie de Nietzsche* (Paris: Éditions du Seuil).
Granier, Jean, 1977: "Nietzsche's Conception of Chaos" in Allison: *The New Nietzsche*, op. cit.
Granier, Jean, 1977: "Perspectivism and Interpretation" in: Allison: *The New Nietzsche*, op. cit.
Green, Michael Steven, 2002: *Nietzsche and the Transcendental Tradition* (Urbana and Chicago: University of Illinois Press).
Grimm, Herman Rudiger, 1977: *Nietzsche's Theory of Knowledge* (Berlin and New York: de Gruyter).
Guyer, Paul, 2006.: *Kant*. (London/New York: Routledge).
Haar, Michel, 1996: *Nietzsche and Metaphysics* (New York: State University of New York Press).
Habermas, Jürgen, 1968: "Nachwort" in *Nietzsche's Erkenntnistheoretische Schriften* (Frankfurt a/M: Suhrkamp).
Habermas, Jürgen, 1968: *Erkenntnis und Interesse* (Frankfurt: Suhrkamp).
Habermas, Jürgen, 1971: *Knowledge and Human Interest*. Trans. J. J. Shapiro (Boston: The MIT Press).
Habermas, Jürgen, 1985: *Die Philosophische Diskurs der Moderne* (Frankfurt a/M: Suhrkamp).
Habermas, Jürgen, 1996: *The Philosophical Discourse of Modernity*. Translated by F. G. Lawrence (Boston: The MIT Press).
Habermas, Jürgen, 1999: "On Nietzsche's Theory of Knowledge" in *Nietzsche, Theories of Knowledge and Critical Theory*. Eds. B. Babich and R. S. Cohen (Springer).
Haeckel, Ernst, 1929: *The Riddle of the Universe*. Translation J. McCabe (London: Watts and Co.).
Hales, S. D. and Welshon, R., 2000: *Nietzsche's Perspectivism* (Urbana and Chicago: University of Illinois Press).

Hamacher, Werner, 1990: "The Promise of Interpretation" in Rickels, Laurence: *Looking After Nietzsche*, op. cit.
Hartmann, Eduard von, 1870: *Philosophie des Unbewussten* bd. 1–3 (Berlin: Carl Dunker's Verlag).
Hartmann, Eduard von, 2000: *The Philosophy of the Unconscious*. Translation by W. C. Coupland (London: Routledge).
Hatab, Laurence, 2008: *Nietzsche On the Genealogy of Morality*. (Cambridge: Cambridge University Press).
Heidegger, Martin, 1991: *Nietzsche*, vols. 1–4. Edited and translated by D. F. Krell. (San Francisco: Harper and Row).
Heit, H., Abel, G., and Brusotti, M. (eds.), 2011: *Nietzsches Wissenschaftsphilosophie: Hintergründe, Wirkungen und Aktualität*. (Berlin and New York: de Gruyter).
Heit, Helmut, 2014: "Advancing the Agon: Nietsche's Pre-texts and the Self-Reflexive Will to Truth," in *The Journal of Nietzsche Studies* 45 (Penn State University Press).
Helmholtz, Hermann von, 1856/67: *Handbuch der Physiologische Optik* bd. 1 and 2 ().
Helmholtz, Hermann von, 1893: *Scientific Subjects*. (London: Longmans, Green, and co.).
Helmholtz, Hermann von, 1995: *Science and Culture: Popular and Philosophical Lectures*. Edited by D. Cahan (Chicago: The University of Chicago Press).
Helmholtz: *Physiologische Optik*.
Helmholzt, Hermann von, 1876: *Populäre Wissenschaftliche Vorträge* (Braunschweig: Verlag F. Vieweg)
Hill, Kevin R., 2003: *Nietzsche's Critiques: The Kantian Foundation for his Thought* (Oxford: Clarendon Press).
Himmelmann, Beatrix (ed.), 2005: *Kant und Nietzsche im Widerstreit* (Berlin and New York: de Gruyter).
Hinman, Lawrence, 1982: "Nietzsche, Metaphor, and Truth" in *Philosophy and Phenomenological Research*, 43: 2.
Houlgate, Stephen, 1986: *Hegel, Nietzsche and the criticism of metaphysics* (Cambridge: Cambridge Univ. Press)
Houlgate, Stephen, 1993: "Kant, Nietzsche, and the Thing-in-itself" in *Nietzsche Studien* 22 (Berlin and New York: de Gruyter).
Hoy, David C., 1994: "Nietzsche, Hume, and the Genealogical Method," in Schacht: *Nietzsche, Genealogy, Morality*, op. cit.
Hume, David, 1898: *Dialogues Concerning Natural Religion*, in *A Treatise of Human Nature* and *Dialogues Concerning Natural Religion,* vol. 2 (London: Longman).
Hume, David, 1969: *A Treatise of Human Nature*. London (Penguin Classics).
Hume, David, 1997: *An Enquiry Concerning Human Understanding*. (Indianapolis: Hackett).
Hussain, Nadeem, 2004: "Nietzsche's Positivism". In *European Journal of Philosophy* 12: 3.
Hussain, Nadeem, 2004: "Reading Nietzsche through Ernst Mach" in Moore and Brobjer (eds.): *Nietzsche and Science* op. cit.

James, William, 1890: *The Principles of Psychology*, vol. I-II (New York: Henry Holt and Company).
James, William, 1906: *Pragmatism: A New Name for some Old Ways of Thinking* (Cambridge: Harvard University Press).
James, William, 1909: *The Meaning of Truth* (New York, Longmans and Green).
James, William, 1911: *Some Problems of Philosophy* (New York: Longmans, Green, and Co).
James, William, 1948: *Essays in Pragmatism* (New York: Hafner Publishing Company).
Janaway, C. and Robertson, S. (eds.), 2012: *Nietzsche, Naturalism, and Normativity* (Oxford: Oxford University Press).
Janaway, Christopher, 2007: *Beyond Selflessness: Reading Nietzsche's Genealogy* (Oxford: Oxford University Press).
Jensen, Anthony K., 2013: *Nietzsche's philosophy of history* (New York: Cambridge University Press).
Kail, P. J. E., 2015: "Nietzsche and Naturalism" in Dries M. and Kail, P. J. E. (ed.), *Nietzsche on Mind and Nature* (Oxford).
Kant, Immanuel, 1918: *Critique of Pure Reason*. Translated by Norman Kemp Smith (Houndmills: Palgrave Macmillian).
Kant, Immanuel, 1968: *Kritik der reinen Vernunft I*, in WA 3.
Kant, Immanuel, 1968: *Prolegomena zu einer jeden Künftigen Metaphysik*, in WA 5.
Kant, Immanuel, 1968: Werkausgabe 1–12. Ed.: W. Weischedel. (Frankfurt am Main: Suhrkamp Verlag).
Kant, Immanuel, 1977: *Prolegomena to Any Future Metaphysics*. Translated by P. Carus (Indianapolis: Hackett Publishing Company).
Kaufmann, Walter, 1974: *Nietzsche: Philosopher, Psychologist, Antichrist* (Princeton: Princeton University Press).
Kaulbach, Friedrich, 1982: *Immanuel Kant*. (Berlin, New York: Walter de Gruyter).
Kemp S. Norman, 1950.: *A Commentary to Kant's "Critique of Pure Reason"* (New York: The Humanities Press).
Kitcher, Patricia, 1982: "Kant's Paralogisms" in *The Philosophical Review*, 91: 4.
Klein, Wayne, 1997: *Nietzsche and the Promise of Philosophy.* (New York: State University of New York Press).
Kleinpeter, Hans, 1905: *Die Erkenntnistheorie der Naturforschung der Gegenwart* (Leipzig: Verlag von J. A. Barth).
Kleinpeter, Hans, 1912: "Letters to Ernst Mach, 1912." Translation, P. Gori, *Nietzsche Studien* 40 (Berlin and New York: de Gruyter).
Kleinpeter, Hans, 1913: *Der Phenomenalismus: Eine Naturwissenshcaftliche Weltanschauung* (Leipzig: Verlag J. A. Barth).
Koelb, Clayton, (ed.), 1990: *Nietzsche as Postmodenist* (Albany: SUNY Press).
Kofman, Sara, 1972: *Nietzsche et la métaphore* (Paris: Editions Galilée).
Kofman, Sara, 1993: *Nietzsche and Metaphor*, translated by D. Large (Stanford: Stanford University Press).

Lange, Frederick Albert, 1865/2000: *The History of Materialism*. Translated by C. K. Ogden. (New York: Routledge).
Lange, Friedrich Albert, 1866/1873: *Geschichte des Materialismus und Kritik seiner Bedeutung in der Gegenwart* bd. 1 and 2 (Iserlohn: Verlag con J. Daedeker).
Laplace, Pierre-Simon, 1814: *Essai philosophique sur les Probabilitè* (Paris).
Laplace, Pierre-Simon, 1902: *A Philosophical essay on Probabilities*. Translation by Truscott and Emory (New York: John Wiley).
Leiter, Brian, 1994: "Perspectivism in Nietzsche's *Genealogy of Morals*," in Schacht: *Nietzsche, Genealogy, Morality* op. cit.
Leiter, Brian, 2002: *Nietzsche on Morality* (London and New York: Routledge Philosophical Guidebook).
Leiter, Brian, 2007: "Nietzsche's Theory of the Will", *Philosophers' Imprint* 7: 7.
Leiter, Brian, 2009: "Nietzsche's Naturalism Reconsidered." (Electronic copy).
Leiter, Brian, 2014: "On the 'Esoteric' Reading of Nietzsche" (Electronic Copy).
Lenin, W. I., 1906/1909: *Materialism and Empirio-Criticism: Critical Comments on a Reactionary Philosophy* in *Collected Works*, vol. 14. (Moscow: Progress Publishers).
Lichtenberg, Georg C., 2012: *Philosophical Writing*. Edited and translated by S. Tester (New York: Suny Press).
Liebmann, Otto, 1865/1912: *Kant und die Epigonen*, (Berlin: Reuther and Reichard)
Lightbody, B.: "Nietzsche, Perspectivism, Anti-realism: An Inconsistent Triad"; in *The European Legacy*, vol. 15/4, pp. 425–38, 2010.
Locke, John, 1690: *Essay Concerning Human Understanding.*
Mach, Ernst, 1883: *Die Mechanik in Ihrer Entwickelung* (Leipzig: Brockhaus).
Mach, Ernst, 1886/1922: *Die Analyse der Empfindungen und das Verhältnis des Physischen zum Psychischen* (Jena: Gustav Fischer).
Mach, Ernst, 1898: *Popular Scientific Lectures*. Translation T. J. McCormack. (Chicago/London: Open Court).
Mach, Ernst, 1903: *Populär Wissenschaftliche Vorlesungen* (Leipzig: J. A. Barth).
Mach, Ernst, 1906: *Erkenntnis und Irrtum. Skizzen zur Psychologie der Forschung* (Leipzig: Ambrosius Barth).
Mach, Ernst, 1914: *The Analysis of Sensations and the Relation of the Physical to the Psychical*, trans. C. M. Williams (Chicago: Open Court).
Mach, Ernst, 1919: *The Science of Mechanics: A Critical and Historical Account of its Development*. Translation by T. J. McCormack (Chicago: Open Court).
Mach, Ernst, 1926: *Knowledge and Error: Sketches on the Psychology of Enquiry*. Translation T. J. McCormack (Dordrecht: Reidel Publishing Company).
Mach, Ernst, 1959: *The Analysis of Sensations and the Relations of the Physical to the Psychical*. Translation T. J. McCormack (New York: Dover Publications).
Magnus, Bernd, 1989: "Nietzsche and Postmodern Criticism," in *Nietzsche Studien* 18 (Berlin and New York: de Gruyter).
Mauch, Philipp, 2009: *Nietzsche über der Gance* (Inaugural-Dissertation, Maximillian-Ludwig Universitet, München)
Mayr, Ernst, 1991: *One Long Argument: Charles Darwin and the Genesis of Modern Evolutionary Thought.* (Cambridge: Harvard University Press).

McCarthy, Thomas, 1985: *The Critical Theory of Jürgen Habermas* (Cambridge: MIT Press).
Meijers, A. und Stengelin, M., 1988: "Kondordanz zu . . . Gustav Gerbers *Die Sprache als Kunst* . . . und Nietzsches *Über Wahrheit und Lüge*," in Nietzsche Studien 17 (Berlin and New York: de Gruyter).
Meijers, Anthonie, 1988: "Gustav Gerber und Friedrich Nietzsche. Zum historischen Hintergrund der sprachphilosophichen Auffassungen des frühen Nietzsche," in *Nietzsche Studien* 17 (Berlin and New York: de Gruyter).
Mill, J. S. 1991: *On Liberty and Other Essays*, edited by J. Gray (Oxford: Oxford University Press).
Mill, John Stuart, 1865: *Examination of Sir William Hamilton's Philosophy* (London: Longmans and Green).
Mill, John Stuart, 1907: *Auguste Comte and Positivism* (London: Kegan Paul).
Mises, Richard von, 1956: *Positivism: A Study in Human Understanding* (New York: George Braziller).
Mitcheson, Katrina, 2013: *Nietzsche, Truth and Transformation* (Palgrave Macmillan).
Montinari, Mazzino, 1984: *Nietzsche Lesen* (Berlin: de Gruyter).
Moore, G, and Brobjer T. (eds.), 2004: *Nietzsche and Science* (London: Ashgate).
Moore, Gregory, 2002: *Nietzsche, Biology and Metaphor* (Cambridge: Cambridge University Press).
Müller, Johannes, 1838: *Handbuch der Physiologie des Menschen* (Coblenz: Verlag von Hölscher).
Müller-Lauter, Wolfgang, 1999: "On Judging in a World of Becoming"; in Babich/Cohen (eds.): *Nietzsche, Epistemology, and Philosophy of Science*, op. cit.
Müller-Lauter, Wolfgang, 1999: *Nietzsche: His Philosophy of Contradictions and the Contradictions of His Philosophy*. Translated by D. J. Parent (Urbana and Chicago: University of Illinois Press).
Müller-Lauter, Wolfgang, 1999: *Über Freiheit und Chaos: Nietzsche-Interpretationen II*. (Berlin and New York: de Gruyter).
Müller-Lauter, Wolfgang, 1999: *Über Werden und Wille zur Macht: Nietzsche Interpretationen I* (Berlin and New York: de Gruyter).
Nehamas, Alexander, 1985: *Nietzsche: Life as Literature* (Cambridge, MA: Harvard University Press).
Nehamas, Alexander, 2009: "Introduction" in *Nietzsche: Writings from the Early Notebooks* (Cambridge: Cambridge University Press).
Norris, Christopher, 1988: *Paul de Man: Deconstruction and the Critique of Aesthetic Ideology* (London and New York: Routledge).
Norris, Christopher, 1990: *What's Wrong with Postmodernism: Critical Theory and the Ends of Philosophy* (Baltimore: Johns Hopkins University Press).
Parkes, Graham, 1994: *Composing the Soul: Reaches of Nietzsche's Psychology* (Chicago: The University of Chicago Press).
Perelman, Ch. and Olbrechts-Tyteca, L., 1969: *The New Rhetoric: A Treatise of Argumentation*. Translated by J. Wilkinson and P. Weaver. (Notre Dame: The University of Notre Dame Press).

Petzoldt, Joseph, 1900: *Einführung in die Philosophie der Reinen Erfahrung,* Bd, 1–2 (Leibniz: Teubner).
Pippin, Robert, 1998: "Truth and Lies in Early Nietzsche" in Conway, Daniel (ed.): *Nietzsche: Critical Assessments,* op. cit.
Pippin, Robert, 2006: *Nietzsche, Psychology, and First Philosophy.* (Chicago: The University of Chicago Press).
Pippin, Robert, 2013: "Doer and Deed: Responses to Acampora and Anderson." In *The Journal of Nietzsche Studies* 44: 2 (Penn State University Press).
Poeller, Peter, 1995: *Nietzsche and Metaphysics* (Oxford: Oxford University Press).
Prange, Martine, 2013: *Nietzsche, Wagner, Europe* (Berlin and New York: De Gruyter).
Proops, I.: "Kant's First Paralogism." (In *Philosophical Review,* 119: 4, 2010).
Reginster, Bernard, 2001: "The Paradox of Perspectivism" in *Philosophy and Phenomenological Research* 62: 1.
Rehberg, A.: "Nietzsche's Transvaluation of Causality"; in Babich (ed.), *Nietzsche, Epistemology, and Philosophy of Science,* op. cit.
Remhof, Justin, 2018: *Nietzsche's Constructivism: A Metaphysics of Material Objects* (London: Routledge).
Riccardi, Mattia, 2011: "Nietzsche's Sensualism" in European Journal of Philosophy 21: 2 (Oxford: John Wiley).
Richardson, John, 1996: *Nietzsche's System.* (Oxford: Oxford University Press).
Richardson, John, 2004: *Nietzsche's New Darwinism* (Oxford: Oxford University Press).
Rickels, Laurence, 1990: *Looking After Nietzsche: Interdisciplinary Encounters with Merleau-Ponty* (New York: SUNY Press).
Ridley, A. 1998: *Nietzsche's Conscience: Six Character Studies from the Genealogy.* (New York: Cornell University Press).
Rittelmeyer, Friedrich, 2005: *Friedrich Nietzsche und das Erkenntnisproblem.* (Elibron Classics).
Rockmore, Tom, 1999: "Habermas, Nietzsche, and Cognitive Perspective" in Babich/Cohen: *Nietzsche, Theories of Knowledge, and Critical Theory,* op. cit.
Rockmore, Tom, 2004: *On Foundationalism: A Strategy for Metaphysical Realism* (Lanham, MD: Rowman & Littlefiled).
Rockmore, Tom, 2005: *On Constructivist Epistemology* (Lanham, MD: Rowman & Littlefiled).
Rorty. Richard, 2001: "Is Truth a Goal of Inquiry?" In *Truth and Progress. Philosophical Papers* bd. 3. (Cambridge: Cambridge University Press).
Rosenkranz, Karl, 1840: *Geschichte der Kantschen Philosophie* (Leipzig: Leopold Voss)
Rowe, D. E.: "Nietzsche's 'Anti-Naturalism' in 'The Four Great Errors'." *International Journal of Philosophical Studies,* 21: 2, 2013.
Russell, Bertrand, 1929: "On the Notion of Cause," reprinted in Feigl, H. and Brodbeck, M. (eds): *Readings in the Philosophy of Science* (New York: Appleton-Century-Crofts).

Salaquarda, Jörg, 1978: "Nietzsche und Lange," in *Nietzsche Studien* 7 (Berlin: New York, Walter de Gruyter).
Saussure, Ferdinand de, 1916/1975: *Cours de Linguistique Générale*. Edited by C. Bally and A. Sechehaye. Paris.
Saussure, Ferdinand de, 1966: *Course in General Linguistics*. Translated by Wade Baskin. (New York: McGraw Hill).
Schacht, Richard (ed.), 1994: *Nietzsche, Genealogy, Morality: Essays on Nietzsche's Genealogy of Morals* (Berkeley: University of California Press).
Schacht, Richard, 1983: *Nietzsche* (London and New York: Routledge).
Schacht, Richard, 2011: "Nietzsche's Anti-Scientistic Naturalism," in Heit et al: *Nietzsches Wissenschaftsphilosophie.*, op. cit.
Schacht, Richard, 2012: "Nietzsche's Naturalism" in *The Journal of Nietzsche Studies* 43:2 (Penn State University Press).
Schacht, Richard, 2014: "Clark and Dudrick's New Nietzsche," in *Journal of the History of Philosophy* 52.
Scheibenberger, Sarah, 2016: *Kommentar zu Nietzsche's, Ueber Wahrheit und Lüge im außermoralischen Sinne*. (New York and Berlin: de Gruyter).
Schiller, Friedrich, 1985: *On Naive and Sentimental Poetry*, in Nisbet (ed.): *German Aesthetic and Literary Criticism* (Cambridge: Cambridge University Press).
Schiller, Friedrich, 1992: *Theoretische Schriften*, Werke (Frankfurt a/M: Deutscher Klassiker Verlag).
Schiller, Friedrich, 1992: *Über Naive und Sentimentale Dichtung*, in: Theoretische Schriften, Werke, band 8 (Frankfurt a/M: Deutscher Klassiker Verlag).
Schlegel, Friedrich, 1979: *Die Griechen und Römer* in: E. Behler, ed.: Kritische Friedrich Schlegel Ausgabe, vol. 1 (Paderborn: Ferdinand Schöningh Verlag).
Schlegel, Friedrich, 1979: *Gespräch über die Poesie* in: E. Behler, ed.: Kritische Friedrich Schlegel Ausgabe, bd. 1 (Paderborn: Ferdinand Schöningh Verlag).
Schlegel, Friedrich, 1979: *Kritische Friedrich Schlegel Ausgabe*, bd. I (Paderborn: Ferdinand Schöningh Verlag).
Schlegel, Friedrich, 1979: *Über das Studium der Griechischen Poesie*, in: E. Behler, ed.: Kritische Friedrich Schlegel Ausgabe, vol. 1 (Paderborn: Ferdinand Schöningh Verlag).
Schlegel, Friedrich, 1979: *Über der Grieschishe Poesie*, in: E. Behler, ed.: Kritische Friedrich Schlegel Ausgabe, vol. 1 (Paderborn: Ferdinand Schöningh Verlag).
Schlegel, Friedrich: *Selected Aphorisms from the Athenaem*, in: Willson, ed.: German Romantic Criticism, op. cit.
Schlimgen, Erwin, 1998: *Nietzsches Theorie des Bewußtseins*. (Berlin and New York: de Gruyter).
Schmid, Holger, 1999: "The Nietzschean Meta-Critique of Knowledge" in Babich/Cohen: *Nietzsche, Theories of Knowledge, and Critical Theory*, op. cit.
Schmidt, Alfred, 1984: "Schopenhauer und der Materialismus" in Spierling (ed.): *Materialien zu Schopenhauer*, op. cit.
Schmidt, R. (ed.), 1988: "Nietzsches Drossbach-Lektüre", Nietzsche-Studien, 17 (Berlin, New York: Walter de Gruyter).

Schopenhauer, Arthur, 1845: *Über das Sehn und die Farben*, in SW 3, op. cit.
Schopenhauer, Arthur, 1847: *Über die vierfache Wurzel des Satzes des zureichenden Grunde* in SW 3, op. cit.
Schopenhauer, Arthur, 1960: *Die Welt als Wille und Vorstellung* in SW I and II, op. cit
Schopenhauer, Arthur, 1960: *Sämtliche Werke* Bd. 1–5. Ed.: W. von Löhneysen. (Frankfurt am Main: Suhrkamp Verlag).
Schopenhauer, Arthur, 1974: *On the Fourfold Root of the Principle of Sufficient Reason*. Translation E. F. J. Payne. (La Salle: Open Court).
Schopenhauer, Arthur, 1974: *The World as Will and Representation*, vol. 1 and 2. Translated by E. F. J. Payne. (New York: Dover Publications).
Searle, John, 1977: "Reiterating the differences. A reply to Derrida." In *Glyph 1*. (Eds. S. Webster and H. Sussmann. Baltimore: John Hopkins University Press).
Searle, John, 1993: "A World Turned Upside Down" in Working Through Derrida. (Ed., G. Madison. Evanston: Northwestern University Press).
Sedgwick, Peter R. (ed.), 1995: *Nietzsche: A Critical Reader* (Oxford: Blackwell).
Simmel, George, 1907: *Schopenhauer und Nietzsche*. In *Gesamtausgabe* Bd. 10. (2000: Frankfurt a/M: Suhrkamp Verlag).
Simon, Josef (ed.), 1994: *Zeichen und Interpretation*. (Frankfurt am Main: Suhrkamp Verlag).
Simon, Josef, 1972: "Grammatik und Wahrheit," in *Nietzsche Studien* 1. (Berlin and New York: de Gruyter).
Simon, Josef, 1989: "Die Krise des Wahrheitsbegriffs als Krise der Metaphysik," in *Nietzsche Studien* 18 (Berlin and New York: de Gruyter).
Simon, Josef, 1999: "Grammar and Truth" in Babich/Cohen: *Nietzsche, Theories of Knowledge, and Critical Theory*, op. cit.
Small, Robin, 1986: "Boscovich Contra Nietzsche" in Philosophy and Phenomenological Research 46: 3.
Small, Robin, 2001: *Nietzsche in Context* (Aldershot: Ashgate).
Solomon, Robert, 1990: "Nietzsche, Postmodernism, and Resentment," in Koelb, Clayton, (ed.): *Nietzsche as Postmodernist* op. cit.
Sommer, Manfred, 1985: *Husserl und der Frühe Positivismus* (Frankfurt: Vittorio Klostermann).
Sorgner, Stefan Lorenz, 2007: *Metaphysics without Truth-On the Importance of Consistency within Nietzsche's Philosophy* (Marquette University Press).
Spiekermann, Klaus, 1992: *Naturwissenschaft als subjektlöse Macht? Nietzsches Kritik physikalischer Grundkonzepte* (Berlin and New York: de Gruyter).
Spiekermann, Klaus, 1999: "Nietzsche and Critical Theory" in Babich/Cohen: *Nietzsche, Theories of Knowledge, and Critical Theory*, op. cit.
Spierling, Volker (ed.), 1984: *Materialien zu Schopenhauers 'Die Welt als Wille und Vorstellung'* (Frankfurt am Main: Suhrkamp).
Spir, African, 1873: *Denken und Wirklichkeit. Versuch einer Erneuerung der Kritischen Philosophie*. (Leipzig: J. G. Findel).
Spir, Afrikan, 1869: *Forschung nach der Gewissheit in der Erkenntniss der Wirklichkeit* (Leipniz: Förster and Findel).

Stack, George J., 1983: *Lange and Nietzsche* (Berlin and New York: de Gruyter).
Stack, George J., 2005: *Nietzsche's Anthropic Circle: Man, Science, and Myth* (New York: University of Rochester Press).
Stegmaier, Werner, 1987: "Darwin, Darwinismus, Nietzsche. Zum Problem der Evolution," in *Nietzsche Studien* 16. (Berlin and New York: de Gruyter).
Stegmaier, Werner, 1988: "Nietzsches Neubestimmung der Wahrheit" in *Nietzsche Studien* 14. (Berlin and New York: de Gruyter).
Stegmaier, Werner, 1994: "Weltabkürzungskunst. Orientierung durch Zeichen," in Simon (ed.): *Zeichen und Interpretation* op. cit.
Stegmaier, Werner, 1994: *Nietzches "Genealogie der Moral"*. (Darmstadt: Wissenschaftliche Buchgesellschaft).
Stegmaier, Werner, 2006: "Nietzsche's Doctrines, Nietzsche's Signs" in *The Journal of Nietzsche Studien* 31. (Berlin and New York: de Gruyter).
Stegmaier, Werner, 2012: *Nietzsches Befreiung der Philosophie: Kontextuelle Interpretationen der V. Buchs der 'Fröhlichen Wissenschaft.'* (Berlin and New York: de Gruyter).
Strawson. Galen, 2015: "Nietzsche's Metaphysics" in Dries M. and Kail, P. J. E. (ed.), *Nietzsche on Mind and Nature* (Oxford).
Swindal, James, 1999: "Nietzsche, Critical Theory, and a Theory of Knowledge" in Babich/Cohen: *Nietzsche, Theories of Knowledge, and Critical Theory*, op. cit.
Ueberweg, Friedrich, 1857/71: *System of Logic and History of Logical Doctrines*. Translation T. M. Lindsay (London: Longmans, Green, and Co.).
Ueberweg, Friedrich, 1902: *Grundriss der Geschichte der Philosophie: Das Neunzehnte Jahrhundert*. (Berlin: Siegfried Mittler).
Urs Sommer, Andreas, 2012: *Kommentar zu Nietzsches Der Fall Wagner and Götzen-Dämmerung*. (Berlin-New York: de Gruyter).
Urs Sommer, Andreas, 2016: *Kommentar zu Nietzsches Jenseits von Gut und Böse*. (Berlin-New York: de Gruyter)
Vaihinger, Hans, 1901/2002: *Nietzsche als Philosoph*. Porta Westfalica (Gerhard Bleick).
Vaihinger, Hans, 1911/22: *Die Philosophie des 'Als Ob'* (Leipzig: Felix Meiner).
Vaihinger, Hans, 1925: *The Philosophy "As If"*. Translated by C. K. Ogden (London: Kegan Paul).
Vollmer, Gerhard, 1995: *Biophilosophie* (Stuttgart: Philipp Reclam).
Welshon, Rex, 2014: *Nietzsche's Dynamic Meta-psychology-This Uncanny Animal* (Palgrave Macmillan).
Whitlock, Greg, 1996: "Roger Boscovich, Benedict de Spinoza, and Friedrich Nietzsche: The Untold Story." In *Nietzsche-Studien* 25 (Berlin and New York: de Gruyter).
Wilcox, John T., 1982: *Truth and Value in Nietzsche: A Study of His Metaethics and Epistemology* (Lanham, MD: University Press of America).
Zöllner, Johann, 1881: *Transcendental Physics* (Kessinger reprint edition).

Index

a priori, 54, 78, 86, 87, 88, 89, 168, 169, 170, 218n10, 219n18, 226n108; synthetic, 86–89, 196, 218n10, 219n18
A System of Positive Philosophy (Comte), 115
Abel, G., 195n22
abstract constructions, 42
abstraction, 17, 27, 30, 32, 41, 62–64, 111, 130, 135, 140, 146, 165, 168–69, 182, 189–90, 214n173, 242n265
accountability, 13–14, 16
aesthetic theory, 69–71
affirmative Nihilism. *See* Nihilism
agnosticism, 98, 113–116, 120, 124, 128, 140. *See also* epistemological agnosticism
Analysis of Sensations (*Die Analyse der Empfindungen*; Mach), 129, 130, 133, 222n51
analytic philosophy, 133
ancient Greeks, 62, 65, 67, 69, 188
animal(s), 74, 83, 86, 90, 105, 110, 118, 148, 170, 182, 204n46, 207n90, 209n115, 218n2, 222n48, 224n75, 238n230
anthropocentrism / anthropocentric, 7, 37–38, 46–47, 73, 200n15, 219n18; anthropic circle, 92–93, 112
Apollo / Apollonian, 70–71
apparent world, 51–52, 59, 81–82, 94, 100–104, 106–7, 114, 131, 144, 224n75, 227n109, 237n230, 239n230
appearance(s), 9–10, 24, 30, 56, 59, 64, 67, 78–83, 88, 90, 92–93, 100–106, 108–9, 111, 114, 118, 125, 127, 130, 132–33, 140, 147, 151, 159–60, 172, 176, 185, 190, 214n173, 225n92, 227n109
arbitrariness / arbitrary, 4–5, 7, 12, 17–18, 22–23, 29, 33, 34–37, 60, 70, 95–97, 120–23, 136, 166, 169– 71, 175, 178–80, 202n27, 202n29, 203–4n46, 205n51
arché-forms, 30, 52
Aristotle, 35
arrow of time, 96
art, 61–70, 176, 188, 190, 214n173, 216–17n198, 229–30n147; artists, 66, 68, 238–39n230, 243n280
atom(s), 85, 105, 117–18, 158, 228n119, 233n176, 241–42n265; corpuscular, 114, 117–18, 148
Austin, J. L., 194n17
authentic linguistic concept formation, 59
Avenarius, R., 1, 31–32, 84–85, 113, 124, 127–29, 141, 144–45, 156, 160, 162–65, 225n94, 229–30n147, 231n158, 234n186, 236n215, 240n249

Banks, E., 147–48, 150–52, 232n166, 233n178, 234n183, 236n215
beauty, 64, 69–70, 190, 214n173, 216n197
becoming, 8, 19, 24, 31, 39, 50, 52, 66, 68, 70, 75, 78, 81, 90, 96, 104, 110, 130, 135–36, 140, 142, 145, 151, 155, 185, 216n195, 232n174, 237n230, 238n230
Bentham, J., 156
Berkeley, G., 128–29, 140
Beyond Good and Evil / BGE (Nietzsche), 72, 81, 86, 143, 172, 193n5, 195n23. *See also Jenseits von Gut und Böse*

263

binary logic, 102; binary opposition, 102, 107
biological: -perspectivism, 45, 46, 48, 110, 122, 137, 172, 211n133, 212n143; -economic theory, 165; -psychological theory, 79, 144–45; -theory, 85, 141, 156, 160–61, 236n223
Birth of Tragedy, The / BT (Nietzsche), 65, 69–72. See also *Die geburt der Tragödie*
Blackmore, J., 231n157
Bogdanov, A., 129, 229–30n147, 236n215
Boltzmann, L., 163
Boscovich, R., 225–26n97, 228n119
Breazeale, D., 194–95n20, 197–98n37
Brobjer, T., 2–3, 220n30, 222n51, 231n157

Carnap, R., 132, 236n224
categories, 20, 43, 51–54, 56, 80, 84, 86–88, 94, 114, 121, 132, 135, 168, 169, 183, 202, 219n18, 226n108
cause / causality, 1, 17, 19, 20, 21, 22, 23, 30, 31, 55, 56, 57, 77, 78, 79, 80, 84, 86, 88–93, 96, 105, 108, 109, 112, 114, 119, 121, 123, 124, 139, 149, 158, 166, 169, 179, 180, 219n14; causal relation(ship), 21, 24, 77, 83, 93, 122; 185; -effect (and effect), 21–22, 78–83, 89, 93–95, 105, 109, 205n58, 219n14, 220n24; the reversal of cause and effect, 31, 77–81, 83, 89, 94, 105, 166
chaos, 2, 11, 63, 68, 70, 80, 86, 97, 104–7, 110, 142, 147, 150, 152, 189, 227, 238, 240n238; chaotic, 32, 62–63, 70, 80, 105–7, 111–12, 128, 136, 141–42, 146, 158, 166, 189, 21718n2, 225n94, 234n186, 238–39n230; world of, 110
Chladni, E., 23–24, 179; sound-figures, 24, 179
Christian, 4, 6, 37–38, 100, 128, 193n5, 200n15
chronological reversal; 31, 89–95
Clark, M., 13, 98–99, 104, 195n23, 196n31, 211n133, 223n68; and Dudrick, D., 195n23

cognition, 2, 53, 77, 94, 102, 217–18n2; cognitive-linguistic, 42, 44, 237–38n230
communication, 110, 144, 146, 165
Comte, A., 114–16, 131, 167, 223n74
concept: of truth, 10, 11, 13, 43, 55, 99–100, 102–3, 107, 169–70, 172, 226–27n109; conceptual constructions, 22, 34, 42, 53, 59–61, 164, 182, 214n172; -formation, 29, 31, 33, 40, 42–44, 58–60, 163, 180–81, 207–8n91, 210n119; -heaven, 42, 183; as inauthentic metaphor, 31–33, 58–59, 70, 182; and language, 32–33, 44, 60, 127, 200n17; and synthetic judgement, 49, 50; and/or/vs word, 22, 25–32, 40–41, 207n88, 209n113
conceptualization, 25, 26, 30, 58, 70, 152, 171, 213–14n166, 226–27n109, 243n280
constructions, 22, 34, 40, 42–43, 47, 53, 59–61, 75, 164, 173, 209–10n119, 214n172
constructivism, 77, 120, 230n148; as epistemology, 77
corpuscular atom. See atom
correspondence theory of truth, 11–14, 22, 46, 57–58, 70, 98, 108, 170, 196n31, 231n158, 238–39n230
Crawford, C., 203n44, 205n51, 207n83, 242n265
Critique of Kant (Fischer), 56, 213n153
Critique of Pure Reason (Kant), 53, 55, 57, 88, 115, 155, 159

Darwin, C., 3–4, 6, 9, 132, 156, 161; Darwinism, 161, 195–96n25, 234n186
Das Wesen des Christenthums (Feuerbach), 2, 37
Daybreak / D (Nietzsche), 52. See also *Morgenröte*
de Man, P., 63, 93–95, 97, 202n29
dead metaphor(s). *See* methaphor(s)
deconstruct / deconstruction / deconstructionist, 1, 48, 55–56, 86–88, 94–95, 101, 106, 145, 167, 173,

193nn3–4, 194n17, 201n19, 202n29, 210n119, 214n172, 214n173, 239n230
Delboeuf, J., 122–23
Denkökonomie, 142–43, 147
Der Philosophische Diskurs der Moderne (Habermas), 167
Der Wille zur Macht / WM (Nietzsche), 169–70. See also *Will to Power, The*
Derrida, J., 94, 157, 194n10, 194nn17–19, 201n19, 222n56
de Saussure, F., 8, 122, 202n27
Descartes, R., 83, 134
Dialectical Materialism, 162, 230n147, 236n215
Die Analyse der Empfindungen (*The Analysis of Sensations*; Mach), 129
Die geburt der Tragödie / GT (Nietzsche), 243n280. See also *Birth of Tragedy, The*
Die Philosophie des 'Als Ob' (Vaihinger), 156, 195–96n25
Die Sieben Welträthsel (du Bois-Reymond), 116, 200n12
Die Sprache als Kunst (Gerber), 3, 198n3, 203n44
Die Welt als Wille und Vorstellung / SW (Shopenhauer), 2, 25, 49, 199n6, 206n73
Dionysian / Dionysus, 70, 243n280
doer-deed, 82–83
dogmatic Idealism, 95
dogmatism, 56–57
double-deed. *See* doer-deed
Drossbach, M., 21, 80, 117, 228n118
Du Bois-Reymond, E., 3, 6, 22, 84, 114, 116–17, 118–19, 127, 140, 166, 200n12, 242n265
dualism, 107, 114, 117, 128, 147–48, 159, 233n180

economy, 141–47, 162, 163, 165, 234n184; economic expressions, 108, 113
elements, 32, 49–54, 70, 97, 108–9, 111, 130, 134–35, 137–41, 146–54, 162, 165, 212n137, 224n79, 225–26n97, 233nn175–78, 234n183

Elemente der Psychophysik (Fechner), 200n12
emperio-criticism, 120
empirical world, 10, 19, 24, 56, 59–60, 96, 100, 102, 185, 187
empiricism, 128, 223n68, 230n148; empiricist, 22, 48, 93–94, 100, 114–15, 121, 124, 221n30, 231n158
enigmatic X (of the Thing-in-Itself), 19, 23, 33, 43, 57, 98–99, 124, 126, 151, 153, 180, 227n109, 232n174, 239n230
enlightenment (tradition), 8, 157, 167, 170, 197n36, 234n186; enlightenment project, 157, 167–68
epistemic constructions, 42
epistemology, 2, 8, 70, 72–73, 99–100, 107, 111, 125, 127, 128, 129, 132, 140, 146, 147, 152, 154, 162, 167, 168, 212n144, 225n94, 234n184, 236n224
epistemological : -agnosticism, 98, 114, 116, 120; -emancipation, 128; -positivism, 98, 114, 116, 120, 124, 128
equalization, 28, 29, 30, 32, 49; equalizing the unequal, 28, 29, 180
Erkenntnis und Interesse (Habermas), 167
Erkenntnis und Irrtum (Mach), 133
Erkenntnißtrieb, 16–17
Essay Concerning Human Understanding (Locke), 22
essence of things, 30, 100, 102–3, 121, 160, 181, 185
evolutionary biology, 3, 18, 97, 146, 162
Examination of Sir William Hamilton's Philosophy (Mill), 115
existentialism, 133

faculties, 86–87
falsification, 98, 100, 103, 105, 109–11, 135, 143, 152, 157, 204n46, 219n18, 223n68, 224nn82–83, 237n229, 237–39n230
familiar(ity), 32, 41, 50, 63, 85–86, 92–93, 97, 109–10, 118, 128, 146, 152, 164, 165–67, 182, 185, 189, 219n14, 241n254, 242n266; familiarize, 89, 166, 195n22

Fechner, Th., 3, 6, 135–36, 141–42, 200n12, 200n17, 234n186
fiction, 104–6, 135, 145, 158–60, 162, 167, 170, 202n29, 210n119, 213–14n166, 224n75, 237n228, 240n233, 242n266
fictionalism, 120, 155, 157–58, 161–62, 224n75, 230n148; fictionalist, 107
filtration, 141–42
Fischer, K., 3, 55, 57, 72, 121, 213n153
force, 6, 21–22, 78, 81, 117–20, 126, 136, 145, 158, 162–65, 169, 185, 201nn23–24, 208n98, 226n107, 225n97, 227n109, 241n254, 241n265
forgetfulness, 15–16, 142, 178, 182, 235n193, 240n246
Forschung nach der Gewissheit in der Erkenntnis der Wirklichkeit (Spir), 3
Foucault, M., 37, 208n100, 232n172
fragmentary subject, 129
Frank, P., 132, 157, 231n157
Freud, S., 8, 25, 200nn11–12, 200n17, 205n50, 206n72, 234n186
functional relationships, 109, 130, 136, 138

Gay Science, The / GS (Nietzsche), 48, 72, 78. See also *Die fröhliche Wissenschaft*
general economy of signs. *See* economy of signs
genius, 40, 42–43, 60, 66, 69, 110, 183
Gerber, G., 3, 18, 198n3, 203n44, 205n51
Geschichte der Kantschen Philosophie (Rosenkranz), 3
Geschichte der Materialismus (Lange), 55
Geschichte der neuern Philosophie (Fischer), 3
Geschichte des Materialismus (Lange), 3, 4, 84, 199n10
Gespräch über die Poesie (Schlegel), 68
god, 6, 20, 37–39, 40, 42, 62, 66, 74, 92, 108, 125, 128, 183, 188, 200n15, 212n138, 231n157
Goethe, J. W., 65
good will, 10
Gori, P., 139, 198n2, 212n137, 233n175, 233n178, 234n184, 240n238

Götzendämmerung /GD (Nietzsche),106, 107, 223n74, 131. See also *Twilight of Idols*
grammar, 79, 81, 82, 89; grammatical structure, 83
greatest happiness principle, 85
Greeks. *See* ancient Greeks
Grenzbegriff, 97, 115, 160
Grimm, H. R., 226–27n109
Grundriss der Geschichte der Philosophie von Thales bis auf die Gegenwart (Ueberweg), 3

Haar, M., 225n92
Habermas, J., 157, 167–71, 197n36, 231n159
Haeckel, E., 6, 228n125
Hamilton, Sir W., 122–23
Hartman, E. von, 3, 4, 18, 84, 209n115
Hegel, G. W. F., 38, 129, 209n102
Helmholtz, H. von, 3, 5–7, 22, 84, 114, 120–24, 135, 142, 163, 200n12, 200n17
Heraclitus, 103–4
hermeneutics, 96, 133
Herschel, Sir J. F., 6
hierarchical opposition, 102
Historical Materialism, 230n148
Hobbes, T., 11, 201n23, 201n24
homo sapiens, 45, 85, 109, 134, 137, 161, 237n230
human: -ground, 166, 193n2, 237n230, 239n230; -perception, 6–7, 18, 44, 46, 77, 94; vanity, 48, 72
Human, all too Human / HH (Nietzsche), 7, 71–75, 209–10n119, 223n74. See also *Menschliches, Allzumenschliches*
humanization, 77, 84, 89, 91–92, 112–13; of nature, 84, 89, 92; repressed-, 77
humanized, 80, 83–84, 92
Hume, D., 53–54, 77–80, 86, 89, 129, 218n4, 218n10, 218–19n14
Hussain, N., 212n137, 223n68, 224n83

idealism, 50, 52, 53, 55, 57, 95, 102, 121, 126, 128, 129, 149, 152, 154,

156, 185, 186, 203n46, 229n143, 236n215
idealist(ic), 8, 67, 122, 128–29, 140, 156, 203–4n46, 236n223
ideological-religious, 65
Ignorabimus, 10, 22, 113, 119, 120, 127, 140, 228n125
Ignoramus. *See* Ignorabimus
Image(s), 6–7, 9–10, 16, 17, 19–29, 32–35, 38–42, 44–45, 47, 54, 59, 62, 64–65, 75, 89–90, 93, 96, 118, 120–24, 133–35, 138–40, 143, 150–53, 169, 177, 179, 180, 182–85, 206n61, 206n73, 207n85, 207n87, 208n95, 208n97, 209n113, 214n172, 216n196, 221n45, 239n230, 241n265, 243n280
imaginary, 23–25, 38, 42, 91, 138, 140, 180, 195n22, 206n66
impression(s), 7, 17, 20, 22, 27, 41, 53–54, 56–60, 63, 70–71, 80, 90–91, 93–96, 104–5, 111, 117–18, 123–24, 130–31 135, 138, 139, 141–43, 145, 150–54, 182, 187, 190, 214n172, 222n56, 225n94, 230n148, 238–39n230
Impressionism, 154, 230n148
inauthentic conceptualizations, 58; inauthentic scientific concept formation, 59
individual instances, 28–29, 204n46
in-itself, 14–15, 17–24, 26, 39, 51, 58, 73, 77–80, 84, 91, 97–101, 104, 109, 113–15, 120, 123, 125, 127– 28, 133, 146, 149, 158, 172, 186, 205n51, 207n87, 217n2, 225n94, 238–39n30. *See also* thing-in- itself
inner world, 93–95, 117
intellectual man, 61, 64–65, 69
intention(1), 79, 83, 89–90, 92, 95, 128, 173, 194n10; intentional, 79; intentionally, 79, 194n10
interpretation(s), 5, 20, 22, 25, 46, 79, 85, 90–93, 95–97, 99, 101, 108, 110, 114–15, 120, 128–29, 134, 136, 140, 143, 149, 151–52, 157–58, 160, 166, 169, 170, 195n22, 195n23, 202n33, 210n133, 211–12n133, 215, 216n197, 217n2, 220n23–24, 221n30, 223n68,
224n75, 232n166, 240n238, 242n265; -philosophy, 128, 157; -process, 96
intuitive man, 61, 64

James, W., 1, 32, 149, 200n12, 230–31n153
Jameson, F., 47
Jenseits von Gut und Böse / JGB (Nietzsche), 9. See also, *Beyond Good and Evil*
Johnson, S., 140
judgment, 38, 43, 49–50, 52, 79–80, 84, 86–89, 169, 170 , 173, 200n15, 203n44, 204n46

Kant, I., 48–49, 51, 53, 55–58, 67, 80–91, 94, 100–101, 113–15, 124–25, 129–31, 133, 155, 158, 160, 168, 199n9, 201n22, 203n38, 206n73, 218n10, 219n18, 221n42, 225n94, 238–39n230
Kantian, 10, 20, 48, 55, 72, 84, 86, 101, 113–15, 121, 125, 132, 156–57, 159, 161, 166–67, 169, 207n87, 208n97. *See also* neo-Kantian
Kantianism, 1, 3, 210n126, 243n279
Kant und die Epigonen (Liebmann), 3, 56
Klein, W., 222n55,
Kleinpeter, H., 132, 142, 143, 196n25, 230n151, 231n256
knowing, 4, 5, 7, 54, 56, 57, 85, 104, 110, 112, 119, 175, 176, 211n133, 219n18
knowledge, 8, 19, 24, 33, 40, 44, 50, 55, 72, 77, 88, 110, 113, 119, 127, 136, 141, 144, 146, 151–52, 160, 173, 178, 198n2, 206n73, 207n85, 211n133, 212n137, 219n18, 225n94, 226n109
Kofman, S., 63, 209–10n119, 214n173
Kritik der reinen Vernunft / KrV (Kant), 3

Lamarck, J. B. P., 6, 199n10
Lange, Fr. A., 1, 3, 5, 7, 18, 22, 24, 55, 71, 72, 73, 84, 97, 113, 114, 115, 120, 122, 124–25, 128, 136, 142, 155–56, 160–61, 166, 177, 206n65, 212n144, 226n108, 228n118, 228n119, 229n143–44, 231n158

268 • Index

language, 8, 11–12, 14, 17–18, 19, 21, 23–24, 28–29, 32, 34, 36, 37, 41, 44, 46, 47, 58–59, 60, 62, 81–84, 89, 90, 93, 96–97, 101, 105, 106, 107, 108, 110, 113, 127, 128, 135, 139, 140, 144, 146, 152–53, 158, 160, 164–65, 169, 170, 172, 173, 178–80, 185, 187, 200n17, 202n27, 202n29, 204n46, 205n51, 207n85, 207–8n91, 208n95, 208n97, 209n115, 209–10n119, 215n177, 218n2, 224n82– 83, 225n94, 238n230, 242n265, 238n230, 242n265; -constructed metaphysics, 83; private-, 152–53
Laplace, P-S., 113, 116–18
Lemm, V., 202n33, 238–39n230
Lenin, V. I., 129, 152, 162, 229n138, 229–30n147, 236n215, 240–41n249
Leviathan (Hobbes), 201nn23–24
Liebmann, O., 54, 55, 56, 57, 72, 100, 121
linguistics, 2, 18, 146, 202n27, 207n85; linguistic sign, 23, 122
Locke, J., 22, 93
logical positivism, 133, 227n114, 231n159, 236n221

Mach, E., 1, 8, 32, 51, 72–73, 84, 97, 105, 107, 109, 111, 113, 124–55, 212n144, 218n10, 220–21n30, 223n68, 224n79, 225n94, 225n97, 229–30n147, 233n176, 233n178, 234nn183–84
materialism, 113–14, 116–17, 121–22, 125–26, 128, 148, 162, 229n143, 230n147, 230n148, 236n215
Materialism and Empirio-Criticism (Lenin), 152
materialist(s), 21, 128, 129, 226n109, 227n109, 236n215
Menschliches, Allzumenschliches / MA (Nietzsche), 156. See also *Human, All too Human*
Messier, C., 6, 199n9
metaphor(s), 13, 15, 19, 21–24, 27, 33–34, 36–37, 39, 40, 41, 44–46, 50, 52–53, 58–64, 113–14, 124, 130–31, 143, 157, 160, 169, 179–85, 187–90, 202n29, 208n98, 209–10n119, 213–14n166, 215n177, 238–39n230, 240n233; dead-, 33, 37, 40, 60, 160, 240n233; metaphorical, 35, 36, 52, 53, 146, 169, 208n95, 97, 215n177; metaphorization, 27, 143
metaphysical, 1, 8, 9, 11, 17, 29, 30, 31, 51, 55, 60, 71, 82, 83, 98, 100, 107, 108, 110, 113, 115–16, 119, 126, 127, 129, 157, 170–73, 193n3, 203n33, 210n119, 219n14, 18, 225n94, 227n109; anti- metaphysical, 112, 218n4; post-metaphysical, 8, 224n75; metaphysically flat world, 82, 83
metonymies, 33, 61, 181, 188
Mill, J. S., 85, 115
mind-independent elements, 148–51, 219n18, 225n94; mind-world, 93, 147
Moliere, J-B., 87
Monet, C., 131, 154–55
Morgenröte / M (Nietzsche), 52. See also *Daybreak*
Müller, J., 3, 6, 200n12
mythology, 61, 68, 101, 145, 188, 210n119, 239n230

Nachlaß, 13, 32, 81, 169, 206n61
naïve artist(s), 66, 243n280
naïve materialism, 113
naming-process, 29
naturalism, 51, 80, 146, 155, 162, 200n17, 214n173, 225n94; naturalist(ic), 1–9, 16, 27, 48, 60, 68–70, 86, 90, 97, 121–22, 125–26, 129, 157, 161–62, 167, 173, 196n28, 200n12, 201n19, 210n119, 211n133, 218n4, 223n74, 233–34n180, 234n186
nature, 4–5, 7–10, 14–17, 22, 23, 26, 29–31, 37–40, 42, 47–52, 65–66, 68, 79, 80, 83–84, 116, 119, 123, 139, 145–46, 148 151, 168, 210n119; and animals, 9, 14, 110, human-, 37–40, 68, 218n4; humanization of, 80, 84, 89–90, 92, 112; ideal-, 40; and language, 81, 89–90, 105, 152, 210; and perception; 39, 117, 122–23, 149; laws of, 47, 49, 50, 51, 52, 145, 185, 186, 201n22; of

Index • 269

things, 14, 48, 116, 120, 125; of truth / truth of, 16, 17, 31, 40, 116, 155; in *On Truth and Lies*, 175–77, 180, 181, 183, 185, 186, 188
Nehamas, A., 71, 194n19, 196n30
neo-Kantian(s), 3, 20, 33, 46, 51, 54, 55, 90, 94, 97, 114, 115, 121, 123, 124, 155, 156, 158–61, 167, 207n87, 212n144, 224n74, 225n94, 230n149, 236n223, 238–39n230, 242n267; neo- Kantianism, 48, 100, 114, 115, 121, 124, 155, 160, 236n223. See also Kant; Kantian; Kantianism
nerve-stimuli / nerve-stimulus, 16, 17, 19–20, 23–24, 28, 33, 54, 96, 124, 150, 169, 170, 179, 180, 183, 185, 207n85
Nietzsche als Philosoph (Vaihinger), 161, 196n25, 223n74
Nietzsche and Metaphor (Kofman), 210n119, 214n173
Nietzscheanism, 102
Nietzsche-Machean theory of knowledge, 51, 132, 151–53
Nihilism, 124, 128, 168, 170, 171, 230n148, 242n266; affirmative-, 124–29
Norris, C., 222n56
Notebook 19 (Nietzsche), 12, 17, 25, 26, 47, 49, 50, 83, 195n25, 196n28

objectification, 38, 97
objectivism, 100
On the Essence of Christianity (Feuerbach), 37, 200n15
On the Fourfold Root of the Principle of Sufficient Reason (Schopenhauer), 19
On the Genealogy of Morals / GM (Nietzsche), 9, 81–82, 144, 235n193. See also *Zur Genealogie der Moral*
On Truth and Lies in a Non-Moral Sense / TL (Nietzsche), 2–5, 13, 2–28, 31, 40, 46, 48, 50, 52, 68, 70, 72– 75, 91, 96, 98, 100, 120, 121, 124, 129, 137, 143, 152, 169, 171-72, 175–91, 198–99n3, 212n144. See also *Über Wahrheit und Lüge im außermoralischen Sinne*
origin of truth, 9, 10, 15, 74

outer world, 91, 93, 94, 95, 96, 117, 122, 162, 221n45, 224–25n84, 228n118, 236n214

paralogism, 88, 89, 221n42
Pascal, B., 62, 188
Peirce, C. S., 1, 156
perception, 105, 108, 116–25, 138–46, 149–53, 158, 166, 170, 172–73, 184, 185–86, 204n46, 205n51, 206n73, 207n90, 208n97, 212n137, 217–18n2, 224–25n84, 235–36n214, 237–39n230, 243n279
perceptive apparatus; 6, 10, 45, 47, 115, 125, 141, 153, 222n48, 239n230; -cognitive apparatus, 27, 105, 108, 122, 153, 205n50, 207n85; -presence, 30
personification, 77, 84, 130, 241
perspective(s), 14–15, 18, 43, 46–48, 64, 73, 91, 97, 103, 108–11, 128, 130, 137–38, 153, 164, 190, 211–12n133, 232n174, 233n175, 242n267; perspectival truths, 136; perspectival world, 134, 137, 211; perspectivism, 45–48, 100, 108–10, 122, 136–37, 172, 210n133, 211n133, 212n143, 222n48, 230n148, 232–33n174, 238n230
Petzoldt, J., 127, 129, 132, 229n146
phenomenology: phenomenalism, 2, 80, 93, 108, 110, 120–21, 128, 130, 132, 230n148, 231n156, 236n215; phenomenalist, 124, 147, 149–50, 152, 154, 221n30, 230n147, 231n157, 231n158, 233n180; phenomenon / phenomena / phenomenal, 25, 27–28, 55, 99, 107, 134, 146, 219n18, 225n94; physiological, 3, 21–23, 33, 35, 47, 94, 118, 121–22, 138, 150–51, 161, 223n174, 240n246, 254n254
Physiologische Optik (Helmholtz), 121
Plato, 29, 30, 101, 131, 193n3, 193n5; Platonic form, 29
pleasure, 46, 62, 63, 67, 69, 85, 118, 119, 145, 164, 189, 241n254
poetry, 13, 35, 53, 61–68, 208n91, 210n119, 216n195
Pojman, P., 231n158

Populär Wissenschaftliche Vorlesungen (Mach), 133
positivism, 80, 97–99, 101, 107–8, 113–16, 120–21, 124, 128, 130–33, 146, 154–60, 167–68, 170, 197n36, 198n2, 227nn113–14, 230nn148–49, 231nn158–59; positivist, 26, 97, 124, 127, 128, 133, 145, 151, 155, 157, 160, 167, 210n119, 215n173, 221n30, 223n68, 223–24nn74, 224n75, 225n94, 230n147, 230n152, 231nn158–59, 236–37n224, 238n230, 242n266, 233n180, 236n215, 236n224
post-metaphysical. *See* metaphysical
postmodernism, 128, 133, 157, 167
pragmatic, 124, 126–27, 129, 130, 132, 141, 145, 151, 157, 165, 172, 196, 223, 24n74, 225n94, 226– 27n109, 230n153, 234n180, 240n233; concept of truth, 15, 100, 227n109; pragmatism, 80, 121, 132, 146, 155–57, 198, 203n33, 236n223, 230n148, 230nn148–49, 236n215, 230n153
pre-given object, 98–99, 109
priest, 65, 215n176; anti-priest, 171
private language. *See* language
Project to a Scientific Psychology (Freud), 234n186
Prolegomena to any Future Metaphysics (Kant), 131
proto-thinking, 25, 206n72
psychic apparatus, 23
psychology, 1, 2, 45, 53, 73, 85, 96, 158, 206n62, 207n85
psycho-physiology, 3, 97, 115, 198, 233n176, 234n186

qualitas occulta, 30–31, 181
qualities, 15, 31, 38–40, 81, 134, 136–37, 148–49, 206n61, 212n138, 233n175
quantities, 27, 136–37, 146, 206n61

rationalism, 55, 70
rationality, 43, 70; rationalization-process, 42
realism, 100, 139–40, 204n46, 219n18, 225n94, 236n215

reality, 14, 17, 21, 24–27, 29, 34–39, 45, 62, 67, 70, 72, 73, 78, 121, 123, 130, 152, 158–65, 170, 185–86, 204n46, 207n87, 207n91, 208n97, 216n197, 217n2, 225n92, 226n109, 227n109, 229n138, 233n175, 237n229, 238–39n230, 243n279; surface-, 107
reason, 131, 160, 169–70, 176, 179, 183, 187, 200n11, 211n133, 224nn83–84, 234n186, 235–36n214, 243n280
rejection of Truth. *See* Truth
Relations-Welt, 108–9, 140
relativism, 48, 51, 100, 108, 110–11, 132, 230n148
repetition, 26, 78–79, 87, 106, 154, 218n2
representation(s) / representational, 80, 84, 98, 100, 107, 111, 120–22, 124, 134, 138, 151–52, 163–64, 186, 195n22, 206n73, 207n87, 207–8n91, 208n95, 214nn172–73, 219n18, 225n94, 223n178, 138–39n230, 241n254, 242n266, 243n280
repressed humanization. *See* humanization
rhetoric, 35, 53, 93, 94, 215n177; rhetorical, 14, 33–37, 59, 63, 72, 94, 98, 119, 181, 241n265
Riccardi, M., 228n118
Rockmore, T., 219n18, 225n94
Roman columbarium, 42, 59, 182
Romantic(ist), 8, 27, 58, 61, 62, 65–72, 129, 172, 196n28, 208n91, 214nn172–73, 216n195, 239n230, 243n280; Romantic School, 65–66; Romanticism, 69, 70, 72, 196n28, 214n1723
Rosenkranzt, H., 3
Russell, B, 149

Schacht, R., 195n23
Scheibenberger, S., 2, 3, 198–99, 213n160, 215n177
schemata, 41, 62, 63, 210n119, 213n160
schematization, 32, 84, 173; schematize, 80, 137, 146, 147; schematizing, 235n190, 240n238
Schiller, F., 61, 65–66, 69, 214n173, 216n197

Schlegel, F., 61, 65, 67–69, 214n173
Schlick, M., 132, 236n224
Schlimgen, E., 208n97, 222n55
Schopenhauer, A., 2, 3, 5, 7, 19–21, 25–29, 41, 49, 51, 53–56, 59, 61, 69, 71, 80, 86, 90, 91, 121, 129, 155–56, 161, 168, 196n28, 197n35, 199n6, 200n11, 206n73, 209n113, 214n172, 224–25n84, 225n94, 226n107, 236n214, 237–38n230
Science of Mechanics (Mach), 143
scientific-naturalist paradigm, 4–5
Searle, J., 194n17
self-alienation, 37-40
self-deception, 40, 43
sensation(s)(al), 18, 20–23, 32–35, 46, 52–54, 90–91, 93, 96–98, 105–7, 111, 118, 120, 122–24, 129– 33, 135–36, 138–41, 146–54, 158–63, 165, 167, 205n51, 206n61, 233n178, 236n214, 238– 39n230
sensation-world, 130, 132, 141, *150*, 160
sense: -apparatus, 46, 121, 135, 153; -data, 90, 97, 104–5, 123, 134, 143, 152; -impression, 27, 53, 56, 58–60, 90–91, 94, 104, 105, 117–18, 123–24, 130, 135, 150, 152–54, 238–39; -perceptions, 118, 172; -reality, 26, 160, 207
sensible signs, 120–21
sentimental artist, 66
sign-economy, 146–47; sign-world, 18, 110, 146
simplification, 1, 28, 32, 78, 96, 105–6, 111, 129, 141–45, 152, 164–65, 168, 206n61, 235n187; - apparatus, 143; simplify(ing), 29, 30, 32, 37, 77, 84
Small, R., 196n26, 198n1
Socrates, 65, 70
solipsism, 152
space and time, 7, 52–55, 57, 237–38n230
species-specific, 46–47, 81, 91, 97, 109–10, 115, 137, 158, 179, 239n230
speech-act, 153
Spir, A., 3, 72, 120, 123–24
Stack, G., 204–5n47, 210n121, 218n14, 222n52, 226n108, 229n143

stimulus / stimuli, 10, 16–17, 19–24, 27–28, 33–34, 40, 47, 54, 83, 96, 120, 124, 135–36, 141, 150–52, 161–62, 169–70, 205n51, 206n61–62, 207n85, 237–39n230
structural linguistic(s), 106–7
struggle of survival, 9
subject and predicate, 79, 81, 84; subject-predicate logic, 80–82, 84, 90, 92
super-apparent world, 103, 106–7
synthetic a priori. *See* a priori.
synthetic judgment, 49–50, 86–87
System der Logik (Ueberweg), 122

Theologian-Christian paradigm, 4
thing-in-itself / things-in-themselves, 10, 19, 21–22, 24, 26, 33–34, 36–37, 43–45, 48, 53, 55–57, 72, 77, 97–106, 108, 113–14, 120, 122–28, 131–34, 140, 145, 151, 154–55, 158–60, 170, 202, 205n51, 207n87, 212n138, 219n18, 223n68, 226–27n109, 229n144, 237–39n230. *See also* in-itself
thing-representation, 25, 28–29, 31, 33, 52, 54, 57–58, 134, 151, 207n87, 208, 214n172, 204n46
thought economy, 142–43
thought-personalities, 74–75
time-reversal, 90–92
transcendental, 11, 14, 30, 43, 47, 57, 60, 80, 89; aesthetics, 124; concept of truth, 15; idealism, 53, 55, 168; subjectivity, 53, 56, 57
transference / transferences, 17, 19, 21–23, 33, 49, 61, 70, 169
Trieb zur Wahrheit (Nietzsche), 16, 213n166. *See also* truth-drive
true-apparent distinction, 100
[t]ruth, 8, 9, 11, 15, 16, 19, 31, 43, 51, 55; belief in, 15–16, 43, 193n3; defense of, 9; -drive, 10, 11, 16, 26, 42, 62 (*See also Trieb zur Wahrheit*); as illusion, 7, 8, 10, 36, 40; as metaphor, 23, 33–36, 40; origin of, 10; post-Truth, 51, 59, 60, 100; pure-, 19; as truthfulness, 10, 13–14, 16, 17, 31

Twilight of Idols, The / TI (Nietzsche), 25, 89, 100, 103. See also *Götzendämmerung*

Über das Studium der Griechischen Poesie (Schlegel), 67
Über den wille der Natur (Shopenhauer), 2
Über die Grenzen des Naturerkennens (du Bois-Reymond), 116
Über die Natur der Kometen (Zöllner), 3
Über die vierfache Wurzel des Satzes des zureichenden Grunde / SzG (Schopenhauer), 3
Über Wahrheit und Lüge im außermoralischen Sinne / WL (Nietzsche), 16, 215n177, 233n233, See also *On Truth and Lies in a Non-Moral Sense*
übermensch, 8
Überweg, Fr., 200n12, 228n118
understanding, 20, 225n82, 236n214
Unzeitgemäße Betrachtungen / UB (*Untimely Meditations*, Nietzsche), 41. Meditations
Ur-ground, 193n2, 237–39n230

Vaihinger, H., 1, 32, 58, 73, 85, 105, 107, 124, 127, 128, 132, 135, 141, 143–44, 155–65, 167, 197n35, 213–14n166, 223n74, 224n75, 236–37n223–24, 237n228, 240n233
value-hierarchy, 28, 111

Wagner, R., 61, 69, 71, 196n28, 225
weak sensations, 32
will to power, 74, 75, 134; as truth, 75
Will to Power, The / WP (Nietzsche), 25, 93. See also *Der Wille zur Macht*
Williams, B., 203–4n46
word(s), 12–13, 15, 17–19, 21–23, 25–29, 31–34, 36–37, 40–42, 53, 56, 58, 63, 68–70, 124, 143, 146, 153, 163–164, 169; -representation, 54, 59; -riddle, 22, 116, 127. See also language; concept
world of chaos. See chaos
world-elements, 148–51

Zöllner, J. 3, 6
Zur Genealogie der Moral / GM (Nietzsche), 9, See also *On the Genealogy of Morals*

About the Author

Peter Bornedal is professor at American University of Beirut, where he teaches philosophy and cultural studies. He holds doctoral degrees from the University of Copenhagen and the University of Chicago. He has published several books and articles, notably *The Surface and the Abyss: Nietzsche as Philosopher of Mind and Knowledge* (2010) and *Speech and System* (1997). He is currently working on a book critically discussing Jacques Derrida's philosophy regarding its supposed relationship to thinkers such as Nietzsche, Saussure, and Freud.

www.ingramcontent.com/pod-product-compliance
Lightning Source LLC
Chambersburg PA
CBHW050858300426
44111CB00010B/1296